ALKAN

The Man
The Music

Opening of an unfinished string quartet. Autograph signed by Alkan.
(*Courtesy of* Bibliothèque Nationale, *Paris*)

Ronald Smith

ALKAN

The Man
The Music

KAHN & AVERILL, LONDON

First published in 2000 by
Kahn & Averill
9 Harrington Road, London SW7 3ES

Alkan: The Man, first published in 1976 as Alkan – Volume One: The Enigma
Alkan: The Music, first published in 1987 as Alkan – Volume Two: The Music

British Library Cataloguing in Publication Data

A catalogue record for this book is available from the British Library

ISBN 1 871082 73 0

Printed in Great Britain by
Halstan & Co Ltd., Amersham, Bucks

Preface

Some twenty years have passed since the publication in 1976 of volume one of my two-volume study of the composer. During the intervening years perception of Alkan's true stature has become transformed. His major works now form a vital part of the nineteenth-century repertoire, while such compositions as the splendid Trio and Cello Sonata are finding ever-increasing favour with chamber players. To the author's knowledge no significant gramophone record of Alkan's music preceded the advent of the LP. The extensive and ever-growing Discography at the back of the book speaks for itself. How, after a century of neglect, have the long-smouldering embers of Alkan's fortunes been fanned into flame?

Clearly the first recordings in the late 1960s of such large-scale works as the Concerto and the Symphony for Solo Piano played a decisive role. For the first time the musical world was made aware of a major contemporary of Chopin and Liszt. As I implied at the conclusion of Volume One, 'The stage was set.'

The 1970s saw a marked increase in public performances, broadcasts and recordings of Alkan's music, and for the first time his native France and notably the French radio became excited about a composer previously ignored. 1978 saw the formation in London of the first ever Alkan Society, followed a few years later by its sister society in Paris. Details of the aims and achievements of both Societies are discussed in Appendices 3 and 4.

By the 1980s Alkan's genius as a miniaturist was becoming recognised and a previously unsuspected mystical element in his music was emerging from the exploration of his later works for pedal-piano or organ.

One of the more bizarre episodes in my personal involvement occurred in 1984. An invitation to introduce Alkan's music to Russian audiences was to be spearheaded by a lecture-recital to

Moscow's famous Union of Composers. Unfortunately my tour coincided with the last major exchange of spies and diplomats between our two countries and I was told that the lecture had been cancelled and that I should include no Alkan work in my programmes. The official reason? Because of Alkan's French background he should only be introduced by a French pianist. Whether or not the political situation played some part in this change of plan must remain speculative, but I felt I had only one option. To my interpreter's dismay I changed the published programme at each venue to include a sizeable Alkan group. Public reception of this unknown music varied from warmly enthusiastic to ecstatic. In Kharkov, Ukraine a largely student audience chanted "Alkan! Alkan!". On leaving Russia I asked "Was I right to play Alkan?" . . . the reply: "Artistically right . . . diplomatically wrong!" Although a return invitation to that wonderfully cultivated country is unlikely my efforts may not have been in vain. Shortly after my visit *Le Festin d'Esope* was published in Russia for the first time.

Could Alkan's music have always remained unknown in Russia? At the time of my visit his name was not included in the most comprehensive Russian dictionary of music and musicians, yet Anton Rubinstein's fifth piano concerto is dedicated to Alkan, and it has recently emerged that *Comme le vent* and the splendid Funeral March op.26 featured in Rachmaninov's repertoire on his arrival in the USA as an immigré in 1919.

By the mid-1980s plans were already afoot to celebrate the centenary of Alkan's death on March 29th, 1888. On this precise date in 1988 all three of Alkan's chamber works for piano, violin and cello were performed before a near-capacity audience in London's Wigmore Hall. During that whole week BBC Radio 3 was promoting Alkan as 'Composer of the Week'. At the same time, across the Channel, French radio's *France culture* devoted a whole day to Alkan, with recitals, discussions and interviews. Later in the year an International Alkan Competition at Croydon's Fairfield Halls was succeeded by a major South Bank Festival organised by the British Alkan Society. Alongside a generous survey of Alkan's mainstream repertory London audiences were introduced to previously unheard of novelties for voices, woodwind, strings and organ. Such activity is often followed by a lull, but happily in Alkan's case this has not been so. The following years have seen a steady stream of performances, broadcasts, recordings and publications, including an indispensable collection of essays by members of Société Alkan, reappraising the music and shedding new light on the composer's background. A translation of the French text would be most welcome.

Within a generation the solving of an enigma has been overtaken by the reality of the music. It is indicative that many distinguished pianists of the younger generation are performing and recording this music. A word of warning to those pianists coming to the composer's major works for the first time. Like his friend Chopin, Alkan stands outside the mainstream of nineteenth-century Romantic virtuosity. Such works as the Concerto or Symphony for Solo Piano are born of a classical pedigree. Their transcendental pianism is integral to the conception and never imposed for effect. The huge first movement of Alkan's Concerto for Solo Piano will fall apart if subjected to the tempo fluctuations and dramatic posturing that beset so many performances of works by his contemporaries. Marmontel's description of Alkan as the rigorous observer of the metronome provides a salutary warning to all of us. Clearly all music must enjoy a degree of rhythmic flexibility. Acoustic recordings made about a hundred years ago by the veteran Saint-Säens, who enjoyed playing duos with Alkan, should be heard by all aspiring Alkan pianists. It supplies the hallmark of the French *style sévère* of fantasy within discipline.

Ronald Smith
Saltwood, 1999

To my wife

ALKAN

The Man

Contents

Acknowledgments

I would like to express my warmest appreciation to those many friends and colleagues without whose help this book could not have been written. Notably, I must thank Richard Shaw, whose investigation, under the auspices of Edinburgh University, of Alkan's life and background coincided with my own researches. Most generously he placed the fruits of his tireless and imaginative labours at my disposal.

Jean-Yves Bras and Robert Collet also supplied me with invaluable information.

I am equally indebted to the following members of Alkan's family: Madame Rachel Guerret, Madame Jacquéline Cuzelin, Madame Dora Ray and Mrs Elizabeth Pierce.

I must thank Miss Jane Harington of the Royal Academy of Music Library and Richard Christophers of the British Museum for their personal kindness and help.

The Bibliothèque Nationale, Paris, also gave me every assistance.

John and Marie-France Sugden of the King's School, Canterbury translated and summarised over two hundred pages of baffling French handwriting and Alan Ridout and Richard Gorer both read the typescript, offering many useful suggestions.

Richard Gorer helped with the proof-reading and I am also grateful to Gerda Stevenson for her excellent realisations, from old photographs of Delaborde and Marmontel.

Finally, words cannot convey my gratitude to my wife, whose uncanny conversion of her husband's illegible handwriting into impeccable typescript was but one of the many tasks she undertook with tact, patience, fortitude — even enthusiasm.

RONALD SMITH
Canterbury 1975

Introduction

No recent event in the world of piano music has been more remarkable than the discovery by an ever-widening public of the works of Alkan. How is it that this exciting, this powerful, this strangely haunting, often surprisingly modern sounding music could have escaped attention for over a century? Not only has much of it been available in excellent editions but quite spectacular claims have been made for its originality and importance by such musicians as Busoni, Sorabji and Petri, one praising its sombre lyricism, another its biting satire while Isidore Philipp speaks of 'marvellous sonorities and such difficulties that reach the utmost bounds of piano playing.' Enough, one might imagine, to quicken the most jaded appetite. Yet, until the appearance in the late 1960's of the first gramòphone records of such large-scale masterpieces as the *Concerto* and *Symphony for Solo Piano* the musical public had no means of testing the validity of Busoni's claim that Alkan, alongside Chopin, Liszt, Schumann and Brahms was one of the five greatest composers for the piano since Beethoven.

Critical acclaim, led by Harold Schonberg in America and by Roger Fiske and Stanley Sadie in the United Kingdom was immediate and decisive.

'As much of his best music is almost unplayably difficult,' wrote Dr. Fiske in *The Gramophone*, 'it is easy enough to see why he has never received his due as the most original composer for the piano of his century'.

Stanley Sadie, in *The Times,* emphasising Alkan's extraordinary dark power described the opening section of the *Concerto* as 'tough, severe, dramatic music, utterly unlike anyone elses.'

The time was right. An awakening interest was transformed into a consuming passion with urgent demands for more information about this lonely nineteenth century genius and his remarkable music. The purpose of this book is to attempt to fill in the tantalising gaps ... to examine those forces, internal and external, that threatened to tear Alkan apart, and to discuss some of the works the general music lover and student are likely to encounter.

1 Prodigy

'Charles Valentin Alkan has just died. It was necessary for him to die in order to suspect his existence. "Alkan," more than one reader will say, "who is Alkan?" And indeed this paradoxical man is all but unknown to our generation. This incomplete, this interrupted destiny, this living burial of an artist of his calibre ... are they caused by the very character of this artist, by his own desire, by his faults or even possibly by the exaggeration of his qualities? Or can it be that French soil is unsuited to the development of certain rare artistic plants? I cannot decide. I am only required to recall the name and work of an artist infinitely greater than thousands of his more celebrated and praised contemporaries.'

So far as Alkan's life is concerned these words might well have been written today. They are, in fact, quoted from an obituary that appeared on the back page of the Parisian magazine *Le Ménéstrel* on April the first, 1888. Nor was its author, Balthazar Claes, alone in his reaction to this most elusive and misunderstood of all French musicians. The following puzzling sentence, first published in 1877, opens a short account of the composer's life when Alkan was still very much alive.

'S'il est une physionomie d'artiste originale et curieuse à ètudier entre toutes, c'est bien certainement celle de Ch.-V. Alkan, dont l'intérêt se double d'une sorte de mystère et d'énigme à pénétrer.' (Marmontel: *les Pianistes Célèbres*)*

*If ever there were a strange, eccentric artistic personality to study it must surely be that of Ch-V Alkan, in whom interest is quickened by a screen of mystery and enigma which surrounds him.

Antoine Marmontel, head of the piano department in the Paris Conservatoire from 1848 to 1887 may, as we shall discover, have had his own rather special reason for wishing to emphasise the eccentricity of Alkan's personality, but clearly the task confronting the modern biographer is daunting. Published information is scanty and tenuous. Vital family documents were destroyed by fire during the Paris Commune in 1871. Memories of incidents handed down by word of mouth seem often ambiguous or contradictory. But above all there is the man himself, secretive, suspicious and with an almost pathological revulsion against intrusion into his private affairs. Little wonder that speculation and fantasy have filled the vacuum in our knowledge of his life until there is a very real danger of the legend devouring the man. Only persistent research and the elimination of countless false trails has at last revealed, like the completion of a complex mosaic, a design no less remarkable than the myth it was intended to supplant: a character and a career so strange, so perverse that the most febrile mind could scarcely have invented them.

First of all, confusion about the various names by which the composer has been known must be resolved. The two incorrect names Henri and Victorin which crept accidentally into early biographies have proved stubbornly resistant. They are best forgotten. He was registered simply as Charles-Valentin Morhange but quickly replaced the latter by his father's first name Alkan – Elkan in English and meaning 'The Lord has been gracious'. Signing himself C.V. Alkan aîné, he asserted his position as the eldest of five brothers, all of whom, adopting the name of Alkan, were destined to become distinguished Paris musicians.

The family name of Morhange identifies them as Ashkenazi Jews. Their ancestors had migrated from Eastern Europe in the Middle Ages to form a self-governing community in the little Alsatian town of that name. Here they endured conditions of acute privation, the harshest in the whole of France. The more enterprising left their poverty-stricken surroundings to seek their fortune elsewhere. Many gravitated to Paris settling in the ancient area known as the *Marais* which is still the centre of Jewish life and culture in the capital. A few steps from the noisy thoroughfare of the Rue St. Antoine and we are plunged into a lost world of exotic bazaars, sombre bookshops and twilit cafés. This network of narrow streets in which Jewish craftsmen, shoemakers, carpenters, jewellers go about their daily work is delightfully scruffy; its atmosphere secret, timeless and self-contained; vibrant with the gentle activity of going about its business; aware, but quietly aloof. To this day the name Morhange is familiar in the *Marais* and Alkan's paternal grandfather, Marix Morhange, was probably well established there by 1780, the year in which the composer's father, Alkan Morhange was born. Marix's solitary appearance as witness at a family ceremony establishes his date of birth as 1748-49 just fifteen years before the death of his future grandson's beloved Rameau, last of the great French harpsichord composers. Of Marix's background we know nothing, although the subsequent academic and musical career of his son and the remarkable gifts transmitted to his grandchildren and their progeny, is highly suggestive.

Again, nothing seems to be known of Alkan Morhange's education and early career, but he springs suddenly and vividly to life at the age of fifty-two. Writing nearly half a century later Marmontel recalls his close association with the Morhange household; an association as yet unclouded by future events. Alkan's father, he tells us, ran a little boarding-school in the Rue des Blancs-Manteaux in the *Marais*, where young, mainly Jewish children received an elementary education in music and French grammar. He goes on to describe an environment which must have been ideal for the nurturing of a young, phenomenal talent. 'I can still see that little house of Monsieur Alkan Père, that patriarchal milieu in which flourished the talent of Valentin Alkan and where flowered his industrious youth. I was myself a boarder there for several months during a period when a group of young people, including Ravina and Honoré, were coming regularly for lessons in solfège and musical theory. It was a kind of juvenile annexe to the Conservatoire. What happy, carefree evenings spent in Valentin Alkan's company, that is, of course, before he had become the lonely recluse of his maturity. Gay, joyous and full of confidence, he shared all the enthusiasms and happy illusions of youth'.

Marmontel describes Alkan's father as hardworking and

intelligent but, alas, makes no mention of his mother. Her name was Julie Abraham and she was born in 1784 or 5 at Mousigny in the Moselle. Her marriage to Alkan Morhange had taken place on 12th April 1810, when he was about thirty, her senior by five years. Their first-born, Céleste (25.2.1812) was succeeded by five musical brothers of whom the first and greatest was Charles -Valentin born on the 30th November 1813.

Quite clearly a prodigious talent began to emerge at a remarkably early age and one can imagine the young Alkan practising elaborate vocal exercises (doubtless egged on by his big sister who was also in training for the sight-singing 'Olympics') almost before he could walk or talk. Not only was he accepted as a student at the Paris Conservatoire at the age of six, but a mere year and a half later was awarded his Premier Prix for solfège, a form of vocal musicianship considered indispensible in the Conservatoire. The professors themselves, headed by their principal, Cherubini, composed the exercises which often required a highly developed contrapuntal skill and were specially devised for a course of study extending over several years. The Morhange household, it seems, must have devoured and breathed solfège. Sister Céleste and brothers Ernest, Maxime and Napoléon all gained first prizes in this exacting art at the precocious ages of thirteen, fifteen, eleven and eleven. Napoléon in fact, eventually became *doyen* of solfège in which capacity he played an active part, until his retirement from the Conservatoire in 1896, in the training of such famous musicians as Bizet and Sarasate. The other brothers, including the youngest, Gustave Alphonse, each pursued careers as pianists, composers and teachers: that is except Ernest, whose flute playing, noted for its 'neatness of execution', won him first prize in this instrument at sixteen. He went on to play in the orchestra of the Théatre du Gymnase.

In 1821, the year of his solfège triumph, the young seven-and-a-half-year-old Valentin made his first recorded public appearance, singularly enough as a violinist. His choice of an 'Air Varié' by Rode, probably 'La Ricordanza', suggests considerable development, for the piece, like most of its genre, requires an elegant treatment of such skills as *spiccato* and syncopated bowings across the strings as well as a firm security in treacherous double stopping. Presumably he had also been practising the piano in his spare time, for he was now accepted as a member of Zimmerman's class where he began to lay the foundation of that mastery which was later to become unsurpassed.

Joseph Zimmerman (1785-1853) was, from 1826 to 1848, the most celebrated piano teacher in the Conservatoire; but he was much more. As a former pupil of the great Cherubini, esteemed by Beethoven as the finest living stage composer, Zimmerman was a man of the widest culture, an opera composer and a highly respected contrapuntist. When one remembers that his later pupils included César Franck, Ambroise Thomas, Gounod and, in his last ten years, the youthful Bizet, the fact that Alkan remained his favourite can hardly be ignored. A beautiful pastel portrait of the young Alkan, now in the possession of his brother Napoléon's descendants, was commissioned by Zimmerman in honour of his brilliant pupil.

Was Alkan overworked as a child? According to the Conservatoire register he was often away sick, and although there is no reason to suspect more than the usual childish ailments, he does seem later to have become highly neurotic about his health. For the moment, however, nothing seemed to impede his progress, and by 1824 he had scored his second triumph with the even more coveted first prize for piano. It was now becoming obvious that the ten-year-old boy was something quite out of the ordinary, and Zimmerman lost no time in bringing him to the attention of leading musicians like Rossini who described him as 'that wonderful child'. While Zimmerman was arousing the interest of influential benefactors it was Alkan's father whose tactful initiative provided his son with his early and necessary public experience. On the 2nd April 1826 a concert 'Au benéfice du jeune Alkan âgé de onze ans' (he was, in fact 12!) was organised at the showrooms of Monsieur Pape. Thus started a close liaison between Alkan and the piano-manufacturing industry which was to endure for the rest of his long life. Apart from taking responsibility for such administrative chores as advance publicity, printing, and the engagement of supporting artists Alkan's father, probably encouraged by Zimmerman, was at pains to seek the official backing of the establishment. The young artist must have felt highly gratified when he received the following letter and

CONCERT

AU BÉNÉFICE DU JEUNE ALKAN,

AGÉ DE 11 ANS,

Elève de M. Zimmerman,

Dans lequel il exécutera un Air varié de sa Composition.

On y entendra : Mmes. PASTA, SCHUTZ, et Mlle. ALKAN; MM. RUBINI, GALLI, CAMUS, BENAZET, le jeune MASSARD, et d'autres Instrumentistes des plus distingués de la Capitale.

M

J'ai l'honneur de vous prévenir que ce Concert aura lieu le Dimanche 2 Avril prochain, à une heure, chez M. PAPE, Facteur de Pianos, rue de Valois, nº. 10, et rue des Bons-Enfans, nº. 19.

Votre très-humble et très-obéissant Serviteur,

Alkan

Rue Simon-le Franc, Nº. 10.

Paris, le Mars 1826.

Announcement of Alkan's first concert.

testimonial from the Director of Fine Arts, Vicomte de la Rochefoucauld, a few days before the event: 'It is with real pleasure, sir, that I am taking the opportunity of giving you evidence of the quite special interest your talent arouses in me. In accordance with the wish you have expressed, I am subscribing to your concert the sum of 100 francs'. The testimonial reads as follows: 'The young Alkan, whose precocious talent is the subject of admiration for lovers of firm and brilliant technique on the piano, proposes to give a concert on April 2nd and is desirous of obtaining for his musical gathering a subscription from the Department of Fine Arts. This artist, aged only 11 years [*sic*], is granted the encouragement he requests. It is proposed, therefore, to subscribe to his concert the sum of 100 francs'.

Alkan appeared for the first time in the combined role of pianist and composer and one of his supporting artists was his sister Céleste.

Apart from his studies with Zimmerman, Alkan was also established in Dourlen's harmony class and achieved his 'hat trick' with a 'first' in harmony in 1827. He was now a 'veteran' of 13, assisting Zimmerman as repetiteur and being introduced by his proud teacher to the Paris salons. The most important of these 'soirées' were those given by La Princesse de la Moscova. In later years Alkan spoke with tenderness of the reception he received from this influential lady; but he also recalled a dark cloud which descended on one of these brilliant occasions causing him deep, if temporary distress. He noticed the presence of a handsome stranger some two years his senior. Later, this striking youth was also invited to the piano. Imagine Alkan's feelings when, on the very scene of his own personal triumphs, he was now made to witness a display of virtuosity such as he had never even imagined and one which relegated him to second place! Tears of vexation, followed by a sleepless night, were merely the outward manifestations of this first encounter with Liszt. It may well have been his most enduring lesson for, late in life, the ever-generous Liszt declared that Alkan had the greatest technique he had ever known, a view not so surprising to those familiar with such compositions as *Quasi Faust* and the fearsome *Trois Grandes Etudes* op. 76.

2 Virtuoso

Alkan was now 15 and faced with that lonely, often painful struggle to survive the cosseted and transitory glory of the wonder-child. The next five years were devoted to consolidating a reputation that was already enabling him to play with such famous artists as the 'cellist Franchomme with whom he and a leading Paris violinist, Alard, were soon to form a trio. It may well have been Franchomme, five years his senior and the future dedicatee of Chopin's 'Cello Sonata', who first introduced Alkan to the Polish master. Although Alkan's first publications date from the early '30's they were probably written still earlier. Consisting of showy fantasies like *Il était un p'tit homme* op. 3, they display little beyond the all-too-familiar drawing-room elegance of the period. According to Fétis the first real landmark was an orchestral concert in the Conservatoire in 1831 at which the seventeen-year-old soloist scored a big success with a piano concerto of his own composition. Could this, one wonders, have been the First Concerto da Camera, op. 10, and published in 1834? This is the first work of Alkan to show a distinctive creative personality and a grasp of form quite absent from those earlier compositions.

By 1833 a recently founded periodical *Le Pianiste* was closely following his activities: 'Alkan's musical and intellectual faculties have shown a remarkable development for some time' we are told, and shortly afterwards the same paper reviewed another performance of a concerto of his own composition: 'Remarkable for its form and style which are new'. The scherzo, the writer tells us, was encored and there follows an interesting description which tallies with no surviving concerto by Alkan:

'A simple, gracious muted song for strings is accompanied by a series of chords which, passing from octave to octave, sustains the melody and produces an effect as original as it is ravishing'. This is quite sufficient to identify the piano part as the second of Alkan's *Trois Andantes Romantiques* op. 13 which was also published independantly as *Caprice ou Étude* in C sharp'. Sure enough, we find included in one of Alkan's last programmes a study in C sharp for piano and orchestra. Unfortunately there is now no way of identifying the remainder of the concerto played in 1833. The strange habit of interpolating an attractive solo piece with added orchestral background within the framework of a concerto was once the common practice of such artists as John Field, but the whole incident also underlines the difficulty of establishing the identity of some of Alkan's early compositions.

Later this same year, on St. Cecilia's day, Alkan was entrusted with the important piano part in a performance of Beethoven's Triple Concerto with distinguished members of the Paris Conservatoire Orchestra. The conductor, Habeneck, target for some of Berlioz's most sarcastic quips was, nevertheless, one of the most famous and influential conductors of his day, having introduced the Beethoven symphonies in France. The review was not without reservations: 'We must compliment Alkan on having rendered in all its purity, if a little coldly, the composer's text'. In a later chapter we will examine in some detail Alkan's stature as a pianist. For the moment the following notice in the *Revue et Gazette Musicale* of his performance at a similar concert just two years later gives a good idea of those qualities most admired in his playing at the age of twenty-one: 'The piano sings deliciously beneath his fingers and it would be difficult to find more vigour, more clarity or more brilliance than in his distinct, pure playing in which myriads of notes fall like an enchanted shower of pearls and diamonds'.

So far Alkan's career as a virtuoso had been confined to Paris but at nineteen he now felt sufficiently encouraged to embark upon a strangely unlikely adventure ... at least, in the light of his later habits, it would seem utterly out of character. In 1833 he set out for London where he established contact with the publishing house of Cocks and Son which was later to bring out several of his early compositions. Oddly enough there is no evidence of his having played in London, no concert announcement, no review: we do not even know where he stayed, what he did or whom he met — that is with just one exception. Early in 1834, and shortly after his visit, Henry Field of Bath, a celebrated English pianist (not to be confused with John Field, the creator of the Nocturne) gave a first performance of Alkan's second Concerto da Camera in Bath itself. The work, which is dedicated to Field, was also brought out by Cocks that year. So presumably, Alkan met, and probably played with Henry Field but, as far as we know, he neither spoke of his English excursion nor of his return there in 1835. Even less is known about this second visit: just the chance mention in a French periodical of a concert at which he played with Moscheles and Cramer, two pianists worshipped by London audiences. Alkan never left France again and soon became reluctant even to leave the capital. It is significant to read in *La France Musicale* of May 19, 1844: 'One by one the great pianists leave the capital ... Chopin, Liszt, Thalberg ... we do not yet know if Alkan will remain faithful to his beloved Paris'.

Between his two visits to London Alkan consolidated his reputation still further with a final first prize, this time for organ.

* * * * * *

Alkan now decided the time was right to forsake his parents' home in the *Marais* for that most fashionable centre of artistic life in the capital, the Square d'Orléans. Such was the prestige of its inhabitants, from writers like Alexandre Dumas and Joseph d'Ortigue to the ballerina Marie Taglioni, that the colony had been described as 'Une petite Athènes'. Here Alkan would live on equal terms with the celebrated pianists Kalkbrenner and Zimmerman, and later, when George Sand and Chopin moved into the square, he was to become Chopin's next door neighbour. Alkan and Chopin had become lifelong friends since the early 1830's. They were similarly fastidious, shared the same artistic ideals and enjoyed the same entertainments. Chopin gives details of one such outing with his friend: 'I went with Alkan to see Arnal at the Vaudeville in a new play by M. Duvert called 'Ce que femme veut'. Arnal, amusing as ever, tells his audience how he wanted to have a p — when he was in the train but could not get out before reaching Orléans. He doesn't utter a single improper word but everyone understands and it's a scream. He says the train stopped once and he wanted to get out, but he was told they were only "stopping to take in water for the engine" and "that was not at all what he wanted" — and so on.

According to Marmontel, Chopin, who was not prodigious with his affection, counted Alkan high on the small list of his confidants. In 1848 when Chopin was in Britain escaping the Paris revolution he wrote anxious letters about his friend's safety and even remembered him on his death-bed bequeathing to Alkan and another musician his uncompleted piano method. Alkan was, for his part, fascinated by the Polish genius, especially by the fierce national element in his compositions. His opinion of Chopin's playing, which he considered inimitable, will be discussed in a later chapter; and he and Chopin also enjoyed playing together. On one occasion Zimmerman, Chopin and his pupil Gutmann (the giant-fisted dedicatee of his master's 3rd Scherzo) all collaborated with Alkan in a performance of the latter's eight-handed arrangement of Beethoven's Seventh Symphony. Chopin survived this alarming event on 3rd March 1838 but a few years later pleaded insufficient strength to take his part in a repeat performance.

By the time of Alkan's arrival in the Square d'Orléans, he and Liszt were also on friendly terms, earlier rivalry having been forgotten. An article about Liszt published in 1835 mentions that his friends included Berlioz, Hiller, Mendelssohn, Alkan and Chopin; but although Alkan doubtless profited from Liszt's presence and collaboration at his concerts, he certainly shared a little of Chopin's envy at their friend's meteoric rise to fame, and some of his scepticism about his method of boosting it. Few of Liszt's colleagues could resist his spell-binding personality: few remained uninfluenced by his generosity. Yet such fastidious artists as Chopin and Alkan must often have felt their hackles rise at some of the antics with which the 'King of Pianists' would hypnotise his audience — that is, of course, before he became the 'Grand Seigneur' of later years. The following description quoted from Sacheverell Sitwell's book on the composer, gives an impression of Liszt's playing in Paris in 1835:-

'I saw Liszt's countenance assume that agony of expression, mingled with radiant smiles of joy, which I never saw in any other human face except in the paintings of our Saviour by some of the early masters: his hands rushed over the keys, the floor on which I sat shook like a wire and the whole audience was wrapped in sound, when the hand and frame of the artist gave way. He fainted in the arms of the friend who was turning over the pages for him and we bore him out in a strong fit of hysterics. The effect of this scene was really dreadful. The whole room sat breathless with fear, 'till Hiller came forward and announced that Liszt was already restored to consciousness and was comparatively well again. As I handed Madame Circourt to her carriage we both trembled like poplar leaves, and I tremble scarcely less as I write this'.

Liszt was, of course, a great champion of other peoples' music, yet there seems no evidence that he played a note of Alkan in public. As one of the very few pianists then capable of meeting the challenge of his friend's finest works he might well have turned the tide in Alkan's favour. For his part Alkan had a pretty poor opinion of Liszt as a composer. Even so, the two artists were not without mutual influence. Playing, such as Liszt's famous performance in 1836 of his arrangement of the *March to the Scaffold* (a *tour de force* which Hallé tells us surpassed even the splendour of Berlioz's original orchestration) probably taught Alkan more than ten years in the Conservatoire about the possibility of turning his piano into an orchestra. An examination of Alkan's Grande Sonate, on the other hand, soon reveals that the composer of the B minor Sonata must have been familiar with this little-known masterpiece written just six years earlier.

An important batch of compositions from Alkan's pen was published in 1837,including *Trois Études de Bravoure* op. 12, *Trois Andantes Romantiques* op. 13 and *Trois Grandes Études* (later re-named *Trois Morceaux dans le genre pathétique*) op. 15 which he dedicated to Liszt. This extraordinary but strangely uneven work consisting of three pieces entitled *Aime Moi, Le Vent* and *Morte* came in for some pretty harsh criticism from Schumann who described it as 'false, unnatural art ... In *Aime moi* we have a watery French melody with a middle part unsuited to its title; in *Le Vent* there is a chromatic howl over an idea from Beethoven's 7th Symphony; and in the last we have a crabbed waste overgrown with brushwood and weeds, the best of it borrowed from Berlioz ...' Liszt, the dedicatee, could afford to be more generous. In an extended, complimentary but not uncritical article in the *Revue et Gazette*, 22nd October 1837, he finds the first piece 'simple, tender and full of melancholy': the second 'marvellously conveys the sound of those prolonged winds which moan monotonously for whole days.' Liszt analyses *Morte* at some length but concludes that, although it contains some beautiful things, Alkan seems encumbered by detail. Both he and Schumann remark on the fact that the whole work is published without tempo indications and dynamics. To twentieth century ears *Morte*, with its oppressive use of the *Dies Irae* and its sombre bell effects, which so strangely foresadow *Le Gibet* by Ravel, is by far the most telling of these pieces and the one most indicative of Alkan's later development.

On the 3rd March 1838, at that same concert at which Beethoven's 7th was performed, Alkan defied Schumann's accusation of plagiarising the Symphony's Allegretto by playing *Le Vent*. The performance was highly praised by the veteran critic Henri Blanchard as 'a delicious conception of descriptive music' adding, perhaps a little untactfully that Auber, in his ingenious portrayal of snow does not approach so near the truth. Auber was later to become head of the Conservatoire and this comparison could not have endeared Alkan to him. *Le Vent* may not be one of Alkan's best pieces but it caught the imagination of several later pianists like Adela Verne and Harold Bauer whose performance of it, around the turn of the century, was said to be 'electrifying'.

By the end of 1838 Alkan's *Trois Scherzi* op. 16, his *Six Morceaux Characteristiques* and the monstrous *Trois Grandes Etudes*, for the hands separately and reunited — later to be given the misleading opus number of 76 — were all in print. The impressive study for right hand alone must remain one of the most appallingly difficult pieces ever written and although Busoni played the study for left hand, and Rudolf Ganz the powerful moto perpetuo which reunites the hands, no public performance of the right hand study has yet been traced. The Three Scherzi, with their persistant rhythms and bold clean-cut outlines, are among the most attractive of Alkan's early works and are well worth playing, even if only for the irresistible trio of the first scherzo. Again and again one finds oneself returning to this delicate invocation of chiming bells, their falling cadences melting elusively into a shimmering haze of pedal-held sound.

The Six Characteristic Pieces, later incorporated into *Les Mois* op. 74, are early examples of Alkan's genius as a miniaturist and lie well within the scope of the amateur pianist. This is the only other work of Alkan that Schumann reviewed. One of these pieces entitled *L'Opéra* cleverly parodies French Grand Opera of the day and it struck a sympathetic chord in Schumann who had been busily castigating its most likely target, Meyerbeer, during those last two years. Schumann was far less enthusiastic about the other pieces which failed to satisfy his quest for emotional warmth and he adds a sting to the tail of his review, which concludes: 'The composer may be an interesting player who well understands the rarer effects of his instrument, but as a composer only the severest studies will enable him to make much progress, for he sinks too frequently into mere superficiality'. This harsh criticism may be justified in the light of Schumann's own standard of taste: but here a comparison with his review of Berlioz's *Fantastic Symphony* is instructive. Those very elements he found disturbing in Berlioz like 'flat and common harmonies, unclean and vague ones ... and some that sound bad, tormented and twisted' would have seemed to him the very stuff that Alkan's music was made of. The cold, stark realism that we now so admire in Alkan must have struck Schumann simply as tasteless incompetence.

We have no way of knowing if Alkan saw these reviews, which had appeared in the *Neue Zeitschrift für Musik* in May 1838 and May 1839, but he certainly never bore Schumann a grudge on their account. Perhaps, as we shall see in the next chapter, he was far too engrossed in personal matters to worry about bad notices.

3 Delaborde

Delaborde is a name not unknown to connoisseurs of Alkan's music, for it appears on the outer cover of the familiar Costallat-Billaudot edition of the composer's works. Otherwise very little is known about him, which is a pity.

Elie Miriam Delaborde was born in Paris on 8th February 1839 and was destined to become one of France's leading pianists. He studied with Alkan, Moscheles and Henselt, but in certain French musical circles it has been loudly whispered that his link with Alkan was rather more intimate than that of pupil and teacher. The claim that Delaborde was Alkan's natural son has been passed on and accepted by pupils of Isidore Philipp, the other name which appears on the title page of Alkan's music. No one seems ever to have questioned this relationship, yet it has proved stubbornly difficult to confirm. To start with no official document could be traced to prove Delaborde's identity; neither birth, marriage nor death certificate was issued in that name and investigation under the names of Alkan and Morhange has proved equally unproductive. Indeed, from a legal point of view Delaborde seems never to have existed, but such a disadvantage in no way inhibited him from pursuing a distinguished musical and artistic career or from living a highly colourful life as sportsman, amorist and naturalist. He was a champion swimmer, a passion he shared with his neighbour, Bizet. Indeed the death of Bizet seems to have been accelerated by a swimming expedition with Delaborde in the Seine. Furthermore the suspicion that Delaborde was at that very time having an affair with Madame Bizet finds ample confirmation in the recent discovery by Jean-Yves Bras of a marriage announcement which appeared in a French magazine not long after the composer's death, between Delaborde and Bizet's widow.

This event, however, did not take place, and when Delaborde did eventually marry, on the 20th March 1901, at the age of 62, it was to a lady with the resounding name of Marie Thérèse de Courchant des Sablons. One can only hope she shared some of her husband's unusual enthusiasms for it must have been a unique and somewhat unnerving household. Delaborde's steady stream of pupils seemed undeterred, however, by the presence of two mighty apes who roamed his studio; and when the war of 1870 drove him to giving concerts in London he was accompanied by his retinue of 121 parrots and cockatoos. Can one reasonably believe that so extrovert and sturdy a character could conceivably be the son of the ever-ailing, introverted Alkan?

Philipp clearly had no doubts about the relationship and it was from Philipp too, that the veiled suggestion that Delaborde's mother was a lady of high birth gave us our first clue to her shadowy identity. From the same source it was also intimated that Delaborde bore Alkan a bitter grudge for denying him full legal status and that he was only reluctantly persuaded to add his own, illustrious, name to Philipp's on the cover of his 'father's' music.* This being so, it is difficult to understand why Delaborde troubled to introduce Alkan's latest *pédalier* works to London audiences in 1871, gave duet performances with him in Paris or accepted the dedication of his *Bombardo-Carillon*, that monstrous pedal-board duet for four feet alone which caused Rudolf Ganz such embarrassment when he tried it out with a lady pupil. Raymond Lewenthal, who studied with a pupil of Delaborde, accepts the filial relationship without question, adding that father and son shared Alkan's apartment; but he gives no clue as to his source of information. We do know, however, that Delaborde was one of the very few people who had free access to the composer in his later years.

---

*A former pupil of Delaborde, Gabrielle Fleury, told Robert Collet, that her teacher was, indeed, the natural son of Alkan. This was later confirmed by Philipp who added: 'Il détestait son père.'

This is how Alexandre de Bertha, a Hungarian pianist describes his first meeting with Alkan: 'It was at the beginning of 1872 that M. Delaborde, the superb pianist and eminent professor at the Conservatoire introduced me to Alkan with an eagerness all too rare among colleagues'. Nowhere in Bertha's long account of the composer is there the slightest hint of a father and son relationship. Delaborde was, of course, still very much alive in 1909 when this article was published, so either Bertha was unaware of his friend's identity or was preserving a well-guarded secret. Furthermore, there is only one most casual reference to Delaborde in a vast collection of recently discovered letters written by Alkan and spanning the crucial thirty years from Delaborde's early teens:- letters in which Alkan often compares his own personal isolation to others' family responsibilities. He did, however remember Delaborde in his will, identifying him as Elie Miriam dit Delaborde and it may have been this information that set Jean-Yves Bras on the fruitful track of Delaborde's elusive mother. Monsier Bras, whose major investigation of Alkan's life and background is eagerly awaited, has most generously provided the following information: 'Elie Miriam dit Delaborde was born on the 8th February 1839, the son of Lina Eraîm Miriam rentière (a lady of means) living in Paris: father unknown.' The name of Delaborde, M. Bras suggests, may have been adopted from his foster mother who was living in Brittany during his childhood and to whom the boy was very attached. He also confirms that the only known official intimation that he was related to Alkan is his citation in Alkan's will. In the face of such scanty legal information one is obliged to fall back on circumstantial evidence and this is strong. Apart from his musical ability Delaborde was a fine painter, a gift that has persisted up to the present day in the Alkan-Morhange family. Alkan's elaborate *Marcia Funebre sulla Morte d'un Pappagallo* written, incidentally, when Delaborde was about nineteen, suggests that he was also a parrot fancier. Again a penchant for birds and animals persists in the Alkan family. But surely the most conclusive evidence that Delaborde was, indeed, Alkan's son is that no one has ever denied it, no other father has ever been suggested and the family itself has never questioned the relationship, including Elie Miriam dit Delaborde in the family tree.

Elie Miriam Delaborde
(Artist's realisation from a photograph: courtesy of Bibliothèque Nationale, *Paris)*

* * * * * *

During the 1830's Paris had become the centre of a unique explosion of pianistic talent. Stars like Chopin, Liszt, Thalberg and Kalkbrenner could all be heard and compared within the space of a few days, not only separately but often sharing the same platform in a kind of pianistic jamboree. The following event is typical: 'On April 30th (1837) the young César-Auguste (Franck) aged fourteen, is to be found appearing on the concert platform on an equal commercial basis with three of the best known virtuosi of the time, the pianist Pixis, now nearing fifty, the celebrated Alkan and the illustrious Franz Liszt ...'

The 'celebrated Alkan' was himself only twenty-four but fast becoming recognised as the leading French pianist. His future position in the Conservatoire, where his salary had now been increased to 1,000 francs, seemed hardly less assured. It was here, a year later, that he again met César Franck, but in rather different circumstances. Alongside the ageing Cherubini he was one of the examiners obliged to disqualify his young colleague for overstepping the regulations in the piano competition. Franck, eager to show off his transposing powers, had given a perfect rendering of the difficult sight-reading test, but in a remote key. Accordingly he 'failed' to qualify for the coveted first prize, but in recognition of his feat was given a 'Grand prix d'Honneur' as a specially created award. Perhaps Alkan had a hand in placating the rigid, regulation-conscious Cherubini on the boy's behalf, for Franck was not so generously treated three years later when he pushed his luck still further in the organ prize by combining two unofficially related subjects in an improvised fugue.

By the end of the decade Alkan's brilliance as a pianist was being matched by his ambition as a composer and the publication of his latest piano works in 1837 and 1838 marked a bold advance. In his threefold capacity of composer, performer and teacher Alkan had reason to feel reassured. His concert on 3rd March 1838, at which his distinguished guest artists included Chopin, must have been a memorable occasion: 'This brilliant evening' wrote the *Revue et Gazette* 'maintained for M. Alkan the twofold reputation he has already won as instrumentalist and composer. The large audience who flocked to hear him were unanimous in their enthusiasm'.

How little could this large, enthusiastic audience have realised their privilege: for they had just witnessed the end of Alkan's career as a virtuoso. Quite suddenly, without warning, his name vanishes from the pages of French musical periodicals and does not re-appear until he is over thirty. It is most puzzling. Was he suddenly smitten by some strange and protracted illness? If so no one has ever breathed a word of it and there is not the slightest hint that his health, at twenty-five was anything but robust. Could it be that he was becoming increasingly aware of his creative genius and simply felt the urge to devote more time to composition? Indeed, these mysterious and silent six years were highly productive; and not only so far as his music is concerned. Is it sheer coincidence that Alkan's self-imposed withdrawal from the Paris musical fray should date from the months immediately preceding the birth of Delaborde? Assuming he was Delaborde's father, and there now seems little reason for doubting the relationship, is it not feasible that he may have suffered a violent upheaval in his personal life: one which could have set up the preliminary tremors of that gradual change in his personality which would not only throw him off course but would ultimately plough his career into the ground? We can know nothing, of course, about the nature and depth of his relationship with the elusive Lina Miriam. Alkan always kept his private life very much to himself, and it is even possible that his closest associates and family knew little of a liaison which was to remain the composer's most jealously guarded secret.

Alkan never married.*

*Even as this book goes to print the author has just had the pleasure, while introducing Alkan's music in Australia, of meeting Mr. Cyril Ray, the great-grandson of Napoleon Alkan. Mr. Ray adds the following information about Delaborde's mother, which confirm our suspicions. Although her name was never divulged she was understood to have been a pupil of Alkan, a lady of high social standing . . . . and already married.

4 A Lost Symphony

On 14th April 1844, the following notice appeared in *La France Musicale*: 'We are happy to announce that Alkan has at last decided to give a concert on the 29th of April in the Salle Erard. Everyone knows of Alkan's superiority as a composer: now they will have an opportunity to judge for themselves his superiority as a performer'.*

Apart from being Alkan's first and only known solo recital the programme itself is of great interest. He opened with two movements from his *Second Concertino*, a solo adaptation, perhaps, of his *Second Concerto da Camera*, already published in England. But there is clearly some muddle, for although this recital was not reviewed in *La France Musicale*, we are told the following November, in its news section, that Alkan's 'magnificent Concerto, excerpts from which had produced such a huge sensation at his recital last winter, is soon to be published'. No concerto by Alkan *was* published during the 1840's and so the identity of this 'sensational' work must remain a mystery. It was followed by five equally unidentified *Petits Morceaux* which were played without break, and then came a Bach Gavotte, a Scarlatti Allegro and Alkan's own transcription of the minuet from Mozart's G minor Symphony. The Bach and Scarlatti may also have been arrangements but not, one assumes, the next two

*Although this announcement gives the impression that Alkan was a stranger to the Paris public, Hugh Macdonald's researches have yielded information about an earlier re-appearance on 27 Feb., 1844. d'Ortigue's review is of special interest as it mentions hitherto unknown and missing works, including quintets and sextets. According to Escudier, Alkan's April recital was rapturously received by a distinguished audience which included Chopin, Liszt, Sand and Dumas.

items: the Rondo from one of Beethoven's Sonatas op. 31, and Weber's *Moto Perpetuo*. The recital ended with four important first performances: *Air de Ballet, Nocturne, Saltarelle* and *Alleluia*.

As these were all about to appear in print as his op. 22 to 25 one suspects that his publisher may have had a hand in persuading Alkan to break his six year's silence. The *Saltarelle* with its hair-raising leaps and furious energy quickly caught the fancy of a sensation-loving public. Only a month after their publication a certain Josephine Martin introduced all five of Alkan's latest works to Paris including the *Gigue* op. 24, which the composer seems to have omitted from his programme. Playing on a magnificent new seven-octave Pleyel concert grand she produced 'a powerful and elegant sonority' and was given a standing ovation. The *Saltarelle* in particular was 'interrompu à chaque reprise par les applaudissments frénétiques'. This ecstatic notice in *La France Musicale* ends by saying; 'There will soon be no pianist unacquainted with these latest brilliant productions by Alkan'. Few artists can so thoroughly detach themselves from public recognition as to remain indifferent to such appreciation and Alkan was sufficiently encouraged to plan further concerts during the next season and, more important, to throw himself with renewed vigour into his creative work.

On 27th October 1844 *La France Musicale* gives further news of his activities and intentions: 'Alkan's latest compositions are enjoying an enormous success and, encouraged by the enthusiastic acclaim he received at his concert last season, this great artist has consented to appear again this winter with new masterpieces including a four-handed Fantasy based on *Don Juan*, and two important études, *Le Preux* and *Le Chemin de Fer*. Moreover he has just completed two Marches which he introduced to a private audience of friends and we declare them among his finest works yet for the piano. Above all, the controlled verve and power with which he played the *Marche Héroique* are characteristic of a talent which unites all the factions in their admiration.' The two Marches did not appear until December 1846 when they were published separately, with a dedication to his pupil La Duchesse de Montebello as *Marche Funêbre*, op. 26 and *Marche Triomphale*, op. 27 ... an opus number already given to *Chemin de Fer* by a rival publisher.

Alkan must have known Berlioz's great *Symphonie Funêbre et Triomphale* for massed bands, which received several performances in Paris during the early 1840's, yet, apart from their titles and an expression of public, rather than private emotion, Alkan's Two Marches have little in common with the Symphony. The facile description of Alkan as 'The Berlioz of the Piano' should not, in fact, mislead us. Both composers, it is true, discovered unheard-of sonorities for their very different media; both imbued a familiar language with new and disturbing power; yet even a common preoccupation with the darker shades of human experience only highlights the difference in their personalities. Humphrey Searle makes this admirably clear when he speaks of 'that element of "terribilità" which in Berlioz generally takes the form of wild devilment, in Alkan of icy restraint'. The Funeral March, with its spare textures, its hypnotically repeated rhythms and its telling use of a growling bass register in imitation of muffled drums, is a remarkable early example of Alkan's uniqueness in this respect.

So far the composer's growing reputation had been confined to solo piano pieces or works in which the piano played a dominant role. The sole exceptions were two unpublished cantatas dating from 1832 and 1834 and a *Pas Redoublé* for military band dated 1840. The former remain a sad monument to two youthful attempts at the Prix de Rome whereas the occasion that prompted the latter must remain a mystery. Far more important are two fine chamber works which he published in 1840 and 1841 but which seem to have passed unnoticed. Both the *Grand Duo* for violin and piano with its blood-thickening slow movement marked 'l'Enfer' (hell) and the impressive Trio, a favourite with Mendelssohn who enjoyed playing the piano part, are unique in their own special way. Although they made little immediate impact in Paris, due, no doubt, to Alkan's temporary absence from the concert scene, they show that by the early 1840's he was beginning to feel the urge to test his creative powers on a broader canvas.

Yet they hardly prepare us for an arresting announcement in *La France Musicale* on 7th November 1844. 'Alkan has now written a Symphony for full orchestra on which he is pinning his highest hopes. The season will not pass without a performance'

... but the season did pass without a performance ... and the next season and the one after that ... and had it not been that Alkan showed the manuscript to Léon Kreutzer, son of the well-known dedicatee of Beethoven's Violin Sonata, the very existence of Alkan's Symphony, as a completed work, must have remained doubtful. This is how Kreutzer describes it in an extended article about Alkan which appeared in the *Revue et Gazette* in January 1846: 'The unpublished Symphony, which M. Alkan was willing to show me, borrows nothing from the capricious forms which the modern symphony has adopted.' He then gives a detailed analysis of each of the Symphony's four movements. The first, he tells us, is notable for its highly organised development section, and he also singles out a striking effect in the second subject which involves a pedal-point on the woodwind. There follows a spirited Scherzo with a particularly charming Trio. Kreutzer is most revealing when it comes to the Adagio, although he could little have realised the significance for Alkan of certain Hebrew characters in red ink which decorated its first page. It was a verse from Genesis, Alkan informed him, no less: 'God said let there be light and there was light'. In a detailed comparison with the opening of Haydn's *Creation* Kreutzer concludes that where Haydn scores with his extraordinary inspired depiction of 'chaos' it is Alkan who is far more convincing in his announcement of the 'explosion of light'. He writes: 'The crescendo is superlatively achieved. The wind unisons mingled with rapid scales produce the most grandiose effect'. Kreutzer found the Finale less impressive in ideas but highly skilful in treatment. The manuscript of Alkan's B minor Symphony has long since disappeared and although hope of its re-discovery one day has not been abandoned it is likely to remain a tantalising mystery. Only the solo parts of the two Concerti da Camera have survived although we do know that the First was with small orchestra and the Second with strings alone. The manuscript of the *Pas Redoublé* shows a skilled use of heavy brass but it is far too limited, musically, to shed any useful light on Alkan's orchestration. Some imaginative woodwind writing, however, in the *Marcia sulla Morte d'un Pappagallo* of 1859 suggests that his orchestral writing might have been just as pungent and direct as his treatment of the piano.

5 The "Grande Sonate"

At the beginning of 1838 Alkan's career as a virtuoso had reached its peak and collapsed. Now, as 1844 was drawing to its close there seemed every sign that he was to achieve his first real break-through as a composer. Stimulated, no doubt, by the success of his latest piano pieces he was caught up on a wave of creative energy which had just reached its climax with the B minor Symphony. But Alkan's destiny was not written in the stars: rather was it the child of his own complex nature, his ambivalence and his over-sensitive reaction to the vagaries of life.

On March 1st and 30th April 1845, he gave two important public concerts at the Salle Erard. Although appearing in every item, Alkan shared the programme with supporting artists including his brother Napoléon who, at eighteen, was also starting to make a considerable name as a concert pianist. A generous number of his own compositions were interspersed with classical works by Mozart, Beethoven, Schubert and Mendelssohn. We are told nothing of public reaction or support but the only performance to receive unstinted praise from the *Revue et Gazette* was the one with which he opened, the Adagio from Hummel's B minor Concerto performed with its original orchestration of four horns and low strings. After the euphoria of the previous year it must have struck Alkan like a cold shower to be told publicly that his playing 'lacked breadth, passion, poetry and imagination'; that his choice of music was 'old-fashioned' (a Schubert minuet) or 'drily scholastic' (a Mendelssohn fugue); but worse was to follow. His compositions were simply: 'the work of a man stirred by the cold; the systematic ... one who is occupied a great deal more by his own impressions than by those which he might produce on his audience.' Once more Alkan retired into his shell.

The following year saw the appearance of Kreutzer's long article about Alkan, the one in the *Revue et Gazette* in which the Symphony is analysed. Kreutzer also throws an interesting light on some of the adverse criticism of Alkan's latest concerts. 'Artists' he tells us 'appreciate his talent as a pianist better than the public. This was quite clear at the concerts he gave in the Erard "salons".' While applauding Alkan's conviction that he must lead, not follow public taste, both in his playing and in his choice of repertoire, Kreutzer feared that Alkan's zeal in this direction bordered on despotism and that his campaign against 'the false, the convulsive, the affected and the portentous' sometimes robbed him of inspirational freedom when playing in public. He also discusses Alkan's attitude to his career, its virtues, its dangers. He contrasts the worldly reputations of those who nurture their careers with the lot of the true artists whose lives are dedicated to contemplation and study. 'These latter' he writes 'having spent too much time on their work to spend any part of it on publicity and canvassing become a little disgusted with a public which does not come and seek them out. They continue, all the same, to perfect their own works but do nothing to promote them thus dedicating them to obscurity. Some time ago we told our readers of M. Reber who carries this need for obscurity almost to the lengths of a passion. Valentin Alkan is another of these misanthropes of the musical world'.

There is much common sense in Kreutzer's reasoning which is as relevant today as it was then: yet his sympathetic appraisal of Alkan's position and the gentle advice that he should re-think it is surely mistaken. A complete artist can only be true to himself. To ask him to be more 'realistic' is simply an invitation to do just that which he cannot do ... to compromise.

Although Alkan made no further bid to woo the Paris musical élite during the following three years he continued to attract the attention of the *Revue et Gazette*. On 25th July 1847 a further major article was devoted to him and this time the author was none other than its founder, the highly respected Fétis himself. His review of Alkan's latest production, the *25 Préludes* op. 31, as well as the Two Marches op. 26 and 27, is a masterly combination of perception and bigotry. Praising the Funeral March as 'the perfect expression of religious fear mingled with regret' he goes on to challenge several 'unjustifiable harmonic audacities' in the *Marche Triomphale*. His searching analysis of these outrages against a harmonic system of which he was himself the self-appointed guardian makes quaint reading today. There then follows a very full and enlightened discussion of the new Preludes. The form, style, atmosphere and even the interpretation of each piece is considered in turn and Fétis has only one reservation, the composer's tendency to return again and again to an atmosphere of melancholy. Indeed he believes this atmosphere pervades too much of Alkan's work, even the *Marche Triomphale*. In seeking an explanation he echoes Kreutzer's warning: 'When an artist sees himself unappreciated while others with little talent create reputations, he becomes irritated: he retires into himself and despises his century. Then, either he condemns himself to silence, or his work becomes imbued with a melancholy which only indicates his mournful state of spirit, not his natural gifts. He continues: 'Alkan is not just a great pianist, he is an original composer stirred by the sacred fire. Unfortunately too many years have elapsed and still his ability has not been recognised for what it is. But is not this destiny perhaps the artist's own fault? Has he not become discouraged too soon?' Fétis ends with a plea. 'An artist owes it to himself, his time and his century to allow his faculties full rein. God does not grant these gifts without obligation'.

When he uttered these words Fétis was sixty-three, the elder statesman and spokesman of a generation of French musicians who had watched Alkan's career unfold from its early promise to its present uncertainty. He and Kreutzer had sounded Alkan out and their worst fears were confirmed. These public expressions of their misgivings, however, although kindly meant, were probably misplaced and may even have driven the sensitive artist further in on himself. Certainly Alkan took little heed of their exhortations. His public career continued to stagnate while the early promise of a distinguished academic position had also withered, unfulfilled. When, in 1842, the seemingly indestructible Cherubini, for twenty years Director of the Conservatoire, had at last died, Alkan found himself deprived of one of his earliest benefactors. The appointment moreover of the celebrated opera composer, Auber, in Cherubini's place was to prove a further check to his faltering career.

Fortunately Alkan's finest creative achievements were often wrested from a background of dark uncertainty and whatever his psychological condition might have been during this disquieting period, he was not idle. In 1847 he published his important *Douze Études dans tous les tons Majeurs*, op. 35 and then, towards the end of the year he unleashed a great monster of a work, the *Grande Sonate* op. 33. Raymond Lewenthal has described this sonata as 'a cosmic event in the composer's development and in the history of piano music'. Its four epic movements, each slower than the last, represent man's psychological state at the ages of 20, 30, 40 and 50. Fétis must have been dismayed by the Finale, a devastatingly powerful Adagio subtitled *Prometheus Bound* in which man suffers his final disintegration. As William Mann has remarked 'It seems that Alkan, at 30 expected to be an old crock at 50'!

The Sonata was dedicated to the composer's father, Alkan Morhange, now sixty-seven, anything but an 'old crock' and still teaching as vigorously as ever. The following advertisement had appeared only three years earlier: 'Monsieur Alkan Père of 12, Rue des Marais-du-Temple, Paris, is taking boarders for music. The numerous successful pupils trained by M. Alkan Père over the last twenty years who have entered the Conservatoire recommend this skilful teacher to the confidence and kindness of families'. (*La France Musicale, 1844*)

6 Marmontel

The publication in 1847 of Alkan's *Grande Sonate* was a landmark in the history of piano music. Not only was the work quite unlike any other sonata but it also opened up a new world of technical possibilities. One can well imagine the composer's hopes and anxieties as he awaited reaction to this latest and most ambitious work. For three years now the Symphony on which he had pinned such high hopes had been lying in his portfolio untried, unheard. His participation in the public musical life of Paris was becoming tenuous in the extreme. One has very much the impression of a man caught between the opposing forces of ambition and retreat, hovering in a kind of no-man's-land of grey uncertainty. He was now in his mid-thirty's. His prestige as a pianist was almost legendary, yet he seemed unable or, perhaps, unwilling to exploit it. On the other hand his experience as a teacher and his unchallenged authority as one of the leading musicians of his day had still not brought him the expected reward of a major post in the Conservatoire, its financial security and the cachet which always attends such a position. If ever an artist needed a moral and psychological boost it was Alkan in 1848. Would not this latest proof of his originality and mastery surely stifle any lingering doubts about his position as the greatest pianist-composer to have emerged from the French school? At the outset of 1848 the work was hardly in print when Paris became plunged in revolution, its artistic life at a standstill. 'All the Parisian pianists are here in London' wrote Chopin, one of the many fugitives from a turbulent city; and so Alkan's *Grande Sonate* was stillborn, unnoticed, unplayed and, like his

Symphony, condemned to oblivion. Not until after the bloodletting of June 1848 was some degree of social life restored to a city still wracked by political instability. By this time, however, Alkan could give little thought to either politics or composition: for the chance he had so long sought seemed at last within his grasp.

During that stifling summer of 1848, with the thunder of violence still menacing a divided capital, a bloodless, but no less bitter struggle for power was in progress within the walls of the Conservatoire itself. Joseph Zimmerman, sensing a mounting hostility from the establishment, decided to relinquish his position as Head of the Piano Department. As Zimmerman's favourite and most distinguished pupil Alkan was, by common consent, the 'heir apparent' to this important post and the moment the vacancy was advertised he put forward his name. He and three other candidates were short-listed. Emile Prudent and Louis Lacombe were no mean pianists but hardly serious competitors against a musician of Alkan's standing. As for the fourth nominee, Alkan must have let out a gasp of astonishment: Antoine Francois Marmontel, his old pupil and camarade. How was it possible that a musician of so little substance, a mere run-of-the-mill product of the Conservatoire could find his name coupled with those of the celebrated Prudent and Lacombe, not to mention that of Alkan himself? Surely he could not be taken seriously by the selection committee?

Even so, the very presence of so unlikely a name as that of Marmontel among the selected candidates, must have caused Alkan a mild twinge of anxiety. A few discreet enquiries soon resolved the mystery. Marmontel was protecting his position by playing up to Auber, the Head of the Conservatoire, and Auber, in turn, was quite clearly favouring Marmontel with his friendship. Anxiety gave way to panic. The reticent Alkan had to act quickly. He could no longer count on Zimmerman who, as the former teacher of all four candidates, could take no part in the nomination of his successor. He found himself alone, fighting not only for his own future but, as he saw it, the whole future standard of teaching in the Conservatoire. It is always an embarrassment to see a man acting out of character but the following letters must be allowed to speak for themselves. Alkan immediately set about obtaining letters of recommendation to be sent to those concerned with the nomination, notably the recently appointed Director of the Department of Fine Arts, Charles Blanc.

Alkan to George Sand. Monday 14th August 1848.
'Excellent Madam,

I have just read your two letters to my mother and have passed on to M. Ch. Blanc the one that concerns him. If you could have seen my mother's face you would have read on it the expression of thanks you so warmly deserve. I do not yet know what course this affair will take, each day presenting new intrigues, new difficulties: but I tell you quite seriously, whatever happens, I am very happy that it has yielded to me the testimonials with which you honoured me this morning'.

Alkan to George Sand. 23rd August 1848.

'I did not wish to worry you again about myself, Madam ... but, however indiscreet I may seem, I am so worried I can wait no longer.

... My rivals, one above all — the most unworthy — are gaining ground each day. If, amidst all the preoccupations which I appreciate only too well, M. Ch. Blanc were able and willing to settle this matter immediately and in my favour, he could do so ... I see the 'École' [Conservatoire] threatened by the most unbelievable, the most disgraceful nomination. Two have already been made since the arrival of the new Board at the Department of Fine Arts. I see they are very afraid of making a third mistake, and perhaps their fear, together with bad advice, will make them do just this. Come to my help, Madam, by being willing to make your voice heard to M. Ch. B., however distressing the circumstances may be. Otherwise, M. Auber, who does not like me at all, in returning the friendship of him [Marmontel] who will dishonour the Conservatoire, will regain the ground which a new system of nomination, under which I had some chance, had made him lose, and he will ruin my candidature ... I draw my courage from your last letter.'

Despite George Sand's intervention on his behalf it soon became clear that Alkan's position was becoming eroded still further and on 1st September he decided to write direct to the Home Office (Ministère de L'Intérieur) as well as to Charles Blanc.

'Monsieur le Ministre,

I have just been told about the words you exchanged with the honourable representatives, Victor Hugo and Donatien Marquis, about the teaching vacancy at the Conservatoire. I have the alternative of seeming a little discourteous, perhaps, or keeping quiet, which would be stupid. Please understand that I am breaking my silence only as a last resort.

The pupils claimed by M. Marmontel are not his at all. ... For instance Mlle. Malescot, first prize last year, took lessons from Chopin and, moreover Herz ...' A list of similar examples follows and Alkan concludes: 'My heart bleeds, my face is covered in blushes and shame to use such means, but there has never been such a battle between justice and injustice'

To Charles Blanc Alkan pleads time to rally the support of all the leading musicians:

'For example amongst the pianists MM. Liszt, Chopin, Thalberg etc: amongst the critics, MM. Fétis, Berlioz etc: and finally amongst the instrumentalists of every sort, through the most justly famous names in the whole of Europe'.

During the following four days a volley of letters was dispatched, each more desperate than the last:

3rd September 1848

'Monsieur le Ministre,

... If you sound out the opinion of the public, instead of that of just a small clique, I will be elected.

If you collect the votes of all the leading musicians in Europe, I will be elected.

If you judge the competition on three aspects — performance, composition and teaching — I will be elected ...' etc.

The impression that Alkan was waging a lone battle is a little deceptive. He also had his supporters. The writer, Donatien Marquis, comments on the short list of candidates drawn up by the Director of the Conservatoire:

'... I am astonished to get the reply that M. Auber had, in fact, mentioned M. Alkan but that he had put his name third on the list: and Marmontel was No. 1. with a very long note giving the greatest possible details to his claims. As for Alkan, the article about him was much shorter. We have replied that we could not help believing that Auber was under some influence, for public sentiment was so opposed to the order he has adopted that the Director of Fine Arts ought to investigate the matter, and it should be easy to arrive at the truth!'

Extracts from a further long letter from Donatien Marquis to a M. Raynal are still more explicit:

'M. Marmontel is quite simply a solfège teacher who was given M. Hertz's class in his absence ... those pupils obliged to follow his course were forced to seek lessons outside the college ...
M. Alkan does not owe his reputation to publicity, to flattering women, to an 'Air Varié' on popular tunes ... he loves art for art's sake. He has opposed charlatanism for twenty-three years and has confidence in the justice of mankind ...'

Alkan to George Sand Friday ? September 1848

'In spite of my positive rights, in spite of your all-powerful support, Madam. I have failed ...
The Republic, for which I have a most ardent love, allows strange blunders to be made. So far as my own sphere is concerned I felt disposed to educate a whole generation in musical matters and I have to give way, not to a worthy or even unworthy rival, but to one of the most total nonentities I can think of ... '

Auber had taken ruthless advantage of the delicate political climate which followed the 1848 Revolution to wield his powerful influence in Marmontel's favour. It was inconceivable that such politically motivated supporters of Alkan as George Sand would dare provoke an open scandal during the tensions of that summer and so the justice in which Alkan so naîvely believed was not forthcoming. As for Marmontel, his reign as

Head of the piano faculty was long and distinguished and was marked in 1858, with further backing from Auber, by the Légion d'Honneur. His pupils included Bizet and he went on to teach the young Debussy just before his retirement in 1887.

In his book *Les Pianistes Célébres* Marmontel goes out of his way to be magnanimous towards Alkan. This is how, just thirty years after the event, he deals with the Conservatoire nomination: 'We are particularly happy to render this public homage to our illustrious colleague [Alkan] for at a certain moment in our careers, in 1848, a most unfortunate misunderstanding, caused by the struggle for Zimmerman's class, separated us without, however, altering our mutual esteem and without diminishing on my part my sincere admiration for the artist; my deep sympathy for the untiring seeker and powerful creator.'

Had Alkan but realised that, for over a century, our main information about him would be from the velvet pen of this man, the irony would have been complete.

M.A. Marmontel
(Artist's realisation from a photograph: courtesy of Bibliothèque Nationale, *Paris)*

7 Recluse

As Alkan returned to the unproductive routine of private teaching, his main source of income, he had ample cause to brood over the harsh reality of his situation. At thirty-five he had witnessed the triumphs on the one hand and the adulation on the other of his friends Liszt and Chopin. Their names were already written in musical history. Although no less prodigiously gifted as a performer, accomplished as a composer or amibitious as a teacher his whole style must have lacked either the sheer autocratic showmanship of a Liszt and a Paganini or the elusive magic of a Field and a Chopin. Neither could his bluntly honest attitude to his profession have commended him to the smooth expediency of the corridors of power. Like a hammer-blow the Conservatoire deception must have convinced him that he had waited too long: that even his friends in high places were unable to supply that final boost, so indispensable for a career such as his, to ignite.

Alkan may now have had every excuse to take umbrage and sulk in solitude. Instead, he defied his destiny by inviting five of the leading Paris string players to join him, on 5th May 1849, in a public appearance which was to prove his last for nearly twenty-five years. The programme – utterly uncompromising and making no concession to public taste – was described in the press as a 'bold experiment, attempted for the first time, of a concert comprised exclusively of classics and earlier music'. In fact, such unpopular novelties as Bach's D minor keyboard Concerto and Mozart's B flat Sonata for Violin and Piano formed a framework for Alkan's own compositions: several of the slighter Préludes and a new *Zorcico* in quintuple time, as well as the inevitable *Marche Triomphale* into which 'he hurled all the treasures, all the splendours of rich and grandiose harmony and all the effects and contrasts of brilliant sonority ...' ... so wrote Henri Blanchard in the *Revue et Gazette*. In his highly laudatory review he also commented on the rarity of Alkan's appearances and the distinction of his audience which, on this occasion, included such artists as Delacroix, Meyerbeer and Scheffer. Chopin was by now too ill to attend his friend's concert but as recently as April, the Conservatoire affair still ringing savagely in Alkan's mind, he, Chopin and Delacroix had been able to discuss it, the latter noting laconically in his diary 'by standing up to Auber he [Alkan] has suffered, and doubtless will continue to suffer, many great annoyances'.

Only too soon Alkan was to sustain a further blow when Chopin died on 17th October 1849. He was now deprived of the one friend with whom he had always been able to communicate; to discuss his personal and artistic problems; whose approach to his career, whether as composer, performer or teacher had seemed so similar to his own. Like Chopin, Alkan had found it lucrative and congenial to give private piano lessons to fashionable young ladies anxious to boast of a famous teacher before displaying their accomplishments. Both teachers had similar methods — the inevitable use of Clementi's *Gradus ad Parnassum* for instance — and so it is hardly surprising that Chopin's pupils now turned to his next-door-neighbour as their master's natural successor. During most of his long life Alkan's main source of revenue must have come from the teaching of an aristocratic élite drawn from the fashionable circles of Paris and including princesses, duchesses and the wives of distinguished diplomats. We have no information about the amount of teaching he did nor how much he charged but if it was comparable to Chopin's exceptional fee of twenty francs a lesson he was at least spared financial worry for the next few years.

Soon after the death of Chopin further professional links were severed when Alkan moved away from the still famous artistic colony in the Square d'Orléans and from now on his appearances at public gatherings became increasingly rare. Between 1849 and 1853 he was occasionally seen at the first night of a few of George Sand's plays. Thanking her for his ticket for *Francois-le-Champi* on 23rd November 1849, he

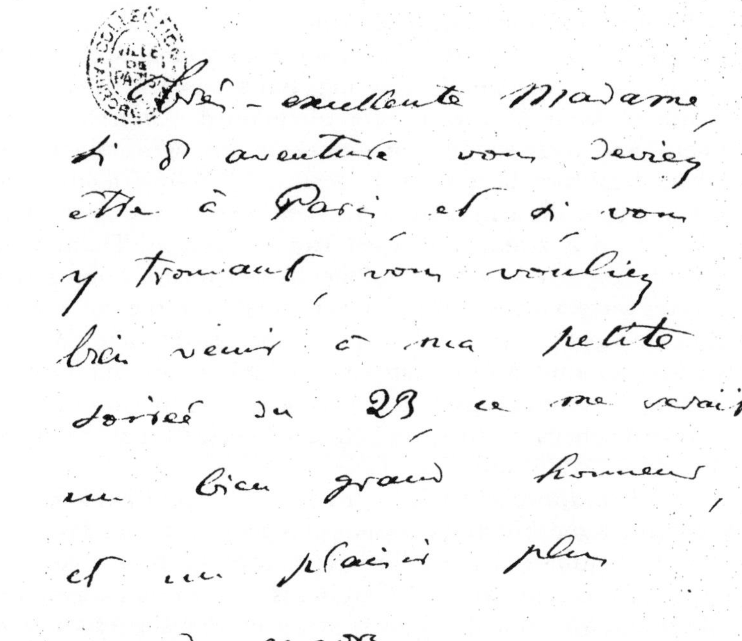

Très-excellente Madame,
si d'aventure vous deviez
être à Paris, et si vous
y trouvant, vous vouliez
bien venir à ma petite
soirée du 23, ce me serait
un bien grand honneur,
et un plaisir plus
grand encore.

C. V. Alkan
aîné
11 r: La Bruyère

10/4/53

A note from Alkan to George Sand

wrote: 'Your note and the performance cured my misanthropy ... I felt my shrunken heart expand'.

Other letters of the period hint at the occasional soirée when Alkan played to a small gathering, but soon even these fitful efforts to keep in touch were abandoned. Unpredictable, moody and increasingly worried about his personal health, Alkan was fast becoming a recluse. Those friends who attempted to drag him from his shell were liable to strange rebuffs. To a kindly invitation from Ambroise Thomas he replied: 'Even if I were to indulge myself for an hour and a quarter you would be obliged to carry me off to the infirmary', while George Sand received the following singular note: 'Thank you for your kind, affectionate letter, dear Madam, but it seems that on no account must I have the pleasure of playing for you this evening because about an hour ago I decided that the music in question could not take place'.

As Alkan approached forty his physical condition was fast becoming a morbid and constant preoccupation and his stock excuse for public inactivity. The extent to which his malady was *imaginaire* is debatable. Probably his constitution was never robust and his clinical faddiness about his diet suggests a poor digestion. No one was allowed near his food which he would prepare himself from his own purchases. One of his maids would refer to her master's invariable and twice cooked diet as 'La ratatouille de Monsieur'.

Early in 1855 the following little note appeared in the *Revue et Gazette* dated January 7: 'M. Alkan Morhange, head of a family which has yielded several distinguished artists amongst whom M. Valentin Alkan, the famous pianist, is first and foremost, has just died aged seventy-five.'

From the mid 1850's Alkan's withdrawal from social life was complete. Only his pupils were admitted at their appointed hour and although it has sometimes been hinted that certain distinguished visitors to Paris, Liszt in particular, would always drop in on their old friend, there seems no real evidence of this. As for others, they were invariably confronted by the concierge with : 'M. Alkan is not at home'. Even the fleeting mention of his name in the press would now always refer to his inexplicable silence: a silence which was only once broken. This isolated exception must, by its very nature, remain an occasion for curiosity and conjecture and one which raises the whole question of the composer's exact relationship with the piano manufacturing firm of Erard. At the International Exhibition of 1855, the year in which his father had died, Alkan was very much in evidence demonstrating the company's latest instruments only to return once more to that obscurity which had now become his way of life.

Apart from his absence from the Paris musical scene Alkan's silence as a creative artist was also becoming ominous. Following the publication in 1847 of the *Grande Sonate* nothing of importance had appeared for nearly a decade. His reputation as a composer still rested on a shallow salon piece, the celebrated *Saltarelle*, which had by now become the inevitable concluding item in every other young French pianist's repertoire and was quickly wearing itself to death. Meanwhile Alkan's splendid *Etudes Majeurs*, op. 35 remained unplayed while his orchestral symphony and *Grande Sonate* had glided gently into oblivion: no great incentive one might assume for a serious and controversial composer unable, or unwilling to promote his own work. Moreover Alkan believed himself to be chronically ill and might well have felt every excuse for remaining inactive; but he was also unpredictable and as capable as ever of springing a surprise. Suddenly, in 1857, the floodgates opened and posterity's debt to Auber was made manifest. A mighty avalanche of important piano works brought out during this *Annus Mirabilis* by the publisher, Richault, supplies all the evidence for Alkan's activity during the lost decade which had followed his rejection by the Conservatoire. Neither warning nor reaction accompanied this imposing release yet it included his most famous work, the *Douze études dans tous les tons mineurs*, op. 39. The two hundred and seventy-seven pages of this masterpiece, which included the Solo Symphony and Solo Concerto as well as the brilliant *Festin d'Esope,* would alone, have provided ample proof that Alkan's withdrawal had been more than justified.

Hardly less remarkable, and more immediately accessible however, is a shoal of smaller compositions which accompanied this historic publication. The two sets of *Chants* op. 38, for instance, pay tribute to Mendelssohn's *Songs Without Words* but in a variety of characteristic and sometimes disturbing ways.

Mendelssohn's original key sequence is adopted and the style of each piece is easily recognisable but seen, as it were, in a distorting mirror, enlarged, broadened or darkened in mood and in one case afflicted by the obsessional repetition of an unresolved foreign note within the texture. The laconic *Minuetto alla Tedesca*, three fine Marches, in turn sprightly, powerful or grotesque and the extraordinary *Trois Petites Fantasies* op. 41, all date from this period. This last work is particularly admired in France for its wry and whimsical humour. Prokofiev himself could hardly have surpassed the rhythmic fury of a final, fulgurating toccata in which Alkan deals surprise upon surprise for all the world like some master card-sharper in whose hand every card becomes an ace ... not at all, one would have thought, the composition of a self-admitted misanthrope! Three further Marches, op, 40, this time for four hands, also display a growing preoccupation with the humorous, the caricatural and the bizarre. These are dedicated to his old friend Hiller, director of the Conservatorium at Cologne.

Writing to Hiller in 1857 Alkan regrets the distance that prevents his trying out the new Marches with his friend. He complains once more of his ill-health: 'I give lessons during the day' he writes 'while in the evening, during those few moments of lucidity, spared me by my illness, I am correcting the proofs of my new Sonata for piano and basse ('cello) which I am having printed myself. (*sic*) I would so much like to play this at Erard's but my poor health prevents it. Still more would I love to play it to you but this is unlikely for, like me you are preoccupied with trying to make ends meet. I only just manage to scrape a wretched living and I haven't, like you, the responsibility of a wife and family'.

Ferdinand Hiller (1810-1885) is remembered not only as the dedicatee of the Schumann Piano Concerto and the teacher of Max Bruch but also as the youthful witness of a famous death-bed reconciliation; that of his master, Hummel with the dying Beethoven. Hiller had lived in Paris from 1828-1835 and had given the first performances there of some of the greatest keyboard works of Bach and Beethoven, including the *Emperor Concerto*. His authoritative 'playing had won him the admiration and friendship of every musician of note from

Cherubini to Berlioz, Liszt, Chopin and, of course, Alkan himself. Later he had returned to his native Germany where he was now making a great mark as a conductor. From the mid-1850's Hiller and Alkan corresponded regularly and the exciting discovery in Cologne of seventy-three letters written by Alkan to his friend, and spanning a period of over thirty years, throws an invaluable light on his tastes and passions, his psychological condition, his domestic problems and even his barbed humour. Indeed it soon becomes clear that Hiller must have filled the gap once occupied by Chopin as the one person in whom he could confide and discuss his problems. Certainly Hiller was one of the few visitors to Paris to whom Alkan was always 'at home' ... except on one occasion which misfired. Hearing the door-bell Alkan hastily sent his servant with the stock plea 'Not at home'. Almost at once he recognised his friend's card and realising his gaffe rushed from the house, but just too late to greet Hiller. Alkan's embarrassment and dismay at missing him is captured in a series of quite desperate notes to various likely addresses attempting to explain, apologise and arrange a rendezvous.

8 Prometheus Bound

Despite constant misgivings about his health Alkan had, by 1857, come to terms with a mode of existence quietly divorced from the reassurance of either professional approval or public acclaim. Wealthy pupils, like the Princess Orloff, provided him with sufficient income for his modest tastes and left him enough time for creative work and for what his friend Hiller humorously called his 'semitic studies'. These included translating the Bible, two or three verses regularly each day, and by 1858 he was claiming to have completed three-quarters of the entire work. In 1865 Alkan was translating the New Testament from the Syriac, and the Bible remained his constant inspiration, spilling over into several of his compositions. Like the Adagio of his lost Symphony the wonderful slow movement of the *'Cello Sonata* op. 47 is prefaced by a few lines from the Old Testament and his piano composition *Super Flumina Babylonis* op. 52 is a kind of wordless operatic scena paraphrasing Psalm 137. 'If only I could have my life over again' he once declared 'I would set the entire Bible to music'.

Other reading in 1858 included the famous treatise on orchestration by Berlioz. Alkan deeply admired Berlioz's orchestral genius but not his music which he associated with the new school of Wagner and Liszt of which he heartily disapproved. His opinion of Berlioz as a writer is succinctly expressed: 'It is always a revelation for me to read that man for alongside interesting and amusing things one comes across utter drivel'.

It speaks highly of the feverish excitement generated by Wagner's presence in Paris at the outset of 1860 that Alkan was reluctantly persuaded to attend the first concert in which Wagner conducted his own compositions in the 'Théâtre des Italiens' on January 25th, an event that caught Paris by the throat and split the musical élite. Alkan sought refuge in the interval excusing himself, with an ironic smile and complaining that it was 'far too noisy'. He later commented 'Wagner is not music; it's a sickness'.

Although taking no personal part in the musical life of the capital he would still cast a quizzical eye at the various celebrities who came and went, especially the pianists. He admired Anton Rubinstein: 'marvellous technique' — that was also in 1860 — but thought he took himself too seriously as a composer. Doubtless, had Rubinstein known this he would not have dedicated his 5th Piano Concerto to Alkan. He also heard but did not see 'the illustrious Madame Schumann'. Writing to Hiller in May 1862 Alkan admitted that although his view of the lady had been unfortunately obscured by a pillar, she had given him considerable pleasure ... 'that is, for a woman'. 'These days' he added 'I see so few people that I have no idea of the impression she has made in Paris, but I have a hunch her admirers overrate her', and then as an afterthought: 'I hope you won't be affronted by my judgment of the excellent Madame Schumann — it's really more a matter of personal temperament. For my taste women never play really well. Either they sound like women or they try and sound like men'.

Such isolated excursions apart, Alkan was now an almost total recluse. 'He locks away his talent as singlemindedly as others in his place would seek to exploit it' wrote a leading periodical in 1860 and a year later a mutual acquaintance was warning Hiller: 'Alkan has now taken refuge in the most complete obscurity'. Even so his retirement from public life seemed to have quickened his interest in public affairs and in 1859 he was writing detailed letters to Hiller fervently defending the French position over Napoléon 3rd's latest military adventure, the Franco-Italian campaign against the Austrians. Alkan's deeper concern for the shallow glory and grim futility of war is reserved for the graphically simple but psychologically complex *Military Caprices* op. 50 of that year.

One of Alkan's most overtly freakish works also dates from 1859, his *Funeral March for a Dead Parrot*, scored for three oboes, bassoon and mixed voices. One may reasonably infer that 'Jacko', deceased hero of this grotesque study in mock pathos, had been a recent member of the establishment: an establishment that clearly afforded Alkan the right degree of stability for creative work. The quaintly neo-classical *Minuets* op. 51 of 1859, the Forty-Eight *Esquisses* op. 63 and the masterly *Sonatine* of 1861 op. 61, all reveal a sharper, at times even abrasive edge to Alkan's pen. Indeed, it is remarkable, given so little encouragement and plagued by ill-health, whether real or imaginary, that he was able for a further four years to sustain the creative peak he had so obviously reached with the op. 39 Studies. The harvest might well have continued but during the summer of 1861 his housekeeper left after looking after his establishment, if not his *cuisine*, for over fifteen years.

Alkan was now in real trouble. Before the end of the year he had rejected fifty-one maids and was still alone. 'Have you ever made your own bed, my dear Hiller?' he wrote. 'I'm becoming daily more and more misanthropic and misogynous ... nothing worthwhile, good or useful to do ... no one to devote myself to. My situation makes me horridly sad and wretched. Even musical production has lost its attraction for me for I can't see the point or goal ... But, enough of my moral infirmities and a thousand pardons for boring you with them'. Ironically enough Alkan might easily have received just that distraction from his moral infirmities he so vitally needed by reading a most enthusiastic article which had appeared in the *Neue Berliner Musikzeiten* about his *Studies* op. 35 by Liszt's son-in-law, Hans von Bulow. Alkan received this article but gave it to somcone to translate who promptly lost it.

To add to his worries he was now obliged to look for a new flat. His constant anxiety about the high cost of living and the danger of having to suffocate himself with too much teaching suggests that several moves in the late 1850's and early '60's were forced on him by financial considerations. In 1863 he was still searching in vain for a flat within his means. Time was running out and he was even considering selling everything and taking a single room in the Latin Quarter where he would divide his life equally between study, preparing his food and doing his own chores. It is impossible to judge the extent to which Alkan liked to exaggerate his physical, financial and 'moral' infirmities. He could certainly not have been destitute for he did eventually find himself suitable accommodation in a fashionable part of Paris. By November 1863 he was established in the Rue de la Croix-du-Roule which, in 1869, changed its name to the Rue Daru and here he was to remain for the rest of his life.

* * * * * *

During the 1860's the long-established 'Concerts du Conservatoire' were being sharply challenged by a new series of 'Concerts Populaires' which took place each Sunday afternoon at exactly the same hour. By 1864 Alkan had not taken part in a public concert for fifteen years and he was somewhat taken aback to receive an engagement from Hainl, the recently appointed conductor of the Conservatoire orchestra, to appear as soloist at one of these famous concerts. Hardly had Alkan recovered from his surprise when there came another invitation, this time from Pasdeloup, the enterprising young conductor of the 'Concerts Populaires'. Would Alkan like to submit an orchestral composition to be brought forward during the coming season? Alkan's *B Minor Symphony* had by now been gathering dust for two decades. Was there, perhaps, a concerted effort to entice the shy artist out of his shell? Despite his long silence there must have remained a lingering curiosity among those who had actually heard him and others to whom he was little more than a vague legend. Perhaps the influential Fétis, the dedicatee of Alkan's great *Studies* op. 35 and 39 had whispered in the right ear. If so he had acted too late. Alkan firmly declined both invitations explaining that his present frame of mind would no more allow him to confront the symphonic public as a composer than his health would permit his undertaking to appear on a fixed day at a fixed hour; and he returned to translating the Bible, except when he was unable to write. During the severe winter of 1865 the cold cracked open his finger tips, which seems to indicate an inadequate diet.

Alkan was over fifty, the final age of disintegration he had so graphically prophesied in his *Grande Sonate* of just seventeen years earlier. In his letters he now refers constantly to his 'old age' and to the consolation to be found in religious studies. Of his compositions there is never a hint. His final creative period, approximately from the early '60's to the early '70's contains three further sets of *Chants* and a large number of finely wrought transcriptions. Otherwise his later compositions, like the thirteen *Prières* op. 64 and the *Eleven Grands Préludes* op. 66 show an ever-increasing preoccupation with religious subjects and with the *pédalier*, a normal piano with pedal-board attached. Alkan's wizardry on this hybrid instrument must have been awe-inspiring. Several other French musicians followed in his footsteps, notably Saint-Saëns and, of course, Delaborde, who created a deep impression when he introduced several of 'his master's' latest works for *pédalier* in the Hanover Square Rooms, London, in 1871. Despite the advocacy, however, of a small nucleus of French musicians, the *pédalier* never really caught on outside France and was soon forgotten, as, inevitably was much of the finest of Alkan's later work, which can only make its right effect on this now obsolete instrument.

If Alkan was reluctant to speak about his latest compositions, his letters often provide a sardonic slant on the musical world at large, especially when his literary style reflects some of that barbed subtlety so familiar in his music.

'What do you make of this latest development in our old friend Liszt's career?' he asked Hiller. This was in 1865. Liszt was in Rome, a guest of the Vatican. On April 25 that year, he had become an Abbé and thenceforth wore the Abbé's frock. Alkan seems highly sceptical about the sincerity of Liszt's 'conversion': 'For my part,' he comments, 'should I ever decide to become a Rabbi it would not be for the sake of high office in the Synagogue but rather would I wear the frock with disinterest' adding shrewdly ... 'if Paris was worth a mass perhaps a position at St. Peter's is worth a cassock'.*

As the decade was drawing to a close Alkan's letters began to take on a new and significant turn. 'Old age', 'illness', 'moral infirmities' ... even his 'semitic studies' give way to a re-awakening interest in performing problems. On 1st April

*In 1593, when the opportunist Henri IV of France re-united his people by turning Catholic, he is said to have remarked 'Paris is worth a mass'.

1869 he expresses concern about the debatable 'return' in the First Movement of Beethoven's *Hammerklavier* Sonata. Has he and everyone he has ever heard play the work, he asks Hiller, mis-read the two preceding bars as 'A naturals' when, in fact, they are 'sharps' in the signature? Only four days later he is asking his friend about the possibility and style of cadenzas in the Adagio of Bach's Triple Concerto in C* and in the same letter, requests the manuscript of Hiller's own early Trio in F sharp minor adding: 'I feel I would like to appear in public again'.

Why should Alkan, having sheltered these last twenty years under the cloak of ill-health suddenly get the urge to give concerts? Is there, perhaps, a more plausible explanation than the naive assumption that his health had suddenly taken a turn for the better? Apart from the Bible, Alkan had three passions in life; composing, playing and teaching and the importance of the latter to Alkan should not be underestimated. Had not the Conservatoire intrigue robbed him of the opportunity 'to educate a whole generation in musical matters'? Had not his last concerts back in the 1840's taken on more and more an educational as well as artistic function? Could it be that by the late 1869's Alkan found his creativity on the wane and realised that his final mission in life was to perform and introduce those great works he had studied but which were still virtually

---

*Alkan had heard an account of a performance in London of this Concerto in which Mendelssohn, Moscheles and Thalberg improvised cadenzas: but he was misled. S.S. Stratton (*Mendelssohn*: The Master Musicians. Dent 1901) quotes an eye-witness account of this extraordinary performance which took place in 1844 in the Hanover Square Rooms. According to Charles Horsley the work was the Bach Triple Concerto in D minor, not the C major, and the three cadenzas were improvised in the Finale. Mendelssohn's cadenza, the last, he tells us, exploded in a veritable storm of double octaves which sustained its climax for a full five minutes (sic) bringing to a conclusion 'an exhibition of mechanical skill and most perfect inspiration, which, neither before nor since that memorable Thursday afternoon has ever been approached. The effect on the audience was electric'. Mendelssohn later remarked 'I thought the people might like some octaves so I played them'.

Strange to relate there is no place for improvised cadenzas in the D minor Concerto while in the C major they are written out in full, forming an essential part of the fabric and accompanied by orchestra. Music must have been fun in those days!

unknown in France? In this way, perhaps, he would not be finally denied the chance to educate a generation. Before Alkan's dream could be realised, however, other and alien events were afoot, and of such magnitude that anything less than the most firmly conceived resolution would have been irrevocably crushed.

* * * * * *

In the summer of 1870 Napoléon 3rd launched his final, disastrous military fling, and within weeks, his armies routed and capitulating to the Prussians, had fled to England. On September 4 a Republic was declared in France, but despite the improvisation of new armies the Prussians had, by September 23 reached Paris. Inevitably France was forced to surrender but not before the besieged capital, with its two million inhabitants, had been subjected to four months of constant bombardment, famine and disease, exacerbated by one of the severest winters of the century. Worse was to follow. Humiliated and stripped of their Eastern provinces the French now started a campaign of self-destruction and by May 1871, Paris was convulsed by a hideous orgy of carnage in which 20,000 perished, many of the finest buildings were burnt and, incidentally, vital official documents relating to the Alkan-Morhange family were lost.

How did Alkan fare during these months of tribulation in which food became so desperately short that cats sold at six francs a carcase, dogs at one franc a pound while, for the less squeamish, there was a thriving black market in rats at a mere one franc each? Once peace was restored he wrote to Hiller, himself a German: 'For forty-nine days and nights without respite I have been living in the midst of cannon balls and bullets. All I have is a shutter and a piano with a hole through them. I have hardly eaten at all'. Even Alkan's fervent patriotism had been tested beyond endurance and his dilemma, like that of so many artists in times of stress, is summed up in his own words: 'Do I renounce my friends because they are Prussian?' ... and he added grimly 'I no longer feel French: only old age'.

Miraculously enough, the heart-searching experience of the Siege of Paris seemed only to have strengthened Alkan's resolve to play in public again. Once more he was pestering the life out of Hiller for the score of his friend's early F sharp minor Trio. 'I would like to play this in Paris next season' he writes, adding enigmatically: 'Delaborde must be told nothing about it' ... and, singularly enough, this is the one solitary mention of Delaborde's name in the whole of this voluminous correspondence which spans three decades.

At the outset of 1873 the Paris musical world must have read with mingled wonder and curiosity the following paragraph in the *Revue et Gazette:* 'Ch.-Valentin Alkan, the eminent pianist and composer who has condemned himself to retirement for too long, returns to the fore with the announcement, which will be received with great interest, of six 'Petits Concerts' of classical music, devoted to compositions of every school and period for piano solo or duet, for *pédalier* or for piano together with other instruments. These performances will take place on the Saturdays of Feb 15, March 1, 15 and 29 and April 12 and 26 at 9.00 p.m. precisely, at the Salle Erard.'

9 Les Petits Concerts

On Saturday evening February 15, 1873 Charles-Valentin Alkan stepped on to the podium at the Salle Erard. It was his first public appearance for nearly a quarter of a century. The programme was formidable. It spared neither audience nor artist and considering the circumstances, and the fact that Alkan, now in his sixtieth year played from memory throughout, it must have taxed him to the limit of his capacity. The following review well captures some of the electricity in the air: 'After a silence of twenty years Ch.-Valentin Alkan, one of the masters of the piano, has made a reappearance. His great talent has remained unchanged ... restrained, learned, accurate ... although he seems to have lost a little of his technique. Moreover, the whole atmosphere, which was if anything still more highly charged than a début, seemed to paralyse the eminent artist at this, his first 'Petit Concert' and was undoubtably responsible for two unfortunate memory lapses, in a study by Stephen Hiller (*sic*) and in the *F major Toccata* by Bach. Alkan also played the *Sonata* op. 110 by Beethoven, three pieces by Rameau, the Allegro from a Concerto by Handel, several studies by Chopin and Hiller and some of his own compositions which are remarkable in every way: a March for Four Hands (with E.M. Delaborde) the first piece from his *Premier recueil de Chants* and the Prière *Deus Sabbaoth*. He still plays the *pédalier* with assurance and perfect clarity as of old. To end the performance he was joined by Alard in the *Introduction and Rondo*, op. 70, by Schubert. The audience, consisting largely of artists, gave the virtuoso and composer one of those warm ovations one never forgets'.

SALONS ÉRARD; 13, RUE DU MAIL.

TROISIÈME ANNÉE.

SIX PETITS CONCERTS DE MUSIQUE CLASSIQUE,

POUR

PIANO SEUL, A 2 & A 4 MAINS;
PIANO CONCERTANT, OU AVEC ACCOMPAGNEMENT,
& PIANO A CLAVIER DE PÉDALES; *

DONNÉS PAR M.

CH: V^{IN} ALKAN AÎNÉ,

LES VENDREDIS SOIRS : 19 FÉVRIER; 5 ET 19 MARS; 2, 16 ET 30 AVRIL 1875, A 9 HEURES *très-précises.*

* *Cembalo a Pedale;* Pedal-Flügel.

PROGRAMMES : **

PROGRAMME I.

Première Partie

I. LA FINE MADELON, etc.: Pièce de . . . COUPERIN. (1668-1733.)
II. VIVACE, de . . . . D: SCARLATTI. (1683-1757.)
III. LES SAUVAGES, de . . . . . RAMEAU. (1683-1764.)
IV. ADAGIO, d'un CONCERTO, pour Clavecin, de . . . . . . HANDEL. (1684-1759.) [illegible]
V. 1er MOUVEMENT, de la 6e SONATE de : . . . . J: S: BACH. (1685-1750.)
VI. POLONAISES, de : . . . . . . FRIEDMANN BACH. (1710-1784.)

Premier Intermède :

A. N° 1, du 1er RECUEIL de CHANTS, pour Piano : }
B. N° . du 4e RECUEIL id : ibid : } CH: V^{IN} ALKAN.

Deuxième Partie :

I. N° 61, du GRADUS, de : . . . . . CLEMENTI. (1752-1832.)
II. 1er MORCEAU de SONATE, de : . . MOZART. (1756-1791.)
III. LARGO, de l'œu : 10 de . . . . BEETHOVEN. (1770-1827.)
IV. ETUDE, en *Mi b sol mineur*, de : MOSCHELES. (1794-1870.)
V. ROMANCE en *Mi bemol*, de: . . . FIELD. (1781-1847.)
VI. SCHERZO, en *La bemol*, de : . . WEBER. (1786-1826.)

Deuxième Intermède :

A. MARCHE des GRANDS-PRÊTRES, de l'ALCESTE: et: }
B. CHŒUR des SCYTHES, de l'IPHIGENIE EN TAURIDE : avec Clavier de Pédales obligé :. } GLUCK.

Troisième Partie :

I. PRESTISSIMO, de l'œu : 7, de :. . CZERNY. (1791-1857.)
II. PENSÉE MUSICALE, de : . . . . . SCHUBERT. (1797-1828.)
III. 2e POLONAISE, de l'œu : 25, de :. KESSLER. (1800-1871.)
IV. ETUDE, en *Fa min :* de : . . . . MENDELSSOHN. (1809-1847.)
V. POLONAISE, de l'œu : 26, de : . . CHOPIN. (1810-1849.)
VI. FANTAISIE: de l'œu : 111, de :. . SCHUMANN. (1810-1856.)

PROGRAMME II.

Première Partie :

I. SONATE, œu : 78, de :. . . . . SCHUBERT.
II. FANTASIA: op : 77, de : . . . . BEETHOVEN.
III. POLONAISE, en *Mi bemol*, de :. . . . . WEBER.

Intermède :

A. DEUX MORCEAUX RELIGIEUX pour Piano à Clavier de Pédales . . . . }
B. 3 NUMÉROS des 48 MOTIFS, pour Piano seul. . } CH: V^{IN} ALKAN.
C. UNE TRANSCRIPTION, du SAMSON, de :. . . . . HANDEL.

Deuxième Partie :

I. FANTAISIES, pour Clarinette et Piano; œu: 73, de: SCHUMANN.
II. PRÉLUDE, ADAGIO et PASTORALE, pour Piano à Clavier de Pédales, de : . . . . J: S: BACH.
III. FANTAISIE, en *La min :*, de : . . . . MENDELSSOHN.

PROGRAMME III.

Première Partie :

I. SONATE; œu : 110, de : . . . . BEETHOVEN.
II. PRIÈRE PENDANT LA BATAILLE; Chant et Piano : WEBER.
III. CHORAL, et FUGUE en *Ré*, pour Piano à Clavier de Pédales, de :. . . . . J: S: BACH.

Intermède :

DUO, pour Piano et Violoncelle : . . . . CH: V^{IN} ALKAN.

Deuxième Partie :

I. DEUX PRÉLUDES, de l'œuvre 28, de : . . . . . CHOPIN.
II. RÉCITATIF, et AIR, pour Voix de Basse et *Cembalo obligato*, de :. . . . . J: S: BACH.
III. MENUET, et 3e POLONAISE, de l'œu : 25; pour Piano à Pédales : . . . . HANDEL, & KESSLER.

PROGRAMME IV.

Première Partie :

I. TRIO, pour Piano, Violon et Violoncelle, de :. . MOZART.
II. CHŒUR de l'OBERON, transcrit pour Piano à Clavier de Pédales . . . . WEBER.
III. DEUXIÈME SONATE, de . . . . CHOPIN.

Intermède :

A. IMPROMPTU . . . . }
B. MARCHE FUNÈBRE . . . . } CH: V^{IN} ALKAN.
C. MENUET SYMPHONIQUE : . . . . }
D. FANTAISIE, pour deux Pianos à Clavier de Pédales : SAINT-SAËNS.

Deuxième Partie :

I. SONATA, pour Piano et Violon, de : . . . . J: S: BACH.
II. MAZURKA, et 1re BALLADE, de :. . . . . CHOPIN.
III. DEUX TRANSCRIPTIONS, pour Piano; de l'ARMIDE, de : . . . . GLUCK.
et de la SYMPHONIE en *Mi bemol*, de : . . . MOZART.

PROGRAMME V.

Première Partie :

I. *A.* CHORAL, et :
B. CANON, pour Piano à Clavier de Pédales, de : . . . . BACH, & SCHUMANN.
II. SONATE : op : 109, de : . . . . BEETHOVEN.
III. *A.* CHORAL, et :
B. VARIATIONS, pour Piano à Pédales; de : BACH, & HANDEL.

Intermède :

A. PRÉLUDE VI, pour Piano à Pédales : . . . . . }
B. *La Chanson de la bonne Vieille*. . . . du 4e RECUEIL de CHANTS pour Piano :. . . } CH: V^{IN} ALKAN.
C. L'ETUDE en *Ut dièse*, avec accompagnement d'Orchestre :. . . . . }

Deuxième Partie :

I. CONCERTO, en *Si min :* avec accompagnement d'Orchestre : œu : 89, de : . . . . HUMMEL.
II. MENUETS, de : . . . . RAMEAU.
III. *A.* CHORAL, et :
B. ANDANTE, pour Piano à Pédales, de : BACH, & HAYDN.

PROGRAMME VI.

Première Partie :

I. SONATE, à 4 Mains, de :. . . . . MOZART.
II. DEUX TRANSCRIPTIONS pour Piano à Clavier de Pédales, de :. . . . . WEBER, & J: S: BACH.
III. PRÉLUDE, et FUGUE V; de : . . . . MENDELSSOHN.

Intermède :

I. MARCHES, à 4 Mains; et . . . . }
II. SONATE, pour Piano et Violon :. . . . . } CH: V^{IN} ALKAN.

Deuxième Partie :

I. MAZURKA, et 3e BALLADE, de :. . . . . CHOPIN.
II. ROMANCE SANS PAROLES, de : . . . . MENDELSSOHN.
III. CHORAL, et FUGUE, en *Sol;* pour Piano à Pédales, de :. . . . . J: S: BACH.

** Des Affiches et des Programmes, Ultérieurs et Spéciaux, donneront, pour chacun des Six Petits Concerts, les Indications complémentaires de la plupart des Ouvrages exécutés; ainsi que les Noms des Artistes qui se feront entendre dans les Morceaux Concertants, etc.

On pourra se procurer à l'avance des Billets, Simples ou d'Abonnement, aux Adresses suivantes :

MM. BRANDUS et Cie, Éditeurs de Musique, 103, rue de Richelieu ;
DURAND, SCHŒNEWERK et Cie, Éditeurs, 4, Place de la Madeleine ;
M. E. GIROD, Éditeur, 16, Boulevard Montmartre ;
Et Maison ÉRARD, 13, Rue du Mail.

Prix du Billet (numéroté) : 6 francs.
Abonnement, pour les Six Séances : 30 francs.

IMPRIMERIE CENTRALE DES CHEMINS DE FER. — A. CHAIX ET Cie, RUE BERGÈRE, 20, A PARIS. — 11034-4.

Although encouraged by his reception Alkan was deeply exercised by this newly discovered tendency to stage fright. Only two weeks separated him from his next encounter with a sophisticated public: something had to be done, and quickly. Since his youth a salon had always been placed at his disposal in the Maison Erard, and realising that his nervousness could be simply a matter of rehabilitation, of acclimatising himself once more to the disturbing presence of an audience, he decided to give an informal recital there twice a week. From now on acquaintances and their friends could drop in at Erard's any Monday or Thursday afternoon and hear Alkan range spontaneously throughout his vast repertoire or give an impromptu preview of an impending concert. This discipline evidently paid off for at his second 'Petit Concert' on March 1 he found his old form. Unabashed by his recent, unhappy experience he ran the gauntlet once more of Bach's *F major Toccata*, this time with impunity, and Delaborde and another pianist joined with him in a performance of Bach's *Triple Concerto in C* (presumably Alkan had solved the problem of cadenzas) and among a group of his own compositions he included the early *Study in C sharp* with string accompaniment which still remained one of his favourite party pieces. This time the review was unequivocal: 'The eminent composer, the noble, austere pianist, the masterly *pédalier*-player was acclaimed by a public of connoisseurs, the public of great artists'. So, it seems, Alkan still played, as he always had for an élite. At no time are we told the size of the audience at the 'Petits Concerts', only of its quality.

The organisation of these concerts was taken in hand by Alkan's youngest brother, Gustave, who seems to have inherited some of his father's business flair. He master-minded the whole enterprise from booking the hall and dealing with the publicity, to numbering the seats and supervising the audience during the performances. Alkan himself, of course, devised the programmes and, although prepared to consider the layout with a few intimate friends, he was quite dictatorial about their content. One of these friends was Alexandre de Bertha who first met the composer at a time when the concerts were still being planned. He assures us that Alkan was never above discussing the problems of interpretation of the music he was about to

SALONS ÉRARD; 13, RUE DU MAIL.

30 Avril 1874.

à 9 heures *très-précises.*

PROGRAMME VI.

DES

SIX PETITS CONCERTS

DE

M. CH : V^{es} ALKAN AÎNÉ.

(DEUXIÈME ANNÉE.)

Durée approximative des Numéros.

PREMIÈRE PARTIE :

I. **Quintetto**, en *Mi bémol*, pour Hautbois, Clarinette, Cor, Basson et Piano : . . . . **MOZART.** — I. *a.* 9 à 10 Min. *b.* 7 à 8 Min. *c.* 5 à 6 Min.

a **Largo** et **Allegro moderato**; *b.* **Larghetto**; *c.* **Allegretto** :

Exécuté avec **MM. LALLIET, GRISEZ, DUPONT** et **ESPAIGNET.**

II. *a.* **Nocturne**, en *Ut min.* (*Moderato espressivo*). . . . . **FIELD.** — II. *a.* 3 Minutes.

b. **Nocturne**, également en *Ut min* : Nº 1, de l'œuv : 48 : (*Lento*). . **CHOPIN.** — *b.* 6 Minutes.

III. **Menuet**, en *Trio*, et **Passacaille**, pour Piano à Clavier de Pédales. . **HÆNDEL.** — III. *a.* 2 Minutes. *b.* 5 à 6 Min.

INTERMÈDE :

Duo, pour Piano et Violon, op : 21 : . . . . **CH : V^{es} ALKAN.**

a. *Assez animé.* — *a.* 6 Minutes.

b. *Lentement.* — **L'Enfer.** — — *b.* 4 Minutes.

c. *Vivacissime.* — *c.* 9 Minutes.

Exécuté avec **M. LEONARD.**

DEUXIÈME PARTIE :

I. **Larghetto**, en *Mi*, du 1er **Concerto**; op : 11, de : . . . . **CHOPIN.** — I. 6 à 7 Minutes.

II. **Les Nonnettes** : — **Les Blondes et les Brunes** : — Nº 13, du 1er Livre, des **Pièces** de Clavecin, de : . . . . **Fr : COUPERIN** (DIT LE GRAND.) — II. 2 Minutes.

III. *a.* **Choral** :

« Ich ruf' zu dir, Herr Jesus-Christ : » . . . . **J : S : BACH.** — III. *a.* 2 Minutes. *b.* 8 Minutes.

b. **Toccata**, en *Fa*, pour Piano à Pédales. . . . .

IMPRIMERIE CENTRALE DES CHEMINS DE FER. — A. CHAIX ET Cie, RUE BERGÈRE, 20, A PARIS. — 5192-4.

play: 'It was thus that I came to understand the immense horizon of his musical knowledge' he writes, adding that not only was Alkan conversant with every school of the past, but that his extraordinary memory found no difficulty in dredging up works he had not encountered since his youth. So far as his contemporaries were concerned he was severely selective. Liszt and his school held no fascination for Alkan who reserved his enthusiasm for composers like Weber, Mendelssohn, Schumann and Chopin, who had not entirely broken with classical tradition. Add to this his insatiable exploration of the German classics, both as an original subscriber to the *Bach Gesellschaft* and as an impassioned apostle of late Beethoven, and the framework of his programmes becomes inevitable.

As well as devising his programmes Alkan was also responsible for setting them out in the utmost detail down to the quaintly fastidious timing of each piece or movement, an innovation prompted by the advantage to concert-goers of indicating in advance when their carriages should arrive, but one which has apparently not outlived the *pédalier*.

Once established, a series of 'Six Petits Concerts' was given each season for the next five years with a break in 1876 caused by alterations to the Salle Erard. Apart from Delaborde and Alard, such celebrities as Saint-Saëns, his old friend Franchomme and the famous Madame Viardot all took part. Tantalisingly enough, not one of those major piano works on which Alkan's reputation now rests was included, complete. Thus, during the first season he played exerpts from his great *Solo Concerto* and the following year the Funeral March and Minuet only from his *Solo Symphony.* Instinctively, it seems, Alkan had always feared that these gigantic works would be misunderstood even by his own reasonably sophisticated audiences. There was also, perhaps, an additional hazard. 'His technique,' wrote one reviewer, 'is not quite what it was, which is hardly surprising in a man of his age'. Although Alkan's command was still equal to the toughest sonatas of Beethoven and Chopin and could encompass the intricacies of Bach's organ fugues played on the *pédalier*, he may, at sixty, no longer have felt himself physically capable of the terrifying and sustained demands of his own most powerful works. Significantly enough, he had no hesitation in including such large-scale chamber compositions as the Violin and 'Cello Sonatas with their taxing piano parts. Could it be that the presence of a distinguished colleague like Franchomme gave the composer Dutch courage during these later years?

Bertha claims that the series of 'Petits Concerts' came to an end in 1877 with the premature death of Gustave, but recent research suggests that Gustave died five years later. It now seems that the concerts may have been phased out over a season or two.* Almost certainly however, the last complete series was that of 1877 and, as if to make amends for the deprivation of the preceding year, a special concert was organised in Alkan's honour on January 21st. The programme included his *Duo for Violin and Piano* and the *Second Concerto da Camera,* accompanied by a distinguished quintet of strings. Before launching his final season of 'Six Petits Concerts' Alkan was also persuaded to give a preview in the Salle Pleyel on February 14 to which the public and press were admitted. 'Nothing could be more interesting' wrote the *Revue et Gazette* 'than this glimpse of the history of the piano as summarised by M. Alkan's playing. The most characteristic pieces from all centuries and of all the masters from Couperin and Scarlatti to Schumann are reviewed and each is played in the style appropriate to it and with the expression which suits it. In M. Alkan we still find those supreme qualities we have so often had occasion to praise', and a week later: 'The gallant artist is now gathering encouraging proof of public esteem and interest in his work'.

At last Alkan was receiving, in some small measure, the recognition that had somehow, always eluded him: but, inevitably, at sixty-four and in poor health, the colossal effort of preparing and giving this yearly series could not continue indefinitely. The last concert of the 1877 season may not have been his final bow to the Paris public but he was soon to return to the shadows of an even greater obscurity than before.

*Dennis Hennig, in an Oxford B.Ph. thesis completed in 1975, claims that a certain number of 'Petits Concerts' did indeed straggle into the 1880's, after a further break in 1879. He adds the interesting information that Alkan even included a performance of the complete *Solo Symphony* on 18 April, 1880. This was not, however the work's première. A certain Mademoiselle Poitevin, a former pupil of Delaborde, had already introduced both *Ouverture* and *Symphonie* to Paris audiences in 1876 and '77.

10 The Final Years

Unlike Alkan's earlier periods of reclusion our scanty knowledge of his final years suggests that even the urge to compose must now have dried up. Despite their high opus number *Les Mois* op. 74 and the *Trois Grandes Etudes* op. 76 are reprints of early works, and the virile little *Toccatina* is also probably not as late as its Opus number of 75 suggests. Most likely Alkan's last compositions were the 4th and 5th *Recueil de Chants* op. 67 and 70 which were almost certainly completed by the time the 'Petits Concerts' were launched in 1873.

During his brief return to the limelight it had occasionally been possible to coax Alkan to appear as guest of honour at a social gathering, a brave but risky undertaking for the organisers. Inscrutable and unpredictable he was quite capable of taking his leave before the party got into full swing; even while distinguished guests, anxious to meet the celebrated artist, were still arriving. According to Bertha, Alkan was a most lively conversationalist, expressing himself with delightful ease on an inexhaustable variety of topics. Unfortunate were those caught up in the full flight of an absorbing discussion with him as the clock struck ten for then, surely enough, Alkan would make his exit brusquely and without apology, leaving the group in bewildered embarrassment. He was, of course, almost grotesquely fastidious about time-keeping; witness the precision with which each item is timed in programmes advertised to begin a 'Neuf heures très precise'. Even so, ten o'clock does seem to have held a special, even mystical fascination for him; one has only to remember the bell-like strokes which introduce the 'prayer' towards the end of the third movement from his *Grande Sonate*.

Alkan, doubtless, paid a high price for his social indifference. He was an artist who instinctively recoiled from the obligation of getting to know the 'right' people and the one time he had repudiated his natural inclinations by seeking their help the effort had foundered and humiliated him. Bertha tells us that as late as 1879 Alkan still harboured a deep and bitter grudge against Marmontel 'for whom he had been sacrificed at the Conservatoire'. As a result, he was convinced he had been robbed of the chance of being decorated — the supreme honour normally reserved only for those who occupied an official position. Bertha decided to draw attention to this injustice and approached a highly influential diplomat, Prince Orloff, husband of one of Alkan's favourite pupils, who promised to set matters right at once. With one leap the enthusiastic Bertha was at the Salle Erard to inform Alkan: but he felt surprised that beneath an outward show of gratitude the older musician looked both displeased and humiliated. The Prince went to Alkan's house nine times without finding him 'at home'. For his part Alkan felt obliged to return the visits also nine times but failed to meet the Prince. Finally he was told by the usher that it was useless to come in the afternoons as His Excellency always left at 2.00 p.m. 'How tiresome' replied Alkan 'I like to rest after my meal' ... and the Légion d'Honneur fell by the wayside. Bertha seems to have been strangely insensitive: Alkan should never have been told about such an initiative. How, one wonders, might Beethoven have reacted in similar circumstances?

Unabashed, the doughty Bertha again allowed himself to become involved in an attempt to satisfy another of Alkan's unfulfilled desires. Towards the end of his life the old man became ever more convinced that there was a plot afoot to defraud him of his life's savings. Suddenly he made up his mind that he would give everything to the Conservatoire for the foundation of a chair in the instruction of the *pédalier*. Once made, the decision was final and irrevocable. On Alkan's behalf, Bertha approached the administration and a meeting was arranged. On the appointed afternoon Bertha and a high official of the Beaux Arts waited, but in vain. The meeting broke up in embarrassment and a few minutes later Bertha discovered his old friend at Erard's calmly seated at his piano.

His excuse was simple. He had changed his mind.

The difficulty of approaching Alkan in these last years is graphically underlined by the experience of Friederick Niecks, for twenty-three years Reid Professor of Music at Edinburgh and the author of a classic biography of Chopin. When, in the summer of 1880 Niecks visited Paris, the sixty-seven year old composer was one of the musicians whose acquaintance he was most anxious to make. What happened is so strange and so enlightening that it must be told in full and in Niecks's own words:

'Having heard much of his strange ways and the difficulty of approaching him, I procured a letter of introduction from a friend of mine who, during a sojourn of several years in Paris, had wooed the shy artist with unusual success. But even thus armed I knew that I was undertaking an enterprise that called for much circumspection. After careful consideration of the possibilities of a safe plan of campaign, I decided to begin by calling at his house. My question whether M. Alkan was at home was answered by the concierge with a decisive 'No'. To my further enquiry when he could be found at home, the reply was an equally decisive 'Never'. And in spite of all the expenditure of diplomacy and eloquence I lavished on the powerful functionary, this was all the knowledge I could obtain. My next move was to write a respectful and propitiatory letter to the great man, asking for an interview, and enclosing our common friend's letter of introduction. The result of this petition materialized into a missive such as was perhaps never before received by mortal man. A brief scrawl of a note, written on an odd scrap of paper, stuck into a cheap envelope. The handwriting so shaky that it could be described only by the epithet vermicular, and the style so curt and awkward that it was impossible to say with certainty whether the writer was rude or clumsy in expression. But the predominant effect of the letter on the receiver was that of a hard repulse. The next time I saw Mme. Dubois, she asked me how I had fared with Alkan. I told her my doleful tale; but instead of condoling with me, she laughed and thought my story good fun. 'What are you going to do next?' she asked. 'Do next?' I asked, much surprised. 'How can I, after having been so rudely repulsed, take another step to approach him? I must respect his desire, and preserve my self respect' 'No, no; nothing of the kind. He plays every Monday and Thursday at Erard's. You go there, without ceremony, and make him a fine speech — don't talk of Chopin, talk of Alkan'. The advice went much against the grain, but Mme. Dubois' powers of persuasion overcame my reluctance. The next Monday or Thursday found me soon after three at Erard's. The spacious room, apparently used for solo recitals and chamber music, had no other furniture than chairs and two instruments — an ordinary grand piano and a pedal grand. There were present Alkan playing, and two listeners, a lady and gentleman — English, I think. As soon as the master had finished the piece in hand he rose to meet me. I felt somewhat nervous. How would he receive me? But my fear was soon dissipated. His reception of me was not merely polite, but most friendly. And what was my astonishment when after a few formal words the venerable white-haired, white-bearded, stooping (almost hunchbacked) old man began to talk freely and with the greatest amiability about Chopin and other matters. In fact, it came out that the reason of his reluctance to see me was hyper-conscientiousness — he was afraid that the information he could give me was not important and accurate enough'.

Although still in his sixties one has the impression of a very old man: yet the rigorous routine of Alkan's life continued, unchanged, for a further eight years. Day by day, immaculate in black frock coat, white cravat and top hat he would arrive at the Salle Erard where his room was always reserved. Week by week he would fetch his produce from his favourite shop in the Halles-Centrales district of Paris: nothing would entice him to entrust such sacred matters to a paid servant who, he would argue, must inevitably swindle him. As ever, he continued to prepare his own meals using only ingredients of the highest quality, and despite his solitary life would always eat at a neatly-laid table placed next to his piano. The composer's great-nephew, the artist Jacques Nam who died in 1974 aged ninety-three, was taken as a boy to visit the great man. He vividly remembered his uncle as 'un vieux célibataire' who bowled paper balls under his pianos and his bed in order to check that the cleaner was not scrimping her work. Madame Rachel Guerret, Jacques Nam's sister, and herself a fine miniaturist is, happily, alive and well at ninety-seven. She actually remembers being taken by her grandmother, Céleste Marix (née Morhange) to hear her great uncle play at the Salle Erard, presumably at one of his Monday or Thursday matinées. As she was seven or eight at the time this must have been during his last years and although she was too young to comment on the performance she clearly remembers that Alkan habitually played in the old-fashioned position with his back to the audience.

Those who survive a life of sickness often find the resilience to face old age with equanimity. Alkan might well have continued to play his *pédalier* well into the next decade had it not been for the bizarre, and possibly apocryphal, event which, until recently, had seemed so essential a part of the whole Alkan legend. His death, on 29th March 1888, is so entangled with contradiction that it requires a chapter on its own.

11 The Death of Alkan

No event in Alkan's singular life has been savoured with greater relish than the one which is generally believed to have ended it. 'He was found crushed beneath his upturned bookcase from which he had been extricating a Hebrew religious book' ... and, as if to confirm the solemn nature of Alkan's final act we are told that he was discovered still clutching the *Talmud*, his beloved book of Jewish law, which is traditionally kept on the top shelf so that no other book can be sacrilegiously placed higher. Fate could hardly have contrived a more apt conclusion to a remarkable life and so entrenched is the story of the falling bookcase that the drab suggestion that Alkan might, after all, have died like other men, of heart failure for instance, comes as nothing short of an affront. For this reason alone, those few scholars who had chanced upon Alexandre de Bertha's article about the composer, published in 1909, had conspired to keep silent on his disconcertingly mundane account of Alkan's death: that is until Hugh Macdonald spilt the beans in a persuasive challenge to the whole bookcase theory in the *Musical Times* of January 1972. This is Bertha's description of Alkan's end as quoted by Mr. Macdonald, 'He was found stretched out, lifeless in his kitchen in front of his stove which he was probably about to light to cook his evening meal having spent the afternoon as usual at Erard's'. At first glance his version could hardly be more sober and concise but it neither tells us how Alkan died nor who discovered him, and Bertha's preceding sentence, not quoted by Mr. Macdonald, suggests that the possibility of an accident cannot be ruled out even in the context of this account: 'He died suddenly on the 30th March 1888 in a situation caused by his unusual habits'. Bertha may, of course, simply mean that there was no one at hand to help the old man when he collapsed, but the ambiguity of this account and an error about the date which was, of course March 29, does make one wonder if Bertha actually had first-hand knowledge of the event.

The earliest published suggestion that Alkan did not die naturally appeared in H.H. Bellamann's article of 1924, in which he baldly states: 'An accident in his apartment caused his death'. This and later variants of the same story are all traceable to the same source, Isidore Philipp, who gave a full açcount of Alkan's death to Robert Collet in 1937. Philipp, who at twenty-three had already embarked on the teaching career which was to make him famous, claimed to have been one of the party that dragged Alkan's body from beneath the bookcase. As Philipp was also responsible for other unique snippets of information about Alkan, such as his relationship with Delaborde, it is important to examine his reliability. Phyllis Sellick studied with him and knew him well. That he could be capable of such a deception, even in jest, was to her out of the question. Robert Collet renewed his acquaintance with him shortly before Philipp died in 1958, aged ninety-four. Collet does not consider it in Philipp's character to concoct such a story but admits that he was a marvellous raconteur with a penchant for grotesque detail. He obviously relished the bookcase story which he related clearly and specifically. The seemingly naive embroidery that Alkan was reaching for a Hebrew religious book need in no way discredit Philipp's account. As we have seen, such books are customarily lodged in high places and Alkan was constantly referring to them. He was also short and bowed. Philipp, seeing the toppled bookcase would immediately put two and two together. The macabre claim that Alkan was still clutching the Talmud is surely a colourful later addition and not to be taken seriously.

Surviving members of the Alkan-Morhange family also confirm Philipp's account. Both the grand-children of the composer's sister, Céleste, who were nine and seven when Alkan died, remembered their great-uncle well. Neither had ever questioned the cause of his death and Madame Guerret who, at ninety-seven, is the last surviving link with the composer, has sent the author several valuable souvenirs. She is quite definite about the nature of his death: 'Oui à ma connaissance c'est bien son armoir qui lui est tombé dessus et qui a causé sa mort'. So dramatic an end to her celebrated uncle's life would undoubtedly have captured the imagination of a young child and remained firmly engraved on her memory.

Unfortunately, quite apart from Bertha's article, there still remains one serious obstacle to our acceptance of the famous legend. The police archives contain no record of an accident, and so it seems that the whole mystery is still wide open. Is it conceivable that a violent accidental death could be hushed up? ... and if so, why? On the other hand it seems just as unlikely that Philipp would have passed on so absurd a story unless he had good cause to believe it himself, Hugh Macdonald's canny suggestion that the ever resourceful Delaborde sold Philipp the tallest of tall stores about his father is a non-starter. Not only was Delaborde out of Paris at the time of Alkan's death but he did not show up at the funeral either, and this brings us full circle to the final paradox in this whole enigma. Apart from the immediate family only four mourners were present at Montmartre Cemetery that bleak, wet Easter Sunday afternoon of 1st April 1888. These were the cóffin-bearers consisting of Blondel, head of Erard's, the violinist Maurin ... and the authors themselves of these two contradictory accounts of Alkan's death: Bertha and Philipp.

12 Rescue of a Lost Cause

As Alkan was being buried with full Jewish rites, the Paris musical world was expressing surprise that he had lived so long. 'He had to die' wrote his obituarist 'in order to prove his existence'. This cynical epitaph to Gallic indifference becomes the more ironic when one remembers that, despite his solitary habits, it had been possible those last fifteen years to slip quietly into Erard's any Monday or Thursday afternoon and eavesdrop on one of the greatest masters of the keyboard of his century. Yet, apart from his own strictly confined circle, Alkan had remained an outsider. His creative genius had largely passed unrecognised. Even his fitful efforts to promote himself as a pianist were either too little or too late to make any real impact. Alkan had become a lost cause: an artist who had 'locked away a talent' which might have brought honour to his country. The French do not easily forgive those who fail to acquit their debt to society. Now they banished Alkan to the archives as one of those 'interesting historic figures' whose identities melt so conveniently into the shadows of their immortal contemporaries; and there he would undoubtedly have remained had it not been for the powerful advocacy of two men.

The first rescue-operation was mounted at the turn of the century with a series of Alkan performances by Busoni in Berlin and with the re-printing by Costallat in Paris of many of his important piano works. The inspiration behind this massive project came from Isidore Philipp who chose the music, wrote a stimulating preface and persuaded the reluctant Delaborde to add his illustrious name as co-editor. For once Alkan was in luck. His music was re-printed from the original plates and its startling appearance, so different from that of any other composer, is a constant reminder both of its originality, and of the pains he took over the clarity of its presentation. Copyright problems alone explain the regrettable omission from Costallat's generous catalogue of the *25 Preludes* op. 31, the *Etudes Majeurs* op. 35 and the *Grande Sonate*. Happily all these works have recently become available and M. Gérard Billaudot, who has taken over the Costallat edition, has ambitious plans for a complete Alkan edition in the foreseeable future.

Meanwhile, in the German capital, Busoni was infuriating the reactionary critics by including such works as Alkan's implacable study *En Rythme Molossique* from op. 39 and several of the Etudes Majeurs at his historic recitals in 1901/2 and 3. 'Preposterous French rubbish' was how they dismissed the satirical Military Caprices, op. 50 and the *Allegro Barbaro*, a virile octave study on the white notes alone. These Berlin critics, already hostile to Busoni for his championship of Liszt, looked upon this latest discovery ... and French at that ... as the last straw. Busoni returned to the attack in 1906 by playing Alkan's cadenza in a performance of Beethoven's *C minor Concerto*. How, one wonders, did they contain themselves as this monstrous *tour de force* reached its peroration converting the Concerto's opening theme into a famous tune from the Finale of the Fifth Symphony? The mind boggles. As a peace-offering Busoni handed them Alkan's Grande Etude for the Left Hand Alone from op.76, but the olive branch was not taken. It is tempting to believe that Busoni set about baiting his critics with sardonic glee, but artists are irrationally sensitive to adverse notices and when, twenty years later, Philipp challenged him to give further Alkan performances he remembered the Berlin critics and refused. Busoni, it seems, had played the wrong music in the wrong place at the wrong time.

Despite hostility in Germany and apathy in France the mere fact that an artist of Busoni's authority was playing Alkan began to arouse interest in the music and curiosity about the man. Several articles spread over the next thirty or so years attempted, with varying success, to assess the one and satisfy the other. We have already referred to Alexandre de Bertha's reminiscences of 1909 and to Niecks's description of his meeting with Alkan published in the *Monthly Musical Record* of January 1918. Both Bertha and Niecks also included a brief discussion of the music, the former showing little understanding of Alkan's creative originality and regarding his true value as that of a custodian of tradition. Niecks, on the other hand, made a close study of the works published by Costallat, quoting the opinions of Schumann and Liszt on the early compositions. He seems reluctant to commit himself, however, and argues that where there is neglect on the one hand there must surely be shortcomings on the other. 'Perhaps', he suggests 'Alkan's talent was speculatively inventive rather than spontaneously creative.'

A fuller discussion of the music was published in the American *Musical Quarterly* during 1924. The writer, H.H. Bellamann discovered much that excited him. *Morte* op. 15, for instance, with its 'great bell effects and rolls of muffled drums', and the *Etudes Mineurs*, op. 39, which he found 'completely astounding'. Unfortunately Bellamann, like Niecks before him, could never have heard these works performed by a real virtuoso. No piano music is more misleading in appearance than Alkan's especially as he approaches the climaxes of such movements as *Quasi Faust* from the *Grande Sonate* or the finales from his Sonatine, Concerto and Symphonie for Solo Piano. These baffling pages 'black with marching regiments of notes' become in performance a Pandora's Box of demonic power to which only the most fearless player holds the key. Bellamann's opinion that the *Grande Sonate* would never be performed, his curt dismissal of the marvellous *Trois Petites Fantaisies*, op. 41 and his comparison of the great Study for Left Hand Alone from op. 76 with a transcription by Sydney Smith, suggest that, like many others, he was deceived by the very look of the notes on paper. Is it not significant that the only musicians of the period who accepted Alkan as a great composer were themselves great performers: Busoni, for instance, who had no hesitation in placing him alongside Liszt, Chopin, Schumann and Brahms as one of the five greatest post-Beethoven writers for the piano. Now came an uncompromising affirmation of this greatness in a remarkable book by a remarkable man.

Kaikhosru Sorabji is reputed to be a complete virtuoso. Certainly, if he can play his own astonishing piano music, perhaps the most difficult to have been published this century, he must be. No student of Alkan is now unfamiliar with the arresting opening of Sorabji's compelling essay on the composer's works as it appeared in his book *Around Music* in 1932: 'Few remarkable and astounding figures in music have been the subject of such persistent misunderstanding, denigration and belittlement as Alkan'. Of the Etudes, op. 35 and 39 he has this to say: 'These amazing works place him among the great masters of piano music ... the prodigious, teeming richness of invention the vivid originality, the very individual harmony, the superb mastery of these works cannot be too highly admired'.

Three years later Bernard van Dieren in *Down Among the Dead Men* was making equally spectacular claims, but whereas Sorabji had praised the epic, the uncanny, the grotesque and the sardonic, van Dieren was more concerned with the descriptive and psychological elements in Alkan's music. Commenting on *Le Tambour Bat aux Champs* (The drum beats a salute), one of the two *Capriccii* op. 50, he writes: 'I seriously doubt whether there is another short composition which, in an equally simple form, conveys so overwhelmingly a sense of concentrated tragedy'. Such powerful advocacy as that of Sorabji and van Dieren could not pass unheeded and in 1938/9 the B.B.C. invited Egon Petri to give three Alkan recitals in commemoration of the fiftieth anniversary of the composer's death and the 125th of his birth. Petri, like his teacher Busoni, had all the intellect, temperament, size and technique to match this demanding music. In these historic broadcasts he included two of Alkan's largest solo works, The Symphonie and Concerto from the *Etudes Mineurs* op. 39. It is interesting to note that Petri's pioneering performance of the Solo Concerto took fifty minutes which suggests that on this occasion, at least, he cut several of the seventy-two pages of its gigantic first movement. The London critics were sharply divided about the quality of this unfamiliar music: one was ecstatic, while another considered it 'a monumental fraud'. Petri's recitals are still vividly remembered as a landmark in pre-war music broadcasts and he would undoubtably have recorded some of Alkan's major works had it not been for the intervention, in 1939, of the Second World War. Even fifty years after his death, it seems, Alkan could still fall victim to his inherent bad luck. Within a few months of Petri's last broadcast the composer's fate was once more vested in the hands of a few *cognoscenti*, mainly pupils of Petri and Philipp both of whom were now living in America. There, interest would doubtless have grown more rapidly but for the serious illness, in the early 'forties, of Petri himself.

* * * * * *

Artistic climates rarely survive a cataclysmic social upheaval. Post-war Britain sought musical consolation in the comparatively cool detachment of the Baroque revival and a fugitive quest for pure style in the classics. Inevitably, the bold romantic gestures and massive sonorities of the nineteenth century rang hollow in a world still dazed by its own epic struggle. For the next two decades Alkan became one of the casualties of a hostile musical environment. His own single-handed crusade to bring baroque and classical masterpieces before a pleasure-seeking Paris public in the 1870's was, of course, quite unknown: in fact, the very little that was still known about Alkan now associated him with the very byways and backwaters of nineteenth-century virtuosity he had himself so resolutely opposed. Is it surprising that in so alien an atmosphere his torch flickered, reluctant; that his admirers, forced on to the defensive, sounded muted and apologetic in their anxiety not to overstate a doubtful case? Performances became few and far between and one brave attempt to re-kindle interest, a B.B.C. series in the late 1940's, took place in the early experimental days of Third Programme before it could reach a wide audience. Yet even in this, Alkan's darkest hour, his admirers waiting patiently in the wings for the passing of a generation, there came a revolution in the gramophone industry which was to grant him an ally perhaps more formidable than the verbal or pianistic persuasions of a Sorabji or a Petri.

In 1960, a young and enterprising gramophone company invited the author to record the first long-playing records of Alkan's music including both the Symphonie and Concerto for Solo Piano. As it turned out the courageous policy of this enlightened company was premature and before the project had taken wing *Triumph Superfi* was in the hands of the Receiver. Meanwhile Alkan had found a passionate, fiery and committed evangelist on the other side of the Atlantic: a man with a mission and the sense of occasion to promote it.

Raymond Lewenthal had studied with the colourful Olga Samaroff, an erstwhile pupil of Delaborde at the Paris Conservatoire, and so Lewenthal could claim the distinction of being a great grand-pupil of the composer himself. He now set about giving recitals and broadcasts of Alkan's music, providing a highly entertaining commentary to an excellent new edition of his works, writing a long-promised book about the composer, but, most important, recording several of his masterpieces including the Symphonie for Solo Piano. At last a young and unprejudiced audience could judge for themselves this legendary piano music which had so long remained seen but not heard. This new generation was already acclaiming the Symphonies of Bruckner and Mahler: pianists were discovering through the re-issue of historic gramophone records, the undreamt-of technical powers of some of their nineteenth century precessors. Played for all it is worth Alkan's Solo Symphonie can be a shattering pianistic experience. It also anticipates in a most startling way the music of Brahms, Bruckner and Mahler. Reaction to Lewenthal's performance was immediate and decisive. 'Some of the writing is prophetic' wrote Harold Schonberg in the *New York Times*, 'some is inspired: all of it attests to a remarkable imagination'.

Britain was quick to respond to the American initiative and an L.P. devoted to a quite different aspect of Alkan's many sided talent, his genius as a miniaturist, appeared in 1969. 'He has a mind of astonishing originality' wrote Roger Fiske in *The Gramophone*: but this selection of short pieces was only a preliminary canter. In January, 1970, one hundred and thirteen years after its publication, came the first recording of the gigantic Concerto for Solo Piano and any lingering doubt about Busoni's claim that here was one of the five greatest composers for the piano since Beethoven was silenced. Leading critics greeted the work as 'a masterpiece ... intriguing, eccentric and disturbing;' as 'the most difficult piano work of its century and one of the most original'. In a perceptive article in *The Times*, (14th March, 1970) Stanley Sadie draws particular attention to 'the curious mixture of extreme severity and profound passion that characterises this music'. 'What of the actual style?' he continues. 'It is not easy to describe, still less easy to compare with others. The *tutti* sections are tough, severe, dramatic music utterly unlike anyone else's ... possibly the most remarkable passage comes in the first movement's development section, with cold, granitic textures, austere harmonies, the music poised and motionless. The Concerto has an Adagio starting quite conventionally, but constantly devolving on to the keyboard's extremes, with the left hand suggesting funereal drum beats and there is a Finale of demonic energy, music of extraordinary dark power and fiendish difficulty.'

The unique technical demands and the sheer size of such compositions as the *Concerto*, the *Grande Sonate* and the *Trois Grandes Etudes* op. 76 must inevitably forbid their frequent public performance. By the mid-1970's, however, a sizeable proportion of Alkan's major works for piano has become steadily available on record. When the first complete recording of the *Grande Sonate* was released in 1974 it was at once acclaimed as a masterpiece indispensable to an understanding of nineteenth century piano music as a whole; yet this work had taken a hundred-and-twenty-five years to reach the public. Can it be that Alkan's message, stark and uncompromising as it is, has more relevance today than it had for his own generation a century ago? Is this the strange case of an artist using the language and techniques of one period to communicate with another? Significantly enough his music appeals to musicians of widely contrasted persuasions. It has recently been rumoured that Dr. Gordon Jacob is working on an orchestral paraphrase of the brilliant *Festin d'Esope* Variations from op. 39 and, apart from such long-standing admirers as Busoni, Sorabji and Humphrey Searle, a growing number of contemporary British composers, including Robert Simpson, Alan Ridout, Ronald Stevenson, John McCabe and Roger Smalley are all discovering something unique and vital in Alkan's many-sided genius.

* * * * * *

If recognition of Alkan's genius in Britian and America was delayed by nearly a century, so far as his native France was concerned he might just as well never have existed. During this same period of eighty or so years — an era which witnessed the successive triumphs of Fauré, Debussy, Ravel, *Les Six*, Messiaen and Boulez — Alkan's eclipse was total and enduring. Unlike his younger contemporary, César Franck, whose creative career made similarly little impact during his lifetime, Alkan left no distinguished pupils, such as Vincent d'Indy, to rally round his cause after his death. Despite his vast repertory, Delaborde no longer peformed his father's music and we do not even know if Alkan continued to teach during those last, shadowy, years. Probably it was no longer necessary for, despite his earlier complaints of trying to scrape a meagre living from teaching, he left a sizeable estate of 100,664 francs. Some of this money was left to Jewish charities such as the Conservatoire Israélite. 'Elie Miriam dit Delaborde' received a small annuity of 400 francs; but by far the most interesting bequest was the following: 'to the music section of the Institute': (ie. the Conservatoire)

1) Annual sum of 800 francs for the foundation of a yearly competition for *pédalier*.
2) Annual sum of 1,800 francs for the foundation of a yearly competition for the composition of a cantata (conditions to be expressed by the executor of his Will).

Even now, though, Alkan's desire to make his posthumous peace with the institution that had rejected him was frustrated. The secretary of the Conservatoire informed his lawyer that the Institute could not accept the two legacies.

We can read the detailed inventory of Alkan's chattels and property at the time of his death in Brigitte François-Sappey's 'Dossier de pièces d'archives' in François-Sappey's *Alkan* (see Bibliography). In his Will (made in August 1886) Alkan noted that the various bound volumes and boxes of his manuscripts could be found in his house and in his studio at Maison Erard. He bequeathed his books, printed music and all these manuscripts to his brother Napoléon*. In his reminiscences

*Isidore Philipp told Robert Collet that he managed to acquire Alkan's *pédalier* but that his neighbours complained so bitterly that he was forced to part with it. No wonder Alkan had found it expedient to maintain two flats, one above the other.

Bertha informs us, however, that the two musicians were permanently 'at daggers drawn', and for reasons neither was willing to divulge. It is certainly odd that Napoléon, fine pianist that he was, took no part in the 'petits Concerts'. As we have seen, Alkan had enjoyed his brothers' collaboration back in the 1840's, and Napoléon had, for his part, championed Valentin's earlier compositions. Perhaps Alkan was vexed that this younger brother, whom he had taught and encouraged, had succeeded just when he had failed; for Napoléon had become the most academically distinguished of the entire, gifted family. His long, illustrious reign as head of the Solfège department at the Conservatoire was crowned in 1895 by the Légion d'Honneur. 'How furious Alkan would have been' wrote Bertha 'had he lived to witness the decoration of his younger brother Napoléon'. Alkan's legacy to Napoléon of 1,000 francs, however, must mean that the brothers had eventually buried their differences, and this is also borne out by the handing-down in Napoléon's family of such personal souvenirs as Alkan's *Prix de Rome* medallion and the beautiful early portrait by Dubufe.

Jean-Yves Bras, is convinced that Alkan's manuscripts were, indeed, entrusted to Napoléon and that any search for the missing *B minor Symphony* should start on this assumption. In 1906, the eighty-year-old Napoléon, wealthy owner of three fine Paris houses, married his housekeeper, Eva Flesch, but died a few months later. Eva was a staunch Catholic, and this alone must have proved a stubborn obstacle to their earlier marriage. It seems probably that one of Napoléon's final acts was to grant full legal status to their two children, Adolphe and Emma-Christina, aged thirty-three and twenty-seven, as well as to the woman who had been his wife in all but name. On Napoléon's death his music library, including his brother's manuscripts are believed to have passed to his son, Adolphe, a brilliant concert-pianist but, strange to relate, Adolphe only survived his father by a few months. He also died in 1906, quite suddenly, quite unexpectedly of septicaemia, after being thrown from his horse. That his wife was having an affair at the time and that she married her lover not long after the event adds a speculative dimension to the whole tragedy. Family recollections of an auction sale at which Adolphe's personal effects were disposed of suggest that Alkan's manuscripts may have been dispersed. During the German invasion of France, in 1940, other valuable papers in Emma-Christina's possession were hastily stuffed into a tin chest and buried in the garden of her country home. After being occupied by German officers the house was eventually sold. No attempt has yet been made to recover the box and so its possibly valuable contents remain for the moment tantalisingly out of reach.

In the early 1970's, prompted, no doubt, by Alkan's rising star in Britain and America, French radio (the O.R.T.F.) mounted an important series of discussions and performances of his music in the course of which a plea was broadcast for information about the possible whereabouts of manuscripts, including the missing Symphony. The sole response was from the artist, Jacques Nam, who came forward as Alkan's great-nephew. Although unable to produce the elusive manuscripts he represented a further branch of Alkan's family, that of the composer's sister, Céleste, the artist's grandmother. Through Céleste's two daughters, Marie and Albertine, the musical and artistic traditions of this remarkable family have been passed on to the third and fourth generations. Marie sang at one of her uncle's 'Petits Concerts' in the 1870's and her husband, a Morhange cousin, kept a flourishing musical instrument shop in Paris at which a prize exhibit was a harmonium invented by Céleste's husband, Mayer Marix. Both Albertine's children became distinguished artists. Madame Rachel Guerret, now in her late nineties, was a fine miniaturist while Jacques Nam's remarkable portrayal of cats, familiar to collectors of Sèvres porcelain, won him the Légion d'Honneur, as well as the admiration of Colette.

Like his cousin, Delaborde, who was as celebrated a painter as he was a musician, Nam had a flair for animals, including monkeys (remember Delaborde's pet apes!). Jean-Yves Bras, who was fortunate enough to have met Jacques Nam during his last years was enchanted by his personality, fascinated by his reminiscences of the Alkan family and captivated by his long memory of artistic life in the capital. It is to the author's great regret that he missed him. Just as a meeting had been arranged by the O.R.T.F. in Paris, illness struck. He died soon afterwards, aged ninety-three, having lived to see the music of the great-uncle he had always remembered so vividly at last catching the imagination of their fellow countrymen.

13 Personality and Appearance

Eye-witness accounts of meetings with Alkan, confined as they are to his later years, all agree that there was something quite unusual about his personality. 'He had a most impressive presence', wrote Niecks who had met the composer in 1880, 'the face of a noble Jewish type, the capacious head and the penetrating and refined expression all spoke of the thinker. And the venerable appearance of his presence was heightened by his dress which was clerical in cut and colour.' Marmontel drew a similar picture. 'His glance was shrewd, a little sly ... his stooping gait and puritanic dress give him the appearance of an Anglican minister or Rabbi'.

Alkan spent his entire life in the more secluded parts of Paris clinging tenaciously to the sober dress and stiff formality of the July Monarchy of Louis-Philippe (1830-1848), the age of his youth. In many ways he sensed himself an intruder into the second half of the nineteenth-century and must have felt utterly lost amidst the gaudy extravagances of the Second Empire. Perhaps it is not entirely by coincidence that the reign of Napoleon III (1852-1870) also marked the boundary of Alkan's largest and most decisive withdrawal from what he considered an increasingly tasteless, meretricious and alien society; a society in which artistic ambition seemed to be ever widening its horizons by lowering its sights. He became more and more puzzled and disillusioned. Commenting on Gounod's success in Germany he asked Hiller if his fellow-countrymen had fallen into their second-childhood. Of Hiller's own latest productions, however, now utterly forgotten, he exclaimed 'It warms my heart to know some good work is appearing in the face of so much muck. I mean it, so much muck. How can there be so many to make it and so many to take pleasure in it?' This was in 1859, a year before Alkan dragged himself, in his own words: 'as a matter of duty for a misanthropic musician ...' to Wagner's concert on January 24 1860. 'It was worth it' he declared 'for my indignation. What brutality, what base materialism'.* His delight, on the other hand, in the compositions of such contemporaries as Mendelssohn and Schumann shows that 'sour grapes' was not at the root of his hostility towards Wagner. Such is the measure of Alkan's objectivity that although he utterly rejected the music of his friend Liszt, who had earlier supported and encouraged him, he sprang angrily to the defence of his own harshest critic when 'some high-priest of criticism too imbecile to understand or appraise him' classified Schumann with the new school of 'Wagner, le Listz [*sic*] and Co.'

Of Alkan's basic modesty there can be no doubt. One may scan the wide-ranging Hiller correspondence in vain for all but a glancing reference to his own work. Not one word, for instance, about the historic publication of his monumental Studies op. 39, in 1857. Yet Alkan is constantly asking for details about his friend's compositions, and his letters are liberally peppered with astute asides about other people's music. As we have seen, his programmes tended to leave room only for a modest group of his own shorter pieces amidst an array of those great, unfashionable classics in which he so ardently believed, but which he knew would bring him neither fame nor fortune. Alkan's accusation of 'base materialism' in Wagner's music is a significant indication of his own puritanic attitude to life in general and to music in particular. Four years later, after attending the first performance of Rossini's swan-song, The *Petite Messe Solennelle*, he described it as 'the work of a genius, but a genius called Rossini: from the religious point of view, Vulgo — Anti-Christ'.

---

*Many other musicians, including Auber, whom Wagner admired, found his music both derivative and vulgar. Their own artistic framework, which stemmed from Cherubini, was far too severely circumscribed to allow them to enter such an erotic and highly-charged emotional world. In any case, an orchestral concert consisting of 'bleeding chunks' could only have seemed to dot its dreadful i's and cross its terrible t's, while giving little indication of Wagner's true stature.

The little we know of Alkan's religious outlook – his scepticism over Liszt's admission to Holy orders, his habit of translating the New Testament and his spontaneous use of the expression 'Anti-Christ' – all these point to the free-thinker unlikely to pay lip-service to established creeds, whose deepest convictions express themselves in private study rather than through public gesture. 'How is it we have never discussed religion together?' he asked Hiller, a professed agnostic, in 1866. 'I don't mean Christianity or Mosaism, but *Religion*.' On the other hand Alkan's profound knowledge of the Old Testament together with his constant study of the Talmud made him an authority on Jewish law. 'He has the learning as well as the appearance of a Rabbi', wrote Marmontel, who also

Alkan in his last years
(Oil painting by Rubach; courtesy The Musical Times*)*

emphasised Alkan's solitary, insatiable thirst for knowledge. His all-embracing culture must have stemmed from shrewd observation and wide reading and even thirty years after Chopin's death he was still expressing concern over his friend's lack of intellectual curiosity. 'Chopin was not a reading man' he told Niecks in a deprecatory tone. 'Pierre Leroux, the philosopher and socialist who loved him tenderly, brought him all the books he published, but his friend left them unread, nay, uncut. Victor Hugo's writing he did not like, nor George Sand's.'

'The reputation Alkan had as an intellectual we already saw documented in his face' wrote Niecks; and this is confirmed by all three of the best known portraits of the composer. The most familiar is a medallion reproduced on the outer cover of the Costallat edition of his music; the most impressive, an oil-painting by Wilhelm Rubach, of Alkan's eagle-like profile, looking for all the world like one of the ancient Hebrew prophets. But with the pencil sketch shown on page 91, we enter once more the inescapable realm of mystery and paradox that colours so many aspects of his affairs. The National Library of Canada, who acquired this portrait as part of the Percy Scholes collection, claims that it is signed and dated on the back: 'A. Osborne Campbell, 1926'. But this makes nonsense, unless the artist, about whom nothing seems to be known, copied it from an earlier source. Yet there has never been the slightest evidence for the existence of a full-face portrait from Alkan's later years, and his quaint reticence before the camera makes the possibility of a lost photograph singularly unlikely.

'We will not confine ourselves to a description of Alkan's appearance as he is depicted in certain photos,' wrote Marmontel in 1877, 'that is, taken from behind'. As though to lend substance to Marmontel's strange assertion just such a long-lost photograph has recently come to light. It is reproduced on the front cover. Why should Alkan refuse to expose his 'intelligent and striking physiognomy' to the camera? Was he inordinately shy? There happens to be one, slender, piece of evidence from his teaching days at the Conservatoire that he might have been. In a dissertation undertaken at Harvard University in 1941, its author, J. Bloch, relates how Alkan used to peer furtively out from his studio, drawing back,

Medallion of Alkan
(Bibliothèque Nationale, *Ottawa, Canada*)

hastily, should he catch sight of someone in the corridor. Only when he was quite sure the offender had disappeared would he make his own exit. Unfortunately Bloch gives no reference for this curious example of Alkan's unsociability. If the story is true, it may have been handed down by either Philipp or Petri, both of whom were in America at the time Bloch was writing.* But, to shed a clearer light on Alkan's reticence before the camera we must turn once more to the Hiller correspondence. Commenting on a recent photograph he had just received from his friend, Alkan explained why he could not reciprocate. 'La postérité' he declared 'se passera donc de mes traits sacrés et de mes sacrés traits' — this was in 1863, when he was approaching fifty. Although his sly play on words defies translation, the meaning is clear. Posterity, would have to do without knowing what Alkan looked like ... and the explanation? ... His last two or three appointments with a photographer had coincided with such misfortunes that he dared not tempt Providence again.

As it happens, Alkan did not completely cheat posterity of his photographic likeness. The full-face, but undated portrait

*As early as 1844, Joseph d'Ortigue, a close neighbour of Alkan in the Square d'Orleans, had described him as shy but craggy; diffident and too proud to seek public favours.

Pencil sketch of Alkan by A. Osborne Campbell
*(*Bibliothèque Nationale, *Ottawa, Canada)*

(page 92) shows him relaxed and seated on a chair handed down in Napoléon's family, and adorned with a gigantic button-hole. Like the back-view photograph it was discovered among Jacques Nam's family souvenirs and has now been presented to the Bibliothèque Nationale in Paris. So firmly entrenched is our traditional image of the world-weary old recluse, as he is depicted by Campbell, that this comparatively youthful presentation of him may come as a surprise. If so, it will certainly require a further degree of mental adjustment to turn to the little known pastel portrait by his friend Edouard Dubufe (1820-1883) showing Alkan as he must have looked around the time of those early concerts with Chopin and Liszt. Like his brother-in-law, the composer Gounod, Dubufe had married

Photograph of Alkan
(Courtesy of Bibliothèque Nationale, *Paris)*

Pastel portrait of Alkan by Dubufe
(Courtesy of Madame Dora Ray and Madame Jacqueline Cuzelin)

one of Zimmerman's four daughters and it is a mark of the famous teacher's esteem for his favourite pupil that he asked Dubufe to capture the young virtuoso's striking features just as he was embarking upon a brilliant public career — albeit a career that was soon to wither and die that he might fulfil his greater, if less glorious destiny.

14 The Reluctant Virtuoso

Alkan's reputation as one of the greatest pianists of the nineteenth century is remarkable, for apart from the evidence of his fantastic piano writing it rests, solely, on the testimony of his colleagues. With the vague exception of his two youthful visits to England, which passed unnoticed, he was never heard outside Paris, and even then. only in strictly limited circles. Within these narrow confines Alkan's concert career falls naturally into three periods; the young virtuoso who retired at twenty-five, four sporadic appearances as pianist-composer during his thirties, and his phoenix-like return to the concert platform in 1873.

Until his long retirement in 1849 Alkan's technique was probably second to none and it is, doubtless, the young virtuoso whom Liszt remembered when he told Frits Hartvigson, himself a well-known pianist, that Alkan possessed the finest technique he had ever known but preferred the life of a recluse. Marmontel, in his *Histoire du Piano* (1885), gave a further twist to Liszt's remark: 'Owing to his horror of fuss and publicity' he wrote 'Alkan has lived misanthropically; but all those musicians capable of appreciating him consider him a genius!' The slight note of reservation hidden in the phrase 'those musicians capable of appreciating him' may supply one of our clues to Alkan's lack of public acclaim. As the supreme guardian of the French *style sévère* his playing was noted for its clarity, sobriety, logic and Gallic tightness of rhythm. A gramophone record made in 1904 by the sixty-nine-year-old Saint-Saëns playing excerpts from his pocket concerto, *Africa* gives a very good idea of the virtues and limitations of the *style sévère* as it survived into the twentieth century. The high speed clarity is remarkable, the rhythmic drive stimulating, the control undeniable: yet the criticisms of Alkan's own early playing, that it was cold, that it lacked 'breadth, poetry, passion and imagination' could just as easily be directed against the veteran Saint-Saëns, on the evidence of this recording alone: and remember, Saint Saëns was one of those artists Alkan invited to play with him at his 'Petits Concerts'. The attributes of transparent honesty, detachment and total lack of self-indulgence so often admired as the hallmark of maturity are just as frequently frowned upon in a younger artist as his 'lack of emotional involvement' or his inability to 'see beyond the notes'. The young Busoni was dubbed 'an intellectual without a soul', and the not-so-young Schnabel dismissed, in some quarters, as a 'scholarly' pianist. Although certain critics of Alkan's earlier playing may have been similarly blinded by its ruthless intellectual glare, no one, one hastens to add, denied him his absolute mastery.

The most casual glance at the scores of such works as the *Etudes Mineurs* suggests that double-notes, octaves and the most towering conglomerations of fat chords were to Alkan what scales and arpeggios are to lesser mortals. His colossal technique, however, was never paraded and, consequently, only his fellow pianists could have had any idea of the feats being accomplished before their eyes and ears. One has, altogether, the impression of a lofty, somewhat puritanical artist: the bringer of light rather than warmth or, as Léon Kreutzer intimated, the musicians' pianist rather than the public's idol.

Besides his uncompromising integrity, the austerity of his programmes and the general lack of glamour associated with his concerts, there may have been a further aspect of Alkan's public performances that could sometimes have reduced his power to woo the Paris audiences. Léon Kreutzer spoke of his occasional loss of 'inspirational freedom' when playing in public, blaming it on the pianist's fierce campaign against the affected, the exaggerated, etc. But perhaps Kreutzer's diagnosis is wrong. Maybe the root cause of Alkan's lack of spontaneous inspiration on the podium should be sought elsewhere, within his highly complex, hyper-sensitive, vulnerable psychological make-up —

that dangerous compound of authority and humility, conviction and doubt, fervent enthusiasm and basic caution which must on occasions have robbed him of the armoury so vital to those who appear in public. Despite his fabulous facility and wonderful memory, one has the impression that he was never really at home on the concert platform. It is not always appreciated that anxiety in the prodigiously well-equipped performer is seldom apparent in loss of technique but tends to manifest itself in other ways: over-speeding and lack of equilibrium in some cases, decrease in warmth and an exaggeration of the cerebral aspect in others. This may well have happened with Alkan throughout his life. Furthermore, as his fastidious timings suggest, he was probably the 'definitive' rather than 'inspirational' type of artist, his interpretations representing a crusade towards an ideal conception rather than an impromptu, never-to-be-repeated gesture. Although no great performance is possible without both discipline and inspiration, in Alkan's case, if he were not 'on form', the inspiration would probably have evaporated leaving only the discipline.

At his best, Alkan must have been a unique pianist combining all the finest attributes of the French school — its equality of touch, clarity, lucidity and rhythmic severity with the intellectual penetration of a Busoni. Little wonder even Liszt, himself, is reputed to have felt ill-at-ease when playing in his presence! Reviewing the 1849 concert which preceded his long absence from public life, the seventy-year-old Henri Blanchard tried to describe Alkan's style — its energy, fullness, clarity, refinement and sensitivity. He spoke of graduations of sound which Alkan possessed to a remarkable degree and considered his ability to stir the emotions by applying the singer's art to the keyboard as 'a modern conquest'. Marmontel was similarly impressed by Alkan's infinite variation of touch which, together with his uncanny sense of style, enabled him to re-create the music of widely differing periods and schools, giving to each work — be it Scarlatti, Couperin, Mozart, Beethoven or his contemporaries Schumann, Mendelssohn and Chopin — its own distinctive character. Again, Marmontel stressed Alkan's rigorous and rhythmic precision which scorned the abuse of *tempo rubato*, that lingering freedom of pulse, so closely identified with Chopin's playing, which had become almost universal by the second half of the century.

It is doubtful, however, if any musician was more familiar with Chopin's playing or more qualified to comment on it than Alkan himself, and his factual account of it can hardly be ignored. 'Not only did Alkan answer all my countless questions about Chopin's playing' wrote Bertha 'but he played me all his immortal friend's masterpieces one after another, and more than once. He initiated me into most of the secrets of Chopin's playing which were lowered into the grave with him sixty years ago' – Bertha was, of course, writing in 1909 – 'They compel one to the conclusion that Chopin should never be treated as a romantic or a revolutionary but, on the contrary, as a staunch classicist who had, involuntarily, opened up new frontiers of his art which had lain dormant until his arrival. Consequently a classical style of playing is imperative to the correct interpretation of Chopin's music. The decorations, however inspired, must not be treated as accessories but rather as part of the whole fabric of the composition. It also follows that the *tempo rubato* the majority of pianists impose wholesale upon Chopin's music is only valid where expressly indicated by the composer. To underline the truth of this assertion Alkan would repeat again and again Chopin's own axiom that 'the left hand must act as conductor, regulating and tempering any involuntary inflexions of the right hand.'

Alkan considered Chopin's nuances inimitable, for, owing to his lack of physical strength, he obtained his gradations by an infinite extension of his *piano*. Alkan concluded that although an ample sonority has its rightful place in Chopin's compositions, the exaggerated *fortissimo* with which certain modern virtuosi assail the ear is utterly out of place in his music and can only destroy its homogeneity'.

So far as Alkan's own playing of Chopin was concerned Bertha admired its comprehensive technical command but felt it was slightly lacking in brilliance and elegance. It may be that a profound study of the German classics had gradually weaned Alkan from the graceful polish and facile glitter of the Paris salon style to a more monumental breed of pianism appropriate to the sober polyphony of Bach or the rugged austerity of late Beethoven, the twin gods of his later years. Or was it, simply, that his fearsome technical armoury and icy precision that must once have chilled the heart of many a famous rival was, after a quarter of a century of comparative neglect, already on the wane by the time Bertha knew his playing in the 1870's — the period of the 'Petitis Concerts'? Once or twice during the reviews of these concerts we may detect small reservations which suggest that his technique no longer supplied him with a complete insurance against the stresses and strains of nervous tension and the additional burden of ill-health.

'It was obvious' wrote *La Revue et Gazette* 'that indisposition was robbing the artist of his ability at his third 'Petit Concert'. This was in 1873 during his first season. Alkan's bowed and aged appearance in his sixties indicates the encroaching hazard of rheumatism which would, doubtless, have affected his hands. Even so, in Marmontel's opinion his 'magisterial command' at sixty-four was unimpaired. How, one might ask, did Marmontel know this in 1877? Had he run the gauntlet by slipping into one of the 'Petits Concerts' under the eagle-eyed surveillance of Gustave Alkan? Fortunately there are other reliable accounts of Alkan's playing during those later years which substantiate Marmontel's claim. The pianist was already in his late sixties when Niecks heard him on the occasion of his second visit to Erards. 'About a dozen ladies and myself formed the audience' wrote Niecks 'and we had the privilege and pleasure of hearing him play for nearly two hours compositions of his own, of Mendelssohn, of Bach, and of Bach-Vivaldi. Much of this music he performed on the pedal-piano, of which he was very fond and for which he wrote a good deal (for instance op. 64, 66, 69, and 72). Of the character of his truly masterly playing I remember this. It was free from any kind of extravagance and of over-accentuation of his individuality: loyalty of interpretation seemed to be his chief aim. Firmness, repose, and sobriety in rhythm and dynamics struck me as outstanding features. But the playing was as much distinguished by the clearness of phrasing and the richness of delicate shading, as by the avoidance of the abuse of *tempo rubato*. The legato element may be said to have been the predominant element. In the main I agree with Marmontel's estimate of Alkan's admirable style of playing, inclusive of some austerity, "the austerity that suited his Puritan and convinced nature".'

'In the intervals and at the conclusion I had some more delightful conversation with Alkan – during which his face was now and then illumined by a kindly, sly smile – of which I remember especially our discussion of Bach's arrangement of Vivaldi's *Concertos*, in which, and its relation to the originals, he was greatly interested'.

Niecks's emphasis of the *legato* element in Alkan's playing at this time is rather interesting. Many of his earlier works, and some from his maturity, seem to demand a highly pungent and detached style of playing – The *Allegro Barbaro* and *Le Festin d'Esope* spring immediately to mind. One wonders, again, if his pre-occupation with Bach's organ works, played on the *pédalier*, had led Alkan to change his earlier style in favour of a smoother manner of performance.

The most authoritative musician who heard Alkan towards the very end of his life was Isidore Philipp, himself a brilliant virtuoso familiar with the playing of all the greatest pianists of the era, from Liszt to Busoni. His impression of his uniqueness as a performer never faded. In response to the spontaneous requests of his listeners, claimed Philipp, Alkan, now in his seventies, would still find no problem in drawing from the vast store-house of his amazing memory works of every period from Couperin to Chopin. Philipp gave Robert Collet the impression that, in these familiar surroundings, at any rate, Alkan's technique had remained equal to anything.

But what, exactly, were the surroundings in which Philipp, and perhaps Madame Guerret as a small child, remembered hearing Alkan? The more one ponders on the vague and sometimes conflicting accounts of his last appearances at Erards the greater becomes the impression that, apart from his private bi-weekly matinées, some kind of fitful concert activity continued, possibly in the form of invitation-recitals, to the end of his life. Philipp spoke of 'elegant gatherings' frequented by 'des dames très parfumées et froufroutantes'. Who were these elegant, perfumed ladies with their rustling skirts? Were they all that remained of Alkan's highly selective audience 'the audience of great artists?' The following extract from the early recollections of Vincent d'Indy contains the veiled suggestion that the 'Petits Concerts', themselves, may have continued in some form or other, right up to the time of Alkan's death. But, quite apart from speculation about his possible concert activities during these later years, the whole account is of unusual interest. Not only does it throw a unique light on Alkan's playing and personality in the mid-1870's as it impressed this highly sensitive and informed musician, but it is also psychologically revealing, coming as it does from an avowed anti-semite writing just fifty-five years after the event:-

'One day I was passing by the small rooms on the first floor of the Maison Erard, reserved only for great pianists, for their practice and lessons. At the time the rooms were all empty, except one, from which could be heard the great *Triple-Prelude* in E flat by Bach played remarkably well on a *pédalier*. I listened, riveted to the spot by the expressive, crystal-clear playing of a little old man, frail in appearance, who, without seeming to suspect my presence, continued the piece right to the end. Then, turning to me: 'Do you know this music?' he asked. I replied that, as an organ pupil in Franck's class at the Conservatoire, I could scarcely ignore such a fine work. 'Play me something' he added, giving up the piano stool for me. Although somewhat over-awed, I managed to play quite cleanly the *C Major Fugue* — the one affectionately known as *The Mastersingers* because of its similarity to a certain Wagnerian theme.

Without comment he returned to the piano saying 'I am Charles-Valentin Alkan and I'm just preparing for my annual series of six 'Petits Concerts' at which I play only the finest things'. Then, without giving me a moment to reply: 'Listen well, I'm going to play you, for you alone, Beethoven's *Opus 110* — listen ...' What happened to the great Beethovenian poem beneath the skinny, hooked fingers of the little old man I couldn't begin to describe — above all in the Arioso and the Fugue, where the melody, penetrating the mystery of Death itself, climbs up to a blaze of light, affected me with an excess of enthusiasm such as I have never experienced since. This was not Liszt — perhaps less perfect, technically — but it had greater intimacy and was more humanly moving ...

'Without giving me a chance to speak, Alkan shoved me violently over to the window and looking straight into my eyes, pronounced these words — words which are precious to me and whose well-meaning bluntness I have never forgotten: 'You —

you're going to be an artist, a real one ... farewell, we will not see each other again ...' Indignant, I protested that I would be in the front row at his next 'Petit Concert'. He replied, more sadly: 'No, we will never see each other again'.

Some compulsory occupation connected with my life in Paris prevented me from being present at the first 'Petit Concert'; on the evening of the second I had an engagement in the provinces; other obstacles on the third. In short, several years passed before I managed to find a free evening and then, at the moment I was about to go to one of these concerts, I read in a paper that Charles-Valentin Alkan had just died'.

15 The Music

A companion volume will be devoted to an examination and analysis of Alkan's music but the present work would seem sadly incomplete without some discussion of its style and flavour.

It would be surprising if the amazing wealth of contradictions that colour Alkan's character did not enrich his creative work. Indeed, the very diversity and range of his compositions has proved a frustrating obstacle to the filing-cabinet mind. Like Beethoven, he seldom if ever repeats himself. His music belongs to no recognisable school, period or place; and it stubbornly refuses to wear its convenient label of identity. To start with, Alkan's harmonic language itself presents a paradox. On the surface he is a severe conservative whose purpose is well served by the harmonic small change of such contemporaries as Mendelssohn and Schumann.

To the unprepared ear he can sometimes sound impersonal – even faceless; his lyricism charming, but faded. On the other hand, his disturbing and unpredictable use of this familiar language may seem freakish, foreshadowing the wilful eccentricity of certain twentieth century composers like Satie and Ives. Apart from Alkan's genius for parody and caricature, such an impression is wholly misleading. Imagine the entire output of Berlioz being withheld until the late twentieth century and then appearing in the impersonal black and white dress of the solo piano. Would he not emerge as a similarly perplexing and controversial figure – and for the same reason, that his language is conservative, his manner radical? Alkan has, in fact, been dubbed The Berlioz of the Piano but although kinship of spirit and background is sometimes obvious, to label him thus is deceptive. Alkan did not care for Berlioz's music. He can be understood only on his own terms and resemblances to the many other composers, earlier, contemporary or even later with whom he has been compared are useful only as descriptive guidelines. Ultimately they melt away.

Alkan's music is romantic, in the Berlioz tradition – highly imaginative, colourful, pungent, displaying a sober, unsensuous but deeply moving lyricism – yet within a framework firmly rooted in the classics. His large-scale structures reveal a profound, almost instinctive awareness of the subtlest inflections of sonata-form as understood by Haydn, Mozart, Beethoven and Schubert. A constant and supple variation of phrase length adds tensile strength to his paragraphs – a characteristic he may well have inherited from Haydn. He establishes his mood immediately: witness the desolate drum beats at the outset of his *Funeral March* op. 26 (1844) or the laconic opening of his splendid *Minuetto alla Tedesca*, a work which seems to combine characteristics of Bach, Haydn, Mozart and Beethoven in a crucible of originality. This piece also displays a bold, uncompromising style of piano writing typical of him. We know, from accounts of his own playing, that Alkan would take the most fearsome hurdles in unflagging tempo. Certainly anyone listening to the relentless finales of his *Solo Concerto, Symphonie* or *Sonatine* for the first time must experience an exhilarating sensation of something unique in piano writing, for here virtuosity is the outcome of a white-hot creative energy. In the finales of both the *Symphonie* and *Sonatine* the musical argument could hardly be more cogent. Not a note is wasted and they both have an obsessive, almost suicidal drive.

If Alkan's language is basically diatonic, simple and direct – even severe – his manner can be startling. Take, for instance, the *Allegretto in A minor*, one of his *Chants* from op. 38. It looks just like Mendelssohn: but the whole piece is obsessed by an inner pedal point. The sub-mediant note F, repeated 414 times, cuts icily into its texture producing some powerful clashes. In the final bar it hovers, suspended, having established a tenuous stability of its own. Several of the *Chants* (there are five sets of six pieces published between 1857 and 1877) give the impression of Mendelssohn gently refracted in the distorting mirror of Alkan's mind. The *G minor Barcarolle*, for example, contains some quaint inflections which give a plaintive ambiguity to the tonality, as though Gershwin had re-written one of Mendelssohn's *Songs without words*.

Against an almost naively simple background Alkan will sometimes plunge into an alien, comfortless environment — a region of disquieting darkness. This happens with uncanny effect in the *Scherzo-Minuetto* from his *Sonatine*, op. 61, where one is led by a series of baffling modulations into a bleak twilit world of suspended tonality. Still more astonishing is the middle section of the fourth in his *Onze Pièces dans le Style Religieux* op. 72, where, without warning, a brief page full of the darkest fantasy occurs. The left hand gropes in widely spaced intervals like a 'cellist in search of a tune, while a monotonous ostinato rises and falls above an obstinately recurring pedal note. The effect is both eerie and hypnotic, and quite unlike anything else of the period — or of any period, for that matter. Doubtless it was passages such as these that Sorabji had in mind when he wrote in *Around Music* (1932) of that 'eerie, bizarre and somewhat eldritch quality that makes this master's work so irresistable'. Sorabji also emphasises satire as an essential ingredient of Alkan's style, describing the brilliant military parody *Capriccio alla Soldatesca* op. 50, as a 'piece of grotesque mocking caricature'. A less abrasive species of grotesquery spills over into the little-known and delightfully freakish *Funeral March for a Dead Parrot* scored for mixed voices, three oboes and bassoon, which dates from the same year, 1859. At the anguished climax of this masterly study in mock pathos, the voices become afflicted by a continuous, wailing lament. Yet a casual glance at the score reveals the strictest fugal discipline beneath the grief-stricken countenance, for Alkan's structural sense is never more vigilant than when he is givng fullest rein to his emotions. The satirical vein in Alkan can be studied in essence in a singularly bizarre miniature entitled *Les Diablotins*, one of his *48 Esquisses* op. 63. A constant pattern of parallel tone-clusters foreshadowing the experiments of Henry Cowell is twice interrupted by an unctuous hymn-like fragment marked, according to its register, *quasi santo* and *quasi santa*. So strange is its appearance in print that Alkan has been accused of writing 'paper music'.

Of all his miniatures the *Esquisses* are probably the most consistently rewarding. There is hardly one of these little pieces which does not explore some curiosity of texture, harmony or rhythm, and several – the *First Love Letter*, for instance – suggest a shrewd and quizzical awareness of the subtlest of human relationships strangely at odds with our traditional image of the man. The series ends with an impressive *Laus Deo*, one of a large number of specifically religious pieces which appeared throughout his life and culminated in the splendid *Prières* op. 64 for *pédalier*. Several of these display an overtly Hebraic element, a further essential ingredient of the composer's complex style and one which will be explored in the companion volume. The jubilant optimism of some of these pieces is an added reminder of how little we still know about Alkan's real character.

If his smaller pieces display a bewildering variety of moods and styles, the sheer range of Alkan's output as a whole must prove still more disconcerting to those who would seek to pigeon-hole him. How are they to reconcile the quaint charm of a three-line fragment like *Les Cloches* (also from op. 63) with such epic structures as the great piano studies op. 39? These gigantic works, disarmingly entitled *Douze Etudes dans Tous les Tons Mineurs*, appeared in 1857. Although published six years after the final version of Liszt's Transcendental Studies, they are as far removed from these as Liszt's are from Chopin's. They are, in fact, studies in the production of orchestral textures and sonorities on the piano. Three of them constitute the three movements of the colossal *Solo Concerto* recently described by Roger Fiske as one of the most original piano works of its century. Four more comprise the *Symphonie for solo piano*. As each study is in a progressively darker minor key (C, F, B flat and E flat), the whole work gives a prophetic impression of the 'progressive tonality' of Mahler and Nielsen. Each movement also becomes progressively shorter: the first, sombre, impassioned and powerful, has already been admired for its striking anticipation of Brahms; the second is an impressive funeral march; the third a rough-hewn minuet with a haunting trio; while the Finale has been aptly described by Raymond Lewenthal as 'a ride in hell'. The final study from op. 39, *Le Festin d'Esope*, is a fantastic and colourful set of variations 'stuffed with every conceivable device of keyboard fiendishness', in the words of Peter Stadlen.

The tremendous scope of Alkan's op. 39 studies has tended to overshadow the op. 35 set in all the major keys and published ten years earlier. This is a pity. While in no way on the same epic scale they contain, nevertheless, some remarkable pieces. The seventh – a descriptive fantasy entitled *Fire in a Neighbouring Village* – has been compared to Berlioz, but it also invokes some of the childlike power of Beethoven's *Pastoral Symphony*. The fifty study – the furious *Allegro Barbaro* – may have given Bartok the idea for his own piece of that title. Despite the key signature of F major this virile octave study is entirely on the white notes, its outlines crudely sharpened by the harsh B naturals.

Like the *Etudes Majeurs*, Alkan's *Grande Sonate* op. 33 also dates from his early thirties. That it could remain, for well over a century, little more than a tantalising legend is a sad and disquieting commentary on professional indifference. In many ways it is the most significant piano sonata of its age. Certainly, as Raymond Lewenthal has rightly claimed, it is the strangest one until the Ives sonatas. Doubtless, many virtuosi glancing through its forbidding pages would blench at the daunting prospect of ending so epic a work with two slow movements. But, as William Mann has pointed out, this strange layout in no way spoils the formal balance or hangs a millstone round its musical effectiveness. The four movements of the sonata are headed *twenty, thirty, forty* and *fifty* years and each corresponds to that particular stage in a man's development. The first, a whirlwind scherzo, seems to represent the ebullient man of action seeking maturity. The second, subtitled *Quasi Faust*, unleashes a pianistic eruption of unprecedented fury. The black, satanic forces that sweep through this gigantic movement are controlled, contained, and finally exorcised by a central chant-like motif which forms the basis of a fugal exposition of bewildering complexity. Hushed, mysterious, it seems to float outside time itself. In a riot of sharps, double sharps and a unique treble sharp, it modulates to the arctic region of E sharp major in a spider's web of eight independent parts plus three doublings – eleven sharps and eleven voices in all. The peroration which follows is vibrant with the peal of celestial bells as the movement approaches its triumphant conclusion. If domestic bliss, portrayed in Alkan's third movement *Un Heureux Ménage* provides the perfect foil to *Quasi Faust*, the finale is its malignant sequel. Sub-titled *Prométhée Enchâiné* it is prefaced by seven lines from Aeschylus's *Prometheus Bound*. Here principal ideas from earlier movements are reduced to their essence in a rondo of uncompromising severity, powerful as granite; implacable as fate.

As we have seen, a first encounter with Alkan's music can produce a variety of reactions. The very stuff it is made of — its relentless drive, its cutting dissonances, the tart astringency and brusqueness of such pieces as the *Minuetto alla Tedesca*, the finale from the *Sonatine* or the *Allegro Barbaro* — will find little response among those who would seek a cosier breed of Romanticism. Again, the stark gulf that separates the mocking satire of *Les Diablotins*, for example, from the brooding loneliness of *Prométhée Enchâiné* can come as a disturbing shock to those as yet unprepared for such widely contrasting styles.

First impressions are similarly divided about the design or uniqueness of Alkan's major works, though few would deny them their vast range and power. For instance, the opening bars of the solo *Concerto* compel attention, but until one has become familiar with the movement as a whole an uneasy impression may well persist that the driver has lost his way or is taking an unnecessarily circuitous route. A stranger to Bruckner can be similarly deceived by his far-flung strategy and unaccustomed expansiveness — the very qualities in fact, which, until recently, proved so severe a stumbling-block to appreciation of Schubert's spacious forms. On the other hand, some of Alkan's finest works have a Beethovenian terseness; the *Sonatine* and the *Solo Symphonie* are succinct examples. In these cases, however, owing to a classical objectivity, their originality may only reveal itself on repeated hearings. Busoni and the Danish symphonist Carl Nielsen sometimes present a similar problem. At first, the substance can seem unworthy of the conception; an impression which tends to dissolve on deeper acquaintance. The casual listener, or the impatient one, may find himself deflected towards other aspects of the composer's bewildering diversity —

the quaintly pictorial or the satirical elements for instance – and decide that, after all, Alkan is simply the odd-man-out of his times; a fascinating eccentric – slightly mad, perhaps, whose grotesquery merely provides a smoke-screen for his inherent anonymity.

It is part of Alkan's fascination, of course, that he can command such widely conflicting opinions. It must not be forgotten, however, that although the mists which have so long enveloped his genius are at last being dispelled, the picture that emerges is far from complete. Much of his piano music, including the *Trois Grandes Etudes* op. 76 and most of the *Etudes Majeurs* op. 35, beckon us impatiently. Among the *25 Preludes*, the *30 Chants* and the *48 Esquisses* there is a goldmine of miniatures waiting to be plundered. Some of these lie well within the grasp of the fluent amateur and many of the *Preludes* and *Esquisses* would provide the younger pianist with a rewarding introduction to his larger works.

The compositions for *pédalier*, alas, present their own unique problem; but how is it possible that Alkan's splendid chamber music continues to remain silent – above all the wonderful *Sonate de Concert* op. 47, for 'cello and piano? A performance by two great artists should prove a revelation for it is possibly Alkan's most personal and impassioned work. Cast in four broadly conceived movements it opens with a luminous Allegro full of bold, soaring outlines but shot through with darker turbulence. The second movement is an enchanting *siciliano* and the third a meditation on the following quotation from the Old Testament prophet *Micah* (Ch. 5, verse 7); ' ... as a dew from the Lord, as a shower upon the grass, that tarrieth not for man, nor waiteth for the sons of men ...' Words cannot convey the rapt, mystical atmosphere of this central adagio in which a haunting 'cello soliloquy invokes passages of strange, unearthly beauty as the piano floats and shimmers above hypnotically repeated pizzicati. By contrast, the finale is a devilish, pulverising *saltarello*, calculated to raise any audience to its feet. It is a matter of urgent concern that works like the *'Cello Sonata*, the *Duo for Violin and Piano* and the powerful *Trio* should be publicly performed and recorded. One word of warning, though: like all great music Alkan's demands masterly and dedicated playing. Anything less would be sacrilegious and damaging to his cause.

Demand for his music is growing. Informed critical opinion is open-minded and favourable. In short, the stage is set. If the enigma of his lonely life can never be completely explained, there now seems every sign that the veil of mystery that has so long engulfed so much of Alkan's music will soon be completely and finally lifted.

Index to Alkan: The Man

Index of Alkan's Works

List of Illustrations

FAMILY-TREE OF ALKAN MORHANGE

(Confined to those mentioned in this volume)

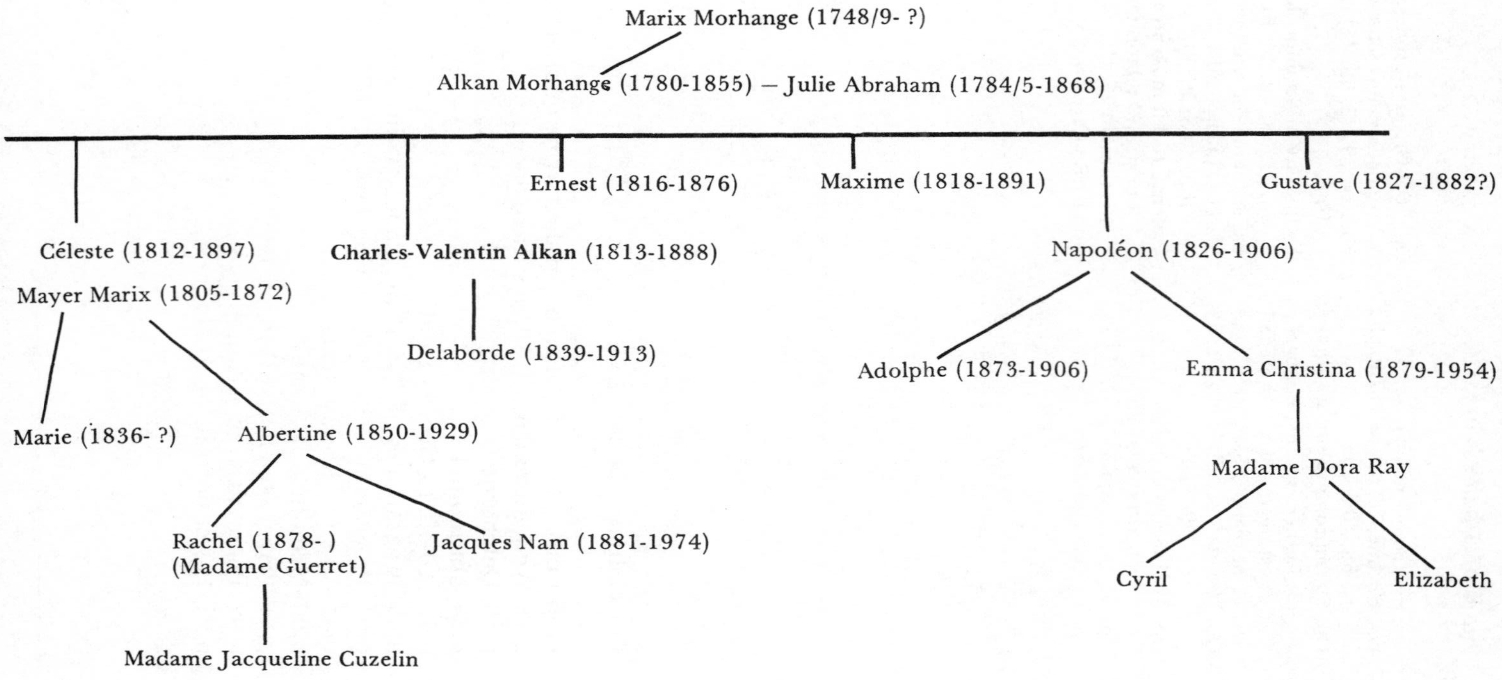

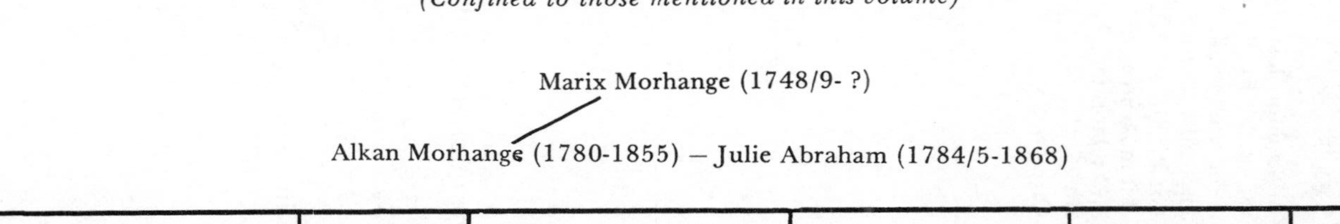

To Richard Shaw

ALKAN
The Music

Contents

Introduction and Acknowledgments

Since the publication in 1976 of the biographical part of my two-volume study of the composer, curiosity about Alkan's enigmatic life has been replaced by a widespread upsurge of interest in his music. Public performances, broadcasts and gramophone records have whetted the appetite, especially on the American continent where enthusiastic admirers will travel a thousand and more miles to hear a live performance of one of his major works. In the United Kingdom the London-based Alkan Society has been promoting a broader spectrum of his music as well as providing a valuable archive of rare scores and recordings housed in the library of the Guildhall School of Music. A similar society has now been formed in the composer's native Paris.

Alkan was a prolific composer. Apart from important works at present unavailable, the catalogue of compositions listed by Billaudot is imposing. Several publications are of epic dimensions. Opus 39, for instance, runs to 277 pages and there are many shorter works of substantial proportions. Moreover major technical problems often have to be surmounted before a particular work is willing to reveal its secrets. Liszt's claim that he read and re-read Alkan's *Trois morceaux dans le style pathétique* time and again before reviewing them is a salutary warning against press-button criticism. What is good for the master is good for the man and I consequently delayed completion of this volume until I felt ready to give a sound and sufficiently comprehensive account of Alkan's entire output.

The book falls naturally into the following sections. The first three chapters trace the composer's early development from wonder-child to the kindling of an individual style in his mid-twenties. Each of the following ten chapters deals with a particular type of composition while chapter fourteen, a more generalised survey of Alkan's unique repertoire for pedal-piano, should prove essential reading for organists and duo-pianists alike. In the final chapter I have tried to summarise the principal ingredients of Alkan's style and discuss the impulse that compelled him to produce music that is essentially different from that of his contemporaries.

Without the gentle but firm persuasion of my publisher, Morris Kahn and the help and encouragement of many friends and colleagues this book would not have been written.

Harold Truscott and Richard Gorer were among the first to introduce me to Alkan's music and to convince me of its uniqueness. I shall ever remain in their debt.

Alan Ridout has not only provided the foreword but read the first draft, chapter by chapter, making invaluable suggestions. Richard Shaw, the dedicatee, most generously placed the fruits of his own researches at my disposal as well as offering indispensable advice on questions of scholarship, style and presentation.

I am also indebted to Nicholas King for demonstrating how so much of Alkan's writing for the pedal-piano can be converted into effective organ music and to Roger Smalley for his analyses of two of the composer's major works for this medium.

I must thank Jane Harington of the Royal Academy of Music library, Richard Christophers of the British Museum and Paul Holden, librarian of the Guildhall School of Music, London, for their personal kindnesses. I am also indebted to Madame Florence Getreau for providing the excellent reproduction of Alkan's pedal-piano.

The Bibliothèque Nationale in Paris gave me every assistance in making manuscripts and printed scores available for study and for reproduction. Monsieur Gérard Billaudot also granted permission to use his publications as a basis for the many music references. Robert Scott photocopied these examples and illustrations under the auspices of the King's School, Canterbury, whose language department also assisted me with some difficult translations.

I must thank my wife for her patience in lending a critical ear to my reading of the entire book before converting her husband's baffling handwriting into elegant typescript.

Richard Shaw kindly assisted with the chronology of Alkan's compositions and list of documents, while the late Charles Hailstone supplied the original Discography. Following the spate of recent recordings and reissues the Discography has been greatly extended by Richard Shaw, assisted by François Luguenot's quite recent *Discographie* for the Société Alkan and Kim Burwell's Discography of my own recordings.

LES OMNIBUS

Variations

Pour le Piano Forte

DÉDIÉES

aux Dames Blanches

Par

Opéra 2.

C. V. ALKAN

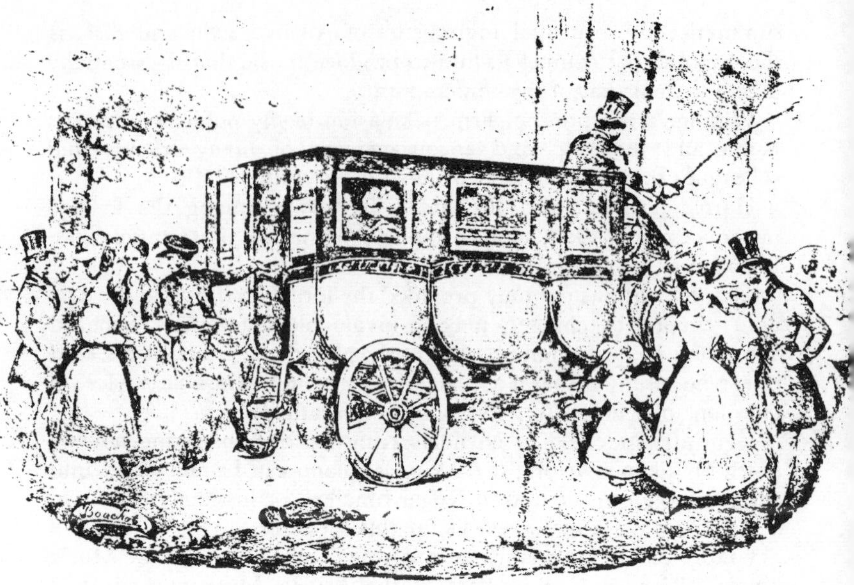

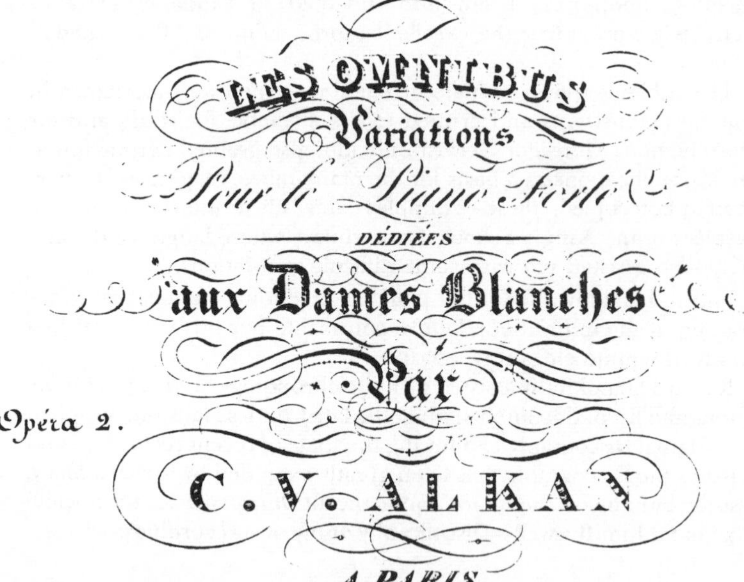

A PARIS

Chez Maurice SCHLESINGER, Md de Musique du ROI, Editeur des Œuvres de Mozart, Rossini, Hummel, Moscheles &

Rue de Richelieu, No. 97.

1 Early Works

Alkan's remarkably precocious talent is firmly engraved on the records of the Paris Conservatoire: first prize for solfège aged seven, first prize for piano aged ten, first prize for harmony aged thirteen. There can be little doubt that Alkan, in his early teens, was a formidable musician but as yet an industrious rather than a creative one. Like Liszt, and unlike Chopin, he gives little hint in his earliest surviving compositions of things to come, of that dark and turbulent genius that was to erupt so challengingly in works like the *Grande sonate* or the great collection of Studies op. 39.

His first published composition, Variations on a theme from Steibelt's Orage concerto, was probably written in 1827. Musically shallow but dazzlingly effective it graphically demonstrates the fifteen-year-old pianist's comprehensive grasp of pre-Lisztian techniques. Vertiginous scales and arpeggios abound and the imaginative use of trills suggest that he was already familiar with the later piano works of Beethoven. It was very likely this work which young Alkan displayed on his concert tour of Belgium in the Spring of 1827, attracting very favourable reviews for his performances in Liège and Brussels.[1]

Alkan's op.2, entitled *Les Omnibus*, is also a set of variations for solo piano. It appeared in 1829, two years after the Steibelt variations and it bears the puzzling inscription 'dédiées aux dames blanches'. The revelation that these elusive dedicatees were neither sisters of mercy nor ladies of more worldly persuasion provides an early example of the fifteen-year-old virtuoso's bizarre sense of humour. 'Les dames blanches' was the name given to the once familiar carriages of a Paris omnibus company, and to make sure there would be no confusion the final page conveys a crude parody of the postillion's horn. Unfortunately the piece itself hardly lives up to its colourful title. Comprising a short prologue, theme, three variations and final hectic galop it parades its shallow formulae in the guise of rapid octaves, brilliant repetitions and a variety of glissandi, doubtless devised to show off the mechanical advances of the latest instruments, not to mention the young pianist's own specialities.

Alkan's next composition followed about a year later. *Il était un p'tit homme* op.3 is an extended rondo suggesting concerto style replete with showy passage work, cadential trills and a mock tutti. Pianistically it suffers from cautious left-hand writing; musically its

[1] See Constance Himmelfarb's 'L'interprète à travers la presse musicale' pp.25-6 in François-Sappey's *Alkan* (see Bibliography).

style is reminiscent of Weber, Hummel and Rossini. Only the catchy first episode over a pedal bass gives the faintest inkling of that harmonic quirkiness that lends such character to Alkan's mature works.

Ex.1

From his early teens the young virtuoso was already attracting attention as a composer. As early as January 1828 Fétis, the learned music historian and critic, was writing enthusiastically about a 'concerto rondo' composed and performed by Alkan 'with an energy and perfection which belied his age'. 'There are many fine things in his Rondo' continues Fétis 'and one would never suspect this is the work of a child'. If, as seems likely, the piece in question was the *Rondo brillant*, later published as op.4, it would be a remarkable achievement for any student, let alone a boy of just fourteen. The musical interest may be fragile but its technical demands are prodigious. Some twenty pages of lightly brushed octaves, skips and sudden volleys of rapid scales vie with experimental passage work that doesn't always justify its difficulty. On paper it looks for all the world like the work of some fiendish, nightmare John Field and its overall accomplishment suggests that op.2 and op.3 could date from a still earlier stage in Alkan's development. It must be emphasised, however, that quality with Alkan is no sure guide to chronology. Throughout his long life he remained capable of an unselfconscious reversion to a style that denies its period and, like Sibelius, his greatest work is occasionally punctuated by productions that seem, by comparison, naïve, perfunctory or even banal. Paradoxically it is this very tendency that gives some of Alkan's smaller pieces their anachronistic charm.

A further performance by Alkan a few months after his 'concert rondo' triumph, this time of a rondo for solo piano, certainly finds Fétis in a less indulgent mood: '. . .notes, notes and more notes' he writes, '. . .of style and expression, nothing. Perhaps this will come later; let us wait until his heart speaks'. In the light of our knowledge of Alkan's creative development up to his mid-teens this may not seem too harsh a judgement. It is easy to dismiss Fétis as a laborious pedant with musical tunnel vision while forgetting that such was his standing in Paris that Liszt himself felt compelled in 1832 to attend his lectures on the Philosophy of Music. Furthermore Fétis was one

Alkan: from *Rondo brillant* op.4

of the first to recognise Alkan's true genius as it began to emerge, and his anxiety about the direction in which the composer's developing talent might be taking him is amply confirmed by an independent review of Alkan's op.3, 4 and 5 which appeared in a new periodical, *Le pianiste*, in 1833. 'One must not judge the composer of today by these samples', we read; and the writer adds significantly: 'His intellectual and musical faculties have shown a remarkable development for some time'. In short Alkan had crashed the maturity barrier that divides the wonder-child from the artist. In Alkan's case this painful but vital transition is spotlighted by a single event that took place the previous year; an event that proved a watershed in the composer's development and one that might have placed him high in the hierarchy of a brilliant generation that also included Mendelssohn, Schumann, Chopin and Liszt.

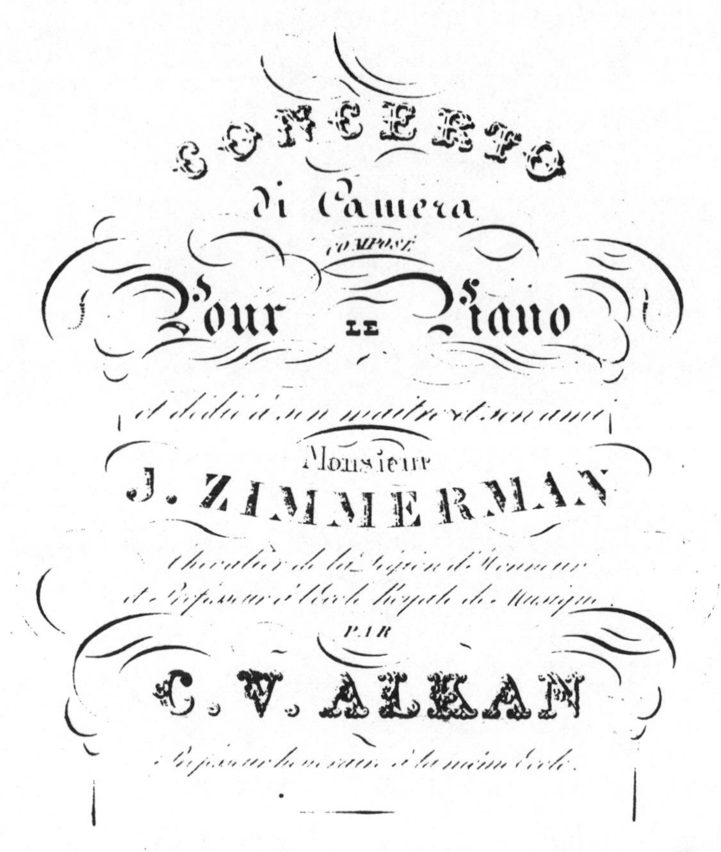

CONCERTO
di Camera
COMPOSÉ
Pour LE Piano
et dédié à son maître et son ami
Monsieur
J. ZIMMERMAN
PAR
C. V. ALKAN

Op: 10.

Prix { Piano seul 12f. Net 4f.
{ l'Orch.e seul 12f.

N.B. [illegible]

à PARIS, chez S. RICHAULT, Boulevard Poissonnière, N.o 16.

2 The Concerti da Camera

The year, 1832; the city Paris; the occasion, an afternoon concert by the Société des Concerts du Conservatoire. The background, the outset of the Romantic explosion in Paris from which Chopin and Liszt were to fashion their pianistic empires. Concertos by Hummel, Moscheles, Field and Weber were all the rage. On May 20 Chopin, introducing the first movement of his F minor Concerto, met with a frosty press. The twenty-three-year-old Mendelssohn, parading his newly-minted G minor Concerto around Europe, ruefully declared Paris to be the graveyard of reputations. This was the backcloth against which Alkan, at the age of eighteen, also presented a concerto of his own composition. The event took place on April 29, three weeks before the Chopin début. Fétis, among other distinguished contemporaries, bears witness to a triumphant success – a success, it seems, that Alkan proved unwilling or unable to repeat. How is it that such a work could have completely vanished from the repertory?

For many years the identity of this concerto remained a mystery. Either it was lost or it should have been identified as one of two early compositions listed by the Costallat-Billaudot edition as *Concerti da camera* op.10 nos.1 and 2. They have remained in the firm's catalogue in the form of solo versions prepared for publication by the composer himself. Any good sight-reader may acquaint himself with these attractive, pocket-sized concertos; but woe betide the investigator set on unravelling their background and origin. It was not until the early 1980s that research by the tireless Alkan scholar, Richard Shaw, managed to dispel some of the mysteries surrounding them. We now know that the second and shorter work in C sharp minor, with string accompaniment, postdates Alkan's Conservatoire début and so must be eliminated from our search for the elusive concerto he played there in 1832. The earlier work, dedicated to Alkan's friend and teacher Joseph Zimmerman, is altogether more robust and ambitious. It might well have seemed a likely contender for the 1832 performance but, curiously enough, the official history of the Conservatoire concerts states that Alkan played only a 'fragment d'un concerto'.[1] Vapereau, on the other hand, writing some years after the performance, remembered the work as a 'grand concerto'.[2]

Speculation about the concerto's identity, however, was finally silenced by the discovery in 1983 of the first edition of the *Concerto da camera* stating not only that it was indeed the work played by Alkan at the Conservatoire concert but that it was also chosen for the *concours de piano* in 1832. The subsequent and surprising discovery by Hugh Macdonald of a complete set of parts throws considerable light on the seemingly contradictory descriptions of the work. A score produced from the parts shows that Alkan's requirements are far less modest than his title suggests: strings, double woodwind augmented by two extra bassoons, four horns, two trumpets, three trombones and timpani. No wonder Vapereau described it as 'grand'; no wonder Alkan was forced, on economic grounds, to abandon it in favour of his more modestly scored C sharp minor work. But it is not simply in its orchestration that the youthful composer demonstrates his independence. The work behaves like no other concerto and its unique shape may well explain the puzzling suggestion that he performed only part of it. There is in fact no reason to believe that the 1832 performance was anything but complete in every detail.

The work is continuous, but it clearly displays three sections corresponding to the three movements of a normal concerto. A brief but powerful orchestral prologue presents a handful of sharply defined motifs – a classical ritornello, in style if not in scope.

Ex.2

[1] A. Elwart, *Histoire de la Société des Concerts du Conservatoire impérial de musique* (Paris, 1860), p.158

[2] *Dictionnaire universal des contemporains* (Paris, 1858)

The soloist's arresting octave entry launches an expansive solo exposition in which ideas seemingly tumble from Alkan's pen in spontaneous abandon. The wealth of such romantic modulations as the following may at first suggest a parallel with Chopin's F minor Concerto, but it is an impression that fades on acquaintance. Certainly the piano writing does not feel like Chopin's under the fingers and the frequent tramp of low, pizzicato strings with the pianist's basses does not permit the waywardness suggested by Chopin's lyrical writing.

Ex.3

These opening pages display a fiery optimistic passion suggesting the direction Alkan's music might have taken had it not been for those psychological changes that were to set him on a more disturbing path. Strangely, by the time the orchestra crashes in on the crest of this ardent exposition one has hardly noticed that not one motif has been repeated or developed. One might well ask whether Alkan's development section can bring such seemingly diverse elements into focus; the answer is that this is the wrong question. Quite naturally, and with an oblique allusion to a phrase from the soloist's second subject, we are guided gently but firmly into a central Adagio in E major. This short-circuiting of development, recapitulation and coda probably stems from Schubert's 'Wanderer' Fantasy by way of the Weber *Konzertstück* and Mendelssohn's G minor Concerto – a work that Mendelssohn almost certainly introduced in Paris earlier that same season – but Alkan's solution is far more drastic.

The Adagio, comparatively short, falls into two halves introduced in turn by soloist and strings. From its still, cool opening the textures become increasingly elaborate until the piano is set vibrating in eager anticipation. For a few enchanted moments it flutters and hovers beneath falling woodwind cadences before a hazardous contrary motion scale flings us headlong into a brilliant rondo. Only now is the introductory nature of Alkan's opening section seen in perspective. This finale is by far the most substantial part of the work. Its infectious rhythms and vertiginous triplets again bring Chopin to mind – this time the finale of the E minor Concerto – but the impression is quite different; there is at once a rugged masculinity about the Alkan, and that fierce, inexorable drive that makes his music unique. Again he throws out fresh ideas with rash prodigality but here, as in the earlier sections, the sequence of events is so purposeful and the tonal framework so convincing that matter seems to beget form. The following example showing the rondo subject as it returns, eagerly encouraged by agile pianism, gives a good idea of the style.

Ex.4

The dactylic rhythmic figure with its inversion plays a vital role in unifying the various features as it propels the work to its exhilarating conclusion.

As one might expect the piano writing throughout is brilliant and demanding and already there is evidence of Alkan's preoccupation with some of the rarer effects available on his instrument: this featherweight cascade of repeated notes in the left hand remains unique.

Ex.5

No less startling is the use in the finale of 'blind' octaves, an innovation rediscovered by Brahms in his Paganini Variations some thirty years later.

Ex.6

This final rondo also provides evidence of the eighteen-year-old pianist's mastery of pre-Lisztian techniques. Imagine Weber's intricate filigree and perilous leaps interspersed with Hummel's double trills and those volleys of chunky chords familiar from Alkan's later piano writing. In performance such devices are held captive to a rigorous orchestral discipline that brooks no rhythmic licence, for

Alkan's accompaniment plays a far from passive role. He parades his impressive forces to capacity in the tuttis, and elsewhere frequent pizzicati and the quartet of bassoons lend an unfamiliar tang, while high woodwind writing provides competition for the pianist's coruscating semiquavers. Chopin was drowned by the same orchestra in his more modestly scored F minor Concerto a few weeks after Alkan had successfully introduced this work – though this may tell us more about the two pianists' relative muscular powers than their orchestration.

Alkan's second *Concerto da camera* was the most fruitful outcome of his visit to England in 1833. This is truly a concerto in miniature and is dedicated to Henry Field of Bath who gave the first performance there on April 11, 1834. It plays for a modest nine minutes and the *Bath and Cheltenham Gazette* aptly described it as a concertino, adding that it was 'especially delightful for the novelty of its style and technique'. Structurally Alkan carries the unbroken fast-slow-fast scheme of his first concerto a stage further by unifying the outer sections. The idea is ingenious: a terse string prologue introduces rhythmic features that form themselves into a swaggering main subject announced by the soloist.

Ex.7

It dominates the outer sections, swallowing up a fragile second subject and fairly fizzing with self-confidence in a second tutti; and it finally catapults the work to its heady conclusion. In between all this activity an appealing Siciliano moves in and out of keys with unpretentious delight. This central section is most skilfully textured and varied. The following version crosses the hands in elegant anticipation of Liszt's *Au bord d'une source.*

Ex.8 Adagio

After a more elaborate embellishment the colouring becomes tinged with regret before we are hustled into a truncated resumption of the opening section. Here Alkan adds immeasurably to the unity by cleverly weaving the Siciliano into a hostile environment.

Ex.9

Allegro moderato

Despite its over-abbreviation the Second Concerto is a piece of marked character: lyrical, brilliant and effective, and its thirty-five-year-old dedicatee must have been a highly skilled player to have encompassed the various technical problems Alkan had set him. The piece abounds in punishing leaps and its sheen of elegant filigree fans out into lightning arpeggios and machine-gun tremolos at the flicker of an eyelid. Although Alkan was only twenty it remained a favourite concert piece of his throughout his life. Later reviews and a set of MS. parts (now in the Bibliothèque Nationale, Paris) suggest that he played it with string quintet (quartet with double-bass) – perhaps more for commercial expediency than from artistic preference.

Did Alkan plan or even compose a further concerto on similar lines? The première of a third *Concerto da camera* was announced as the novelty in a programme he was to give on March 3, 1838, the sixth item being an *Etude* in C sharp major. Tantalisingly, in an otherwise generous review, no concerto is mentioned... and this brings us to a stranger puzzle. Towards the end of 1833, some eighteen months after the premiere of the first *Concerto da camera* and about six months before Henry Field introduced the second, the periodical *Le pianiste* reviewed an Alkan concerto 'remarkable for its form and style, which are new'. There follows a description of the scherzo (which was encored); it tallies with no surviving concerto by Alkan. 'A simple, gracious muted song for strings is accompanied by a series of chords which, passing from octave to octave, sustains the melody and produces an effect as original as it is ravishing'. This is sufficient to identify the piano part as the second of Alkan's *Trois andantes romantiques* op.13 (1837) which was later republished independently as *Caprice ou Etude* in C sharp major, the piece played in March 1838. Sure enough, although no concerto is mentioned in the 1838 review, it is noted that Alkan's performance of the *Etude* was accompanied by muted strings. In this form it seems to have remained a favourite alternative on the pianist's programmes to his second *Concerto da camera* and was still being encored as late as 1877. There can be little doubt that this was a piece incorporated into a concerto in 1833. The strange habit of interpolating an alternative solo piece with added orchestral background within the framework of an established concerto was a common practice among such artists as John Field. Could the C sharp major study possibly have been used in this way in either of Alkan's existing *Concerti da camera*? Both key and orchestration would surely place the first concerto out of court, and although the key and light scoring of the second might accommodate the piece there is still a serious drawback. As we have seen, the normal central section of this concerto is cleverly woven into its final section; so either the second *Concerto da camera* already existed in a form substantially different from the one we know, or the *Etude* in C sharp major is all that has survived from an otherwise discarded concerto by Alkan. The mystery of this missing or incomplete work may never be solved, but we can rejoice in the possession of two complete concertos by Alkan from an earlier phase than any of his more familiar works.

TROIS ETUDES DE BRAVOURE

(IMPROVISATIONS)

Ex.10

3 The Crystallisation of a Style

The period immediately following the completion of his second *Concerto da camera* was one of consolidation and reassessment for Alkan. The originality of his early concertos lies rather more in their manner than in their substance. Although nurtured on French soil they display precisely the same influences that provided Chopin with his models but they do not yet speak with an equally unique and homogeneous voice. Like Liszt, Alkan was still seeking his creative identity. It required a powerful catalyst to focus his precocious talent and the most rigorous process of assimilation and rejection to harness it.

Following the formation in 1828 of the Société des Concerts du Conservatoire, its founder, Habeneck, set about introducing the Beethoven symphonies to a hostile public. Though viewed by the Establishment with pitying contempt they made an overwhelming impact on Berlioz and many of his younger contemporaries. By 1837 Liszt had already started transcribing them for solo piano. During that same year Alkan made an eight-handed arrangement of the Seventh, and then proceeded to publish a challenging series of piano pieces known collectively as *Caprices ou Etudes*. The twelve pieces were issued in 1837 as *Trois études de bravoure* (subtitled *Improvisations*) op.12, *Trois andantes romantiques* op.13 and *Trois morceaux dans le genre pathétique* op.15, and the sequence was completed by a further *Trois études de bravoure* (*Scherzi*) op.16.

At once one is struck by an abrupt change of style. The very first piece in op.12, a monolithic scherzo abounding in ferocious leaps and widespread octaves, springs out from the printed page like a lightning flash. Here, an altogether tougher spirit has swept away every lingering trace of salon elegance. For one brief moment the spell of Beethoven's Seventh Symphony becomes inescapable as the familiar dactylic rhythm of its vivace is punctuated by pregnant silences followed by an abrupt modulation (see Ex.10, line 4).

The opening bars demonstrate a stark contrast between forearm and wrist techniques (see Ex.10). Note the sadistic glee with which Alkan finally slams the door on admirers and detractors alike. The explosive slap at the extremities of the keyboard, an almost Stravinskian gesture, was to become something of a trademark in his later works.

Ex.11

The second piece from op.12, an Allegretto in D flat is even more indicative of things to come. Starting rather bleakly with an insipid melody of the boating-song breed, it soon slips in and out of remote keys. A bold modulation to C major rouses an angry chromatic response full of stinging dissonances, but the real surprise comes with a rhythmic transformation from 3/4 to 6/8 for a furiously hotted-up version of the opening song, chromatic outburst and all. A coda, in which rhythms are opposed in double counterpoint, yields a charmingly pastoral close over a double drone: vintage Alkan – but the piece remains unconvincing for its substance fails to justify its elaborate treatment.

Throughout his creative life Alkan was fascinated by march rhythms, a penchant he shares with Schubert and Mahler. The final study from op.12, an *Allegro marziale* in B minor, is one of his earliest examples. It is quaint, it is naïve, it is gauche, it is banal... and it brings us face to face with a problem that must embarrass many a random explorer of his music. Alkan's obsession with the clichés of popular music seems to belie the reputation he enjoyed among certain of his contemporaries as the sworn enemy of bad taste. Alongside their pre-Mahlerian use in parody these overtly trite elements seemed to hold an almost cathartic fascination for him – a fascination he never succeeded in exorcising, and one that leads us to the frontier where music ends and psychology begins.

As their modest title implies, the *Trois andantes romantiques* are the least demanding and most lyrical of the *Caprices*. Apart from some Weberesque filigree in the first piece they also display a healthy disregard for the pianistic clichés of their time. The first, in B flat, invites an innocuous little tune into an alien environment with more than a hint of the sinister transformation that is to occur in Alkan's *Chant d'amour... chant de mort* op.35 no.10 of 1847. The reappearance of the melody in B flat minor above a chromatically disturbed accompaniment gives rise to a page of grinding dissonances before subsiding into the following cadential snarl.

Ex. 12

Again, the vapid opening hardly justifies such heady treatment and one has the impression that Alkan is not yet in full artistic control of his darkly disturbing vision.

We now come to the mysterious C sharp major composition which, as we have seen, already existed with muted string accompaniment in 1833. The idea is ingenious: a series of lightly brushed chords in a lilting 6/8 rises and falls over three octaves so that harmonic resolution occurs in constantly changing registers.[1] As accented passing notes and suspensions come and go an implied melody emerges and is later transferred to the bass beneath sweeping arpeggios *senza pedale*. Here there is a veiled foretaste of Fauré and, as the mood intensifies, more than a hint of Liszt. Had Liszt heard Alkan play it, and it is most likely that he did, he would doubtless have been particularly impressed by the return in which the formerly hushed

Ex. 13

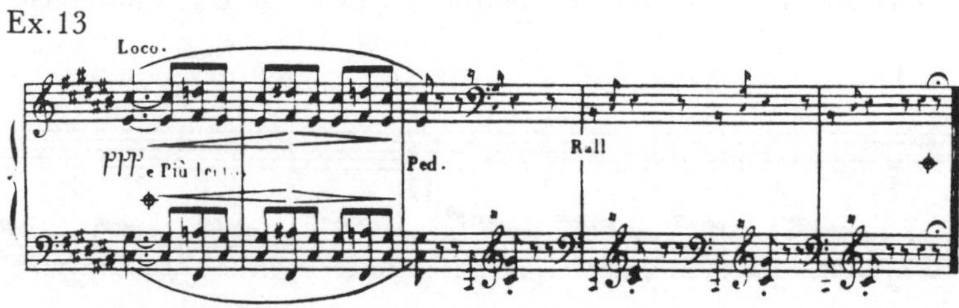

[1] It would be interesting to know if Alkan completed the upper harmonies at his later concerts by the addition of notes unavailable on his instrument before 1844.

chords of the opening are struck with full sonority before billowing out into shimmering figuration. A strangely-spaced cadence hovering bleakly between the major and minor must surely have been delivered by the muted strings in Alkan's concerted version.

Pianistically and musically the piece is a remarkable achievement. It looks right, it feels right, it sounds right, and its schematic simplicity ensures that, on repetition, it stays right. The contrast with its successor underlines the Jekyll and Hyde duality in Alkan's creative personality. As a gentle exercise in controlled trill technique the final Andante in G flat could form a valuable pendant to Cramer's similar study in B flat. Its rightful place must surely remain in the classroom of the Conservatoire.

With the third set of *Caprices* we encounter yet another lurch in style. The *Trois grandes études dans le style pathétique* were probably renamed *morceaux* to distinguish them from the *Trois grandes études pour les mains separées ou réunies* which followed in their wake. Dedicated to Liszt, and reviewed both by Schumann and Liszt, they form the most ambitious and controversial triptych of the series. Against the fifteen pages of op.12 and the twenty-one pages of op.13 the *Trois morceaux* sprawl over fifty-odd sheets 'packed with notes and devoid of expression marks' as Schumann has it. Perhaps the omission was intended as a subtle tribute to Liszt's intuitive artistry; if so the compliment backfired on Alkan. A benevolent review by the dedicatee was also tempered by irritation at the total lack of tempo indications and dynamics.[1] All three pieces have fanciful titles. The first, *Aime-moi* consists of a sombre procession of operatically shaped themes accompanied by proliferating figuration that is systematically increased, over several pages, from crotchets to demisemiquavers while the tempo remains constant. A dramatic climax, collapse and *alla breve* wind-up completes a loose-knit scheme which still manages to engender a certain degree of sustained intensity. Pianistically Alkan falls prey to his own invention. Much of the writing sits awkwardly on the keyboard requiring an expertise disproportionate

Ex.14

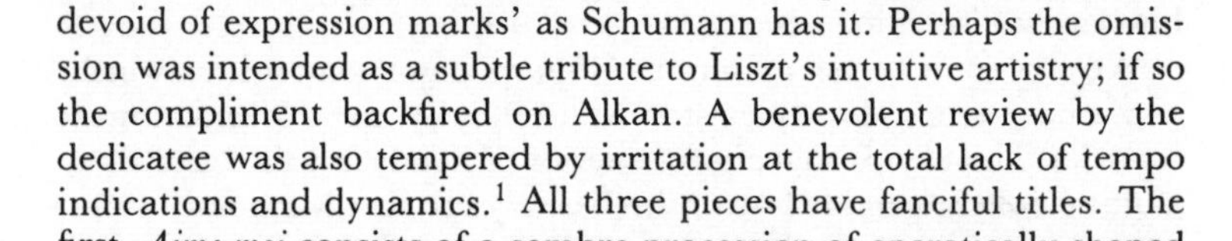

[1] *Revue et gazette musicale*, Oct. 1837, pp.460-1.

to its effectiveness. The above passage was surely intended for an extinct race of seven-fingered pianists.

Liszt passed no comment on Alkan's piano writing but he may well have learnt a thing or two from the next piece. *Le vent* was once a familiar *pièce de résistance* in the recital programmes of Harold Bauer and Adela Verne. Sorabji's complaint that most people only think of Alkan as the composer of *Le vent* must fall strangely on modern ears that have never caught the most fleeting snatch of this superannuated war-horse. On the face of it *Le vent* appears to be no more than a period piece of pyrotechnics: 'a chromatic howl over an idea from Beethoven's A major symphony' was Schumann's unkind description. Despite, however, a superficial resemblance to the Allegretto from Beethoven's Seventh the true ancestry of the dirge-like chorale that inhabits its outer sections should be sought elsewhere, for example in the great slow movements from Schubert's last two sonatas. The spine-chilling appearance on paper of a merciless stream of sextuplets is misleading. Their constant rise and fall should sound impressionistic until Alkan unleashes the elements in two pages of unthematic, chromatic storm. His subsequent combination of chromatic volleys with tremolando must have impressed Liszt for he used both devices at a similar point in the 1851 revision of *Chasse-neige*, but more concisely. Henri Blanchard's description of the composer's own performance of *Le vent* suggests a style of delivery familiar from the finale of Chopin's B flat minor Sonata, completed three years later. 'All the sounds of the wind are depicted and varied in the most delightful manner' he tells us.

Morte, the last piece from op.15, is the most prophetic of all Alkan's early compositions. Its form is simple; prologue – allegro – epilogue; its content, harrowing. The introduction of the plainsong *Dies irae* in the works of Berlioz and Liszt is explicit; with Alkan it remains veiled. In *Morte* it only appears twice, introducing both prologue and epilogue, yet it casts its spiritual shadow across the entire work, shaping its motifs and menacing its harmonies. Note how Alkan detaches the last three notes of the plainsong, planting indelibly in our minds that cogent descent through a minor third to the tonic that lends such dark power to the theme itself.

Ex.15

Its rhapsodic descent is echoed by the following mournful comment . . .

Ex.16

. . . and succeeded by a sombre lament 'for Wagnerian Tubas' which dominates the rest of the prologue. I quote this fine theme in its remarkable sequel as the accompanying tramp of funereal triplets reveals its plainsong origin in the form of a palindrome. The irregular tolling of a church bell in melancholy anticipation of *Le gibet* by Ravel, completes a vision of Mussorgskian power and Ives-like daring.

Ex.17

Despite the concentrated discipline of these opening pages the impression remains improvisatory and introductory. Soon the oppressive minor third starts to vibrate, signalling action; a jagged fragment rises from the bass forming itself into the principal motif that is to dominate the central core of the work. On first acquaintance the agitated allegro seems blighted by its main subjects; the one short-winded and repetitive, the other a static melody that sits heavily on its main beats. Their common plainsong parentage adds a degree of unity to a scheme that with all its romantic fervour seems somehow incapable of generating true organic growth. Liszt may well have realised this when he singled out two transitional developments for criticism as 'a bit careless'. Despite its weaknesses the movement accumulates an unsuspected, demonic energy as it sweeps headlong to its climax. The final phrase, with its tightened confirmation of the prologue, its ghostly recollection from *Aime-moi* and an astonishingly prophetic short-circuiting of its harmonic resolution is, in the words of Sorabji 'as weirdly uncanny as it is original and daring'. The closing bars are vividly orchestral suggesting the sombre majesty of Sibelius just a generation before he was born. In this piece, for the first time, the twenty-three-year-old composer taps a source of necromantic fantasy that he was later to harness to sinister effect in such works as *Chanson de la folle*, *Le tambour bat aux champs* and in the chilling finale of his *Grande sonate*.

Despite the power and originality of the finest parts of *Morte* the most startling evidence of Alkan's newly found creative energy must be sought in the final set of *Caprices*, the *Trois études de bravoure* op.16, subtitled *Scherzi*. Here, for the first time, the composer seems able to brand his personality on to every aspect of his invention, whether he is exploring new paths or wringing new meanings from well-worn ones. Their manner is brusque, their style tough and, like the first study from op. 12, they are fuelled by tight, rhythmic cells which form themselves into ever larger units adding momentum to vitality. Alkan probably learnt this method of construction from studying Beethoven and it becomes a vital, unifying factor in many of his greatest works.

The first Scherzo, in C major, contains one of Alkan's happiest inspirations, a quaintly evocative imitation of a musical box *Scampanio*, which forms its trio. One wonders if the French Impressionists themselves produced anything more atmospheric than the following remarkable sequence, its dominant-supertonic swing, out of phase with the prevailing harmonies, as it weaves its spell above a fundamental A flat.

Ex. 18

The first section itself is less immediately compelling, its originality only making itself apparent on repeated hearings. From its almost casual opening 'l'appetit vient en mangeant' as Alkan proceeds to breathe life into a dry, academic tag and a commonplace refrain. Their combination in a trenchant ostinato yields more than a hint of Mahler, a composer with whom Alkan sometimes shows a surprising affinity.

Ex. 19

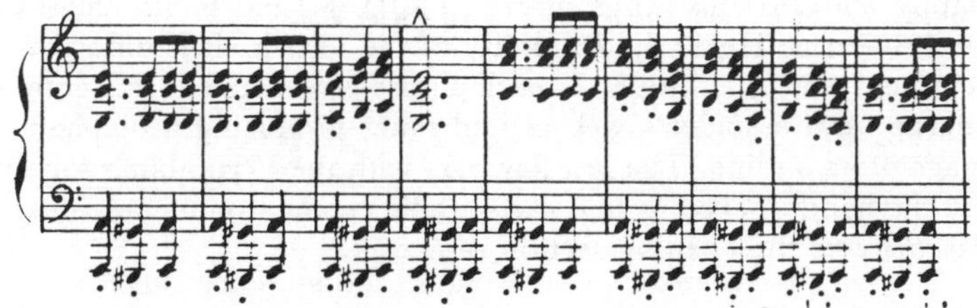

The continuation, chunky, belligerent and full of dense chromatic clusters produces the following pianistic avalanche in anticipation of Chopin's second Ballade completed two years later.

Ex.20a Alkan

Ex.20b Chopin

With all its prescient ingenuity the Scherzo is not altogether convincing. Perhaps it suffers most from the incompatibility of its main sections, a fact only exacerbated by Alkan's continuation of a strand from the magical trio as counterpoint to its earth-bound return. As a sophisticated piece of compositional engineering it looks effective enough on paper, but it requires interpretive pleading of a high order if it is not to sound contrived.

The second Scherzo, the most compact of the three, is a rough-hewn minuet. Its rude masculinity and key of C minor emphasise Beethovenian strength. For those stout spirits capable of hurling themselves at its cascades of double octaves, thirds and similar devices it engenders a satisfying sense of physical well-being. Others must confine themselves to a subsidiary episode in Alkan's favourite 'happy and glorious' rhythm 3/4 ♩♩♩|♩. ♪ ♩ and to its naïve but deceptive trio. Here, the insipidity of the idea itself is offset by its treatment which is unique. As each phrase is repeated its dulcet tones emerge from a spider's web of tied notes producing a diaphanous image of its outline. The last few bars with their crumbling tonality and the hands locked as in a cat's cradle create a moment of fragile insecurity as the opening section returns.

Ex.21

The coda affords a striking comparison with its counterpart in the first movement of Alkan's solo *Symphonie*, also in C minor. In an attempt to reconcile his delicate trio with its robust surroundings he weaves it into a massive climax of tortured Neapolitan pathos which devolves on to the following strangely 'orchestrated' chord of C major – *mirabile dictu*, the selfsame eccentric chord that ended the first Scherzo.

Ex.22

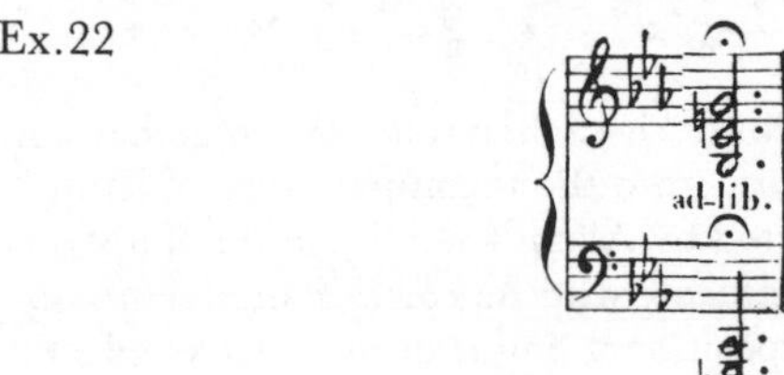

An explosive compound of pedantry, daring and genius makes the last Scherzo, in B minor, one of Alkan's most extraordinary creations. Like the *Scherzo diabolico* from op.39 it goes at a blood-curdling prestissimo in 3/4 time, its impetuous progress punctuated by an incursive 2/4 bar; a warning of things to come.

Ex.23

It continues with exciting sequences, some wildly improbable modulations and such derivatives as the following examples.

Ex.24

Ex.25

A richly polyphonic episode in B major promises a trio and it is not only in its key that it foreshadows the trio in Chopin's B minor Sonata of 1844.

Ex.26a Alkan

Ex.26b Chopin

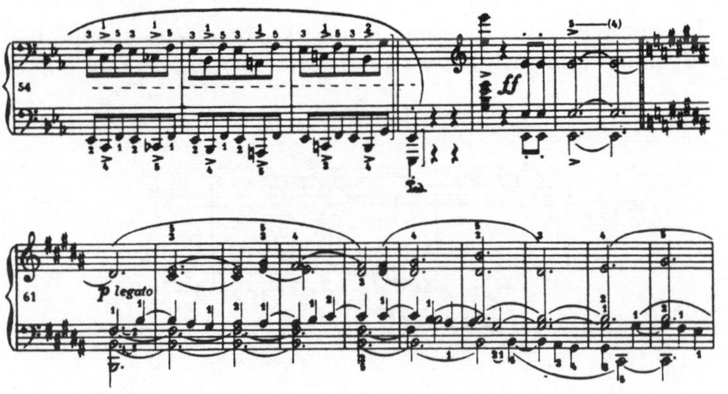

This is, in fact, a false alarm for we are soon involved in further developments of the opening rhythm and the quaver derivative (Ex. 25). Now comes the fulfilment of that intrusive 2/4 bar as we are hustled into the real trio, a fleet-footed *prestissimamente* with two of its 2/8 bars equal to one 3/4 (or 2/4) bar of the preceding scherzo section. The abrupt changes of register add an almost Schönbergian angularity.

Ex.27

Ex.28

A bravura climax invokes the following remarkable rhythmic conjunction . . .

Ex.29

. . . followed by a still more bizarre augumentation as the opening motif makes fitful attempts to gain a foothold, fails and makes way for a return of the Chopinesque episode in C major. Undeterred by a momentary threat from the 2/8 trio and a nudge or two from the quaver derivative (Ex.25) it finds its way back to the 'correct' key of B major. The ensuing development now becomes afflicted by a whole rash of 2/8 contradictions.

Ex.30a

This rouses the quaver motif, its position usurped, to thirty-eight bars of whirlwind gyrations leading to the long-delayed return of the opening. Even now the hostile 2/4 bar makes a final bid to overthrow the prevailing 3/4 rhythm but is angrily cast aside. The piece ends as it began, in a fever of sabre-rattling defiance. Unfortunately at a true prestissimo it must seem well-nigh unplayable!

Collectively the twelve *Caprices* chart Alkan's discovery of himself both as a creator and as a pianistic innovator. Ruthlessly purged of the clichés of romantic pianism they pursue an altogether tougher course; one rooted in the classics but expanded beyond recognition. Musically, they demonstrate that by 1838 Alkan had burnt his compositional boats. They systematically display his new creative attitude: restless, questing, questioning, experimental and obsessive; squeezing every conceivable meaning out of his invention; searching for new meanings along well-trodden paths. It is the exploitation of these qualities that make him one of the most original and prophetic composers of his century... and one of the most maddeningly uneven ones. Such dissimilar masterpieces as the early *Marche funèbre* op.26 or the late *Toccatina* op.75 rub shoulders with work that seems merely mechanical, scholarly, speculative or even downright banal. Yet there is still hardly a piece from Alkan's maturity that does not surprise us with some unsuspected twist or sudden delight. Without warning, a flash of genius will spring forth from unfertile soil only to be mocked by a hostile environment. From its very nature, however, Alkan's music requires powerful advocacy. Its technical demands, alone, take little heed of human frailty. Unparaded keyboard daring is of its essence, particularly when Alkan generates a musical overdrive that brooks no licence. Major works call forth a Beethovenian control of large-scale structures, the more so where an inherent classicism means that the impact of a work as a whole may far outweigh our emotional reaction to any part of it. Again, the very appearance of the printed page is often misleading; what may look rambling on paper can become concise when presented with clarity and comprehension and at the correct speed. For these reasons alone it is especially difficult and dangerous to evaluate any composition by Alkan in the absence of a committed performance. His massive *Ouverture*, for instance, was once universally denigrated (with one or two notable exceptions)[1] as the Cinderella among the minor-key Studies op.39 and I must admit that I had little inkling of the work's extraordinary power and originality until I had penetrated its

[1] 'A fine example of Alkan's orchestral pianistic style; here again crop up Beethoven-like turns of thought and expression.' K. Sorabji: *Around Music* (London, 1932).

technical armour-plating to tap the darkly-turbulent undercurrents that lie locked within.

The publication, in 1838, of the final *Caprices* marks the watershed between apprenticeship and maturity. Alkan's creative equipment was now complete and he had laid the foundation of a transcendental pianism equal to that of Liszt.

Album leaf dated Oct. 9, 1847 (see p.44)

4 The Miniatures

With the exception of a handful of short pieces such as Song of the Mad Woman (from op.31), *La vision* (op.63) or Barcarolle (op.65) Alkan's importance as a miniaturist has remained largely unexplored. There are well over a hundred tiny pieces, nearly all unusual in one way or another, many of them astonishingly advanced for their time, and all beautifully written for their instrument. The whole series displays a kaleidoscopic range of style and scope that makes Alkan such a difficult composer to classify; yet familiarity reveals an unmistakable thread of unity just as resilient as that which identifies his great contemporaries, Chopin and Schumann. If a few of these pieces occasionally recall the innocent appeal of a Haydn or a Mendelssohn, for the most part they strike an altogether different chord or, rather, series of chords. At times they seem more attuned to the austere and visionary world of late Beethoven; at others they offer a fugitive portent of such twentieth-century masters as Bartók or Prokofiev but without ever forfeiting their classical shape and style. Some of the finest of these vignettes invoke an unmistakably numinous atmosphere which may be darkly disturbing, or, on occasions, reassuringly spiritual – a quality that sets Alkan apart from his more familiar contemporaries. Among pieces that are immediately compelling there are others, particularly among the preludes, whose cool sober depths only reveal themselves on closer acquaintance. Only now, as this vital and attractive repertoire is becoming more widely known, can the composer's true stature as one of the greatest miniaturists of the nineteenth century be properly realised.

Paradoxically Alkan's earliest set of miniatures enjoys one of his highest opus numbers. The *Six morceaux caractéristiques* were published during the late 1830s, probably as op.8, in Paris, and as yet another op.16 in Germany. They were soon joined by a further six pieces and entitled *Les mois* in which form they remained in the Alkan catalogue without opus number until ultimately being awarded the misleadingly high one of 74. They are of special interest, not only because the original six pieces once more attracted the critical attention of Schumann, but because they adumbrate, in the simplest possible way, many of his later miniatures as well as the relaxed lyricism of some of the *Chants*.

The pieces reviewed by Schumann are those we now know as nos. 1, 4, 5, 7, 8 and 12. Consistently less sharply etched than the later ones, their bare simplicity could easily be mistaken for naïvity and their short-breathed melodic cells for a compositional lack of breadth. 'The composer of these pieces might be an interesting player' writes Schumann, 'but only the severest studies will enable him to make much progress, for he sinks too readily into mere superficiality'. All the same Schumann finds at least half the pieces very much to his taste, including, surprisingly enough, the first one, *Une nuit d'hiver* – and this despite its emaciated textures, desultory progress, and a stilted melody that gropes its way from phrase to phrase. Add to its deliberately sere outlines a touch of *frisson* and Schumann's vain search for *gemüth* (warmth) in the series as a whole is easily understood. The next two pieces are from the later vintage and so remained unknown to Schumann. *Carnaval* is an entertaining galop employing the double octave acciaccatura, an invention of Alkan's played glissando from black note to white. It is packed with amusing high-jinks such as a can-can poised for sixteen bars on an unresolved dominant seventh as well as a rumbling pedal point and some hectic changes of register. *La retraite*, which follows, is an absolute oddity. Consisting of the fourfold repetition of a stark, military formula it might be described as rhythm and texture without music. The whole piece, but especially its end, affords a remarkable parallel with a much later masterpiece, *Le tambour bat aux champs* of 1859. *La Pâque* (the Passover) makes an innocuous contrast. The 'milk and water' impression of its pastoral opening remains unredeemed by a short-lived Jewish declamation that forms its climax. For the month of May Alkan offers a *Sérénade*, rather undistinguished in substance but laid out with expertise. An abrupt Neapolitan resolution lends a bitter-sweet edge to the final bars.

Schumann remained unacquainted with the following piece, *Promenade sur l'eau*. More is the pity, for he would surely have seen the genius behind its classical facade. On paper, this simple song, with echoes rising from within a limpid accompaniment, suggests Mendelssohn; but with Alkan appearances can be misleading. The sober harmonies and a certain grave depth in the spacing are unique to Alkan. Halfway through, a strangely disturbing shadow darkens the outline to provide a focal point, while the gruff, deep texture of the close makes its authorship unmistakable. Schumann would have preferred a warmer, more fragrant *Nuit d'été*. The resemblance of its lacy parallel sixths to the 'enfants' episode in the *Grande sonate* of 1847, makes one wonder if Alkan had the children's July holiday in mind. Some conflicting inflections (F natural/sharp) find a parallel in Chopin's posthumous Prelude in A flat written for Pierre Wolff in 1834. *Les moissoneurs* (the reapers) is full of Alkan fingerprints, like the deceptively anxious introductory bars and such piquancies as the following.

Ex.31

A central dominant pedal point in the stern middle section repeats the rhythm ♩♩♩| ♩.♪♩ in fierce anticipation of a particularly memorable passage in the solo Concerto. The piece affected Schumann 'as delightfully as country after city air'. Alkan celebrates September in peremptory hunting style with a piece entitled *L'hallali* (the bugle call). It consists of a powerful fanfare with brilliant pianistic affirmation featuring, once more, the chordal acciaccatura. If the assertive style anticipates the fifth prelude from op.31 (also in D major), the sharply etched grace notes look even further ahead to *Les diablotins*, one of the forty-eight *Esquisses*, published in 1861.

The next two pieces are among the simplest and most startlingly original of Alkan's early compositions. *Gros temps* exemplifies the 'icy restraint' that Humphrey Searle so rightly claimed sets Alkan aside from the more overt terror of, say, a Berlioz. As a type it is unclassifiable and there is nothing else like it even by Alkan himself. A mysterious, wavy tremor begets a self-generating lament, all held in a tense pianissimo. The briefest climax is sufficient to fulfil the sense of impending tragedy before the piece evaporates in a spectral wisp of an arpeggio. The brooding atmosphere is given a further sinister twist in *Le mourant* (the dying man). A nagging ostinato with oppressive harmonies is relieved first, and appropriately, by a hymn and later by a bass recitative. This is immediately repeated in the minor, detached and choked to provide a revealing portent of the *Chant de mort* in the ninth étude from op.35. The ostinato returns, falters and fragments while the final bars suggest the death-rattle followed by a sharp painful release. After such morbid realism the last piece of the collection and of the original six, comes as a shock. *L'Opéra*, a virtuosic send-up of the operatic clichés of the time, requires a brilliant technique in octaves and chordal leaps to bring it off convincingly. Schumann loved it; but he had also been lambasting such fashionable operatic favourites as Meyerbeer and must have sensed an unlikely ally in Alkan with his light-hearted parody. Elsewhere he damned with faint praise and it is a thousand pities that, apart from his denunciation of the *Morceaux* op.15, Schumann's pen only encountered six comparatively trivial pieces quite unrepresentative of the twenty-five-year-old composer's potential and accomplishment. Had the second Andante from op.13, the third Scherzo from op.16 or the later pieces in *Les mois* come his way his assessment of Alkan might have been very different.

Les mois includes some of Alkan's most accessible pieces and they probably provided excellent teaching material during his life. In *Les pianistes célèbres*, his erstwhile pupil and later rival, Marmontel, describes them as 'douze morceaux poétiques, pièces charmantes, accessibles aux pianistes de moyenne force'.

The peculiar discipline imposed by writing miniatures seems to have fascinated Alkan thoughout his creative life and it must have afforded a refreshing change in perspective from such monumental projects as the *Trois grandes études pour les mains séparées ou réunies* which occupied him during the late 1830s. One can imagine that as they accumulated he would organise them into sets, often with ingenious key sequences.

Although a number of short pieces – some highly characteristic – appeared in 1844 the next important collection of true miniatures came in 1847 with the publication of *Vingt-cing préludes* in all the major and minor keys, op.31. Following in the wake of Chopin's twenty-four preludes, also in all the major and minor keys, Alkan's title might suggest either homage, or a challenge to his friend's work. It comes as a surprise to discover how little these two publications, with their almost identical titles, really have in common. Few would deny that Chopin's famous set contains some of his most concentrated and highly-wrought miniatures. If others (11 or 18 for instance) give the impression of unfulfilled digests for larger projects the character, nevertheless, of every piece is stamped with the essence of Chopin's unique genius. Alkan's preludes are, by comparison, more relaxed, less virtuosic and harmonically, less highly-charged – not to say severe; yet the originality of many of these pieces is undeniable, their enduring attraction implicit.

Two curiosities; the one simple, the other baffling, cannot go undiscussed. Why twenty-five preludes? Following the example of Bach's 'forty-eight' both Chopin and Alkan start their series in C major. Alkan proceeds through F minor, D flat major, F sharp minor and so on, completing a cycle of rising fourths and falling thirds in E minor for his twenty-fourth prelude. One step more and he achieves the satisfaction of ending as he has begun, in C major. Both here and in his late *Esquisses* op.63, Alkan's religious conviction compels him to sign off with a devotional fragment; in this case a *prière*. The second eccentricity is not so easily dismissed. Each prelude is preceded by the singular direction 'piano ou orgue' and many of the bass lines carry the instructions 'pieds', 'pieds ou mains' or 'pédale'. Fifteen years earlier Alkan had crowned a brilliant Conservatoire career with the coveted first prize for organ. Although his background may have denied him an organ post he must have remained an expert performer; yet many of these pieces are ineffective on the organ, requiring the piano's attack and sustaining pedal to bring them to life. One or two are impossible and the fifth prelude is unplayable on either instrument as Alkan has written it. My own hunch, that the entire series was originally intended for the pedal-piano and that a publisher's commercial instinct persuaded Alkan to substitute 'orgue' for the somewhat esoteric *pédalier*, was slightly undermined by the discovery of an early edition ascribing registrations to certain preludes. On the other hand this very omission elsewhere, only confirms that these other pieces were never intended for the organ. The *pédalier* or pedal-piano, with which Alkan was to become obsessionally identified, is certainly the only single instrument capable of doing full justice to the complete set. Fortunately, however, the medium is far less important than the music and pianists will find that many of the pieces go splendidly on the piano while the remainder are all possible, given a little rearrangement of parts, a few minor omissions and an imaginative use of the pedal.

Fétis, who reviewed the preludes shortly after publication[1] expressed concern at the composer's tendency 'to return again and again to an atmosphere of melancholy'. If true, this need hardly disturb the modern listener. Alkan conveys his moods with an objectivity that never becomes self-indulgent or self-pitying. Many of these pieces are gravely reflective suggesting the timeless atmosphere of an old church or synagogue. Some are wistful, others playful – several passionate or even fiercely jubilant... and all are presented with a chaste and classic simplicity. At the outset a ten-bar meditation leads us gently into the darkly reflective world of the first four preludes. As so often in these pieces an intangible, almost mystical power seems to invest their apparent naïvety. In this opening prelude the most

[1]His full and often perceptive account appeared in the *Revue et gazette musicale*, July 1847.

primitive elements of melody, harmony and rhythm are held captive to a bell-like pedal point. A telling modulation from A major back to C major in the penultimate bar provides a convincing focal point. The left-hand pedal should only be released for the two central bars marked 'forte' and the dotted figure must contrast effectively with the triplet. Both repeats seem essential. The stark contrast between two apparently unrelated ideas provides the novel layout of the second prelude marked 'assez lentement'. The left hand alone introduces a lugubrious song in 6/8 only to be contradicted by a quaintly obsessive march. Alkan's instruction, 'même mouvement' must mean that the 6/8 dotted crotchet should match the ¢ minim. Soon the march becomes afflicted by restless harmonies before the song returns, this time in contrasted registers. A further snatch of march, ever more anxious, gives 'pause for thought', then in a three-line coda Alkan spells out the subtle relationship that has always existed between these seemingly ill-assorted ideas, the march having the last word. Several preludes have retrospective titles. *Dans le genre ancien* (no.3) is baroque in style and Mendelssohnian in counterpoint; but as the mood intensifies, with grinding ninths and false relations, the creator of its inner pathos is never in doubt.

The next three preludes are overtly Hebraic in character and origin. *Prière du soir* (no.4) is a childlike devotional fragment, charmingly harmonised but hardly preparing the listener for the triumphant outburst of its successor. This jubilant paraphrase of Psalm 150 (Praise God in His Holiness) is written on three staves throughout. It demands the resources of a pedal-piano to make its proper effect, especially in the middle section which invokes a fourfold 'shout of human voices'. The organ lacks the incisive attack necessary to fulfil Alkan's instructions 'with enthusiasm', 'resolute', 'passionate' while the final tremolo would be utterly ineffectual. A normal piano, with the adroit use of pedal and some redistribution of parts in bar ten should come close to realising Alkan's intention. No.6 is entitled *Ancienne mélodie de la synagogue*. Plaintive outlines and oriental colouring reveal their traditional Hebrew sources, while rhythmic freedom suggests the cantor's declamation, with its punctuation of pauses and mournful cadences. No.7 is aptly described by Fétis as 'a graceful banter'. This prelude makes considerable demands on the player's flexibility of wrist in the execution of double notes. The piece falls into two halves. The first, with its persistent rhythm and bland harmony suggests Schumann. The second and final section is conversational. It contains the only brief departure from the home key, E flat, and it highlights a return to the opening above a drone bass. The piece has a classical poise and a subtle ambiguity of phrasing that raises it above its rather commonplace material.

Alkan reserves the dark key of A flat (or G sharp) minor for some of his most cogent inspirations: think of the grimly oppressive finale from his *Grande sonate* or the first movement from his solo Concerto. *La chanson de la folle au bord de la mer* (song of the mad woman on the shore) never fails to capture the imagination, yet its substance could scarcely be more ordinary. It is in its spare texture and in its spacing with a great gulf fixed between the hands, that we must seek its strange, hypnotic power. Deep in the bass the monotonous repetition of a simple half-close paints the vast solitude of the sea. High above, the woman's song rises to its frenetic climax and cuts out in a haze of pedal. As it fades the ear may just catch snatches of the song as they vanish into the continuing ground-swell. Readers of Goethe's *Wilhelm Meister* might sense a parallel with Mignon's 'bereft' mother who, lonely and deranged, wanders the lake side seeking the remains of her lost daughter. Despite its Haydnesque innocence, a touch of wistfulness also creeps into the second half of the next piece causing Fétis to doubt the aptness of its title: *Placiditas* (*dans le style fugué*) (no.10) is a robust toccata alive with mock-fugal devices, inversion and double counterpoint. It calls for dexterity and a resolute attack. As its title suggests *Un petit rien* is over in a flash, its finger-twisting contours and carefree counterpoint dispelling the briefest hint of darker thoughts. On the contrary *Le temps qui n'est plus* (no.12) is a plaintive song without words in which a sonorous climax in the major key only enhances a pathetic return to the minor. Despite its Chopinesque cadence Schubert seems to me the inspiration behind this prelude. Its successor, *'J'étais endormie mais mon coeur veillait...'* (from *Cantique des cantiques* – Song of Songs v.2) became a special favourite with Busoni around the turn of the century. Delicately repeated chords support an undulating melody in quintuplets, its gently vibrating rise and fall clouded by the pedal. The unusual disposition of familiar harmony adds to a sense of unreality as the opening is repeated above an alternating tonic and dominant pedal. The mood darkens; the chords hover and float into silence over an unresolved six-four harmony.

No.14 is another song without words, but in a turbulent B minor. The fierce challenge of a hearty refrain, brave as the 'Men of Harlech' is rejected for a more diplomatic solution. An ingenious combination of both its elements compresses the form and resolves the conflict at a stroke. Its successor *Dans le style gothique* dances straight out of the nursery, starlit and twinkling. The incursion of a low, impertinent E flat near the close is deftly brushed aside. In so untroubled a context its bizarre title, which also puzzled Fétis, must surely remain yet another enigma! The atmospheric charm of the sixteenth prelude is more difficult to describe. The slenderest of fugal openings droops sadly into a fragile pattern of undulating double notes, wayward as drifting cloud. The process is repeated, the undulation taking a surprising turn. Two further repetitions with the subject inverted and its sequel casually unpredictable completes the scheme. By comparison *Rêve d'amour* (no.17), a melodramatic fantasy, seems rather undistinguished despite a charming sequence marked 'avec volupté'. Had Tchaikovsky rewritten Schubert's *Ständchen* he might have produced something like the eighteenth prelude, a sensuous romance in which the constant crossing of hands suggests the advantage of a double keyboard. Played on a normal piano it calls for the most cunning compromise of technical prowess and pedal dexterity if the melody is not to be broken. The robust *Prière du matin* (no.19) is just rescued from banality by its varied phrase lengths and mildly interesting dissonances above a drone bass. There follows a dogged but vigorous octave study in the Dorian mode. A characteristic coda, furtive and spiky, is cut short by a final, resounding flurry of octaves. In complete contrast the next prelude is as relaxed and carefree as a child day-dreaming in its swing, whereas *Anniversaire* (no.22), with its pervasive dotted figure, is an impressive elegy equal to the finest of Mendelssohn's Songs without Words. Note how the mood becomes ever more oppressive as the bass grinds its way downwards. Despite a modulation to the major, the final bars only confirm its spirit of grim resignation. Light relief, in the shape of an airy, tuneful 'entr'acte' (no.23) suggests that an orchestrated selection from Alkan's shorter pieces might produce a highly successful ballet-score. In the middle section some unpredictable syncopations would catch any dancer on the hop.

So far there are few weak links in Alkan's chain, and it is sad to relate that the last two preludes hardly form an adequate climax to the series, although one might not wish to go as far as Fétis in his condemnation of the twenty-fourth prelude. 'The ceaseless, prodigious velocity is so different from the other pieces' he declares 'that it can only be considered a debauchery of the author's talent'. This 'moto perpetuum' *alla Paganini* lacks the pianistic sophistication of a Chopin or a Liszt, yet it might still make an effective concert study. For the closing *Prière* the humblest elements of melody, harmony and rhythm weave a hymn-tune of self-effacing naïvety; yet despite some consciously crude doublings and consecutives the piece retains a plain and wholesome dignity that forbids too facile a judgement.

Should the *Préludes* be played as a set? Alkan's bold key sequence is tempting and with customary foresight he devised a series that would fit snugly on to a record or compact disc. I can only admit that each time I toy with the idea of a public performance doubts creep in; uncertainty about the quality of nos. 7, 17, 19 and 24; misgivings about the naïvety of the *prières*, which seem designed only for private consumption and, above all, fear of insufficient contrast between pairs or groups of preludes, notably the first four which are all reflective. On the other hand the best of these pieces inhabit a unique world unlike that of any other composer. Their classic perfection makes them absolutely enduring and should have ensured their indispensable place in the piano repertoire. I would, personally, single out nos. 1, 2, 3, 6, 8, 9, 12, 13, 14, 15, and 16 as the most characteristic, with 5, 10 and 11 providing the essential foil to an otherwise reflective style.

About a year after the *Préludes* came two sets of *Impromptus* op.32 (nos. 1 and 2). As their title suggests these are relaxed, uncomplicated pieces designed more for private enjoyment than public exposure. At this level they are well worth exploring. The first, *Vaghezza* (beauty) would make a useful pendant to the much-loved A flat study from Chopin's *Trois nouvelles études*. The second, *L'amitié*, with its striding bass, sounds uncommonly like a revivalist hymn; that is until taken at Alkan's 𝅗𝅥 = 92, when it becomes a stirring marching song. Its bold modulations and harmonic side-slips confirm the composer's debt to Schubert. For his third impromptu, *Fantasietta alla moresca*, Alkan sends us an exotic 'musical picture postcard' from North Africa, though the following curiosity would hardly sound out of place in one of Bartók's Rumanian Dances.

Ex.32

The fourth piece *La foi* (faith) strikes a valiant stance but remains undistinguished until its central revelation, hushed and forbidding, its stalking octaves and smouldering trumpets threatened by a triplet ostinato.

Ex.33

This awesome episode marked 'divoto' only exacerbates the ordinariness of the opening section which returns with a sense of crushing anticlimax.

The second set of impromptus is schematic. Headed *Trois airs à 5 temps et un à 7 temps* it constitutes one of the most curious collections ever published and is the fruit of Alkan's encounter with the Zorcico, a Basque dance in 5/4.[1] Each piece repeats a rhythmic formula throughout and the first one corresponds precisely in rhythm to Alkan's previously unpublished *Zorcico* discovered in the Bibliothèque Nationale in 1969 by Georges Beck. The tempo, ♩ = 144, is indicated in a Zorcico episode in the composer's *Petit caprice, réconcilia-*

[1] See Appendix 1, p.251

tion of 1857. Had Grieg and Bartok conspired to write a Chopin mazurka for quintupeds they might have produced something like this first impromptu. The following example gives some idea of its teasing harmonisation.

Ex.34

The second piece, in a languid 5/8, is less interesting, but conflicting accentuation in the third produces a catchy, five-legged rumba. In the final impromptu, in 7 time, a melancholy obsession with the rhythm ♩♩♩♩𝅗𝅥. generates a hypnotic spell akin to the style of certain 'repetitive' composers of the late twentieth century. The Alkan piece, though, is cemented into an entity by a cunningly contrived harmonic scheme.

Alkan published his last and most important collection of miniatures in 1861, the year that also saw the appearance of his last extended work for solo piano, the *Sonatine* op.61. At forty-seven he was turning more and more to the pedal-piano as his ideal medium, yet the *Esquisses: 48 motifs* (sketches) op.63 are, unlike the preludes, piano music pure and simple. The discovery, in the Bibliothèque Nationale, of a manuscript dated Oct. 9, 1847 of an earlier version in D of the E major *Esquisse Délire* (see p.32) suggests that the contents of op.63 probably accumulated over a period of fifteen years before Alkan organised them into a sequence. Issued in four volumes, they pass through all the major and minor keys twice, in a series of rising fourths and falling thirds followed by one of falling fourths and rising fifths. The final, unnumbered *Laus Deo* returns to the opening key of C major.

These tiny pieces establish a seemingly endless variety of mood and character, their small-scale discipline lending a keen edge to Alkan's harmonic, rhythmic and pianistic specialities and bringing his formal mastery into sharpest focus. They also pinpoint Alkan's historic importance, comprehending both past and future in the continuity of French keyboard music. As Richard Gorer shrewdly observes 'he stands like some musical pithecanthropus as a link between the *clavecinistes*, and the impressionists of the early years of the twentieth century'.[1] Indeed, the first piece *La vision* has a somnambulistic charm, its wistful song floating wraith-like above a motionless accompaniment that anticipates the *Gymnopédies* by Erik Satie. Its ancestry, on the other hand, may be traced, like that of the thirty *Chants*, to Mendelssohn's Songs without Words. Several of the more lyrical *Esquisses* pay oblique homage to Mendelssohn, and *Notturnino – innamorato*, no.43, is of special interest for it invites direct comparison with Mendelssohn's Venetian Gondola Song op.30 no.6. Both pieces are in F sharp minor, both are barcarolles, and both sing their languid song above similarly undulating accompaniments.

Ex.35a Mendelssohn, op.30 no.6

[1] Article in *The Listener*, Nov.14, 1946.

Ex.35b Alkan, op.63 no.43

Paradoxically, such inescapable parallels only serve to focus their basic differences. Whereas Mendelssohn sets the stage with a six-bar preamble, Alkan's song plunges straight in. Where Mendelssohn's melody proceeds in symmetrical four-bar phrases Alkan groups his opening section in pairs of five- and two-bar phrases ending with a four-bar phrase fractured down the middle. Mendelssohn sustains his sombre mood by remaining inescapably anchored to F sharp minor, while Alkan from the outset opposes F sharp and B minor, making great play with Neapolitan returns. His second half is in the major and contains a stunning modulation to A sharp (B flat) and he also anticipates the 'blue-note' technique of the 1920s by clashing the flattened leading-note against its true harmony. Further rhythmic and tonal ambiguities and the reversal of parts add an insubstantial, dreamlike quality before the piece slots unexpectedly and pessimistically back into the minor on its penultimate note. The essential differences of approach in these two pieces become crystallised in their final notes. Mendelssohn holds a bleak F sharp in the treble. Alkan also holds a solitary note, but a low C sharp, the piece extinguishing on an inconclusive 6-4 chord. An even stranger example of the same species is the fifteen-bar *Barcarollette* in 18/8 time, the twelfth of the series. Beneath a thin, wavy accompaniment tenuous wisps of melody curl languidly down in search of their elusive root, only to be mockingly echoed from within a cavernous void. Emaciated and restless they find resolution in a final *tierce de Picardie* coloured by an enigmatic seventh.

There are other *Esquisses* of the *chanson* genre, all worth exploring. They include two slumber songs *En songe* (no.48) and *Fais dodo* (no.33) the briefest and drowsiest of all such pieces. But the absolute masterpiece among the lyrical *Esquisses* is no.46, *Le premier billet doux* (the first love letter) – a highly sophisticated cameo of twenty amorous bars in the most fugitive E flat major one could imagine. Volatile, unpredictable yet inevitable, it flits past so nonchalantly that it must, surely, have been thrown off at a sitting.

The *Esquisses* contain several pieces of the étude or toccata type. *Le staccatissimo* and *Le legatissimo* (nos.2 and 3) are twin studies in miniature contrasting pin-pricked agility with delicately caressed legato. 'Notes fall from his hands like an enchanted shower of pearls and diamonds' – so reads an eye-witness account of Alkan's playing and it suggests the perfect realisation of such pieces as no.25, a capital little study in perpetual motion. Nos.16, 28, 29, 36 and 44 are all pianistically rewarding. No.36, a *Toccatina* (not to be confused with the marvellous late *Toccatina* op.75) is one of Alkan's punishing finger drillers, of no great distinction, whereas no.29, *Délire* (frenzy) which, as we have seen dates from 1847, is an ecstatic study in wide-spanned agility with left hand leaps.

Several *Esquisses* revert to a pre-nineteenth-century style and some, no.34 for instance, embrace the old modes. No.26 is a distilled fragment in the Phrygian mode, perhaps an over-spill from the *Petits préludes sur les 8 gammes du plain-chant* for organ of 1859. No.6 is an emphatic four-voice *Fuguette*, a miniature text-book model, stretto, pedals and all, while in no.17 Alkan's classical pen furrows deep and chromatic to fashion a minuet in the style of a string trio. His quizzical homage to earlier masters yields an extraordinary pre-echo of Stravinskian pastiche in a fleet-winged two-part invention, *Duettino* (no.14). It abounds in contrapuntal devices, trilled cadences *alla D. Scarlatti* and such sly syncopations as the following:

Ex.36a

. . . which a twentieth-century writer might easily have notated with displaced barlines.

Ex.36b

The series also contains a brilliant *Contredanse*, a jolly little *Rigaudon* (no.27) suitable for young players, a *Petite marche villageoise* (no.20) – harmonically a very slippery customer – and two marvellous little scherzi. No.37 is a darkly conspiratorial *Scherzettino*, its wide-spaced textures made more sinister by the dry rattle of tremolandi in tenths; a little piece for big hands. No.47, in B flat minor, is a baleful frolic, its arrow-like motifs darting hither and thither, its neo-classical guise mocked by wildly improbable modulations, its fierce rhythmic contractions exacerbated by the empty spacing. A grimly comic '*Trioletto*' (Beethoven would surely have approved) starts with a joke. Alkan wrenches his key-centre up a notch, to B minor, but leads off in an explosive B *major* only to correct his 'mistake' second time round. A passage of rasping bravura brings about the return in this miniature firework display of Alkan *hardiesses*.

Many of the *Esquisses* have fanciful titles. Some are mood paintings: *Pseudo-naiveté*, *Confidence*, *Le frisson*, etc. Others are purely descriptive like *Les cloches* (no.4), a three-line fragment devoted to Alkan's insatiable fascination with bells; or no.23 *L'homme aux sabots* (the man in clogs), a piece of jaunty grotesquerie with a tramping, grimacing accompaniment to frighten the children. On an altogether deeper level *Le frisson* (no.7) conjures up a Mahlerian fantasy haunted by funeral drums. Its successor *Increpatio* (rebuke) is prefaced by a few searing arpeggios sounding like the rending of garments. Smouldering quintuplets supply the motive power and form a spring-board for a violently rhythmic feature which fairly splutters with venom. In absolute contrast, the delicately-brushed arpeggios of no.9 *Les soupirs* (sighs) weave an unsuspected link between the harmonic worlds of Schumann and Debussy. The most extravagant rhythmic contortions produce a minefield of booby-traps in *Musique militaire* (no.35) in which Alkan reveals a rash mastery of the most jejune material: a blank, four-note oscillation, a handful of detached chords and a triplet twiddle. Organic growth is constant and unpredictable and the whole effect is arrogantly bizarre. Prokofiev provides the only parallel. *Héraclite et Démocrite*, (no.39) confronts the dark by the laughing philosopher in an astounding double portrait involving the opposition and combination of 2/4 (♩ = 63) and 4/4 (𝅝 = 63) time. Alkan first introduces his characters independently but they soon start to bicker. Democritus quickly up-stages his rival, even debunking him to his face before he finally dismisses Heraclitus in a peal of ribald laughter.

How ironic that Mussorgsky's double portrait Goldenberg and Schmuyle in Pictures at an Exhibition is accepted for the masterly innovation it certainly is, while Alkan's equally audacious *tour de force*, published thirteen years earlier, should have passed unnoticed.

Ex.37

It was Sorabji who first drew attention to the extraordinary appearance of Alkan's music on the printed page. No.45 *Les diablotins* (imps) would certainly fit his description of 'an entirely novel and unfamiliar system of decorative design' (see p.49). The example of Berlioz could easily be held responsible for the fanfare-like opening with its jeering embellishments, just as Henry Cowell would surely have answered for the continuous pattern of mocking tone-clusters had he not inconveniently been born ten years after Alkan's death! Two hymn-like interruptions marked 'quasi santo' and 'quasi santa' (according to register) sound too derisive in their context to suggest exorcism.

The few remaining pieces include two poetic paraphrases. *Quasi coro* (no.5) is headed by a quotation from Aristophanes's The Frogs. Its bland, scholarly opening proves deceptive as it unfolds in generous modulations, semitonal clashes and rhythmic contradictions. The quotation from Horace that inspires no.34 might have

LES DIABLOTINS.

struck a particularly sympathetic chord in Alkan: 'Odi profanum vulgus et arceo: favete linguis (I loathe and shun the profane rabble)'. In fact the Latin text calls forth a somewhat impassive little hymn-tune in the composer's favourite dotted rhythm, its modality confirmed by a few spartan bars in the Dorian mode resembling plain-song. The effect is as impersonal as it is austere; one is neither attracted nor repelled.

Three final oddities comprise the opening of a string quartet (no.31), a freak concerto tutti in baroque style with the abortive solo entries parodying the Mendelssohn G minor concerto (no.15) and, most remarkable of all, *Les enharmoniques* (no.41). This riot of false relations, baffling modulations and harmonic *double ententes* seems to teeter on the brink of atonality; but the piece is far more than a speculative experiment. Its stern, yet uneasy depths are laid bare in the following awesome descent, menaced as it is by two final subterranean rumbles.

Ex.38

Characteristically Alkan ends his greatest collection of miniatures with an unnumbered *Laus Deo* (Praise to God) – a sober chorale, framed in mystery, announced and dismissed by an arresting peal of bells. What could be simpler, stranger... or more unique?[1]

[1] The reader's attention is also directed to Raymond Lewenthal's admirable edition: *The Piano Music of Alkan* (Schirmer, New York, 1964). This includes an entertaining, enlightening and highly practical discussion of a representative selection from the *Esquisses*.

5 The Thirty Chants

Alongside the *Grande Sonate*, the *Trois petites fantaisies* and the *Sonatine*, the five volumes of *Chants* op.38, 65, 67 and 70 are among the works of Alkan most admired in his native France. Their publication spans a period of some fifteen years, from his creative 'high summer' of 1857 to a collapse in production that seems to coincide with the advent of the *petits concerts* in the early 1870s. Whether or not op.70 witnessed the last flame of Alkan's failing inspiration it certainly contains music of a disturbingly valedictory nature. Strangely enough, the Hungarian pianist Alexander de Bertha, who became closely associated with the composer in the 1870s, dismisses the *Chants* as slavish imitations. In an article published in 1909 he writes: 'Did he not imitate the first book of Mendelssohn's Songs without Words in his first book of *Chants* using the same keys, the same speeds, and the same devices?'[1] Bertha might reasonably have added that not only did Alkan imitate Mendelssohn's key sequence: E major, A minor, A major, A major, F sharp minor and G minor in his four subsequent suites, but he ended all five suites with a Barcarolle in dutiful reverence, it might seem, to the well-known Venetian Gondola Song that ends Mendelssohn's first set. Even Mendelssohn's own remaining suites (there are seven of them) all adopt different key sequences and only two contain further Venetian Gondola Songs, neither of which are in G minor and only one of which is a final item. Clearly the idea behind these pieces by Mendelssohn fascinated Alkan, providing both catalyst and framework as he viewed them from ever more oblique angles and in different lights, refracting, distorting and amplifying while always leaving sufficient clues, apart from key, to identify their origin.

In our own day Robert Simpson has provided a striking parallel by deliberately basing his 4th, 5th and 6th string quartets on

[1] *Bulletin français de la Société Internationale de Musique*, Feb.15, 1909.

Beethoven's Razumovskys, submitting analogous material in his own twentieth-century idiom to Beethoven's compositional procedures. While Simpson's audacious experiment throws a revealing light on his Beethoven models, his three quartets retain their own personality as independent works. Had not the author, himself, spilt the beans their pedigree might well have passed undetected. Alkan's venture is more risky for he shares the same harmonic language with his model; yet his strange turn of mind yields similarly independent results as he strives to fulfil what he clearly perceives to be the underlying potential of Mendelssohn's seemingly innocent pieces.

Book 1 op.38

At the outset Alkan takes over the essential elements of Mendelssohn's first piece replacing his urbane melody by a soaring cantilena 'avec grand' passion' and converting his flowing accompaniment into a broad semiquaver sweep of over three-and-a-half octaves.

Ex.39a Mendelssohn

Ex.39b Alkan

Where Mendelssohn politely engages the listener's attention with two preludial bars, Alkan launches his tune without preamble, generating a stream of bold, unsensuous lyricism so essentially Gallic that it might easily pass for Fauré at his most ecstatic. Both pieces modulate eagerly to the sharp side of the key and both glance wistfully back from the flat side in their codas. Alkan's broader canvas, however, requires a focal point. By briefly halting the semiquavers he concentrates our attention on the following novel progression in anticipation of Fauré's pupil Ravel.

Ex.40a Alkan

Ex.40b Ravel, *Le gibet* from *Gaspard de la nuit*

It seems fascinating that two such similar passages, both involving a pedal bell-effect above chromatic shifts, should, according to their contexts, convey such dissimilar moods.

The second piece, *Sérénade*, despite the refinement of its two-part writing and some mildly exotic colouring, makes a somewhat tepid impression. Consisting of a static little tune above a scurry of staccato semiquavers its uniform treatment would make it difficult to bring off convincingly. It ends with a curiosity, a treble B held for three bars in crescendo. Either Alkan desired the impossible or Erards were experimenting with some form of swell! The A major *Choeur* which follows is a grotesque inflation of Mendelssohn's famous 'hunting' piece in the same key. It opens with a vamping introduction of quite outrageous banality and the first section, in dauntless hunting style, yields a Neapolitan cadence of such crude eccentricity that it demands illustration.

Ex.41

Like its model it modulates to C sharp minor calling forth Mendelsohn's hunting horns. Elsewhere the piece bounces along in an ever-increasing whirlwind of virtuosity to land on the now familiar Alkan 'slap' at the absolute extremities of the piano.

No.4 *L'offrande* (the offering) also displays unmistakable links in keys, tempo, melodic shape, texture, style and detail with its Mendelssohn counterpart while remaining a totally independent composition which, from its opening phrase 'knows just where it is going'.

Ex.42a Alkan

Ex.42b Mendelssohn

Both 'songs' are preceded by an introduction of precisely four-and-three-eighths bars but the Alkan, bell-like above a double pedal, has a flattened seventh which favours D major.This tendency is only fulfilled when, like Mendelssohn, Alkan returns to his introduction for the close but, unlike Mendelssohn, interpolates a suggestion of the opening tune itself in D major to form a plagal cadence. Within this framework Alkan's lyricism although marked 'ingenuamente' is far less ingenuously harmonised than the Mendelssohn and it has some exquisite pungencies leading up to and continuing into the return.

Ex.43

For his fifth piece Alkan carries Mendelssohn's somewhat cautious 'poco agitato' to the ultimate in a headlong *agitatissimo* marked 'disperato' at the suitably desperate speed of 𝅗𝅥 = 84; yet far from being an *alla breve*, the non-stop torrent of triplet semiquavers enjoys a time signature of 24/16. Presumably Alkan requires crystal clarity not a vague wash. Under the composer's fingers the piece may have taken on an obsessional, almost frightening quality despite its conventional, unvaried figuration. Occasionally the angular chromaticism anticipates Schönberg in its constant change of register.

Ex.44

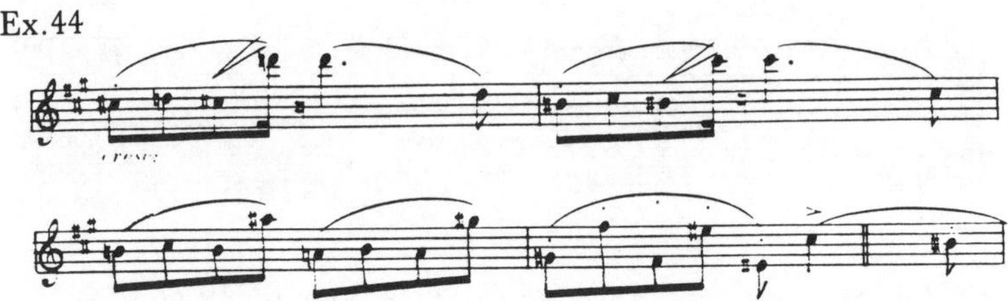

The piece ends enigmatically, with two major chords slipping back into a minor six-three chord in the final bar. Should the very opening sound vaguely familiar compare it with the Trio in the second movement of Brahms's E minor cello sonata; but the poignant clash of E natural against E sharp could have occurred to either composer when playing the following phrase from the great adagio, in the same key as the Alkan, from Beethoven's *Hammerklavier* Sonata:

Ex.45 Beethoven

If the G minor Andante from Beethoven's little G major Sonata op.79 begat Mendelssohn's first *Venetian Gondola Song* in the same key, the Mendelssohn in turn must be held responsible for the five Barcarolles, one of which concludes each set of Alkan's *Chants*, not to mention such later progeny as the Arabian Dance in Tchaikovsky's *Nutcracker Suite* and the second movement of Sibelius's Third Symphony. The peculiar brand of wistful indolence shared by the Beethoven and Mendelssohn pieces is probably induced by the constant rise and fall of parallel thirds (and sixths) above a rocking accompaniment.

Ex.46a Beethoven: Andante from Sonata op.79

Ex.46b Mendelssohn: Venetian Gondola Song op.19 no.6

Alkan takes over Mendelssohn's undulating bass but discards the thirds in favour of a supplementary internal pedal. He presses incidental figures from Mendelssohn's outline to more sinister purpose, intensifying the plaintiveness with acciaccaturas and false relations. The stark atmosphere is further enhanced by an austere texture strangely akin to that of the magical second movement in Ravel's Piano Concerto in G. Although a central *maggiore* section pays unmistakable tribute to Mendelssohn's later Venetian Gondola Song in A minor op.62 no.5, the whole piece remains an independent minor masterpiece of disturbing originality. If its Mendelssohn model engenders a mood of gentle melancholy, the Alkan breathes bleak pessimism. Dark, brooding and resigned, its final bars teeter precariously on the brink of major, minor and mixolydian modes, its tonality only to be resolved with the uncertainty of the roulette table.

Ex.47.

Book 2 op.38

The first piece, *Hymne*, retains Mendelssohn's domestic style but little more. A rather insipid idea is rescued from banality by its originality of texture and some arresting modulations, including a brief excursion to the flattened minor supertonic that Schubert might have appreciated. It is followed by one of Alkan's most famous (or notorious) creations. The Allegretto in A minor, subtitled 'Fa', became a test case for the erstwhile accusations of 'speculative invention' and 'paper music'. The originality of its scheme arises not so much from the use of a persistent pedal note, of which there are earlier examples, as from the choice of the note F (the flattened sixth) in an A minor context. Alkan's shrewdness, however, in selecting this far from arbitrary note becomes increasingly apparent as the piece modulates freely through C, B flat, A flat and other distant keys. F is, of course, essential to both the augmented sixth and Alkan's favourite Neapolitan colouring and, as the minor ninth, it adds spice to the dominant harmony while explaining itself away as an appoggiatura around the tonic and its relative major. It even enhances a remote key like A flat, by colouring its dominant with the exotic major ninth *à la Grieg*. Repeated 414 times, this bell-like note 'Fa' cuts icily into the texture with the ruthless precision of a laser beam. In the final bar it emerges from the surrounding A major harmony suspended and unresolved, having acquired a strangely convincing if transitory stability of its own. In this, one of the most remarkable short pieces to come out of the nineteenth century, Alkan's pedal-note discipline produces some of his most telling harmonic situations, just as Bach's strictest and seemingly most restrictive counterpoint can call forth his most trenchant harmonies. This is what lesser mortals call the luck of genius.

Like the corresponding number in the first book, *Chant de guerre* takes up the bold hunting style of its Mendelssohn prototype. A handful (one might say fistful) of embarrassingly well-worn clichés are treated with unpredictable freedom and bravura. Fierce harmonic tensions abound and the impression that Berlioz might have had a hand in it increases as a hushed, grotesque fugato rises from a subterranean 'valley of dry bones'. Like the earlier *Marche triomphale* op.27, it provides an imposing display of swaggering pianism – leaps, octaves, massed chords and explosive clusters of grace notes that most audiences would love. *Procession-Nocturne* suggests a sober marching-song with pizzicato accompaniment, dogged and monochrome, while no.5 wrings the last ounce of meaning out of three commonplace ideas, an arid, two-part invention in double counterpoint, and two more generously-textured waltz-like motifs.

Although its rhythmically flat style becomes tiresome the piece repays private study for its harmonic inventiveness, esoteric rather than compelling. Surely no-one but Alkan could have conjured up the following curiosity:

Ex.48

In the final *Barcarolle en choeur* we seem to eavesdrop on a Venetian choir singing in close harmony; a Christmas carol perhaps. Those treacly German sixths, so favoured by male-voice choirs, and a pervasive rhythmic stagnation make this the least distinguished barcarolle of the series.

Book 3 op.65.

Alkan's third set of *Chants* is possibly his most consistently rewarding. Although he gives no title to the opening *vivamente*, he might reasonably, have called it 'Svolgimento' for it unfolds a seemingly endless stream of curiosities, both harmonic and textural, with such disarming felicity that they could easily pass unnoticed. Key centres are volatile, modulations far-ranging while the constant chime of appoggiaturas with their resolutions provides the palate with unaccustomed piquancies.

Ex.49

The pianistic layout, superficially Schumannesque, is also deceptive, for the fingers seldom find themselves running along accustomed tracks. The last three bars, threatened by a gong-like pedal note, require a sensitive ear and agile foot to sustain tension without sacrificing clarity.

Ex.50

Esprits follets (goblins) must go like the wind, as light as a feather. A kind of supersonic Mendelssohn scherzo, it also affords a fleeting glimpse of the finale from Beethoven's Sonata in E flat, op.81a (*Les adieux*) but is more closely related to the first movement from the composer's own *Sonatine* of 1861. Indeed both here and in the previous piece this strong family resemblance confirms that they also date from the early 1860s. No.3, framed by an artless prelude and postlude, is in strict canon at the octave. Its opening again reveals a striking melodic and harmonic affinity with the fourth piece in Book 1 and, consequently, with no.4 from Mendelssohn's own first book, and both pieces are of course also in A major. The harmonisation throughout is exquisite and the gentle lurch to A minor and momentary flirtation with F major near the end, ravishing.

Ex.51

Each of the five suites features one piece of grotesquerie. Op.65, no.4 is a sturdy Polonaise undistinguished in matter but abounding in bizarre detail of unmistakable pedigree – wry counterpoint and unpredictable modulations. There is a particularly uncomfortable jolt home from C to A major via its supertonic (B minor) and a virtuosic wind-up that ends, rather unconvincingly, on a thumping six-three chord.

All honour to Dr. John White for identifying the inspiration behind the following paraphrase, *Horace et Lydie*. Horace wrote three books of odes between 20 and 30 BC. Among these are four odes featuring Lydia, three in the first book and one in the third. Here, for the only time, he uses a special form in which the second speaker in the dialogue must reply to the first in the same number of verses and on the same or similar subject and also, if possible, 'cap' what the first speaker has said.

Book 3, ode 9 Donec gratus eram tibi... (translated by Lord Dunsany).

H. When that I was acceptable to thee
And round thy white neck never arm would cling
Of any young man luckier than me,
Then was I prouder than a Persian King.

L. When that thou burnedst with no other flame
Nor Chloe was preferred to Lydia,
Then did I live with a more splendid name
And more renowned than Roman Ilia.

H. Well, Thracian Chloe is my mistress now,
Skilled in soft notes and on the harp to play,
For whom, if the three Sisters would allow,
I would give up life to prolong her day.

L. I burn for Calais as he for me,
The son of Ornytus in Thurii,
And if those Sisters would allow that he
Should so survive, twice for him would I die.

H. What if the old love should come back again
To bind us once more with its yoke of brass?
Blond Chloe cast off, what if should remain
Open those lost doors where I used to pass?

L. Were he more lovely than the evening star,
Thou lighter than a cork and more awry
Than billows of the Adriatic are,
With thee I'd love to live and gladly die.

Alkan follows the scheme meticulously. He switches registers between the stanzas and sets the first pair in the Dorian and the second in the Phrygian modes. The third verse, starting off in F sharp major, soon becomes afflicted by anxious D naturals but Alkan adds a final peroration in which he fans the old flame into a furnace.

The set ends with the most familiar and charming of Alkan's Barcarolles. Its quaintly modal inflections provide a fascinating pre-echo of the 'Twenties' within a framework of cool, classical economy. It remains in two voices throughout, the wavy accompaniment being cunningly derived by imitation from the right hand's opening phrase. With its flattened sevenths and false relations it might well be described as the piece of Mendelssohn that Gershwin forgot to write!

Book 4 op.67

With this fourth suite one has the growing suspicion that Alkan's creative fires were burning low. Still, when they do spark forth, his experience, sense of experiment and a profound knowledge of his instrument bring into being some of his finest work, if increasingly intermittently. He introduced the second, sixth and probably fifth numbers from this set at a *petit concert* on April 12, 1873, before their publication.

The first piece *Neige et lave* (snow and lava) contrasts a pallid andante with a fast middle section, fierce in manner but thin in substance. *Chanson de la bonne vieille* (Nannie's song) is far more characteristic. Sharp acciaccaturas add spice to a doleful folk-like melody which also serves, its contours inverted, as a central *maggiore* episode marked 'quasi rimembranza'. Once more Alkan isolates a six-three for his final chord, this time marked *ppp*. As the titles *Bravement* and *Doucement* suggest, Alkan links his next two A major pieces as a contrasted pair, though few artists would dare risk presenting them this way today. Both betray their respective sources. The former debases its well-worn 'hunting' contours into a nagging parody, repetitive and contrived. Even some resounding 'timpani' strokes, and other occasional eccentricities sound oddly unconvincing in this context. *Doucement* is quite another matter. It adds a devotional glow to the basic design, bestowing its confidences with affection, its textures warm but airy, its modulations bold yet reassuring. It also contains some vintage pungencies. Only Alkan would have thought of smuggling in this chromatic descent which so enhances the return.

Appassionata (no.5) takes wing in an anxious, fiery 6/8 but soon runs out of steam. Sequential developments and a cosily pious episode

Ex.52

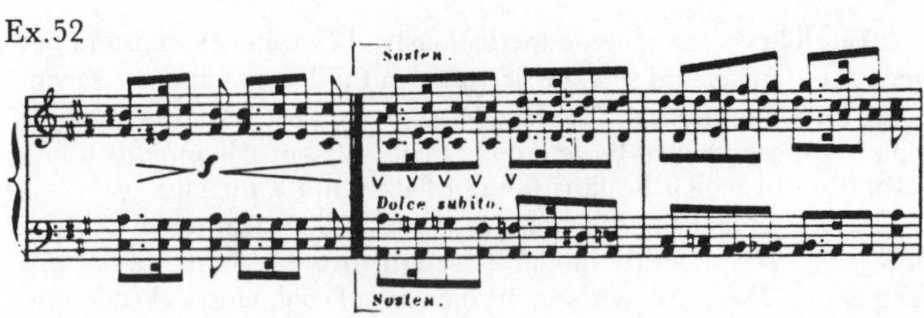

render the final plagal cadence, with both chords in second inversion, peculiarly incongruous. This is probably the piece described as 'Allegro con bravura' that Alkan introduced from manuscript at his *petit concert* in 1873.

Having proved the least rewarding, as yet, of the series, op.67 ends with one of the most impressive of Alkan's Barcarolles; a piece of dark, mysterious power. In a strangely monochrome *maggiore* episode the pianist finds his hands locked as securely as in a cat's-cradle. Note the almost surrealist return. The spirit of death seems to hover over

Ex.53

the final phrases as they rise, phantom-like, from a smouldering vibration deep in the bass.

Alkan's last volume of *Chants* also follows the key sequence adopted by Mendelssohn in his first set of Songs without Words but unlike the earlier examples op.70 forms an integral whole. Before his final Barcarolle Alkan inserts an interlude in which he reviews the five preceding pieces; an idea that may have stemmed from Beethoven's Ninth Symphony but one that shares a far closer affinity both in function and atmosphere with a similar device in Ravel's *Valses nobles et sentimentales* of 1911. If, as one suspects, op.70 was one of Alkan's last creative efforts it is, like the final harvest of an old fruit tree, a most rewarding one. All but one of the pieces are first-rate, three must be counted among the finest of the series and the link passage adds an altogether new dimension to the overall impression.

Exasperatingly, the opening piece entitled *Duettino* is the least compelling. Perhaps it took the ageing Alkan a little time to get going. Although pianistically grateful its homely lyricism, with harp-like accompaniment, demands a remarkably persuasive performance to raise it above the commonplace. Near the close, however, where the arpeggios break into a more impetuous descent, the innocent ear might easily identify Fauré as its author so unmistakably French is the style. The second piece, *Andantinetto*, is altogether in another class. A plaintive, duple melody in the right hand chimes throughout in direct conflict with its left hand accompaniment in triple time. The effect must on no account be allowed to sound fussy or congested, or to draw attention away from natural growth and balance in a piece that is self-developing and indivisible. Harmonic as well as rhythmic subtleties abound and there is more than a hint of oriental colouring.

The *Allegro vivace* that follows is one of the most bizarre and technically demanding of the series. A peremptory flourish of triplet and trill introduces a grotesque vamp-like motif. A martial refrain soon forms the spiky accompaniment to a marching song. Now Alkan breathes fire into these seemingly arid ingredients. In development of symphonic propensity an inversion of the vamp-like motif becomes increasingly obsessed with the opening flourish as it is forced through a series of baffling modulations. There follows a reversed recapitulation of song and march culminating in an outburst of chromatic fury, the final fling of virtuosity landing headlong on the outer extremities of the keyboard. Although the piece may border on the absurd it remains highly original, dramatically exciting and pianistically hair-raising.

La voix de l'instrument (no.4) has an old-world lace and lavender charm which must surely have won the hearts of those 'dames très parfumées et froufroutantes' who, according to Isidore Philipp, frequented Alkan's later concerts. Although the title mentions no specific instrument the piano naturally springs to mind. Did not the great J. S. Bach, himself, after some preliminary flourishes to test the mechanism of an instrument, break into a more sustained or lyrical style exclaiming 'Now let's see if it has good lungs!'? On the other hand the range and layout favours the cello, an instrument for which Alkan reserved a special affection. The soaring cantilena, with its lightly brushed 'pizzicato' accompaniment, strongly suggests string quartet writing, the cellist's colleagues listening with rapt attention until they, too, feel compelled to join in the song.

Alkan calls his penultimate piece *Scherzo-Coro*, but despite its close 'vocal' chording it goes like the wind, prestissimo, its anxious harmonies threatened by rattling pedal notes, its rhythmic urgency still heightened by the constant compression of its phrases. This is the most concentrated of the *Chants*. Note how the following feature 𝅗𝅥 ♩| ♩♩♩ and its rhythmic inversion ♩♩♩| 𝅗𝅥 ♩ is given a variety of meanings within the scherzo itself and is also pressed into service in an expansive trio section. Here again the constant variation of phrase length adds tensile strength as Alkan proceeds to bend our familiar harmonic world into unaccustomed connotations. At times, it seems, the voices themselves have been shaken out of alignment:

Ex.54

... while the following example anticipates the obsessional chromaticism of Franck and Reger.

Ex.55

There is a compressed reprise of the scherzo and a coda that tunnels, balefully, before recalling a phrase from the trio. The final escape from centrifugal control is achieved in a spiralling accelerando notoriously difficult to bring off.

The problem of confronting two pieces in adjacent minor keys, the one a concentrated fast piece, the other an equally concentrated slow one is solved by interposing a modulating transition that Alkan calls *Récapitulation*. Fragments from all five pieces are recalled in a sequence of minor keys until we pause on the threshold of G minor, the now inevitable key for Alkan's last and undoubtedly finest barcarolle. Slight in size, profound in content, its valedictory message is clarified by a classical restraint that stands aloof from place and period. The opening is darkly evocative as the lonely cry of a gondolier echoes to the melancholy rocking of his boat and the gentle splash of the oar. Soon the dying call is gathered up into a sad little refrain while the oar continues its rhythmic counterpoint. A rising sequence *senza pedale* modulates through B and E flat minor as it mounts to an uneasy climax only to fall back into the pervasive field of G minor. Even a delayed *maggiore* episode above a double drone offers little escape from the impending sense of doom as the piece glides inexorably to its close. Its final pessimistic bars seem to invoke a wraith-like memory of the furious chromatic descents that clinch the tragic conclusion in the first movement of Alkan's *Symphonie* for solo piano of 1857.

Ex.56a *Symphonie* for solo piano

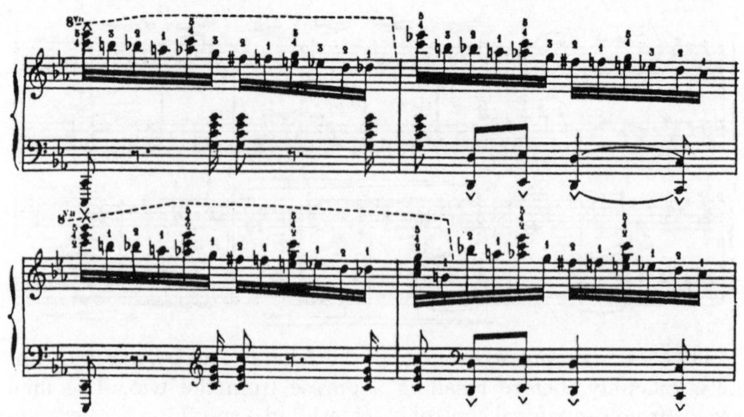

Ex.56b Barcarolle op.70 no.6

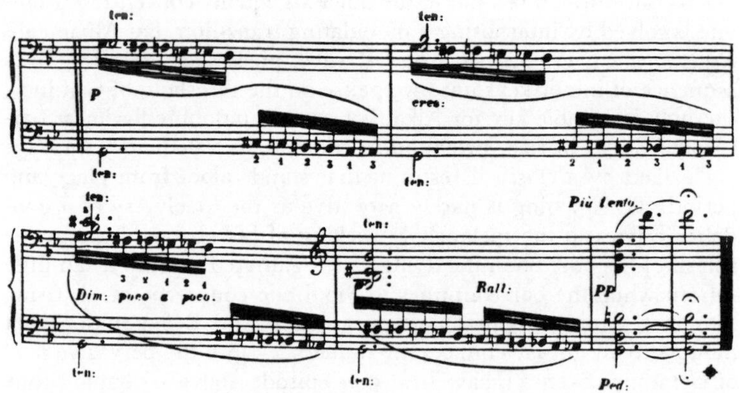

This final Barcarolle casts a deep and disturbing shadow over the fifth and last volume of *Chants*. Its sensitive placing after an improvisational interlude ensures its fullest, psychological impact, a fact that must weigh heavily if it is to be played as a separate item.

6 The Grande Sonate and Sonatine

The *Grande sonate* op.33 appeared in 1847 about six years before the Liszt Sonata and is dedicated to the composer's father. Its publication has been described as 'a cosmic event in Alkan's development and in the history of piano music'.[1] Certainly it is one of the most significant piano works of its century – challenging in its psychological background, impressive in the internal organisation of its four movements, and as for its piano writing, this just about sums up the possibilities of the instrument, reminding us that Alkan at thirty-four must have been a virtuoso of quite frightening powers and profound subtlety. But the most surprising thing about this unique work is the fact that it eluded public performance for over a century and a quarter.[2] So far as we know Alkan never played it; neither did Liszt, although, as we shall see, the work itself provides convincing evidence that he was familiar with it. Its wholesale neglect can hardly be due, as has sometimes been suggested, to its technical problems, though these are real enough; virtuosi, like rock-climbers, like to live dangerously. It seems to me far more likely that the true stumbling block is its design which, from all appearances, seems calculated to wring the minimum effect out of the maximum effort. Such an impression, one hastens to add, is quickly dispelled during a committed performance even though Alkan's *Grande sonate* behaves like no other sonata. Who else would have thought of opening with the scherzo, following this by a magisterial Allegro of symphonic proportions and then setting himself the prodigious task of concluding with two spacious slow movements. . .the one in total opposition to the other? To explain this extraordinary layout Alkan adds a brief

[1] Raymond Lewenthal, *The Piano Music of Alkan* (Schirmer, New York, 1964).

[2] The author gave what he believes to have been the first complete performance in York University on Aug. 10, 1973.

introduction in which he tells us that each movement represents a particular stage in a man's development. The movements are headed *20*, *30*, *40* and *50 years* and although three of them have descriptive titles these are simply to help our understanding of the psychological ideas embodied in the work.

'A great deal has been written about the limits of musical expression' he tells us. 'Without attempting to resolve the far-reaching questions involved I should like to explain why I have given particular titles to these four movements and sometimes used quite unusual terms. Imitative music does not concern us here; still less is this music that seeks to justify itself at an extra-musical level. Each of the four movements corresponds in my mind with a given moment of existence, to a particular mode of thought or imagination. Why not make this clear? The musical content remains unaffected while the performer, without forfeiting his own individuality, is stimulated by the same ideas as the composer; a fact which must surely deepen his understanding of the work'. Alkan concludes by invoking the authority of Beethoven whom, he claims, was engaged towards the end of his life in preparing a catalogue of his principal works, indicating the nature of their inspiration.

Apart from its blazing pianism the two most obvious aspects of the *Grande sonate* that will at once impress the susceptible listener are its bold, far-flung contrasts and the sheer totality of its overall conception. If the proliferation of such directions as 'palpitant'...'diabolique'...'amoreusement'...'Le diable'...'Le Seigneur'...seems to foreshadow the deliberate mystification of late Scriabin, these, together with a certain degree of symbolism and a few pictorial details, in no way diminish the work's organic unity. The second movement is headed *Quasi-Faust* and the third *Un heureux ménage* while the finale bears the ominous title *Prométhée enchâiné* (Prometheus bound). This sombre last movement opens with a pain-wracked prologue full of dark, brooding power, defiant with the rattle of Promethean chains.

Ex.57

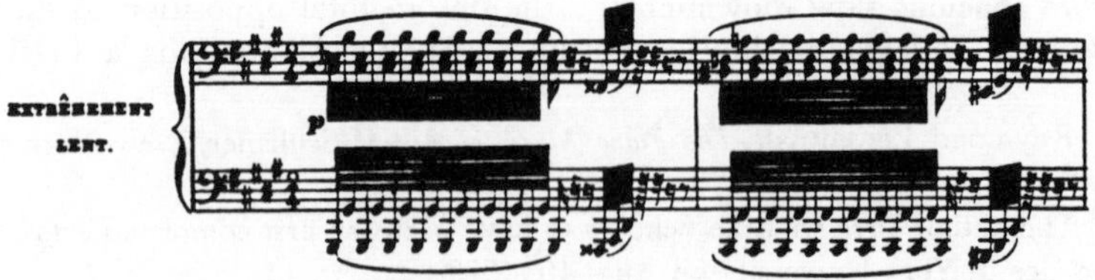

Not only does this final movement cast its fateful shadow across the entire work but it also provides a powerful link with *Quasi-Faust*. In fact the first, second, and fourth movements are all thematically interwoven, but what is still more significant, all four movements form an intriguing key sequence. The first movement opens with a flourish in D major:

Ex.58

The second movement is in D sharp minor while the third and fourth movements are in G major and G sharp minor . . .

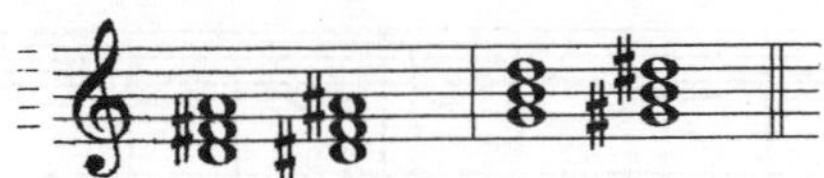

. . . two pairs of movements enjoying the same remote tonal relationship, always moving to the depressive side of the key and each movement slower than the last; a unique example, it would seem, of 'retrogressive tonality'. In performance a considerable breathing space after *Quasi-Faust* should emphasise this division of the work into two balanced halves.

Alkan's first movement is a whirlwind of a scherzo, naïve in substance but unpredictable in manner. It is both the shortest and structurally the most straightforward, being in simple ABA form. But there is nothing straightforward about either the tonality or the rhythm. That opening D major flourish (Ex.58) is constantly rebuked by a stern B minor explosion and the fast 3/4 scherzo rhythm is shot through with fierce cross-accents. The keys change kaleidoscopically before gravitating sharply towards D sharp minor, the remote key of the second movement – the man of thirty. At twenty he is still obviously a pretty restless character, a man of action impatiently feeling his way towards maturity. Suddenly the D major flourish lands on a thumping wrong chord (B flat) rewarded by an abashed pause and apologetic laughter ('ridente') and, second time round, the mercurial figuration takes fright and starts to break up. Some startled F sharps, marked 'palpitant' (breathless), confront fragments of the opening quavers in a 'cat and mouse' game full of questioning silences.

Ex.59

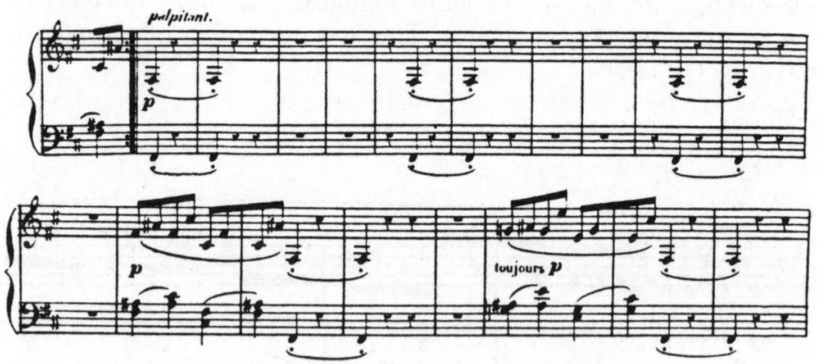

This hushed preparation of fifty-two bars is rewarded by the following ingenuous phrase restricted to notes of the common chord, and we realise the trio is under way.

Ex.60

As our hero of twenty becomes more venturesome that naïve tune, starting 'timidement', gradually sheds its shyness in a flowing melody marked 'amoureusement' and later 'avec bonheur', but it only finds fulfilment in a coda of unsuspected power and excitement.

With a final swaggering gesture marked 'victorieusement' it seems that the youth of twenty has come of age.

Ex.61

Alkan must have felt in a savagely sadistic mood when he followed this taxing first movement by what must surely be one of the twelve most hazardous and tiring minutes in the entire nineteenth-century piano repertoire. But *Quasi-Faust* is far more than a demonstration of transcendental piano writing. An iron discipline controls and contains the black satanic forces that sweep through this gigantic movement. At the centre of Alkan's plan is a chant-like motif very close in shape to the E major fugue subject from Book 2 of the 'forty-eight'.

Ex.62

Lewenthal calls this the 'Redemption theme'. Although it does not reveal its true identity until late in the present movement it wields its influence far beyond the confines of this huge sonata-form structure and is already foreshadowed in that victorious gesture from the first movement (Ex.61, fig.a). Futhermore the Faust motif which opens the second movement is a truncated version of it (note how it is mocked by its own diminution):

Ex.63

The duality of this subject, like the dual nature of man, anticipates by six years a similar duality in the Liszt Sonata in which threatening repeated notes are also a feature of the answering phrase.

Ex.64 Liszt, Sonata in B minor.

Elsewhere, these opening pages, with their bleak harmonies and weird spacings, come closer in spirit to Berlioz in his *Symphonic fantastique*. Soon the Devil makes his meteoric descent. Proud, harsh and implacable he is depicted as an inversion of the Faust motif itself (Ex.63, fig.a), reminding us that temptation comes from within.

Ex.65

Like Liszt, Alkan probably learnt the art of thematic transformation from Schubert's 'Wanderer' Fantasy and the *Symphonie fantastique*, but when we discover that both he and Liszt turn their menacing repeated notes into seductive lyrical subjects the parallel between *Quasi-Faust* and the Liszt Sonata becomes inescapable.

Ex.66a Alkan (1847)

Ex.66b Liszt (1853)

Unlike Liszt, who treats his subject rhapsodically, Alkan is concerned with the severer demands of classical form. His second subject grows into broad paragraphs gradually changing its shape until, finally shorn of its repeated notes, it rounds off the exposition with the following reassuring dialogue.

Ex.67

The white-hot development section, a headlong pursuit of devilish hooves, is led off by the Faust motif set in grotesquely contrasted registers.

Ex.68

The action now becomes increasingly violent and tortured. As the lyrical subject (Ex.66a) makes continued but abortive attempts to assert itself it is marked 'with supplication', 'despairingly' and 'torn apart', before the recapitulation is reached in a passage of unbridled fury. Here the constant crossing of the pianist's arms seems to add a symbolic significance as the Faust motif becomes locked in mortal conflict with salvos of leaping octaves.

Ex.69

Faust survives, and for the first time Alkan applies the brakes in an imposing build-up of orchestral sonority crowned by four huge arpeggios that sweep from the bottom to the top of the keyboard.

Ex.70

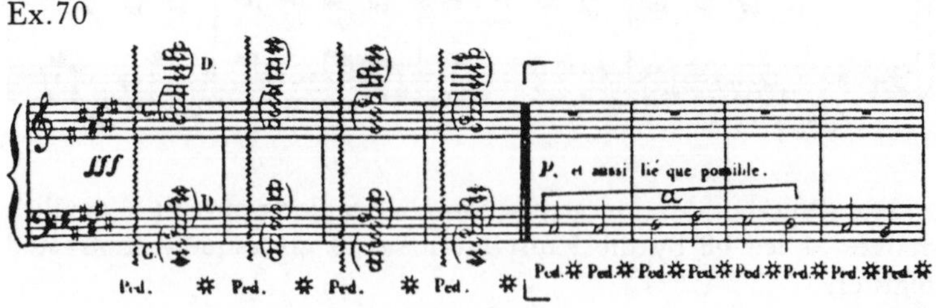

. . . with the devil's assistance they should land on the notes E sharp, F sharp, D sharp and C sharp and, lest we have forgotten that these are the first four notes of the 'Redemption theme' played backwards, Alkan immediately reminds us by spelling them out in their correct order. All is now hushed for the strangest and most complex passage in all nineteenth-century piano music. The chant-like motif (Ex.62) heard complete for the first time, forms the basis of 'exorcism by fugue', its modal flavour adding to the timeless, disembodied atmosphere as voice upon voice weaves a web of mystery. In a riot of sharps, double sharps and one triple sharp this fugal exposition modulates unerringly to the remote key of E sharp major. The final extraordinary combination of six parts in invertible counterpoint, plus two extra voices and three doublings – eleven parts in all – initiates the entry of 'Le Seigneur' (The Lord) symbolised by an open fourth, the outlying notes of the chant.

Ex.71

Lewenthal aptly likens this great pedal point to Atlas supporting the universe. In the wrong hands the whole passage can sound thick as mud, heavy as lead. With bright, clean sonority it should set the heavens resounding to the triumphant peal of celestial bells.

Ex.72

The final pages complete the sonata scheme with a magnificent peroration in which all the warring elements – even the devil himself – are held captive by the omnipresent motif as it mounts inexorably, as a six-note ostinato, to its majestic climax.

Ex.73

For the two massive chords which end this complex drama this great subject, the main-spring of the entire work, is once more reduced to its essential interval of a fourth signifying 'Le Seigneur'.

After the apocalyptic vision comes domestic fulfilment; the man of forty. Alkan never wrote a more unclouded piece than this idyllic expression of supreme joy – a joy which, at the age of thirty-four, he probably realised would be denied him. *Un heureux ménage* (a happy family) is in an expansive ternary form; a gently undulating intermezzo framed by a generous flow of fine-spun melody in which a mood of serene contentment remains undisturbed even during a quaintly picturesque coda. But if formal and emotional simplicity are the natural foil to the hair-raising complexities of *Quasi-Faust* it is equally vital that a movement of comparable size and importance should contain its momentum. Alkan's solution is to build large, unbroken paragraphs from irregular phrases in an ever-expanding design. In the opening song-like section a reassuring answering voice often breaks into the texture.

Ex.74

As the song develops so the harmony intensifies. There is a real Alkan tang about the following 'Neapolitan' inflections.

Ex.75

The central episode introduces 'les enfants' and remarkably gentle, well-behaved children they are as they trip happily along, all three of them, their dulcet voices seldom rising above a whisper.

Ex.76

A recapitulation of the opening song – its contours subtly varied, its harmonies enriched – blossoms into an eloquent duet. As the voices merge in a moment of ecstasy marked 'amoureusement' a clock strikes ten, an hour of strange significance for Alkan. It is said that when he heard the ten strokes he would habitually withdraw, even in mid-conversation (Ex.77).

Ex.77

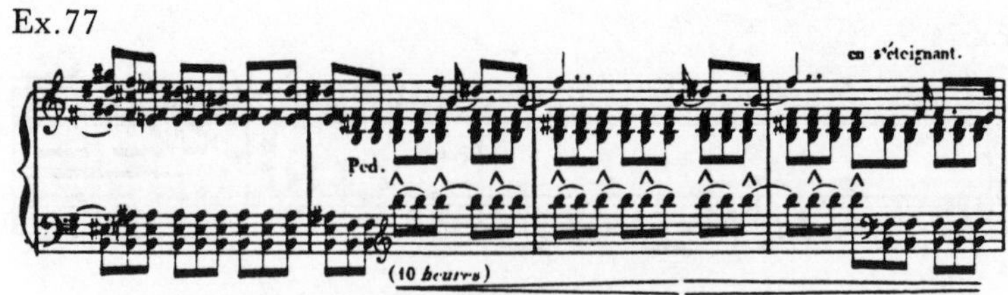

A domestically harmonised hymn-tune announces family prayers. The children join in; the hymn gains confidence. A brief, lingering reference to the opening song provides the cue for an even briefer exit by the children, and the movement ends with a feminine cadence quite impossible to play as Alkan has written it . . . at least without the advantage of a telescopic thumb!

Inevitably Alkan's conception of the ideal marriage must remain a fantasy – a nostalgic dream shattered by the sinister rattle of chains. His final movement *50 ans* is prefaced by seven lines from Aeschylus's tragic poem *Prometheus Bound* (verses 750-754, 1051 and 1091):

'No, you could not endure my suffering.
If only destiny allowed me to die.
To die. That would be the deliverance from my torment.
There will be no limit to my woes while Jupiter's power remains.
I shall live . . .
Look and see if I deserve these torments which I endure'.

The whole legend of Prometheus, the bringer of fire, chained to a rock and enduring exclusion and torture for his gift to mankind must have struck a particularly sympathetic chord in Alkan himself, already set on that lonely path which would ultimately lead him to social and artistic isolation. It generates a rondo of uncompromising severity, harsh as granite, implacable as fate, in which ideas from previous movements are reduced to their very essence. The tempo 'extrêment lent' is equally uncompromising. It exacts an unusual degree of courage and faith to launch and maintain its momentum. The main subject, a sombre augmentation of the Faust motif, appears three times.

Ex.78

It is harshly interrupted by a funereal dotted figure with stabbing accents.

Ex.79

A hymn-like second subject in the relative major is distilled from that 'victorious' gesture which links the opening movements (see Ex.61, fig.a). It is now strangely transmuted, as though in supplication.

Ex.80

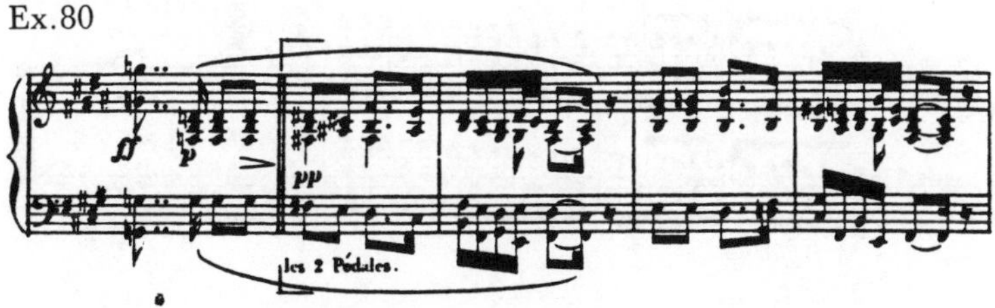

This tenuous shaft of hope is cruelly betrayed when the subject returns in the fateful key of G sharp minor, dwarfed and cowed by its surroundings. At the heart of the movement looms a development of granitic power in which a further variant of the Faust motif grinds slowly downwards beneath the inflexible insistence of the dotted rhythm.

Ex.81

A passage of equally austere grandeur concludes the work as the Faust theme, which has played so vital a part in the whole drama, is finally made to melt into a slowly rising scale. As it mounts, inexorably, through three-and-a-half octaves, smouldering trumpets repeat the funereal rhythm (Ex.77). Implacable, it reaches its apex as two giant chords followed by three quiet ones, all perfectly spaced, end the work in a spirit of mingled defiance and resignation.

Ex.82

Sonatine op.61

When it comes to major works Alkan tended to produce a single example in each genre: one orchestral and one solo symphony, one solo concerto, one trio; and a duo each for violin and cello with piano. A second *Grande sonate* would seem as unthinkable as a second *Symphonie fantastique* and when, at the age of forty-seven, Alkan returned to the form the result was vastly different in kind and scale. During the fourteen years that separate the *Grande sonate* from the so-called *Sonatine* op.61 the composer published much of his most epic music including the formidable minor-key Studies; but from 1857 one finds in such works as the *Trois petites fantaisies*, the magnificent Cello Sonata and the *Esquisses* an increasing economy in texture and style.

With the *Sonatine* this process is taken a stage further. Gone are the dense 'orchestral' sonorities of *Quasi-Faust*, the Symphony and Concerto for solo piano. In their place we find open textures, spare, muscular counterpoint and climaxes of transparent brilliance. Indeed despite, or maybe because of Alkan's ruthless economy, there is hardly a more thrilling example of controlled virtuosity than the impassioned climax that ends its first movement, or the headlong coda in its finale. Although it plays for less than twenty minutes it is in every way a major work. Sorabji describes it as 'vehement, droll, gargoyle-like, childlike and naïve in turn – almost as though Berlioz had written a Beethoven sonata'. If its title is not ironic, and there is no evidence to suggest it is, then this must be the most complex 'sonatina' ever written. Its four movements form a wonderfully integrated and cumulative whole in which not a note is wasted or misplaced.

The first movement, in sonata form, is as subtle in detail as it is bold in outline. It is almost entirely generated from an opening twelve-note phrase which seems to spring, newly minted, from its triadic accompaniment.

Ex.83

The four units that complete its outline – a rising fifth and its inversion (a), a falling sixth and its resolution, a scale fragment and its rhythmic conclusion – all play their part in building larger components. Its immediate continuation already combines these rhythmic and melodic features in an expanding paragraph. Note how the falling sixth (b) is sharpened by the rhythm (d) as it fans out above a persistent inversion of the scale (c).

Ex.84

A more urgent sequel rouses (c) to some anxious dialogue.

Ex.85

Ex.83(c) is now reduced to flickering semiquavers in eager anticipation of a dancing second subject in the bright key of C major but in a deep bass register.

Ex.86

Quite suddenly darker elements erupt in fiery syncopation to end this almost laconic sonata exposition in brilliant concerto style. An equally compact development keeps the pot boiling as further canonic exchanges, derived from the main subject, drive its sequel (Ex.86) into a harmonically dark corner. Its escape route, painful and tortuous, yields the following strenuous series of imitations to bring about an oblique return:

Ex.87

The reprise gives a further twist to the harmonic screw as it hovers, precariously, between the key centres of A and C minor. It recovers its equilibrium, short-circuiting the transition, and to restore the balance we are rewarded by a dazzling coda of unsuspected power and vehemence. Some sonatina!

The directions 'allegramente' and 'con placidità' head the second movement. Their apparent contradiction indicates a finely balanced ambiguity of character and it may shed a fugitive light on the composer's own performance. Alkan is always specific in his requirements. Such titles as *L'inflexibilité* (*Esquisses* no.28) and *Placiditas* (*Préludes* no.9) are self-explanatory. If the further instruction 'carrément', in the former implies a similar inflexibility in *Fuguette* (*Esquisses* no.9), which is also marked 'carrément', the qualification 'dans une mesure très independent' in *Placiditas* can only be a warning by this 'rigorous observer of the metronome'[1] against inflexibility in a piece of Haydnesque innocence. The present movement is an infectious intermezzo in F major, rustic and capricious. Its texture, thoughout, is in three or four independent voices so that no single performance can do it full justice. Successively bland, disquieting, reassuring, wistful and wry, its fleeting moods melt one into the other with volatile facility; its pulse, regular as a heart-beat, must never suggest the soulless ticking of a machine. Structurally it is a kind of self-developing rondo in which the combination of its components

[1] A. Marmontel: *Les pianistes célèbres* (Paris, 1878).

with their sequel promotes constant growth. The four elements that complete its design are indivisible:

Ex.88a

On its final return (Ex.88e) the rondo theme (Ex.88a) has taken the process full circle by combining with its latest progeny (Ex.88d). Thoughout the movement various strands collide within a contrapuntal fabric, rich in pedal-points, to produce such audacities as the following:

Ex.89a Ex.89b

Perhaps most striking of all is the following passage, nineteen bars from the end:

Ex.90

Here, the constant collision of double appoggiaturas, interlocked with their resolutions, produces a sensation of drowsy unreality, but just as the movement seems about to dissolve into evening shadows Alkan impatiently slams the door.

The third movement, a Scherzo-Minuetto in D minor, unleashes a precipitous pursuit of scales accelerated into a nightmare switch-back by the merciless insistence of Alkan's favourite rhythmic device.

Ex.91

The constant foreshortening of phrases heightens their urgency and, at times, frustrates the bar-line.

Ex.92

Stern and impatient, the persistent semiquavers drive headlong into a cadence of three detached chords which is immediately sequestered to form the trio, a piece of quiet self-communion unlike any other music.

Ex.93

One must not be misled by the classical harmonisation; a trifle severe perhaps. Halfway through, it steps down into a world of twilight fantasy, its baffling modulations and suspended tonality made more sinister by a bleak understatement. Note the icy restraint with which Alkan controls his numinous vision.

Ex.94

After an enhanced reprise the trio returns in the reassuring daylight of D major only to be curtly dismissed by its progenitor. Any lingering doubts about the calibre of this so-called 'sonatine' are promptly dispelled by its finale. The arresting opening over a fierce six-four chord, with its obsessive dance-rhythm and stabbing accompaniment, acts like an alarm signal.

Ex.95

It summons from the depths a threatening retinue of turbulent semiquavers and other derivatives which propel the movement on its suicidal course.

Ex.96

Even the resplendent second subject (Ex.97), an outright winner, is quickly swallowed up by converging armies of double notes. Further attempts to gain a foothold at the outset of a tightly-packed development are similarly frustrated and, after an angry outburst, its rhythms re-group as a march (Ex.98).

Ex.97

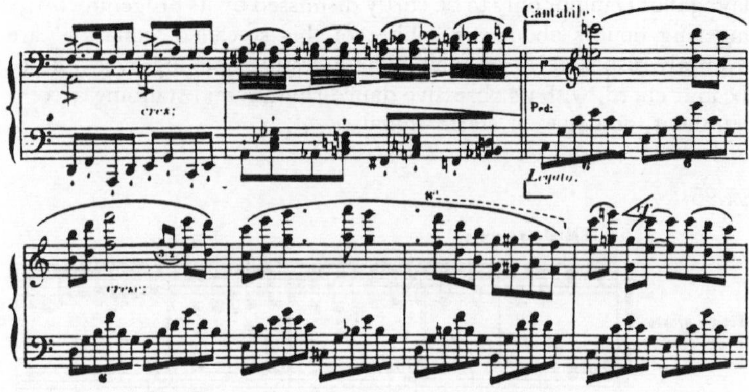

Ex.98

The process is repeated and tension heightens as the opening subject is roused to renewed belligerence.

Ex.99

Unabated, the fury continues as seething diminutions writhe and coil above and below a punched-out quaver rhythm, linking Ex.96 with the march.

Ex. 100

This is true development, cogent and compelling. When Alkan sinks his teeth into a subject he can, with terrier-like ferocity, shake the very essence out of it. This whole passage now boils up to its climax and with a savage lurch from B flat minor to A minor he grabs the reprise by the scruff of its neck, telescopes the action and sends performer and listener, alike, hurtling to its lemming-like conclusion.

7 Trois Grandes Etudes, op.76

The *Trois grandes études pour les mains séparées et réunies*, misleadingly known as op.76, are the earliest of Alkan's major achievements. They first appeared without opus number in 1838, the year in which Liszt completed his twelve *Grandes études*. Although both he and Alkan were, undoubtedly, stimulated by new and undreamt of refinements and amplifications in piano design, the appearance of these two great pianistic manifestos by the two greatest masters of transcendental pianism at just about the same time is a remarkable coincidence, the more so since both composers seem to have been working independently and in comparative isolation. As one might suspect, the two publications, though equally challenging, defy comparison. Liszt's studies, a diabolical expansion of his op.1, are reputed to unleash such appalling difficulties that the composer himself felt obliged to refine their textures and transform their more cumbersome extravagances into his *Transcendental Studies* of 1852. In all fairness one should add that Liszt later withdrew the 1838 versions, looking upon them more as working models for the final definitive version. Alkan's *Grandes études* presented their author with no such problems for, despite their comparable challenge, the far-ranging technical explorations in his twelve *Caprices* of 1837-8 ensured that his knowledge of his instrument and its possibilities was by now absolute. The *Trois grandes études* are designed with consummate authority from their first note to their last, yet they have remained, to this day, a highly specialised and unconquered peak of transcendental pianism.[1]

Although one can trace no record of a public performance of op.76

[1] The young Australian pianist Stephanie McCallum gave what is probably the first complete performance of op. 76 for the Alkan Society in January 1985 and recorded it the same year. My own recording followed in 1987 as did those by Laurent Martin (1990) and Marc-André Hamelin (1994).

no.2, the first study, *Fantaisie* in A flat for left hand alone, was introduced by Busoni in Berlin in 1908. Its form is unique: a spacious prologue linked by its own speeded-up variant to an independent finale; an unlikely enough scheme on paper but completely convincing in performance. Rhapsodic opening phrases are expanded by way of an ecstatic C major gesture into dignified paragraphs. Modulations to the flat side of the key affirm their introductory nature before a brisk adaptation restores the home key and rounds off the section with an exultant dominant flourish and pause. Alkan now tightens his grip. The bass theme that follows (*gravement*, in the minor and in bare octaves), might suggest a military patrol. Stern and laconic it forms the backbone of a terse finale.

Ex.101

On repetition it becomes animated by a dotted rhythm which soon detaches itself into the following unsuspected developments:

Ex.102

Ex.103

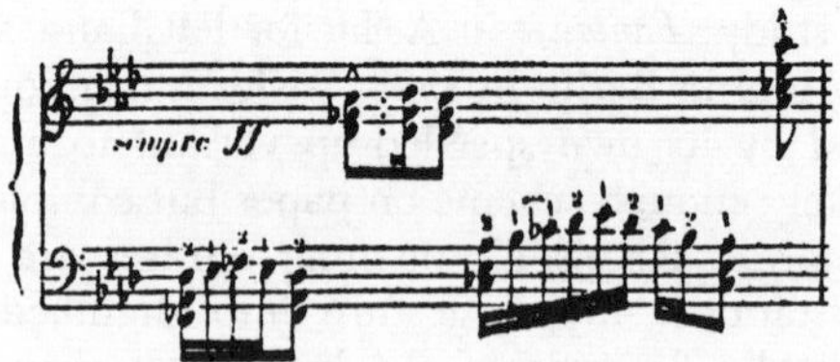

With each return of the main theme the excitement (and technical elaboration) increases until a jubilant stretto and the briefest reference to the introduction brings the work to a majestic close.

Whether or not writing for the hands separately was pioneered by Alkan, and I know of no significant earlier examples, we have in the first two studies of op.76 a seemingly exhaustive exploration of the possibilities imposed by its discipline. Although it might easily be possible for the idle hand to come to the rescue when the going gets tough it is not expedient. The essence of such writing must assume that any two-handed arrangement would falsify and reduce its effectiveness. The left-hand thumb is able to delineate a phrase, to sing out a melody, even to punch out a melodic apex with a projection denied to the two hands combined. This particular characteristic of left-hand writing is exploited to great advantage in Alkan's study as it is in Ravel's Concerto for the left hand, written nearly a century later.[1] The single-handed challenge also creates a sense of strife; of grappling with odds. The writing of Bach, Paganini and Ysaÿe for unaccompanied strings provides the closest parallel. It also imposes momentary rubati and concentrates the right foot in a highly specialised way by training the ear to judge the precise tolerance of pedal-held sound compatible with clarity of texture.

With Alkan's study for the right hand, a still more extended and testing piece than its left hand counterpart, all these characteristics become critical. When Isidore Philipp wrote of 'such difficulties that have reached the utmost bounds of piano playing'[2] he must, surely, have had this piece in mind. It is heroic in proportion, generous in substance and it exacts a daunting measure of technical daring and staying-power from any pianist brave enough to attempt it. One cannot emphasise too strongly the physical advisability of preparing both the left- and right-handed studies side by side and in comparatively short stints. Entitled *Introduction, variations et finale* in D, the right-hand study opens, like the previous study, with an imposing *largamente*, sober, dignified but even more demanding. No two-

[1] A copy of Alkan's study for the left hand has been located in the Ravel archives of the Bibliothèque Nationale in Paris.

[2] In his preface to the Costallat edition of Alkan's works.

Ex. 104

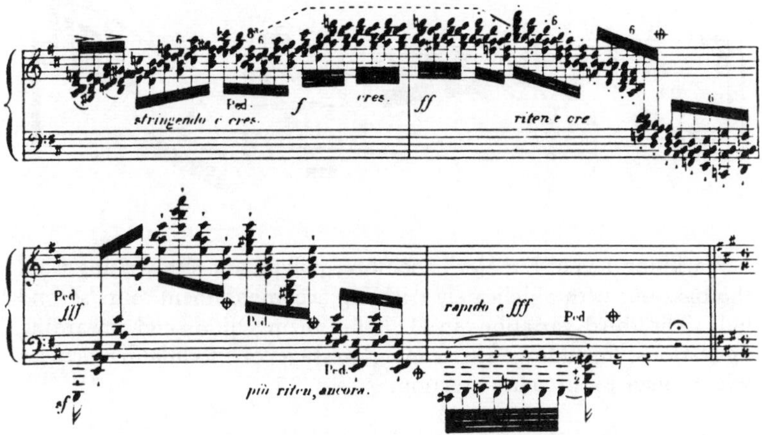

handed adaptation of the following pianistic 'Beecher's Brook' which leads into the variations, could rationalise its challenge.

The variations are on a 6/8 binary theme in A major, its two halves extended to ten bars each, adding breadth to the design. Its ingenuous opening is deceptive, for the second half, while starting in the dominant, contains a startling modulation to C sharp. The simple two-voiced presentation suggests solo violin writing, an impression reinforced by later variations.

Ex. 105

Alkan probably played the first variation, with its light, staccato treatment in constantly shifting registers, from the forearm except for some rapid interjections which require a controlled flick of the wrist.

Ex. 106

Variation 2 is in F major; a sombre, polyphonic study rising from the bass but with a delicately trickling accompaniment to its second half. The third variation, in C, is full of ingenious and rewarding figurations, including this leaping passage of modulating octaves which inspires an acute reaction.

Ex. 107

Both here and in the final variation, which returns to A major, the textures increasingly resemble a bold, pianistic amplification of violin figuration. One can almost catch the swish of Paganini's bow in the following example from variation 3 :

Ex. 108

as in a variety of remarkable invention in the fourth and last variation.

Ex. 109

Ex. 110

Despite his unusually broad hand Alkan was only human and a modicum of rubato seems implicit in this last example lest it induce a sensation akin to medieval torture. The D major finale plunges in with a spectacular apotheosis of the opening bars 'superbamente'. It modulates ecstatically through B minor to E, F, B flat and E flat majors before it is wrenched back to a dominant timp-like roll in preparation for the punishing peroration which combines both themes.

Ex. 111

A remarkable similarity between the final thunderous D major arpeggios spiced with B flats and the end of Ravel's Concerto for left hand (in the same key) must surely be an inspired coincidence!

A turbulent toccata in C minor completes the set. It reunites the hands, locking them together in desperate unison for nearly five hundred bars, with sallies of parallel tenths forbidding all but the largest hands from exploring their vigorous contours. On paper there are few visual landmarks in the implacable stream of wide-spanned semiquavers but any initial impression of mere note-spinning, of some kind of jumbo-sized Kessler study, is quickly erased as powerful sequences build themselves into a strictly organised rondo of some five-and-a-half minutes' duration. The rondo theme itself yields a wealth of figuration, especially in its fourth and fifth bars, earmarked for later development.

Ex.112

Alkan's repetition of the full thirty-one bar theme should not be shirked if its smouldering menace is to make full impact when, later, it flames into a blazing inferno. Third time round its course is drastically cut short with the composer's favourite Neapolitan colouring clinching the home key. There is now an abrupt modulation to the dominant, E flat, and with deft punctuality a melodic outline emerges from the surrounding semiquavers to stake its claim as the second subject.

Ex.113

The exposition ends in brilliant affirmation of E flat, its classical framework focusing attention on the restless central section which follows. After flirting with a sequence of remote keys and dallying with C major it hovers uncertainly on the threshold of E minor from which harmonic limbo the rondo theme claws back its C minor authority. Almost at once the second subject horns in, but in the vulnerable key of A flat, from which unstable tonality it is sucked back into C minor enabling the rondo theme to continue its course in disdainful contempt. Once again the second subject gropes for a foothold, this time in its correct key of C major, but is brusquely swept aside as the rondo theme takes final hold of this tightly compressed reprise. In a dazzling C major coda it is reduced to its essential components before the piece ends with a vertiginous descent in broken octaves, an imperious sweep up the keyboard and a plagal Amen.[1]

[1] The subdominant conclusion to op.76 is the natural outcome of the C to F compass of Alkan's 1838 instrument.

8 Douze études dans tous les tons majeurs, op.35

In their totality Alkan's twenty-four studies in all the major and minor keys op.35 and op.39 embody the fullest realisation imaginable of a lifetime of lonely musical and technical exploration by one of the greatest, but also most isolated keyboard giants of all time. Fétis, to whom the studies are dedicated and who heard the composer play them in private, declared that Alkan, and Alkan alone, possessed the key to their mastery. Certainly, within their 370 or so pages is engraved the most complete evidence of what must have been an almost frightening keyboard command. . . a wizardry that once led Liszt to declare that Alkan possessed the biggest technique known to him. Indeed, several of these works stand on the very threshold of possibility and are only rescued from freakishness by their unfailing expertise. Berlioz has demonstrated how it is quite possible to invent *impossible* piano writing.[1] Everything in Alkan is possible; he simply calls for unrivalled speed in finger techniques, keyboard freedom unaccommodated by rhythmic licence and, in op.39, a physical and mental staying-power unparalleled by any of his contemporaries. All but four of Chopin's twenty-seven studies are modelled on a type of construction used by Bach in several preludes from the 'forty-eight'. Their course is determined by the systematic exploitation of a specific technical feature heard at the outset. In his *Grandes études* of 1839 Liszt replaces this pure genre by displaying his brilliant invention in a series of rhapsodic fantasies. Alkan expands his studies from both types but, as we have already seen, his most free-ranging examples, like op.76 nos.1 and 2, develop their ideas within a classical framework abandoned by Liszt, while the monolithic third study generates an obsessive momentum equally alien to Chopin. It is this unique synthesis of the obsessive and the classical with a transcendental technique that enabled Alkan to create studies of unprecedented size and power in op.39.

[1] *Grand traité d'instrumentation* (Paris, 1843).

The minor-key Studies op.35 are less monumental but still substantial. They were published in two volumes in 1847. The first six pieces, comprising the first volume are pure studies in the Chopin tradition but often expanded in such a way that one might redefine the genre as the systematic *and exhaustive* exploitation of a technical feature. Vol. 2, which is larger, also contains three such studies alongside a robust contrapuntal exercise with an etude-like middle section and quite unexpectedly, two descriptive fantasies which doubtless prompted Hans von Bülow to hail Alkan as 'the Berlioz of the piano'. The composer's ever-tidy mind determines that his op.35 and op.39 studies should proceed through a series of ascending fourths so that the final chord of each piece slots neatly into the new key (A,D,G, etc.). He starts deceptively with a mellifluous but comparatively undemanding prelude, its gently rising terrain giving little warning of the rock-climbing feats ahead. Although Alkan gives this Allegretto in A no title he might well have headed it 'Wallenstadt revisited'. A lazy swing from tonic to dominant above a double drone; an amiable melody rising in quavers and folding, insistently, from F sharp to E – and one cannot escape the impression that *Au lac de Wallenstadt* from the first book of Liszt's *Années de pèlerinage* might have been lurking somewhere at the back of Alkan's mind. But it is towards the end of Liszt's piece, where his limpid accompaniment crystallises into Alkan's widely spread chords, that the resemblance becomes most striking.

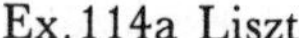
Ex.114a Liszt

Ex.114b Alkan

Here the likeness ends. Alkan spreads his harmonic wings more purposefully as the left hand takes up the quaver motif in a series of bold modulations settling on the dominant. With masterly spaciousness the harmonies remain suspended for four anxious bars before drifting reluctantly towards resolution.

Ex.115

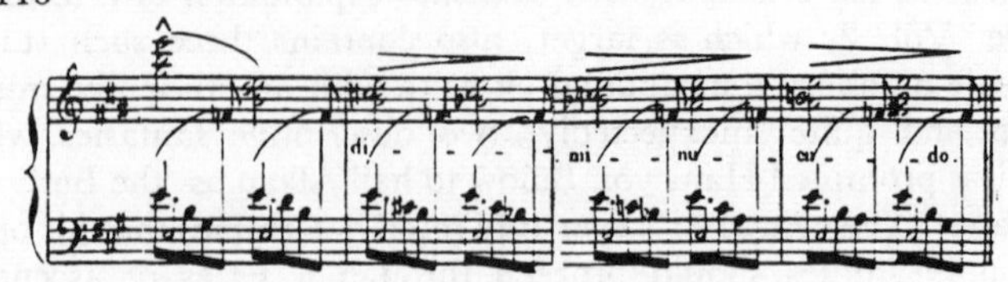

The briefest reprise and a finely-spaced plagal cadence concludes this classic study in third species counterpoint.

The ceaseless pursuit of a staccato tag by its legato shadow provides the motivation for the next study.

Ex.116

Like Siamese twins the motif and its echo remain inextricably bound until the coda becomes too fast for their mutual survival. At first sight this singular device seems meagre fuel to power 180 hectic bars of harmonic intensification; but at the correct speed its persistent gallop creates an irresistible momentum that Busoni and Petri must have relished as they drove the piece to its vertiginous conclusion. Both pianists also included the third study in their repertoire, a richly-textured and inviting Andantino in G. Its suave opening in shimmering octaves soon gives way to more speculative harmonies with just a hint of that darkly-brooding world with which Rachmaninoff would one day become so closely identified. A temporary glance at remoter Neapolitan regions in the glowing key of A flat only serves to nail down the pervasive G major tonality. Now the storm breaks as the left hand leads off in C minor through a series of steeply rising modulations to set the whole piano vibrating in B flat major. This massive octave climax casts its deepening shadow across the reprise forcing it on to the defensive in an anxious G minor. It is, however, soon steered back into the still, quiet waters of G major to recapture the opening mood of calm delight.

Alkan's 𝅗𝅥 = 108, or almost fifteen notes to a second, mercilessly sustained for nearly two hundred bars, makes the 'will o' the wisp' fourth study the most testing exercise in tremolando ever devised.

Ex.117

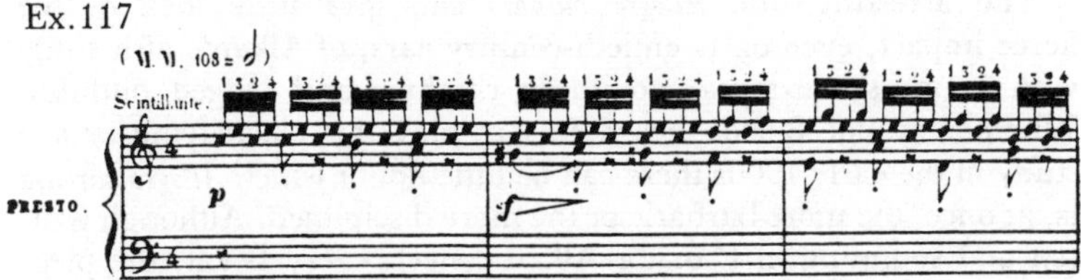

Whereas Alkan's finger substitution 1324 works well for the right hand his left-hand version proves a positive hindrance on modern pianos.

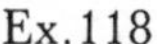
Ex.118

Here most pianists would adopt a constant 21 vibration keeping 3 in reserve for each downward step 3121. Lightness, clarity and artfully placed accents give the impression both of weightlessness and of aerial velocity shot through with fleeting shafts of light. An arresting double episode places a bell-like motif in the extreme treble in confrontation with a stern octave entry deep in the bass. Further antiphonal entries of the octave theme are hastily cut short by restless developments of the opening material involving the following technical freak.

Ex.119

Temptation to rewrite this passage should be resisted; the constant perilous crossing of the hands produces an effect quite different from any more convenient adaptation. This 'false' return is curtly dismissed by a more sonorous version of the bell motif in the exotic key of

E flat. This oblique vantage point enables Alkan to delay the true return by a further twenty-two bars of unresolved suspense to boost the briefest of recapitulations with its precipitous coda.

The arresting title *Allegro barbaro* can give little idea of the fierce impact, even on twentieth-century ears, of Alkan's fifth study with its harsh textures, pounding rhythms and jagged outlines. Whether or not Bartok heard Busoni play this electrifying octave study in the early 1900s there can be little doubt which *Allegro barbaro* is, at once, the more barbaric or the more disciplined. Although written and sounding in F major Alkan cancels every B flat, the piece remaining stubbornly on the white keys, its rondo structure etched out in a series of contrasted modes. Phrygian, Aeolian, and Dorian episodes, in turn, confront the Lydian subject, rousing it to ever increasing ferocity until with a final stampede of semiquavers it explodes into numbed silence.

It was Robert Collet who first suggested that Brahms might have encountered the sixth study, an exercise in flexible contractions, whilst working on his D minor concerto. Doubtless the passage Collet had in mind occurs in the first movement of the concerto.

Ex.120 Brahms

The parallel with Alkan's curious invention is unmistakable.

Ex.121a

. . . And later

Ex.121b

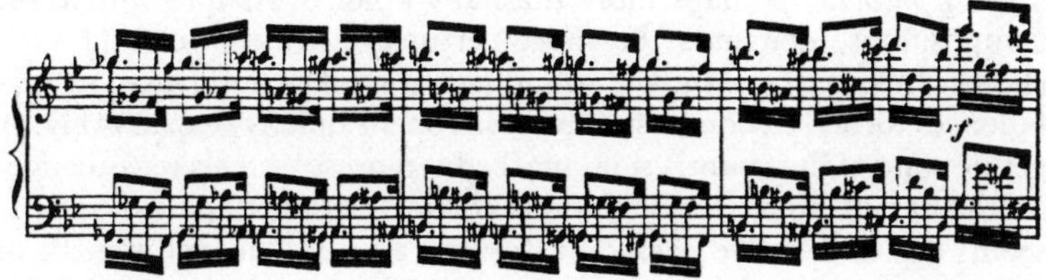

Although a link between Alkan and Brahms might seem unlikely, an appreciation by Hans von Bülow in the *Neue Berliner Musikzeitung* in August 1857 could have drawn Brahms's attention to these studies just at the time he was refashioning the concerto's opening movement from an aborted symphony. I have often felt that the bold, widely spaced texture in Brahms's piano writing and his exploitation of the lowest register has a lot in common with Alkan. Although there is no direct evidence to suggest that either composer knew of the other's existence Alkan's natural son, Delaborde, was on friendly terms with Brahms. The composer of *Le festin d'Esope* would surely have found much to admire in the Paganini Variations, and vice versa. On paper this B flat study may suggest little more than a systematic exercise. A central block of parallel octaves smacks uncomfortably of the Conservatoire. Elsewhere, however, the piece offers many delights; the deliciously perverse harmonisation of the opening eight bars, for instance or, best of all, the artfully deceptive return. Here, after a page of elaborate preparation over a pedal C, with tortured harmonies groping painfully towards the key of F, Alkan jumps the gun by setting us deftly but firmly on our feet in the correct key of B flat.

If the first six studies in op.35 are among Alkan's strictest examples their contrast with no.7 could hardly be more startling. *L'incendie au village voisin* is an unclassifiable extension of the genre, a kind of free-ranging, pictorial fantasy akin to the Lisztian symphonic poem of the succeeding decade. The occasional excursion into a more extravagant realism, with its inescapable twang of silent film music, falls uncomfortably on modern ears and has thrown even Alkan's staunchest admirers into disarray. 'A flat style' declares the French musicologist Georges Beck, 'and effects that are mere noise'.[1] Could this writer have ever strayed upon a pioneering essay on the composer in Bernard van Dieren's *Down among the Dead Men* (1935) in which the piece is described as 'an exquisite tone painting like one of the movements in *Harold in Italy*'? Three years earlier Sorabji had

[1] Preface to *Ch. V. Alkan: oeuvres choisies pour piano* (Heugel, Paris, 1969).

also praised it as 'very remarkable; most original in form'. All the same *L'incendie*, perhaps more than any other of Alkan's important compositions, demands the most persuasive artistry to fulfil such claims. In lesser hands it will sound faded, shallow and naïve, its turbulences turned to bombast. The work opens quietly, expansively. A gentle song of the countryside, marked 'amoroso', steals reassuringly on the ear. Romantic modulations colour the landscape. Nothing it seems can disturb the pastoral calm; not even the distant menace of eight drum strokes. They pass unheeded. The drum insists. The landscape darkens. The drum now raps out its unmistakable warning to the accompaniment of scurrying feet and the whole scene rattles into action as the flames leap, threaten and engulf. This central phase is dominated by an impetuous allegro moderato in 12/8. As the fury intensifies so the alarm signals become more desperate. All at once the distant approach of soldiers promises relief. As they draw nearer fierce trumpets herald action. At first the fire only rages with renewed ferocity but as it continues to mount it is confronted by a series of inexorable advances 'clamando' and with a final defiant burst of energy is brought under control. A few angry eruptions retreat into silence and all is calm. With simple-hearted reverence the villagers join in a six-part *Cantica*.

This song of thanksgiving rises to its climax and the work ends with a majestic plagal cadence.

Ex.122

No-one attempting the following piece should fail to study Raymond Lewenthal's illuminating introduction to it in his invaluable selection of piano works by Alkan.[1] 'This is a perfect work' he

[1] *The Piano Music of Alkan* (Schirmer, New York, 1964).

claims. 'Perfect as music, perfect as the étude it sets out to be.' As music it suggests a love duet with guitar or lute accompaniment. As an étude it deals systematically with the problem of entwining a legato melody within a staccato accompaniment in the same hand. Chopin apart I can think of no other composer who could have wrung inspiration from such a constrictive device. With cunning strategy Alkan introduces the hands successively. Floating airily within a web of delicately plucked accompaniment the right hand leads with an amorous Siciliano. Wistful inflections colour the mood before the right hand makes its graceful exit. The left hand now takes the stage and, in persuasively rising sequences, encourages the re-entry of its partner. Closer exchanges culminate in the inevitable combination of the two hands in ardent fulfilment as they rise to an impassioned climax. But Alkan has yet to play his trump card. A boldly-contrived modulation to his favoured Neapolitan key is made more breathtaking by the pure, diatonic mountain air that surrounds it. This piece is likely to remain a stumbling block to the impatient virtuoso for it requires infinite pains to infuse passion into its thin, pedal-free textures. If it displays Alkan at his subtlest its successor *Contrapunctus*, a ternary structure in C sharp, proclaims its mighty obverse; a monstrous two-part invention with a chattering, canonic trio in staccato thirds. The opening section starts like some craggy academic exercise punched out in double octaves. Later, an affinity with Beethoven's piano writing at its toughest is harshly exacerbated by an ever-widening gulf between the hands. The trio also looks like Beethoven, one of his set of thirty-two variations, but it affords a more immediate parallel with the 'enfants' episode in the *Grande sonate* published at about the same time. Alkan's recapitulations rarely repeat themselves and all but four bars of this reprise are radically refashioned. In place of the vigorous opening the return steals furtively in, stalked by an overlapping trio.

Ex.123

Four bars later the parts are reversed and then displaced, as though shaken out of phase. Strangest of all is a grotesque amplification of the widespread climax now sustained for five extra, strident bars. The piece ends with the briefest reminiscence of its trio unceremoniously dismissed by two sledge-hammer chords. Rugged and uncompromising, *Contrapunctus* is hardly calculated to win its creator new admirers; yet it wields a powerful, if perverse fascination and is unlike any other composition.

The tenth study, in G flat, one of his finest short pieces is entitled *Chant d'amour – chant de mort* (Song of love – Song of death). This grim play on words is complemented by a Latin quotation: 'Et quando expectori lumen, venit caligo' (Just when you expect light there will come darkness). As the title suggests this is a poetic fantasy. It is as original in design and as masterly in execution as it is rewarding to play. The main section, headed *Amor*, seeks to relate two contrasted aspects of love: the passive and the active. Both ideas are unfolded expansively; the first in a melody of classical pedigree, pure as a Mozart aria, the second in boldly-rising contours that spring from a more romantic source. Between their first appearances the mood is momentarily darkened by the enigmatic interjection of a procession of repeated chords. Although it never returns, this one brief appearance, minatory as fate, is sufficient to change the whole course of the work. Undeterred the two principal ideas cajole and pursue each other, the one all tenderness and grace, the other consumed by fervent desire. Twice it rises to a passionate climax. Twice it falls, spent and unfulfilled as uneasy harmonies hover above a deeply ominous vibration. Now comes the master-stroke. The merest wisp of opening melody falters, vanishes and is transformed into a grotesque parody. No description of death could be more graphic than this ghostly caricature, its outlines fractured, its accompaniment reduced to a subterranean rattle. Comfortless, like some macabre funeral procession, it grinds grimly on only to discover final release in a strangely disembodied cadence; a conclusion in which compassion plays no part. From time to time, during a performance of this work the susceptible listener may experience the fleeting sensation of having been here before. If so, a number of quotations, fugitive or hidden within its textures could provide the explanation. The second strain of opening melody traces the unmistakable outline of Mozart's Rondo in D, K485; the chordal transition shelters a cogent phrase from Chopin's 'Raindrops' prelude, an impression confirmed by the insistent upper pedal note, B flat. If, however, the complementary melody also strikes a familiar chord the explanation must be sought nearer home (Exs. 124a/b).

The most surprising of these coincidences occurs in the final *débâcle* where the crushed outline of Alkan's sinister accompaniment to death bears a remarkable resemblance to a rasping ostinato near the opening of Liszt's A major Concerto (Exs. 125a/b).

Ex.124a op.35 no.10

Ex.124b op.35 no.7

Ex.125a Alkan

Ex.125b Liszt

Although Liszt started to sketch his concerto in 1839 it did not appear until 1863, fifteen years after the publication of Alkan's op.35. Whether deliberate or unconscious such cross-pollination between composers in no way affects the value of their work. Alkan's

Chant d'amour remains one of his most original conceptions, made more compelling by the stark simplicity of its presentation. Could it, perhaps, be a musical commentary on Shakespeare's Romeo and Juliet, a tragedy which would undoubtedly have appealed to Alkan's sense of irony and one that had received an historic performance in Paris during his formative years?

'Hunt the melody' might prove an apt title for the penultimate study, a novel and invaluable exercise in the problem of extricating a tune from its surrounding accompaniment. Thoughout its main section a flowing melody lies trapped within a pulsating background so that considerable control must be acquired before it can be made to stand out in relief.

Ex. 126

The chordal pattern itself requires the most delicate handling lest it resemble the mindless beat of a petrol engine. As the piece unfolds the sensitive player will find much to relish in its richly textured harmonies and its picturesque modulations. Half way through the mood darkens for an orchestrally inspired central episode. Here, as though summoned by a trio of 'Eroica' horns, the sombre spirit of Schubert presides banishing the pervasive pulsations to outlying pedal points. Tightly condensed, but enriched by sonorous basses, the recapitulation builds to a sumptuous climax and brief gesture of virtuosity before all is calm. The piece ends quietly with a reminiscence of the opening bars, its harmonies now tinged with melancholy as the melody makes its fugitive escape. The final set-piece, a brilliant octave study, provides a breathtaking conclusion to what Edward Dannreuther describes as Alkan's 'astounding opus 35'.[1] The unfamiliar time-signature, 10/16, so typical of Alkan's preoccupation with quintuple rhythms, adds zest and swagger to its suave contours. At the composer's ♩♪ = 88 the piece becomes a *tour de force* of staying power and we can only thank Alkan for distributing his octaves between the hands and for inventing an ingenious interlocking device in the darkly threatening middle section.

[1] 'Alkan' in *Grove's Dictionary* (London, 1927)

Ex.127

In this way a cumulative momentum may be built up and maintained right through to the grandstand finish.

Pianistically op.35 is an outstanding achievement; the more so when one considers its total independence from the powerful examples by Chopin and Liszt which dominated pianistic development during the nineteenth century. Each of Alkan's studies explores technical specialities quite different from those of his famous contemporaries and each has its own, sharply defined character. Hans von Bülow was quick to discover and proclaim their value; Busoni and Petri included several in their repertoires; yet, despite the novelty and scope of the major-key Studies and a technical challenge equal to that of Liszt's Transcendental Studies, the series seemed destined to become overshadowed by its colossal sequel. Part of the explanation may well lie in its unavailability over a long period when much of Alkan's other music, including the minor-key Studies remained in print. Its recent republication by Billaudot, from the original Brandus plates, should mean that it is now only a matter of time before this indispensable collection will find its place in concert and radio programmes and, more important, attract the attention of the gramophone industry. Only then can an important gap in our knowledge of nineteenth-century piano music be filled.

9 Douze études dans tous les tons mineurs, op.39.

Nearly a decade separates the appearance of Alkan's major-key Studies from the publication in 1857 of their more celebrated sequel. At the time of the earlier series Alkan was still a fashionable virtuoso whose performances, rare though they had become, would be attended by such famous colleagues as Meyerbeer, Chopin and Liszt. By 1857 a combination of professional disappointments and an increasing tendency to reclusiveness had driven him into an isolation which was becoming pathological. In so rarefied an atmosphere it might, perhaps, not seem too fanciful to suggest that this formidable cycle, surely intended to complement the earlier set, must have grown – rather like Frankenstein's monster – far beyond the confines of its creator's original intention. Containing, as it does, a sizeable overture, a monumental symphony and a titanic concerto, the very term 'étude' must seem singularly inappropriate; that is until one considers these works as studies in the translation of orchestral sonorities into their pianistic counterpart. As such they stand alone and may, in some measure, convey the composer's frustration at his inability to mount a performance of his orchestral symphony of 1844. Whatever its origin, however, op.39 is a towering achievement, gathering within its 277 pages the most complete manifestation of Alkan's many-sided genius: its dark passion, its vital rhythmic drive, its pungent harmony, its masterly construction, its occasionally outrageous humour and, above all, its uncompromising piano writing – our only remaining evidence of a technique that caused even Liszt to feel uneasy when playing in Alkan's presence.

The only piece from op.39 which might reasonably be described as a study is the one that opens it. On paper it looks very black, very long and very repetitious. . . not at all encouraging, at least until one looks in disbelief at Alkan's direction 'prestissimamente'. It is entitled *Comme le vent* (like the wind) and like the wind it goes, set at a hair-raising speed of 160 2/16 bars to the minute, or sixteen notes to the second, a kind of nightmare tarantella.

Ex.128

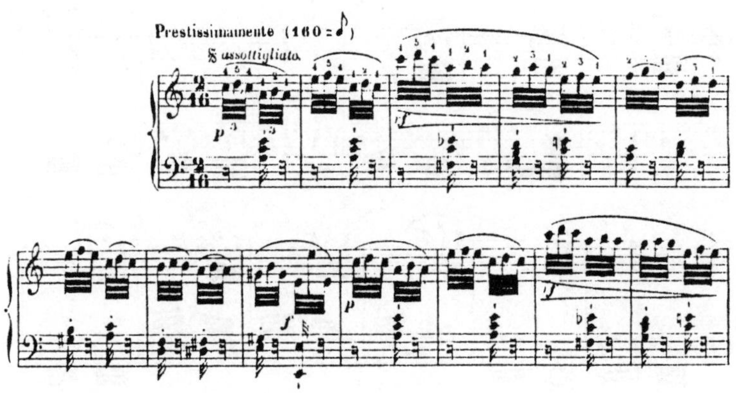

There follow twenty bars of perpetual motion in which a second dancer joins in the fray.

Ex.129

Ex.129 leads off a short development section in which the opening subject is harassed and pursued by its own shadow for, despite its perpetual motion character, the piece falls roughly into sonata form. Its second subject springs to obedience as though at the sadistic crack of a whip.

Ex. 130

Just before that subject returns there is a moment of shimmering anticipation which may sound tantalisingly familiar until one discovers that it is not only the second subject that is being anticipated!

Ex. 131a Alkan: op. 39 no. 1

Ex.131b Sibelius: Violin Concerto

For all its twenty densely packed pages *Comme le vent* only takes four-and-a-half minutes to perform.

En rythme molossique, the second study, is one of Alkan's most original conceptions. Busoni introduced it to Berlin audiences at the turn of the century only to face a stone wall of hostile criticism. The piece is quite substantial, a spacious rondo of some eight minutes' duration and, as its title suggests, rhythm provides the driving force.

Ex.132

A canonic continuation in crude octaves reminds us of Alkan's admiration for the minuet from Haydn's String Quartet in D minor op.76 no.2, also a harsh canon in the same key.

Ex.133a Alkan: op.39 no.2

Ex.133b Haydn: op.76 no.2

After two ruthless pages the mood softens for the first episode but the rhythm remains constant.

Ex.134

For his second episode, in flowing semiquavers, Alkan abbreviates the pervasive rhythm to crotchet-plus-minim before reverting to the original version for an impressive return in which the opening subject is combined in double counterpoint with the second episode.

Ex. 135

Alkan further tightens his recapitulation by cleverly combining both episodes. This sleight-of-hand is so natural that it could easily escape notice.

Ex. 136

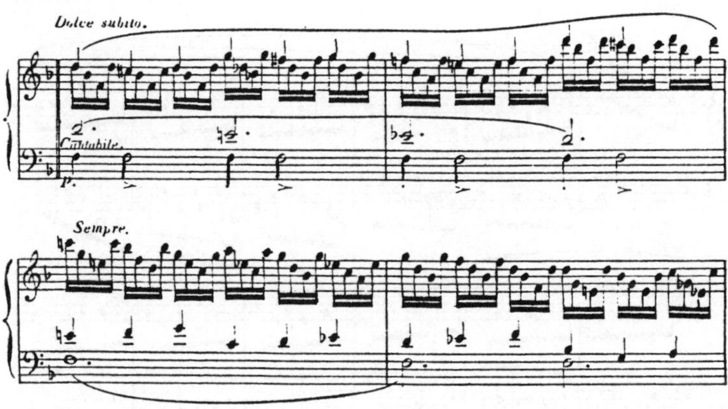

Finally there is a remarkable coda in D major in which the flowing semiquavers are held captive to a continuous molossic drum stroke deep in the bass; but the work ends in D minor with an enigmatic reference to Beethoven's 'Tempest' sonata op.31 no.2 in that key.

The third and shortest of these studies, *Scherzo diabolico*, anticipates Liszt's 'Mephisto' style but is more classical in shape and sterner in character. Although in G minor its leading subject opens with a bold splash of A flat colouring and throughout the main section this constant contradiction of G minor by the Neapolitan sixth, A flat, adds tension to its obsessional drive.

Ex. 137

The same harmonic device also lends a darkly glowing menace to its sequel.

Ex. 138

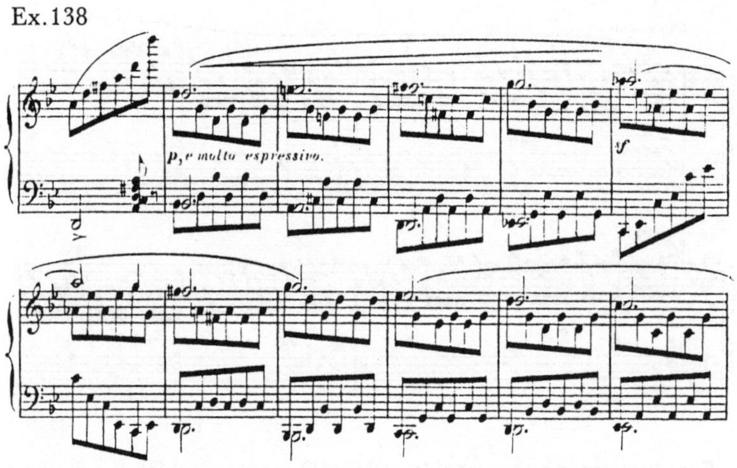

The tempo slackens for a trio in huge fat chords. Then comes the surprise. The scherzo returns but in a breathless whisper and it vanishes, wraithlike, into a sulphurous haze of pedal. Alkan's instruction to hold both pedals throughout this final section is highly imaginative but cruelly exacting, especially on most modern instruments. It should certainly be risked, its success depending on the pianist's ability to tame such wide-spanned velocity into a controlled *ppp*.

Alkan groups the following four studies to form a massive *Symphonie* in four movements. As these are cast in progressively darker keys (C,F,B flat and E flat minor) the work, as a whole, gives the prophetic impression of the 'progressive tonality' of Mahler and Nielsen. The whole notion of a 'symphony' for piano seems to present a paradox, but Alkan knew precisely what he was doing. His unique keyboard sonorities are deliberately orchestral but untranslatable. Their effect is the result of a subtle illusion rooted in the very nature of the piano and its evocative power. No orchestration of the following passage in Alkan's *Symphonie* could produce anything like the cumulative power engendered by the piano.

Ex. 139

That powerful anticipation of a similar ostinato in Brahms's C minor Symphony is from the coda of Alkan's first movement. But

Alkan's tonal conception is equally orchestral, illuminating the discipline imposed on symphonic forms by the very nature of the classical orchestra. Note, towards the end of the finale, how the 'timpani' with their fixed tonic and dominant notes hold a rebellious orchestra to ransom.

Ex. 140

The structural stability imposed by the drums is a totally symphonic procedure. A sonata would behave differently.

The four movements of Alkan's *Symphonie* are closely integrated one with another but, unlike so many cyclic works of the nineteenth century, they never parade their badge of identity. Their relationship is of a subtler order, one that enables each movement to retain its personal independence. Those drum strokes are derived from the finale's opening subject:

Ex. 141

But this is itself a parody of the preceding movement, their outlines being identical.

Ex. 142 Minuet

This close family relationship can be traced to the parent theme which opens the work and which dominates its first movement. That Brahmsian ostinato (Ex. 139) is a development of it. This is how it first appears, sombre and dignified as it rises and falls beneath a pulsating accompaniment.

Ex. 143

Those rising and falling semitones (a) answered by falling whole-tones (b) form the mainspring of this tightly organised movement and subtly relate to the second group to its parent stock.

Ex. 144a

Ex.144b

The exposition ends with a bold cadence theme in which the main subject is mirrored deep in the bass. Notice too how the whole passage is then inverted and how that rising semitone cuts impatiently into the texture as though warning us to make the repeat.

Ex.145

Following the exposition repeat Alkan's main subject stands host to a number of conducted tours, each revealing new aspects of those now familiar rising and falling intervals. Here the falling second (Ex.143b, fig b) is pressed into service beneath a fluttering descant.

Ex.146

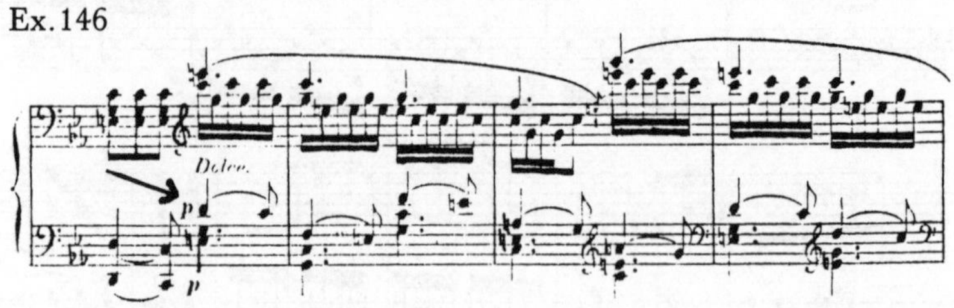

The upper voice provides a further link, this time with the slow movement. It was first suggested earlier in the exposition:

Ex.147

But is destined to complete its emancipation as the trio in the second movement.

Ex.148

After generating a final voyage of discovery, the development section suddenly explodes into a climax of such complexity that one wonders if Alkan kept a spare hand up his sleeve. Certainly ten fingers seem a frail substitute for full orchestra in the towering sonorities that follow this fourfold entry of the main subject.

Ex. 149

The recapitulation is at first tightened, then expanded and after an impassioned coda the movement ends darkly and inconclusively with seven enigmatic chords.

The contained sorrow of the *Marche funèbre* which follows comes close to the mood of Berlioz in its expression of universal, rather than private grief. Its haunting middle episode (Ex. 148), so full of unforeseeable yet inevitable twists of harmony, also grows – despite its long-range origin – from the final phrase of the main section.

Ex. 150

In a brief, but arresting coda, the dramatic simulation of muffled drums rouses a further confirmation of that relationship of rising and falling semitones (Ex. 143 a, fig a) which adds such unity to the entire work.

Ex. 151

The third movement is a craggy Minuet, full of jagged cross-rhythms and punched accents.

Ex. 152

It is marvellously concise; note the following stark inversion.

Ex.153

Despite a ländler-like continuation, in three-bar phrases, the movement has a cosmic swing, almost like that of a Bruckner scherzo. It is remarkable how this rough-hewn music becomes magically transmuted when its opening interval is turned into a haunting melody for the trio.

Ex.154

To bring about the return Alkan reverses the process by syncopating the melodic permutations of three notes.

Ex. 155

Raymond Lewenthal has described the relentless finale as 'a ride in Hell'. Its diabolic onslaught, however, should not blind us to the severe logic of its inexorable progress. It exploits two pianistic ideas. The first, in leaping octaves, is at once developed contrapuntally.

Ex. 156

It later chases its tail in a kind of spectral double counterpoint.

Ex. 157

There is also a mercurial quaver motif, breathtaking at Alkan's 𝅝 = 96!

Ex.158

The composer's mastery of his material is nowhere better demonstrated than in the subsequent development in which both elements are hurled into the structural and emotional apex of the movement. Its explosive climax yields the following remarkable chord, unclassifiable yet utterly logical in its context.

Ex.159

. . . But the nightmare ride continues. Not even the ferocity of that last climax can check its momentum as it rushes headlong to its destiny.

Studies 8, 9, and 10 form the consecutive movements of the celebrated Concerto for solo piano, an even grander conception than the preceding *Symphonie*. It has been described as the nineteenth century's answer to Bach's Italian Concerto. In both works a single player is invited to imitate the impression of solo and massed forces. But the Alkan is on a colossal scale; an isolated masterpiece which cannot be sensibly compared with any other work. The impact of a public performance, an understandably rare occurrence, is immediate and overwhelming; yet its latent depths and subtleties, especially those relating to the overall tonality of the first movement, only become apparent on repeated hearings. Although the huge, classical design of the first movement takes nearly half-an-hour to unfold it is totally convincing. There are two reasons for this: the underlying unity of its principal themes, and a key structure that is basically simple and sound. Like so many other minor-key works (in this case it is in G sharp minor) it concerns the establishment of the relative major, B, its subsequent annihilation and the quest for ultimate fulfilment in the tonic major. This is the tonal backcloth against which the first movement's titanic struggles are enacted.

Alkan requires from his performer the projection, sometimes simultaneously, of two personalities. Throughout the work the directions 'tutti' and 'solo' indicate the opposition, interaction and fusion of two contrasted styles of piano writing, the grandly orchestral and the eloquently pianistic. Taken out of its context, the following example of Alkan's pianism at its most lyrical could be mistaken for Liszt:

Ex. 160

but with its continuation Alkan's thumb-print becomes unmistakable in a persistent bell-like dissonance that clouds the texture.

The orchestrally-conceived writing in the tutti sections is chunky and uncompromising, yet it is equally valid. Its effective layout for the keyboard is immediately demonstrated in Alkan's magnificent handling of the concerto's opening pages. This 'orchestral' ritornello introduces four powerfully contrasted themes in the order in which they might appear at the outset of a symphony. But a concerto is not a symphony and Alkan leaves us in no doubt about the true function of his ritornello, which is the formal and psychological preparation for the first dramatic event: the entry of the soloist. Its opening subject compels attention.

Ex.161

It can change its shape without losing its identity.

Ex. 162

Notice, also, how that striding accompaniment arches up to clinch the climax of this powerful tutti.

Ex. 163

Two further ideas complete the quartet of subjects which generates this most expansive of concerto movements. A lyrical second subject in E major is adroitly turned back to G sharp minor in severe confirmation of the ritornello's introductory nature.

Ex. 164

Finally there is the most 'happy and glorious' consummation of Alkan's pet rhythm:

Ex. 165

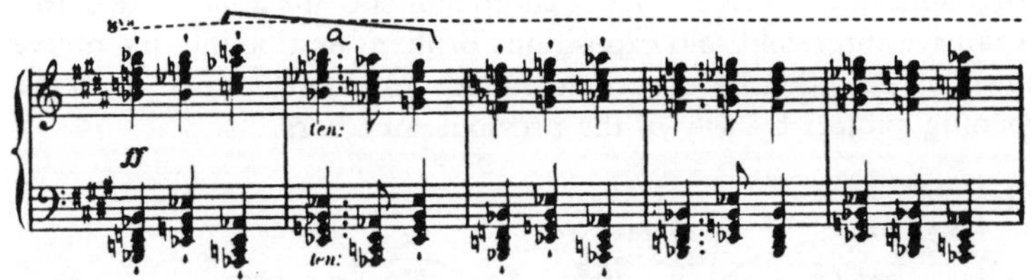

As the opening tutti draws to its close the atmosphere becomes hushed, but alive with anticipation. At the precise psychological moment the soloist enters, establishing his identity in a series of rhapsodic descents.

Ex. 166

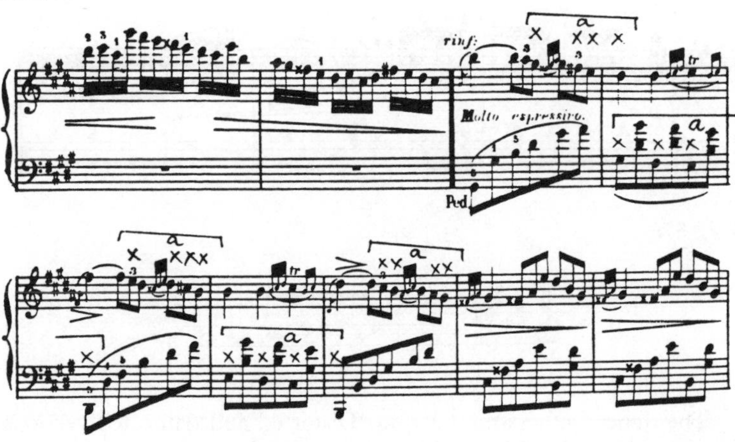

The free, improvisational character of these phrases is deceptive. Their origin in the dynamic opening subject provides an oblique example of the long-range thematic unity derived from its falling fourth (see Exs.161, 165, 166).

Having left his visiting card the soloist proceeds to do what the massed forces of the orchestra could never do; to escape from the gravitational pull of the home key. Brilliantly embroidering the main subject he gradually shifts the tonal centre to B major in which key he can luxuriate in the lyrical second subject (Ex.164). The ensuing paragraphs establish the new key as a base for increasingly romantic excursions until a fierce B major chord launches the final phase of this expansive three-fold solo exposition. Brilliant and taxing, its motive power is provided by a curious dotted derivative, drawn from the opening subject by way of the previous four bars.

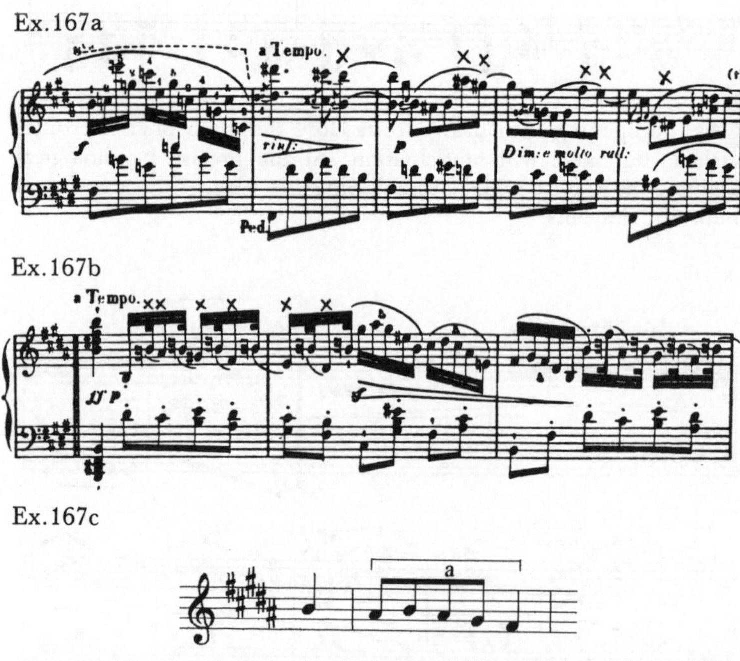

The dance gathers momentum. Distorted and truncated versions of the principal subjects vie for our attention. As the excitement reaches fever-pitch the orchestra, so long held back, crashes in, in triumphant command of B major; and then disintegrates. For a few bewildering moments we find ourselves suspended in a kind of harmonic no-man's-land as a handful of instruments enter in search of the key.

Ex.168

The soloist supplies the solution by planting down a firm G natural in the bass in preparation for the relaxed lyricism of Ex.160 in this remote key of G major. But B major is not so easily dislodged. As it tries to steal in by the back door, however, its tonal reality is challenged by the new key 'G' . . . and this, of course, is the explanation for that strange, bell-like G natural in its texture. A brusque reminder of the dotted motif in the still remoter key of B flat finally dismisses B major and once more the soloist enters, this time modulating romantically to give a first, momentary vision of the promised land of G sharp major. This whole episode, which precedes the development section, forms the tonal fulcrum of the movement. The remaining action is concerned with turning vision into reality.

Reluctantly the tonal centre drifts away from G sharp and we soon find ourselves caught up in stormy developments of the main subjects notable for the appearance of the following dignified descant to Ex.164.

Ex.169

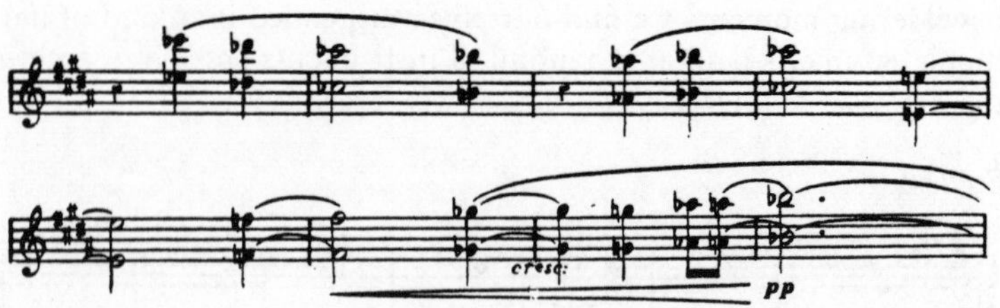

At the heart of the section, and central to the whole gigantic plan, stands a passage of strange and disturbing power. For sixty-six bars the action becomes frozen as the second subject (Ex.164) gropes forlornly around a hypnotic repetition of the key-note G sharp in the rhythm of the first subject. Its bleak textures, persistent pedal note and grinding tritone may transport us to the arctic world of Sibelius's Fourth Symphony; but it also seems to contain the brooding power of dark forces biding their time. Suddenly they are unleashed in a cataclysmic eruption which is sustained for five turbulent pages to bring about the return. The fury of this crisis casts deep Neapolitan shadows across the recapitulation, only to be dispelled by the arrival of the second subject, now gently confident in its key of fulfilment, G sharp major. As confidence increases nothing, it seems, can check its impassioned progress; that is until a still, small voice, in the shape of an almost inaudible chorale, says 'No'.

Ex.170

The lyrical phrase reasserts its passionate plea; again the chorale says 'No'; but this time in the fateful key of G sharp minor. For the last time the lyrical phrase enters; hovers, undecided, then starts to break up, giving way to a monumental coda. Here, against a background of diabolical repetitions, Alkan mounts his final climax in which all four themes are reviewed and integrated as the movement ends in a magnificent blaze of G sharp major.

The following guide may help the unfamiliar listener to keep his geographic bearings during a performance of this vast movement.

Orchestral Ritornello in G sharp minor	3½ mins.
Solo Entry (rising scale) in three-fold Exposition	7½ mins.
A Embroidery of 1st Subject	3 mins.
modulating to:	
B 2nd Subject in B major	2 mins.
C Brilliant final section featuring a dotted derivative of the 1st Subject	1½ mins.
leading to:	
Triumphant orchestral affirmation of B major: cut short.	
Central lyrical Episode (Tonal fulcrum)	1½ mins.
Development Section	6⅜ mins.
Powerful return and reflectively modified Recapitulation	6 mins.
Coda, characterised by diabolical repeated notes rising to peroration of principal themes	4 mins.

The two remaining movements are far easier to describe, their complexities being psychological and pianistic rather than structural.

The Adagio, in C sharp minor, introduces two contrasted ideas. The first, with its drooping outlines, suggests a lament.

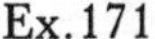
Ex.171

Its sequel starts beguilingly:

Ex.172

But its continuation becomes discursive, its mood more fugitive. Regretful, anxious, reassuring – all in turn – it nevertheless manages to engender a brief sense of well-being before the skies darken for three powerfully-orchestrated entries of the lament. The third entry, which is canonic, erupts in a series of explosions punctuated by funereal drum beats. This grimly realistic episode, over which the spirit of Mahler seems to preside, returns pianissimo in the final, desolate bars.

Alkan calls his finale 'Allegretto alla barbaresca' but it sounds uncommonly like a polonaise. It is in F sharp minor, the key of his friend Chopin's most cogent polonaise; but, unlike the Chopin, this finale is carried through with a fiendish singlemindedness which rides rough-shod over every obstacle. Its main subject is animated by an incisive rattle on its up-beats.

Ex.173

Rapped out with steely ferocity, or reduced to a lightly brushed shimmer, it provides the driving force as Alkan's wild dance gets under way.

Ex.174

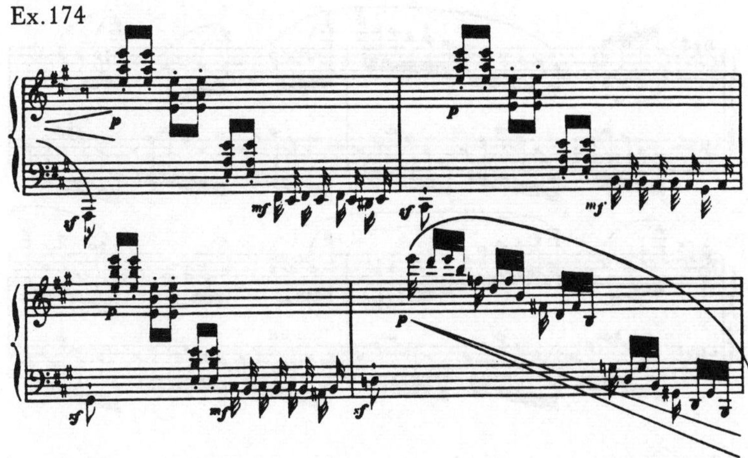

It invades every corner of the development section becoming a continuous murmur as it goes to ground beneath right-hand lamentations.

Ex. 175

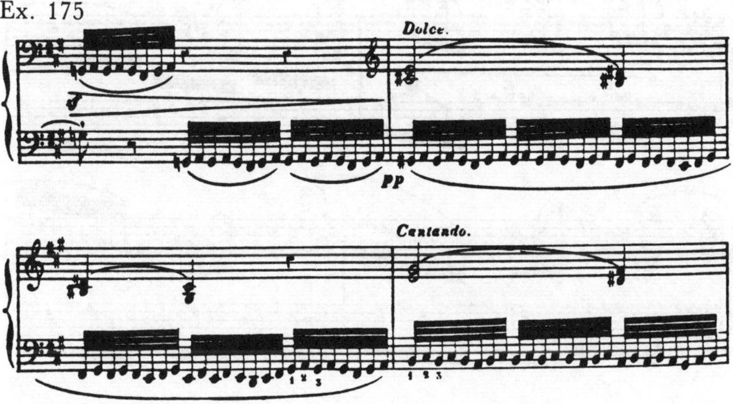

By way of contrast there is this gracefully-spun second subject:

Ex.176

Both subjects become cleverly combined in Alkan's tightly compressed recapitulation:

Ex.177

and reduced to their stark essence at the outset of a spectacular coda.

Ex.178

The finale opens obliquely with a 'Rakoczian' flourish on D which is immediately contradicted.

Ex.179

This added dimension of tonal conflict between D natural and C sharp, the minor second, is of course the very stuff Alkan's music is made of. It lends a wistful inflection to the following cadence:

Ex.180

and it conveys an almost oriental flavour in the coda:

Ex.181

but it is only towards the end of the development section that the smouldering conflict between D and C sharp truly ignites.

Ex.182

Such are the basic ingredients of Alkan's *Allegretto alla barbaresca*. Alone they seem quite harmless; but their combination unleashes the dynamic energy that gives this finale its dark, elemental power and sustains its ruthless momentum.

Apart from the seventy-two page first movement of the Concerto the penultimate study entitled *Ouverture* is the longest, taking about fifteen minutes to perform. It is also the most rarely heard. This may be due less to its lack of surface glitter than to the problem of placing it sensibly in a normal concert programme. Although it makes a marvellous opening item it takes courage to meet its challenge 'cold'. On the other hand its massive style, while tending to dwarf succeeding pieces, is not ideally designed to end a recital. This is a pity, for *Ouverture* is a unique work; stern, sombre and impressive, and despite its cruel technical demands it is intensely rewarding to study. The following example, from the majestic opening section, gives some idea of the implacable piano writing.

Ex.183

Maestoso 100 = ♩

ff

sf

cresc.

sf sf sf sf

With such abrupt changes of register the innocent ear might easily mistake what it is hearing for a duet arrangement of an orchestral score. The overall shape of the work is also unusual though it bears a superficial resemblance to the two early *Concerti da camera*. Like these works *Ouverture* falls naturally into three linked sections. The opening is preludial. It contrasts that powerful procession of repeated chords with an austere dotted motif in the bass.

Ex.184

The process is repeated, but second time round the dotted rhythm gains ascendancy, banishing the repetitions to the extreme bass where they flutter and give way to a childlike theme and variation. The variation casts its magic spell on the upper reaches of the keyboard before melting into silence. Four bare octaves, repeated ominously in the bass, remind us of the opening as they announce the third and most extended section, a fiery Allegro cogently developed from three striking themes. The first raps out its challenge in great fistfuls of chords.

Ex. 185

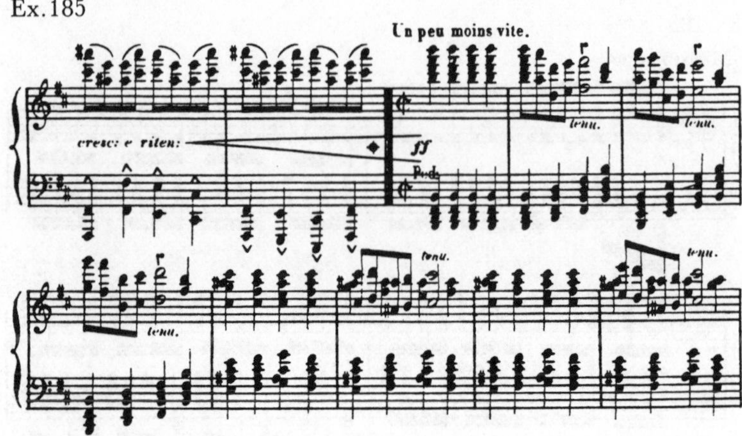

The second, in D major, weaves patterns of figure-eights in octaves.

Ex. 186

Other double-note features, some of them immensely taxing, lead to the sombre third subject in the remote key of G minor.

Ex. 187

A terse development section soon has the figure-eight subject chasing its tail in contrapuntal earnestness.

Ex. 188

The plot thickens as the figure-eights go into partnership with the sombre third subject.

Ex. 189

Sensing a conspiracy the powerful main subject (Ex.185) twice flexes its muscles in anticipation of the return, only to find itself confronted by the new combination.

Ex.190

This failure of the main subject to mount its return reverses the order of events in the recapitulation and when ultimately it crashes angrily in its fury is quickly turned to resignation as, deep in the bass, Ex.187 makes its final bow. The pace slackens but just as the work threatens to yield to the forces of darkness it is rescued by a vehement 6/8 coda in Alkan's brilliant hunting style. It is, in fact, an ingenious transformation of material from the first section.

Ex.191a

Ex.191b

Indeed, not a note is wasted in this closely organised work and even the final, sharply-etched chords outline the principal subject of the Allegro but with the hunting motif having the last word. The orchestrally-conceived piano writing throughout *Ouverture* shows Alkan at his most uncompromising; yet in its context it is absolutely valid and could only have come from the pen of a great performer.

For his final study Alkan chose the most succinct way of summarising his technical invention by displaying it in a classically strict set of twenty-five variations on an original theme.[1] Traditionally the work is thought to represent various animals from Aesop's fables. Raymond Lewenthal discerns 'all manner of creeping, crawling things' within its colourful pages. In reality certain variations offer more than a hint of the animal world; yet the impression remains sporadic and the idea of a 'carnival of animals' in no way explains the title *Le festin d'Esope* (Aesop's feast). Sir Roger L'Estrange's *Life and Fables of Aesop* offers a more plausible theory.[2] He relates how Aesop's master, Xanthus, invited several philosophers to supper on two consecutive nights. Xanthus instructed his slave to provide a banquet first from the choicest and then from the basest of all foods. On both occasions Aesop brought the same delicacy to his master's table, an ox-tongue but prepared in every possible manner; sliced, dressed, fried, boiled, etc. In this way Aesop was able to demonstrate to his master's distinguished guests the absolute power of the word; its responsibility for all good and for all evil in the world. This was 'Aesop's feast' and Alkan not only displays every conceivable manner of treating his theme, from the obvious to the transcendant, but he juxtaposes the complete spectrum of emotions from the naïve to profound. All the same, Alkan's family has retained a penchant for animals and birds and it would be surprising if a work concerning Aesop should not contain some references to the animal kingdom such as the instruction 'abbajante' (barking) and the unmistakable roaring of lions in the 23rd variation:

Ex.192

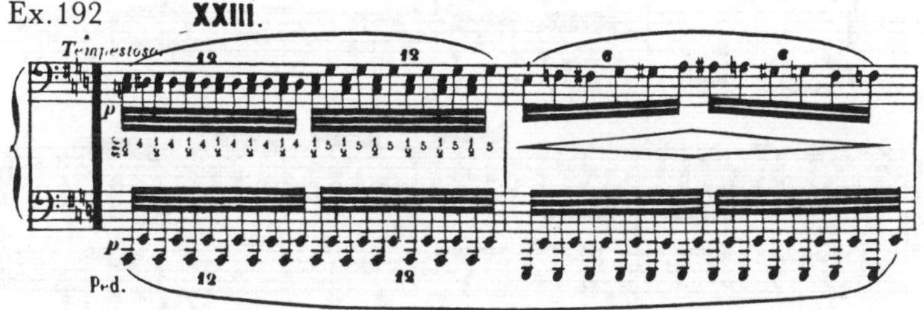

[1] For a further discussion of the ethos of Alkan's theme see Chapter 15, page 240.

[2] Kahn & Averill, London, 1970.

Elsewhere the work seems to evoke echoes from grand opera, military advances and retreats, a hunt and a musical-box as well as a bewildering variety of motifs and textures to remind us of Mendelssohn's claim that the language of music is too precise for words. What makes *Le festin* a work of outstanding genius is the tight discipline that rivets such seemingly disparate elements together. The starting instruction 'senza licenza quanlunque' ♪ = 126 (without any rhythmic licence whatsoever) imposes a fierce continuity that falls little short of sadistic. Alkan's theme is one of those maddening tunes one seems to have known all one's life but cannot identify.

Ex. 193

Var. 1 immediately takes up the challenge of that final phrase and hammers out the theme in the bass.

Ex. 194

That typical overlapping and concentration of ideas makes one wonder why Alkan did not turn more often to variation form. In

Aesop's Feast he snatches hungrily at the varied opportunities it affords him to parade his rhythmic and harmonic specialities. Note the malicious glee with which he will keep the listener harmonically poised on one leg – stork-like – for a complete variation.

Ex. 195

The tenth variation, marked 'scampanatino' (the chiming of tiny bells), could suggest either a musical-box or the distant sound of sheep-bells as they tinkle away regardless of the shifting harmony.

Ex. 196

. . . if so, Alkan's startling contrast of the extreme registers of his instrument in Var.13 could depict a more sprightly beast.

Ex.197

The only variation, however, which makes a specific reference to animals is no.22 when, at the repetition of a hunt, the dogs break loose clearly on the scent.

Ex.198

The rhythmic ingenuity with which Alkan systematically tightens his ejaculation 'abbajante' (barking) will invoke a ripple of laughter from most audiences. A similarly spontaneous reaction is also likely to greet those many other ingenious pianistic effects that led Peter Stadlen to describe the work as 'lovingly . . . and I might add knowingly stuffed with every conceivable device of keyboard fiendishness.' Amidst all this excitement Alkan offers one brief moment of respite in the shape of a supplication ('preghevole'); a plea that falls on stony ground as the ensuing variations (17 and 18) lead off in a blood-curdling torrent of velocity that seems to turn Paganini's perpetual motion into a preliminary canter! Their sequel (var.19)

bewitches the ear while confounding the eye as the unmistakable outline of Alkan's theme emerges from a confusion of flying octaves.

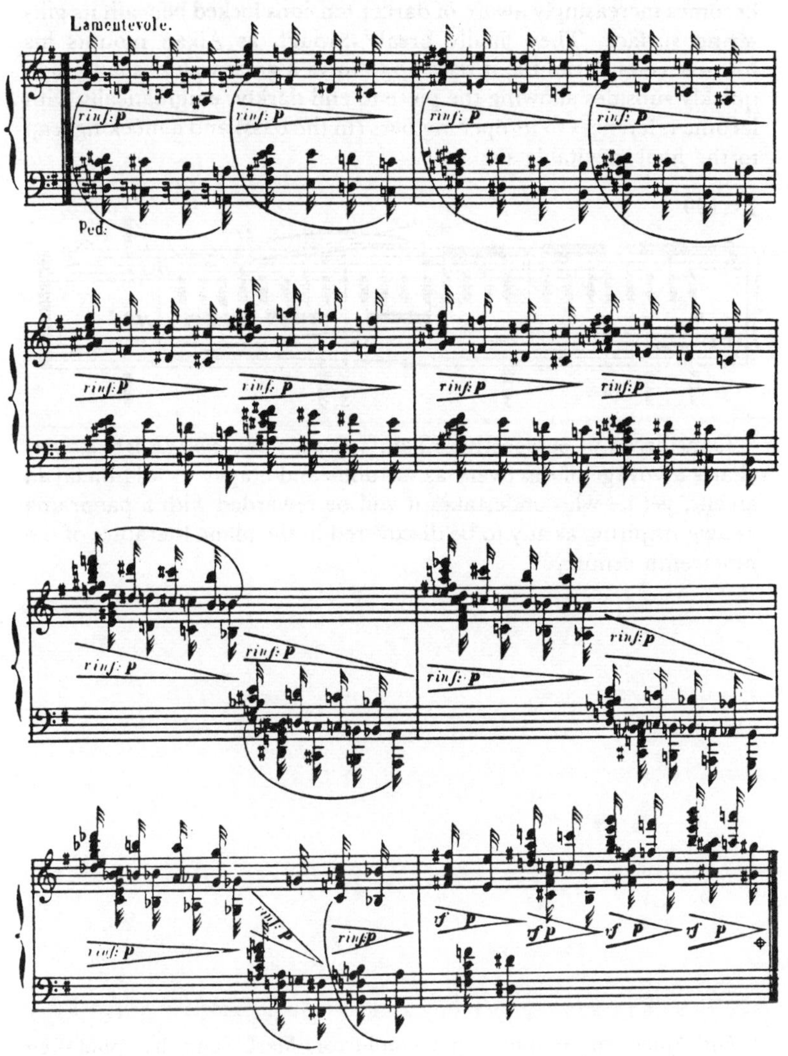

Such are the pungent ingredients of *Le festin d'Esope*; but the work is far more than the sum of its brilliant detail. As it progresses one becomes increasingly aware of darker tensions locked beneath its glittering surface. They finally break through as Alkan mounts his massive coda. Granitic, it rises up to form a great wall of sound then quickly subsides allowing the piece to end darkly, enigmatically with laconic references to its opening bars (in the bass) and a mocking leap to the final inevitable slap.

Ex. 199

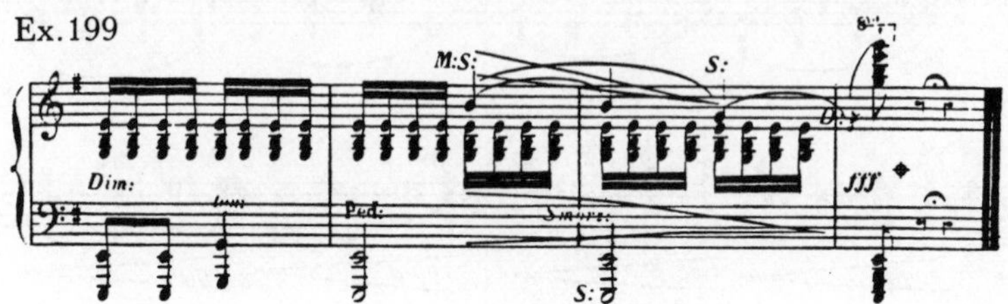

Considered in perspective Alkan's *Douze études dans les tons mineurs* charts a voyage of discovery as tortuous and craggy as a Himalayan ascent; yet he who undertakes it will be rewarded with a panorama as awe-inspiring as any to be discovered in the piano literature of the nineteenth century.[1]

[1] The American composer and conductor, Mark Starr, has published brilliant orchestrations of three major works from op. 39: *Symphonie, Ouverture* and *Le festin d'Esope* (Carl Fischer Inc., New York, 1986). A slightly condensed version of the first movement from Alkan's solo concerto, arranged for piano and orchestra by Karl Klindworth, is in the library of the Royal College of Music, London and University of Iowa, USA. Klindworth's arrangement has recently been recorded (see Discography).

VARIATIONS QUASI FANTAISIE,

Composées

Pour le Piano,

SUR UNE BARCAROLLE NAPOLITAINE,

et dédiées à

Miss Mary Windsor;

Par

C. V. ALKAN,

PROFESSEUR HONORAIRE DE L'ECOLE ROYALE DE PARIS, ET
MEMBRE DE LA SOCIÉTÉ DES ENFANS D'APPOLLON.

Ent. Sta Hall.

Op. 16. _Nº 6.

London. Printed by R.COCKS & Cº Publishers of the Works of
Chaulieu, Czerny, Herz, Hummel, Hunten, Mayseder, Pleyel, C. Pixis, Weber, &c.
20, Princes St. Hanover Sq.re

10 Miscellaneous piano music

Apart from a lost orchestral symphony, two early concertos, compositions for organ or pedal-piano, a little vocal music and some highly characteristic chamber works, the overwhelming mass of Alkan's production is for keyboard alone. Beside his major compositions and collections of smaller pieces there remains a sizeable amount of independent piano music. This includes further examples of the étude type we have already encountered, alongside marches, caprices and various dance forms which are often arranged in pairs or grouped in threes, as well as several lyrical pieces and the odd paraphrase. Appearing at regular intervals between the early 1830s and the composer's involvement in his *petits concerts* in the 1870s they contain some of his most imaginative creations and a few of his worst. Unfortunately the background to their original publication rather than the relative merits of certain compositions determined their republication in the early 1900s. Perversely enough two or three of Alkan's poorest compositions have remained stubbornly in the catalogue at the expense of some of his finest.

In winnowing the chaff from the wheat one must start, chronologically, with the publication in 1834 of three salon pieces by the London firm of R. Cocks & Co. Their only musical surprise is provided by the last piece which anticipates, by some twenty-five years, Liszt's use of a Neapolitan barcarolle in his Tarantella from *Venezia e Napoli*; but note how Alkan's extension of these familiar phrases enhances their wayward indolence.

Ex.200

The comparatively high opus number of these compositions, op.16: nos.4, 5 and 6 (the first three probably never existed) was clearly devised to add substance to the list of honours, such as the 'enfants d'Apollon', displayed on their showy covers. The pieces themselves sound suspiciously like an overflow of juvenilia that the twenty-year-old composer might have kept up his sleeve (or in his portmanteau) and their sole surviving interest is focused on their dedications to various 'Wives (or daughters) of Bath' implying, as they do, an influential entrée into that aristocratic English society. Could it have been Alkan's illustrious pupil, the Duchess of Montebello, one wonders, who provided the key? As dedicatee, her name is boldly engraved on the title page of Alkan's *Rondo brillant* op.4, published in Paris just at about the time of his first visit to England. As Hugh Macdonald discovered, her name before marrying the Duke was Eleanor Mary Jenkins.

Le preux op.17 (the valiant knight) is a hefty concert study full of peremptory gestures but undistinguished in content. A massive octave peroration marked 'du bras' confirms that by the early 1840s Alkan was playing such passages from the forearm just as Liszt, judging by the scoring in his concertos, must have done. *Quasi-caccia* (in hunting style) op.53 and *Une fusée* (a rocket) op.55 both date from one of Alkan's best periods, the late 1850s but both are also blighted by the paucity of their substance. *Quasi-caccia* shares both key (A major) and manner with the third piece in each set of *Chants* and might even have been originally intended for the op.65 series. *Une fusée* opens most invitingly with a 6/8 Andantino recalling the whimsical second movement from the composer's Cello Sonata but it leads to a long and, for Alkan, comparatively uninventive toccata. The following growling tone-cluster near the end looks and sounds rather nasty.

Ex.201

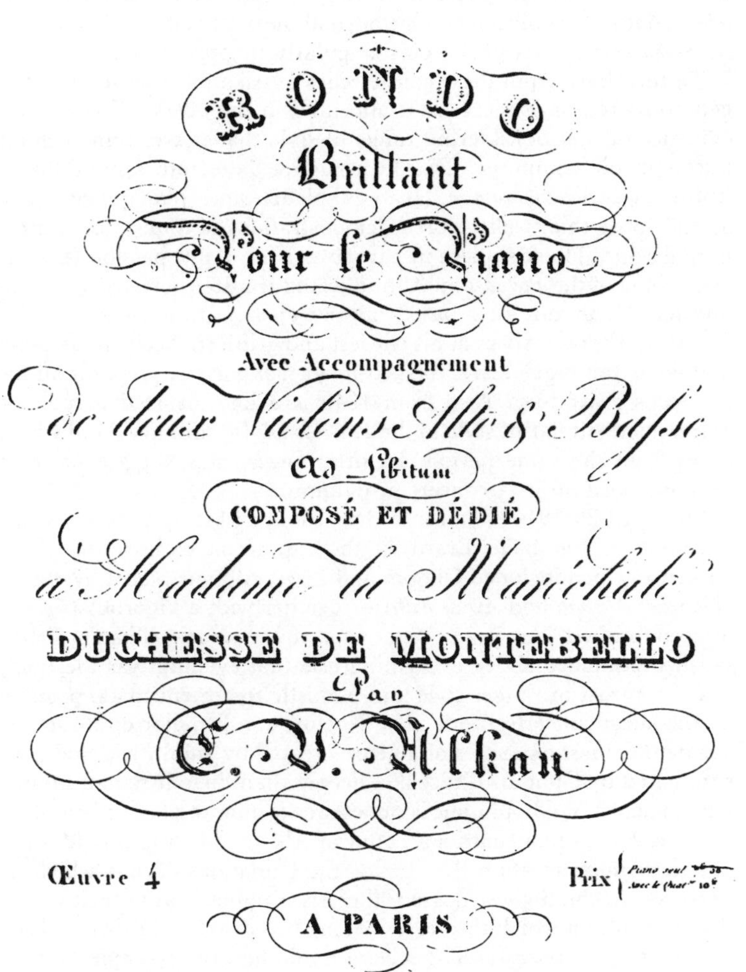

RONDO

Brillant

Pour le Piano

Avec Accompagnement

de deux Violons Alto & Basse

Ad Libitum

COMPOSÉ ET DÉDIÉ

a Madame la Maréchale

DUCHESSE DE MONTEBELLO

Par

C. V. Alkan

Œuvre 4

Prix | Piano seul 38 | Avec le Quat.^{re} 10^{f}

A PARIS

chez Henry LEMOINE, Profess.^{r} de Piano, Rue de l'Echelle, N.º 9.

1126. H.

Of the two *Fantasticherie* dating from Alkan's last period, the first, with a rondo subject in canon, is the stronger. The second spins out a few routine technical formulae beyond their capacity so that its title '*Chapeau bas!*' (Hats off!) seems singularly inappropriate.

To turn back from these sterile relics of Alkan's later years to the generous stream of pieces that appeared in the 1840s offers further evidence of that bewildering range of style that makes him such an unclassifiable composer. Two little fugues date from around 1840. Entitled *Due fughe da camera*, 'Jean qui pleure' and 'Jean qui rit', they are far more than well-tailored demonstrations of four-voice contrapuntal skills. The first piece in particular has a grave passion familiar from some of the *Préludes* op.31 and would transfer perfectly to string quartet. 'Jean qui rit', based on the *brindisi* from Mozart's *Don Giovanni*, displays Alkan at his wittiest and grittiest. Accidentals come and go as the fugue starts to shed its formal garb in preparation for a virtuosic wind-up. Also from 1840 is a light-hearted march for piano duet, similar in style to the *Pas-redoublé* for military band which dates from the same period. Its title, *Finale*, may suggest its most effective position in a concert programme.

On April 29,1844 Alkan introduced four of his most recent compositions in the Salle Erard to the rapturous enthusiasm of an audience which included Chopin and Liszt. All four pieces, *Nocturne*, *Saltarelle*, *Alleluia* and *Air de ballet* – together with a vigorous *Gigue* – were published that year. What must have struck Alkan's distinguished audience above everything else that evening was the bold, sharp contrast in range, style and pianistic treatment made possible by the latest concert-grands. The Nocturne in B major op.22 stands beside the finest examples of a genre created by John Field and consummated by Chopin. If it strikes deeper than Field it remains purer and cooler than Chopin but is no less rewarding to play or beguiling to hear. Henri Blanchard's account of Alkan's playing provides the key to its interpretation: '. . . beside the gradations of tone which he possesses to the highest degree, there is a fullness and sensitivity – that rare gift on which the art of making this instrument sing and stir the emotions is based'.[1] The scheme could hardly be simpler: a limpid melody framing a persuasive middle section with the ingenious combination of both ideas in its closing bars (Ex.202).

In absolute contrast *Saltarelle* op.23 exploits the extreme registers of the latest seven-octave Erards with their piercing high treble and drum-like bass. Played in the strict French 'style-sévère' of which Alkan was a leading exponent, its characteristic mixture of charm and ruthlessness transcends the facile material. Its pianistic fireworks

[1] *Revue et gazette musicale* (May 13, 1849)

Ex.202

and hair-raising skips soon made it a favourite concluding item in the recitals of Alkan's younger contemporaries.

If *Saltarelle* demonstrated the scintillating brilliance of the new French grands, *Alleluia* op.25 projected their massive sonority. High repeated chords and huge bass support evince all the fervent enthusiasm of its title and a cadential obsession with the augmented triad rivals Scriabin in ecstatic energy. Although op.24 links the *Gigue* and *Air de ballet*, both in the 'style ancien', one could scarcely imagine a stranger pair of bed-fellows, this dyspeptic two-part invention and its rondo-companion, four-square, stern and disproportionately long. The *Gigue* with its knotty counterpoint and driving rhythms is well worth playing whereas the *Air de ballet* does not live up to its sententious opening, sounding rather like a routine arrangement of orchestral music.

Also dating from 1844 are three more substantial pieces. *Le chemin de fer* op.27, which depicts a railway journey, is probably the first ever example of 'mechanised' music. It is a brilliant concert study of the toccata genre. A fuliginous stream of semiquavers flickers and surges above the hypnotic beat of wheel-upon-track. From time to time a confident song springs up to confront the danger and anxiety of rail travel in the 1840s. There is even a strident, stylised realisation of the locomotive's whistle. Clusters of acciaccaturas, Alkan's speciality, add extra thrust to the relentless pace which never slackens until a final deceleration brings the momentum to a controlled standstill.

Alkan also performed a contrasted pair of marches before a group of colleagues in 1844. They were not published until 1846 when they appeared with a dedication once more to his pupil, the Duchess of Montebello, as *Marche funèbre* op.26 and *Marche triomphale* op.27 (sic). The funeral march is one of Alkan's most impressive short pieces. With chilling effect it rises from the depths, stark in outline, spare in texture – desolate – hypnotic. Twice the procession approaches;

twice it recedes as it is guided to its destiny by oppressive pedal points, muffled drums and tolling bells. *Marche triomphale* is a huge, swaggering affair, mildly oriental and of pulverising virtuosity. Other oddments of the period include a fiercely oriental *Bourrée d'Auvergne* op.29 with an arresting bagpipe episode. It later degenerates into mere note-spinning before finally committing compositional suicide in a conventional octave build-up, chordal acciaccaturas and all... a pity; the first half with a few minor harmonic adjustments might easily pass for Bartók and must remain unique for its time. *Désir*, a more homely miniature, is rescued from complacency by some surprising turns of key. Alkan's most substantial work for one piano, four hands was also announced as early as 1844. The *Fantaisie sur Don Juan* consists of five variations on 'Venite par avanti' from Mozart's *Don Giovanni*, with a majestic introduction and, like Liszt's *Reminiscences de Don Juan* of 1841, a brilliant finale on the Don's drinking song from the first act. Alkan, however had already based his fugue *Jean qui rit* on this famous 'explosion of licentious energy in which the whole essence of the Don is summed up.'[1] The variations, in alternating minor and major keys, are cleverly contrasted. The fourth variation, a fierce toccata four octaves deep, provides a splendid foil to the dark colouring of the last variation, an expressive adagio. The work contains few of Alkan's harmonic audacities. Instead, it relies for its effectiveness on the formal balance and a masterly handling of the medium which is never allowed to become overloaded. In particular the variations in minor keys rivet the attention by their wealth and variety of texture. For this work Alkan invented novel key signatures for minor keys. G minor, for instance appears as

Happily this particular innovation was not perpetuated.

The decade that followed the appearance in 1847 of Alkan's *Préludes, Grande sonate* and major-key Studies contains a gap in publications of some eight or nine years. In all probability the flood of works issued by Richault in 1857 had been accumulating during the whole of this scantily documented period in the composer's life. In an appreciative letter, dated July 25, 1847 and prompted by Fétis's review in the *Revue et gazette musicale* of the *Préludes* op.31 and *Marches* op.26 and op.27, Alkan goes on to tell the older musician of further works he hopes to see published. These comprise compositions several years old as well as works just finished. 'This does not include chamber music' he adds. 'This I am reserving for later on; but piano works whose development is quite unlike those you have so kindly described. They include a long sonata, a large-scale

[1] H. Berlioz: *Memoirs*, tr. D. Cairns (London, 1969), p.103.

scherzo, an overture for piano and studies, some of which are fashioned on a rather large scale.' The mention of 'an overture for piano' ten years before the publication of *Ouverture*, no.11 of the minor-key Studies makes one wonder how many of these later studies were already simmering in Alkan's mind alongside the major-key Studies.

Besides the *Grande sonate* op.33 and the major-key Studies op.35 1847 also saw the publication of an independent piano work, probably the large-scale scherzo referred to in Alkan's letter. Both its key, B minor, and a hunting-style coda suggest that this odd-piece-out might originally have been projected for the minor-key Studies and subsequently replaced by *Ouverture*. Entitled *Scherzo focoso* op.34 it gives the impression of having been torn off in one fell swoop. At Alkan's ♩. = 120 it provides a remorseless path to pianistic immolation for all but the most invincible techniques. Obsessional torrents of semiquavers, frequent crossings of hands and inflexible leaps offer no respite but, unlike many other very taxing pieces, this one both looks and sounds as difficult as it is and its coda generates a final fling of virtuosity to end all such displays. Nevertheless one can but wonder if the substance quite justifies its elaboration. Only a courageous performance might tell. The following resounding subject provides its corner-stone.

Ex.203a

The publication in 1857 of the minor-key Studies, the first two collections of *Chants* and the *Sonate de concert* for cello and piano was accompanied by a shoal of smaller piano compositions in all shapes and sizes. Possibly the most characteristic and admired of all these works are the *Trois petites fantaisies* op.41. Their lean textures, stark outlines, motor rhythms and grotesqueries seem more attuned to twentieth than nineteenth-century ears; Prokofiev is perhaps the composer who most readily leaps to mind. Despite their modest title they are quite substantial pieces of some six minutes each. The first, *Assez gravement*, has the dry tang of a classic wine. It contrasts two ideas; the one anxious, questioning; the other, a drum-like motif which forms the persistent accompaniment to a flowing melody in right-hand octaves. Later the harmonies intensify as the song rises to a brief, impassioned climax before emancipating itself from its drumming accompaniment in a final page of magically soft chords prophetic of Debussy.

Ex.203b

The second, *Andantino*, grows from its innocuous beginning like some unruly child whose sly ways, wry humour and 'deformed' gait are only kept within bounds by the most rigorous discipline. Who else but Alkan – or Beethoven – could have wrung inspiration from the following rhythmic hiccup?

Ex.204a Alkan: *Trois petites fantaisies* no.2

Ex.204b Beethoven: Sonata in G op.31 no.1

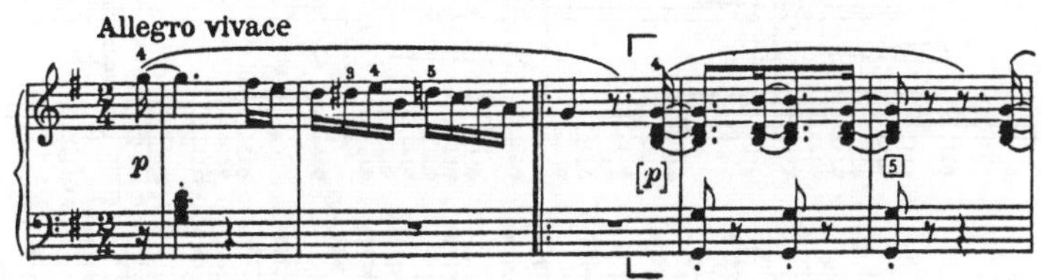

The third *Fantaisie* is a fulgurating toccata loaded with dynamite and powerfully developed from three motifs: brusque, martial and belligerent in turn (Exs.205a, b and c).

Ex. 205a

Ex. 205b

Ex.205c

The above, whose bass may be punched out with a vertical thumb, forms the basis for threatening advances beneath a scurrying derivation of Ex.205a.

Ex.206

Thoughout the piece each appearance of Ex.205a signals a heightening of tension until in an incandescent coda it assumes a jaunty 6/8 to flout its impassioned surroundings.

Ex.207

This final *Fantaisie* might be described as a study in paradox. Cogently argued yet unpredictable; stern but self-mocking; its kaleidoscopic shifts of emphasis are both consumed and regenerated in a single, controlled burst of ruthless energy.

Like Schubert, Alkan wrote a great many marches. Of the two sets published in 1857 op.37, entitled *Trois marches quasi da cavalleria* (three cavalry marches) is for solo piano while the op.40 set is for piano duet. The first march from op.37, in A minor, affords a striking instance of Alkan's genius for transmuting platitudes into visions by generating unsuspected power from the commonplace of musical small change. Driven by a rhythmic ostinato (a) and such baleful derivations as (b) and (c) it gathers momentum in a series of assaults

until the triplet boils up obsessionally, its displaced harmonies conveying the impression that the whole fabric has been shaken by a minor seismic tremor. A fanfare-like trio hammers out its challenge in resonant chords before moving in on itself to reveal a deeply glowing episode on the dominant of G minor. For one brief moment the poetry of personal involvement stands witness to the heartless terror that must engulf it as the sinister march returns, rising above a stubbornly insistent low C. To play this passage in octaves, on the assumption that a restricted bass register forced Alkan to repeat the C, robs it of its trenchant fatalism. Alkan had been making full and imaginative use of the lowest notes of a seven-octave keyboard since its introduction in 1844. Ex.208 shows the last four bars of this grim passage.

Ex.208

The remainder of the reprise is short-circuited and polarised by three blaring fanfares in B flat as the triplets gather and re-form for a final cavalry charge. For the last time they mount their onslaught, rising wave upon wave above the implacable ostinato; but these are not, as Constant Lambert would have it, waves beating angrily on the breakwater of our intelligence but a rising tide that carries all before it.

Neither of the other pieces from op.37 catches fire in the same way. The third is a fleet-footed scherzo, its trio sounding like exotically spiced Mendelssohn; while the following pianistic absurdity in no.2 makes us wonder if Erards were experimenting with a double keyboard.

Ex.209

The *Trois marches* op.40 for four hands, designed to be played with his friend Ferdinand Hiller, should attract the attention of duettists for their wry caricatural humour. The first abounds in abrupt modulations, pedal points and ostinati while its trio is a grotesque parody of the 'Marche-militaire' style, interchanging gruff imprecations with impudent, fife-like responses. The second is notable for its imposing four-handed sonorities, whereas the third contains one of those maddening tunes that will deny its victim a moment's peace until purged from the system.

Of the three remaining solo pieces from the mid-fifties the first is idiomatic but flawed, the second unobtrusively impressive and the third unique. The sensitive musician will find himself returning again and again to the opening pages of *Réconciliation* op.42 with renewed delight as he re-explores their harmonic twists and turns. Later Alkan abandons his lilting 6/8 for a 5/4 *Zorcico* complete with trio. Despite the return of the 5/4 trio to conclude the recapitulation the two main sections refuse to gel. *Salut, cendre du pauvre!* op.45 (Hail, ashes of the poor!), on the other hand, would make an ideal opening piece in an Alkan recital. It conveys its dark message in a most dignified and direct manner and is sumptuously laid out with imaginative exploration of the lowest register, with characteristic drum effects. The abrupt 'take it or leave it' style of *Minuetto alla tedesca* op.46 will hardly commend itself to those in search of a soft-centered romanticism; yet its blunt manner and pulsating energy act as foils to the vehement passions they also hold in check. Particularly arresting is a long crescendo over a lumbering pedal point. Perhaps

Mozart was the first composer to squeeze such anguish from crushed harmonies above a dominant pedal.

Ex.210 Mozart: String Quartet in D minor K421

The fierce impatience of Alkan's sequence stands in sharp contrast both to Mozart and to Mahler who rediscovered its touching pathos in the scherzo of his Sixth Symphony.

Ex.211a Alkan: *Minuetto alla tedesca*

Ex.211b Mahler: Sixth Symphony

A violent wrench from F minor back to A major in Alkan's trio drives him to the frontiers of credibility in the following enharmonic conundrum designed to trip the doughtiest sight-reader (including, no doubt, his friend Ravina, the work's dedicatee).

Ex.212

With one exception the remainder of Alkan's short pieces for solo piano were published in 1859, the year that brought forth such diverse masterpieces as *Benedictus* op.54 for pedal-piano and the Funeral March on the Death of a Parrot for choir and woodwind.

Alkan's allegiance to the era and style of Louis-Philippe never faltered. The grosser vulgarities of the Second Empire, with its outdated jingoism and military pomp, was probably one of the factors that drove him from public life. The two *Caprices* op.50 oppose the romantic illusion of military ambition and its sober reality. *Capriccio alla soldatesca*, described by Sorabji as 'a brilliant piece of grotesquerie, caricatural and mocking', parades the outer trappings of military life. Quicksteps, brazen bugle calls, a self-pitying interlude and a jaunty 6/8 tune of quite outrageous banality marked 'crânement' (swaggering) set the stage for a long and exciting cavalry charge. After a series of frenzied advances a rumbling pedal point arouses our expectancy. Strident fanfares signal our hero's imminent approach... a moment of hushed wonder...and he is here 'quasi conquistatore', swollen with triumph, his huge fat tune celebrated in the blazing splendour of C major. The excitement is sustained for three brilliant pages before collapsing into the self-pitying episode. Now comes a singularly bizarre example of Alkan's imaginative use of the extreme registers in a ghostly parody of a tune that is itself a caricature. The coda, stealthily retreating to the accompaniment of muffled drums, ends tragically, its simulated piety enhanced by a bald, plagal cadence marked 'religioso'.

The companion piece *Le tambour bat aux champs* op.50 no.2 (the drum beats a salute for the dead) appeared a few months after the Capriccio as an independent 'esquisse' before the two *Caprices* were sensibly linked as a pair. It inspired the following claim from Bernard van Dieren. 'I seriously doubt whether there is another short composition which, in an equally simple form, conveys so overwhelmingly a sense of concentrated tragedy.'[1] Stark, hypnotic, nightmarish and obsessed by the most basic of drum rhythms, this piece is uncannily

[1] *Down among the dead men* (London, 1935)

prophetic of Mahler who was born a year after its publication. No analysis can explain the alchemy by which this rare compound is fashioned from the rawest of base metals; how its extraordinary atmosphere of foreboding is nourished and sustained on a diet of tired clichés and sterile formulae. Only twice are the drum beats momentarily silenced as the following glum refrain limps painfully along with grinding inner octaves adding a harsher dimension to its world-weary resignation.

Ex.213

Much of the cumulative power of the piece must lie in its hypnotic rhythmic persistence and in a polarised tonality which moves inexorably from B minor to F minor, returning to B minor for the pitiless climax. This suddenly cuts out, leaving a vision of desolation, empty as a deserted battlefield. The change to B major at this point seems to remove all feeling of human activity except for the fitful distant sound of bugles out of step with the now almost inaudible drum beats as they fade into a chilling silence.

It would be difficult to imagine a greater contrast than that offered by the following work, the neoclassical *Trois menuets* op.51. Less immediately compelling than the earlier *Minuetto alla tedesca* they unfold a wealth of surprises and subtle detail for the connoisseur. In each case a somewhat impersonal classicism provides the starting point for unpredictable harmonic and structural adventures. Austere diatonic dissonances sharpen the clean outlines of double counterpoint that open the first minuet in E flat, but soon a surprising modulation to G minor, with four voices in close imitation, widens our perspective in a strategically contrived crescendo. The trio, also in E flat, behaves similarly, its plain clarinet-like melody stepping slyly in and out of E (natural) major. Both minuet and trio arrive home with telling jolts and the return is quaintly inflected, its elephantine octavation optional. The second minuet, in a languid G minor, makes great play with a Neapolitan cadence, delaying its resolution and deepening its colouring on each reappearance. After a more purposeful *maggiore* trio some stinging dissonances bite into the minuet and there is a final, almost unbearable postponement of the Neapolitan resolution before a reminiscence of the trio clinches the relationship between the two sections with a series of puns. The third minuet is a very tricky piece to bring off. Its opening theme, bland and confident, starts off no less than twenty times leading us up various garden paths. In both minuet and trio the player must guard against any temptation to point out the many harmonic twists by gratuitous rubati which will only make the piece sound esoteric, contrived or arch. The enigmatic bell-like strokes that initiate the rhythm of the scurrying trio are marked 'sostenuto' the *locus classicus* of Alkan's use of this term which never signifies lingering.

Alkan's preoccupation during the 1850s with his translation of the Old Testament yielded one of his finest short pieces. *Super flumina Babylonis* op.52 paraphrases Psalm 137 in the style of an operatic scena and falls roughly into three sections: a lachrymose adagio in G minor, a muted song of Zion with thrummed 'harp' accompaniment generating frustrated developments in an impatient 12/8, and a powerful G minor finale burning with rage. 'Blessed be he that taketh thy children and crushes them against the stones.' From its bleak opening to its fiery close the whole piece takes less than five minutes and would make a novel and arresting concert item.

During this same fruitful year, and after a gap of some fifteen years, Alkan once more turned his attention to the nocturne, publishing his second and third as a pair op.57, with op.60 bis following closely in their wake. All three pieces are more contrasted, one with another, than the examples of Field or Chopin, and though none quite recaptures the youthful rapture of the first nocturne each has its own marked individuality. Comparison between the first two nocturnes is instructive. The ternary shape of the later piece is less clearly defined even though its central section is enharmonically induced by one of Alkan's bell-like calls to attention. The plaintive opening concentrates our thoughts on each drooping contour whereas the earlier nocturne directed our minds forward to the broader perspective of twenty-four unbroken bars of melody. The more introspective nature of the later work is underlined by a wealth of polyphonic detail that never becomes congested but which makes this the most concentrated of the four nocturnes. Once more both sections are cleverly interwoven in the brief coda, and a flattened leading-note adds its touch of mysticism in the penultimate bar. The companion piece is that rare bird, a fast nocturne. It takes wing at a dizzy 𝅗𝅥. = 72 'très vif' undecided as to whether it might soar in F sharp major or swoop in B flat, but settling for both options in F sharp. Its *minore* section, alas, despite some characteristic piquancies, remains earth-bound. Alkan calls his fourth and last nocturne *Le grillon* (the cricket). Also in B major, it is cleverly laid out to suggest that Alkan's 'third hand' supplies the high, metallic chirrup of the little insect as it charmingly punctuates the main section. During a wintry, minor episode it hibernates only to emerge once more at the reprise. Any impression of naïvety however is quickly dispelled by a wealth of picturesque modulations one of which, a cleverly contrived return from C to B, makes the heart miss a beat each time it comes round. *Le grillon* shares its opus number and affectionate lyricism with two lesser pieces *Ma chère liberté* and *Ma chère servitude* op.60. Both are worth exploring at a domestic level though a rather thin middle section in the first becomes obsessive and tiresome.

Two short pieces, both unique and each conveying an utterly different aspect of Alkan's complex genius, complete this survey of his large output of original works for piano alone. *Petit conte* (fairy tale) also dates from 1859. It is one of the composer's most enchanting miniatures, sounding as though it sprang into being complete in every one of it perfect details. The key-scheme (E flat, A flat, E flat) denotes commentary rather than action, its decorative style confirmed by two childlike melodies: a 'cradle-song for musical boxes' and a more skittish refrain like the banter of children at play. The second idea trips happily along, its sly modulations bandied between the hands but never straying far from its central key of A flat. On repetition it becomes more animated before fluttering down to settle with butterfly lightness on the false key of E (natural) major. The opening tune steals shyly in, but realising its mistake deftly sidesteps to the correct key of E flat. This reassuring event is celebrated by the addition of a modest descant and given further encouragement by the continuation of a wavy figure overspilt from the middle section. The discovery that its sequel will go nicely in canon causes this figuration to bubble into triplets of approval. A reflective coda brings both ideas into closer relationship before the triplets, waiting in the wings, chortle their way to a happy ending. The wonderfully economic piano writing throughout is born of a mastery whose consciousness has long been forgotten.

The *Toccatina* in C minor op.75, together with *Bombardo-Carillon* for four feet (sic) was probably the last of Alkan's compostions to be published in the 1870s. Like so many of his greatest miniatures it all looks too simple on paper, yet the effect in performance is unique and will startle even the most sophisticated twentieth-century ears inured though they are to every latest freak of compositional absurdity. From his earliest creative period an obsessional streak in Alkan seemed to drive him into writing toccatas, or pieces in toccata style; the third study from op.76 and *Le chemin de fer* are toccatas in all but name. Now for the last time he spins his relentless semiquavers, but with a difference. Held in a sinister, expressionless pianissimo for over a hundred bars they flicker with the eerie potential of a time-bomb ticking over. Astringent dissonances tease the spare two-part writing as the mercurial figuration collides with biting, staccato counterpoints. An abrupt modulation to A flat major has the right hand weaving more open textures above a timp-like ostinato, in masterly disregard of harmonic alignment. For twenty-seven bars the tonality remains uneasily poised on the tonic and dominant of A flat until, with the first hint of a foreign note (G flat), stability founders. The ostinato is wrenched out of phase. The soufflé-like textures contract. As the pull of C minor, through its augmented sixth, becomes even more critical, the rhythm tightens and, with matchless timing, the right-hand intervals continue to narrow until they converge into the contours of the reprise. Here, their outline still afflicted by the abrasive G flat (F sharp), the harmony is made explicit by the modest incursion of a third voice. The piece has by now run three-quarters of its course held in a breathtaking pianissimo. Without warning it lashes out as twenty withering bars in contrary motion followed by two slashed chords propel the listener into silence. For seven anxious bars the semiquavers flutter, tentatively, before being finally dismissed by an angry flurry as it devolves with the explosive force of both hands on to the blinding light of middle C. If this *Toccatina* were Alkan's last completed composition he could scarcely have devised a more appropriate or grotesque way of signing off than by this self-mocking reversal of his all too familiar slap on the outer extremities of the keyboard.

The manuscript of *Les Regrets de la Nonnette* was acquired by Symposium Records in 1991 to enable it to be heard and to prevent it from disappearing into a private collection. It is dated 1854 and its title and dedication 'To Mademoiselle Louise' are specifically reflected in its character. Was Louise perhaps a favourite pupil about to enter a convent? One can but speculate. The piece may best be described as a miniature tone-poem. Its pervasive atmosphere of cool resignation is highlighted by a brief but telling central modulation. This added dimension of ambivalence is further endorsed by the final bars in which the music hovers between major and minor to the accompaniment of a beckoning convent bell.

11 Transcriptions and Cadenzas

Alkan's solo Concerto demonstrates as never before the dual nature of the piano. The tutti and solo sections in this work bring the contrast between pianistically and orchestrally conceived writing into sharpest focus. Chopin's piano writing is probably the most intrinsically pianistic ever devised, growing it seems from the sensuous exploration of the composer's fingers upon the keyboard. His F sharp minor Prelude is an extreme example, unsuited to any other medium. Much of Schubert's piano music on the other hand, though no less pianistically valid, seems derived from the sound and behaviour of the wind ensemble, while the opening of Beethoven's Sonata op.81a (*Les adieux*) is purely orchestral in style. Paradoxically its simple suggestion of quiet strings summoned by an evocative horn-call might sound less cogent in a straightforward orchestration. Elsewhere Beethoven makes fullest use of the pianistic resources suggested by his 1803 Erard.

The two later composers who most acutely appreciated this fundamental dichotomy in the nature of the piano were Liszt and Alkan. By exploiting its power of suggestion they raised the craft of transcription to an art in its own right. Before the advent of broadcasting and recording, solo or duet arrangements of great symphonic and chamber works were the principal means of their dissemination. During the nineteenth century the provision of such arrangements for purely domestic consumption soon became an industry relying on a treadmill of routine formulae to provide a crude realisation of the original textures. Liszt swept all this aside in 1833 with his monumental transcription of Berlioz's *Symphonie fantastique*. In the light of his subsequent encyclopaedic production of paraphrases, transcriptions and, in the case of the Beethoven symphonies, unembellished adaptations, it is the more tantalising to read the following claim in Isidore Philipp's introduction to the Costallat edition of Alkan's works: 'his marvellous transcriptions which are more orchestral than Liszt's . . .', tantalising of course because these arrangements have become largely unavailable, almost unknown and likely to remain so. This is a pity for, in the hands of an Alkan or a Liszt, such translations stimulate the mind by shedding light on detail that may otherwise pass unnoticed. Comparison, for instance, between the Arioso in Beethoven's Sonata op.110 and Alkan's piano arrangement of the *beklemmt* episode in the same composer's Cavatina from his String Quartet in B flat op.130, may illuminate the interpretation of both passages for string players and pianists alike.

Ex.214a Alkan: Cavatina arrangement.

Ex.214b Beethoven: Sonata op.110.

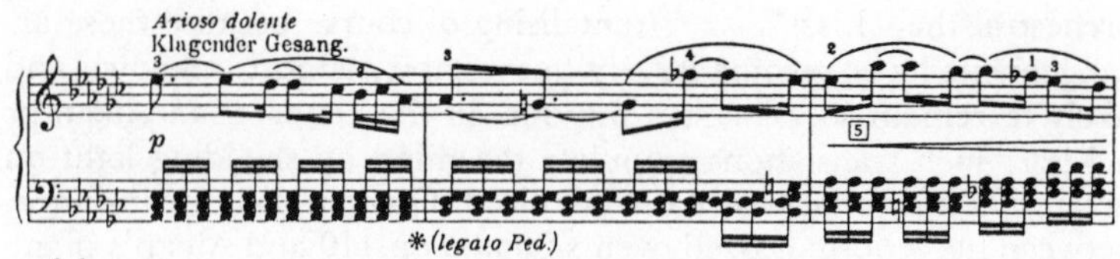

and later:

Ex.214c Beethoven

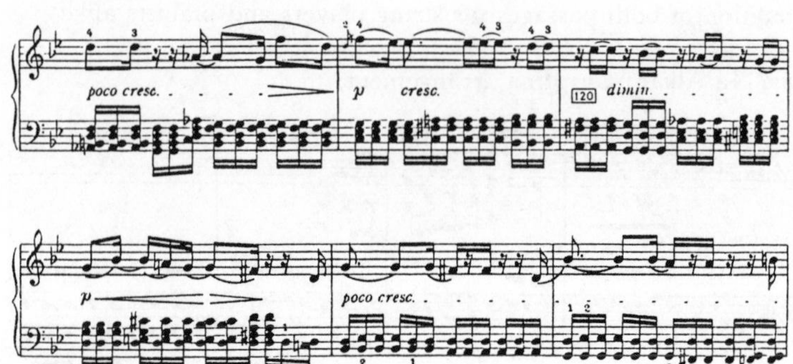

Apart from his arrangement of Beethoven's Seventh Symphony in 1837 for two pianos, eight hands (presumed lost), most of Alkan's transcriptions were issued in 1847, 1861 and in the early 1870s in three collections of six pieces each. The first two series were headed *Souvenirs des concerts du Conservatoire* and the last, *Souvenirs de musique de chambre*. Although the arrangements themselves would hardly find their place in a concert programme today, Alkan's introduction to the first series is of unique interest. Not only does it summarise for all time the principles underlying the art of transcription but it also adds significantly to our knowledge of his own interpretative and pianistic ideals, sharpening our perception of his original compositions. A translation is reproduced here in full:

'Despite the many attempts to reproduce certain major lyrical and symphonic works on the piano I believe that I can offer an approach to the task which is new, or at least developed from concepts more closely linked to the progress made in the manufacture of this instrument and to advances in performance for which we are indebted to various modern virtuosi.

'The first condition for most previous arrangements was that they should lie within the grasp of all pianists, however good or weak. Arrangements for two players, much easier to write, have only in exceptional cases satisfied a delicate ear; apart from other defects, the continual coming-and-going of a single idea, a single theme, between the two performers forms an obstacle to any unity of will and interpretation. Nowadays some artists follow the previous errors; others create transcriptions of exceptional difficulty. For the record one should also mention those 'arrangers' who, under the pretext of improving the work of the great masters, of giving them more sparkle, more effect, decorate them with ill-fitting trappings of their own invention.

'The number of excerpts from operas or symphonies capable of being arranged for a single piano in a manner both clear and complete, yet within the limits of difficulty, must be quite small. Furthermore they require a perfect knowledge of those effects, timbres and 'illusions' of voices and instruments in their innumerable combinations that are made possible by the peculiar sonorities of the modern piano; for these sonorities are wide-ranging if one knows how to obtain them through various methods of attack, through the intelligent use of certain fingerings, hand-crossing etc. The selection of these pieces and the talent to adapt them forms an art on its own, one which demands above all long, hard work, extreme delicacy, sensibility, fine instinct and the appropriation of all available means.

'It is this instinct, this tact which guides the intelligent musician when he wants to make the piano reproduce the great magical accents of an orchestra and a choir; which suggests to him at one moment how to combine the chords in a particular way, at another moment to write some part or other at this octave rather than that, to emphasise this, to lighten that; in fact to use a thousand ingenious methods to arrive not at a mathematical similarity, but a faithful, relative, moral one. So whoever considers dealing seriously in this genre, of bringing his model to life once more, conscious of both that which he wants to reproduce and the facilities he has at his disposal, must force himself to concentrate upon those precious effects revealed to him sometimes by stubborn hard work, sometimes by a happy stroke of chance. In a word, this art lies in making everything heard, knowing which parts to bring out and how to do it, and also how they should be accompanied, lit up or left in the dark; an art, perhaps, with a richer future than might at first seem possible. There is no need to add that, like any other, it must have its rules, i.e. those formulae which everyone can use, but which, without the necessary insight, must remain useless.

'I dare not flatter myself with having rigorously satisfied all such conditions in the six pieces which form this first anthology, despite the trouble I took to arrange them, or even having been helped enormously by the magnificent performances in the Conservatoire concerts to appreciate all their beauty and finesse. I hope that my work will not be considered totally useless. Furthermore, in these few words I want only to indicate the laws which should govern all work of this nature, and at the same time point out some of the faults committed by most of my predecessors, although amongst them there are several whose names and merits will always be admired.[1]

'Others coming after me will probably do better if they take the trouble; as for myself, with a certain number of pieces still held in reserve I can but profit from all judicious comments made to me. All the same I think this first collection should satisfy both those who like to remember and reproduce the beautiful pieces they have heard in the theatre or at a concert without the obbligatos, accompaniment of variations, arpeggios and embellishments of all kinds which should be reserved for the type of music which suits them; and also those who wish to find in one piece material for study with a certain difficulty to overcome but not an insuperable one.

'France is waiting and may yet wait a long time for correct editions of most of the major works of the greatest masters. So far as these six fragments are concerned I examined all the resources offered by public libraries and private collections in order to arrive at the highest possible degree of fidelity. I only decided on this version or that, this or that nuance, after long reflection and meticulous checks. When in doubt, where the choices seemed equally balanced to me, I followed the majority of editions. For lack of a better title, may I be permitted to strive for that of Faithful and Respectful Interpreter of our Divine Genii. March 30, 1847. C.-V. Alkan'.

Of the six transcriptions published in 1847 Alkan's arrangement of the Minuet from Mozart's G minor Symphony K550 may be the earliest, for he had already played it in public on April 29, 1844. A phrase-by-phrase comparison with the original confirms Alkan's scrupulous realisation of every detail. His almost pedantic refusal to sacrifice textural completeness to keyboard practicality, as Liszt does when faced with similar choices in his arrangements of the Beethoven symphonies, leads to cumbersome arpeggiations and ungainly leaps.

[1] 'I wish to quote just one example here, namely the outrage Weber committed upon himself in the sublime overture to *Der Freischütz*. Who does not feel his heart swell with emotion at the memory of this beautiful song:

Well, this is how Weber himself arranged it for the piano:

and the rest is just as bad. One must say in his defence however, that Weber was writing for the Viennese pianos of his day, and not for those of our day'.

His own broad hands may have been able to grasp the left-hand chords in bar 7; others will discover various redistributions, all equally frustrating.

Ex.215

Woodwind entries in the trio slot more naturally into the hand but further awkwardnesses, after the double bar, suggest a degree of compromise unacceptable to Alkan.

Ex.216

Ex.217

Alkan's full, factual, slightly abrasive treatment emphasises the severe masculinity of the original and most musicians, having grappled with his solution, will come to realise that compromise will simply not do. His arrangement is not the best, but the *only* possible one.

Pianists who wish to sample further examples of Alkan's fastidiousness as a transcriber might turn to the widespread elegance of his perfect arrangement of the *Choeur des filles de la mer* from Weber's *Oberon* which would make an effective encore. By far the most important of his arrangements however are the two solo reductions, commissioned by his publisher Richault around 1860, of the first movement from Beethoven's C minor Concerto and of Mozart's D minor Concerto K466. As one might expect, his realisation of the purely orchestral passages combines integrity with bold pianistic imagination. Who else would have devised the following daring hand-crossing to bring out the crucial bass notes at this lead-in to the cadenza of the Beethoven?

Ex.218

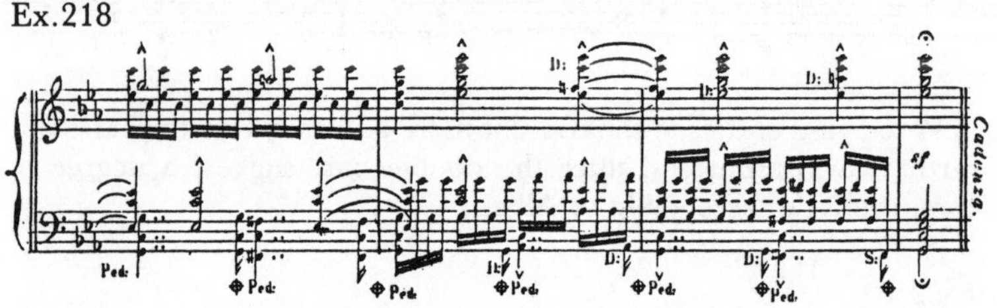

Of still greater interest, however, are the cadenzas Alkan provided for the first movement of the Beethoven and the outer movements of the Mozart. The Beethoven cadenza in particular has remained something of a legend since Busoni incensed the Berlin critics by playing it at a Philharmonic concert in 1906; and no wonder, for this is no ordinary cadenza. Almost two-hundred bars in length and shorn of all the improvisational trappings normally associated with cadenzas, it unfolds in eight linked sections, a fiercely argued commentary on the movement as a whole. From its laconic opening to an apotheosis of the cadential trill it probes every nook and cranny of Beethoven's masterpiece, enlarging its perspectives in a continuum of far-flung tonal relationships. An arresting modulation to E major anticipates both the remote key of the Largo and the comprehensive tonal procedures adopted by Beethoven himself in such middle-period works as the 'Appassionata' Sonata, the 'Emperor' Concerto and the Seventh Symphony. Central to Alkan's strategy is a sombre canonic development of the main subject, its internal vibrating pedal-point inviting comparison with two parallel passages in the first movement of his solo concerto. Here, however, the process is given a further twist by the systematic tightening of its phrase lengths forcing the voices out of phase. In mounting tension they contract from three to two and then to one-and-a-half bars, their diverging paths encouraging the vibration to burgeon into interlocked octaves. The compression continues, the phrases narrowing still further until with white-hot intensity the whole passage blazes into a towering C major combination of the concerto's principal subject and the triumphant theme that leads off the finale in Beethoven's Fifth Symphony (see Ex.219b). Eyebrows may leap at its punning audacity, but let us not forget that here, as in the symphony, the famous paean rises from a preparation of darkest mystery. Beethoven would surely have appreciated a further pun in its continuation which identifies the concerto's rising scale with the piercing piccolo flourishes in the symphony.

Ex.219 Concerto

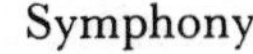

In Alkan's strategy such cross-references fall naturally into place in no way impeding the sense of continuous growth. Perhaps the most astounding passage in this most alarming and controversial of cadenzas results from Alkan's extension of his cadential trill as fragments of the second subject grope their way along twenty-four bars of harmonic tight-rope. Unaligned voices blur the outline; multiple appoggiaturas threaten the key-centre; yet the tonality never wavers thanks to a fearsome, cold logic that controls and guides its progress towards ultimate resolution.[1] The composer Roger Smalley concludes a full and perceptive article as follows: 'In this cadenza Alkan almost miraculously matches the power and originality of Beethoven's concerto'.[2]

The two cadenzas for Mozart's D minor concerto are also highly characteristic though far less monumental. In the absence of cadenzas by the composer himself those by Beethoven are most often played in this concerto. Like Beethoven, Alkan makes no attempt to assume Mozart's style and his cadenzas are full of abrupt switches of key and gruff humour. Alkan's modulations are even more challenging. In his cadenza to Mozart's first movement the unstable Neapolitan region of E flat witnesses the metamorphosis of the main theme into the opening of the 'Jupiter' symphony, while the concerto's second subject is recalled in the even remoter key of B major.

[1] For further discussion of this strange passage see Chapter 15.

[2] *Music and Musicians*, May 1972.

Ex.219b Alkan: from Cadenza to Beethoven's C minor Concerto

Alkan also makes fullest use of his seven-octave compass ending the cadenza with a rasping scale, two octaves deep, from bottom to top A. His cadenza to Mozart's finale opens in an arresting, cavalry style before combining themes from all three movements in an infectious display of contrapuntal high jinks.

In their context these cadenzas should prove exciting novelties; but only a committed performance could demonstrate how well the later movements in Beethoven's C minor concerto would survive the seismic tremors set up by Alkan's tremendous cadenza in the first.

150

Pour Monsieur
Léon Jacquard
de la part de l'au

Ch. V. Alk

à Monsieur James Odier

SONATE

DE

CONCERT,

pour Piano et Violoncelle,

PAR

CH.s V.in ALKAN

aîné

ŒUVRE 47.

PARIS.

A.V.

12 Chamber Music

According to Fétis the seven-year-old Alkan already played the violin well enough to give a public performance of a show-piece by Rode. It would have seemed surprising had he not composed chamber music involving strings and it is disappointing that a promising opening for string quartet was never brought to fruition. Much of Alkan's piano writing suggests this medium; just think of the second movement from his *Sonatine* op.61 or, better still, *Les enharmoniques* from the *Esquisses* op.63.[1] We can, however, rejoice in three major contributions to the chamber repertoire: the Duo op.21 for violin and piano and Trio op.30, both from his early maturity, with the *Sonate de concert* op.47 for cello and piano representing the high summer of his creativity. All three works have been scandalously neglected although the splendid Trio was recorded in America in 1975 and the *Sonate de concert* is starting to attract the attention of those cellists lucky enough to find a partner equal to its taxing piano part.

Grand Duo Concertant for Violin and Piano in F sharp minor, op.21

Alkan's only sonata for violin and piano appeared in the early 1840s, probably in 1840 itself when the composer was still in his late twenties. Set in a series of somewhat uncouth keys it fairly bristles with sharps and double-sharps and is altogether a tough, severe but impressive work unlike any other essay for the medium. Of its three movements the first, in telescoped sonata form, is the shortest. The opening, with its angular counterpoint and suggestion of plainchant, begets a chain of subsidiaries.

[1] Roger Smalley has arranged several of the *Esquisses* for string quartet, and others for brass ensemble.

Ex.220

VIOLON.

Assez animé.

PIANO.

p

soutenu.

Ped.

largement et en augmentant.

Motifs (a), (b) and (c) all play an important role (Exs.221 and 222).

Ex.221

Ex.222

Having scarcely gained a foothold in F sharp minor we are hustled within the space of a dozen bars through a restless key sequence that defies the tonal principles of sonata form. Having had his fling Alkan now settles for the 'correct' key of A major, welding this disparate trio of motifs into a true second group and, in wry homage to propriety, rounds off his exposition symmetrically with a backward glance at the opening subject. With its tight compression this exposition must be repeated before proceeding to the even terser development. This is dominated by two powerful octave entries of the main subject in G and D minor before a violent wrench to G flat major invokes an augmented version of (b), relating it to the 'plainsong' motif. To our surprise this bold splash of colour dissolves quite naturally into its enharmonic equivalent as we find ourselves caught up in the briefest of recapitulations in F sharp major. Such contraction, however, enables (c) to spread its wings before a decorative celebration of the opening subject brings the movement to a jubilant close.

A musical representation of the underworld that avoids melodrama or parody requires a master. Alkan heads his second movement 'L'enfer' (hell) and his plan is drastically simple. A stark prologue and epilogue in C sharp form the framework for a broader episode in G sharp. Here, high above a murmuring accompaniment, a muted yet impassioned violin melody stands in severe contrast to its chilling surroundings. The movement opens with a series of tortured chords rising from the bass of the piano. A peremptory call to attention invokes a chromatic entreaty from the violin. The process is repeated; the violin rhythm is converted into a fragile hymn tune marked 'évangéliquement' which, in turn is refashioned as the central melody 'avec la plus grande expression.' This brief illusion of hope, however, is ruthlessly shattered as the opening dissonances return, diabolically amplified. Throughout the movement Alkan's exploration of the lowest register of the piano is unprecedented as can be seen from the final uncompromising bars (Ex.223).

Ex.223

The elaborate finale, sadistically marked 'aussi vite que possible' is in F sharp major, a pianist's rather than a violinist's key; but it opens with a twenty-bar flourish in the minor.

Ex.224

Here the melodic shape defies the bar-line in a series of track-shunting contradictions which might be expressed as follows: two bars of 2/4, ten bars of 3/4 and three bars of 2/4. Such was Alkan's fascination with rhythmic ambiguities that, according to a contemporary review, he re-accented the familiar opening of Chopin's third Ballade from 6/8 to common time (presumably by pairing the quavers and denying the bar-line.)[1] Alkan's stern, unison opening launches the rondo theme, a toccata-like subject for the piano in contrary motion. At first the violin marks time by repeating a leaping sixth from the opening unison but quickly upstages its partner with an inverted 'pre-echo' from the finale of the solo *Symphonie* of 1857:

[1] *Revue et gazette musicale*, March 25, 1880.

Ex.225

which is cleverly turned into:

Ex.226

The piano's toccata-like figuration continues to add vitality, the prevailing tonality of F sharp major confirmed in a huge unison descent immediately repeated a minor third lower. Having established its F sharp major base the toccata is now free to set out on a series of tonal adventures, passing through B major, G minor, A flat major and minor, and E major, devolving by way of a circle of fifths on to a tuneful and harmonically engaging transition in A before alighting on the orthodox key of C sharp for the second subject. 'Airborne' violin syncopations and piquant colouring make this one of Alkan's happiest inventions.

Ex.227

At this point the toccata is resumed. Its mood quickly darkens but its root remains firmly grounded in C sharp as this complex exposition ends with the powerful unison descent in that key.

A brief but concentrated development combines the syncopated second subject with a new triplet motif as we find ourselves caught up in a web of contrapuntal infighting. The triplets threaten to take over, provoking a petulant outburst. Once more the syncopations take the stage; once more the triplets break in but tinged with regret as the key centre starts to give way in a harmonic landslip. The toccata flickers mysteriously in twenty bars of tonal ambiguity until the piano discovers the dominant of the home key and descends from a great height in an arresting display of unresolved appoggiaturas. As it comes to rest in a mysterious oscillation derived from the opening sixths, the violin delineates ghostly reminders of the triplet motif and we are home. Nothing, however, can be anticipated in this richly inventive movement and despite a characteristic tightening of his reprise Alkan still finds room for a fiery new episode based on a diminution of Ex.225.

Ex.228

Elsewhere all the exposition motifs, with the exception of the A major transition, become accounted for but in a revised order that enables Alkan to build a commanding climax from which the excitement never flags. A terse reminder of the opening unison and some explosive chordal exchanges bring the work to its resounding close.

I have yet to hear a performance of this unique sonata, a work hardly calculated to ensnare the speculative violin virtuoso on the scent of luscious tunes and facile effectiveness. It is tough and uncompromising and would take an outstanding artist to compete on equal terms with his partner, especially in the first movement. With characteristic perversity Alkan has tailored the piano part to his own prodigious skills, placing it beyond the accomplishment of all but the elect. Although I have still to discover a review of Alkan's own performance with the Belgian violinist Hubert Léonard[1] on April 30, 1874, Léon Kreutzer, son of an even more famous violinist, published the following impression in the *Revue et gazette musicale* in January 1846: 'The opening allegro is treated in a severe yet grandiose manner. The adagio, with a series of chords low down on the piano; strange chords which, by the introduction of an inner pedal, seem to float amidst unknown and mysterious tonalities. Shortly afterwards the violin has a melody, plaintive and passionate, the sad cry of a desolate wandering soul... The rondo finale of this sonata abounds in piquant effects and varied rhythms. If it were not necessary to exercise considerable caution in one's judgement of modern works we should pronounce this composition a work of art.'

Trio in G minor for Violin, Cello and Piano, op.30

None of the practical problems that may have contributed to the neglect of the Duo for violin and piano beset this masterly work, completed about a year later. Like Marschner's admirable trios and like so many other fine works by Alkan it has until recently vanished from the repertoire simply by default. The lack of a modern edition has much to answer for, but until this omission is rectified, there should be no difficulty in obtaining photocopies from a national library.[2] The work is brilliantly effective; varied, colourful and concise. It is also expertly laid out for the medium; as stimulating to play as it is rewarding to hear, and there seems no reason why it should not stand beside the trios of Mendelssohn, Brahms and Dvořák as one of the handful of nineteenth-century masterpieces after Schubert for this testing combination.

Exceptionally for Alkan all four movements are in the same key (G minor or major.) The first movement 'Assez largement' displays

[1] Léonard gave the Berlin première of Mendelssohn's Violin Concerto with the composer conducting.

[2] The Trio has been reissued by Billaudot.

some of the stern intensity of Bach's fugue in the same G minor key from Book 2 of the 'forty-eight' and is even terser than its corresponding movement in the Duo. Like his classical predecessors Alkan is never averse to using a musical formula should it serve his structural purpose. The opening subject grows from a three-bar aphorism in the Dorian mode. Abrupt and concentrated it is given out by the piano alone, the strings adding their encouragement in the third bar.

Ex.229

A more tuneful second subject in a restless B flat calls forth a running semiquaver accompaniment which enlivens the texture for the remainder of the movement. Tonally discursive, it dallies with C minor and flirts with G flat major and A flat minor, all in the course of a few bars, before finding itself back in B flat. Wisely opting for the latter it celebrates its decision in a daring piece of harmonic brinkmanship (Ex.230), followed by an expositional wind-up of brilliant cadential sequences for all three instruments.

Ex.230

There is no repeat and the listener must keep his wits about him for both the development and recapitulation are drastically concentrated and absorbed into the continuous flow of semiquavers. The return, heralded by a stern convergence of sequences from Ex.229, is accomplished by a master-stroke. With a sudden drop to *piano* and a switch to the major Alkan telescopes his reprise with the following skilful combination of both subjects:

Ex.231

Here the cellist must project with laser-like precision if Alkan's legerdemain is not to pass unnoticed, though it could hardly have failed to catch Mendelssohn's eye when he received a presentation copy from the composer.[1] It might even have inspired the famous identical combination in the finale of Mendelssohn's own Violin Concerto of 1844. Alkan's cadence-theme displays further contrapuntal skills with the interchange of its violin and cello sequences. After a brief touch of retrospective pathos there is a concise coda. The opening subject bursts forth in a fiercely syncopated E flat unison followed by some sonorous G minor flourishes four octaves deep. The movement ends as it has begun, its octave Gs hammered home by all three instruments.

Mendelssohnian lightness, Beethovenish humour and Haydnesque rhythmic caprice: such are the hallmarks of Alkan's pedigree scherzo. It opens with an aerial descent of three bars, pizzicato, answered by a five-bar refrain (Ex.232).

[1] Now in the Bodleian Library, Oxford.

Ex.232

The pianist's continuation is held firmly in check by the cellist who plants down the opening rhythm *forte* every third bar, in rude violation of his partner's mercurial filigree. The game continues until the violinist intervenes imposing the first four-bar discipline on this rhythmically volatile movement. Harmonically, the whole section is poised, insubstantially, on a dominant pedal and it may be interpreted with puckish, or spectral delicacy. The pianist now decides there is nothing like a fugue for concentrating the mind and he leads off the central trio section with the grouchiest of fugal expositions.

Ex.233

The violinist, waiting patiently in the wings, will have none of it. Taking up the fourth entry he slyly twists its fourth note into the upbeat of a more homely tune, thereby broadening our horizons by lowering our sights. The cellist adds his 'Hear, hears!' and the pianist, completely upstaged, has no option but to supply a modest accompaniment. He soon regains the initiative, however, blinding his colleagues with harmonic science and then, with true pianistic egotism, taking up the tune himself as though he had thought of it all the time! After the return of the Scherzo the pianist is allowed his final fugal fling.

In this work, perhaps more than any other, Alkan assumes the mantle of Beethoven, transforming it to his own strange purpose with Jewish intensity and Gallic skill. The abrupt contrast of string and piano entries in the third movement, for instance, bears a superficial resemblance to the stark exchange that characterises the central movement of Beethoven's G major Concerto; but the effect is quite different. With Alkan it is the piano that storms and the strings that pacify (the opposite of Beethoven's scheme). The benevolent opening bars could easily come from a string trio by Haydn.

Ex.234

With the entry of an impassioned piano recitative, however, all thought of Haydn is banished as though the whole instrument is set vibrating with Hebraic fervour.

Ex.235

Several of Alkan's slow movements have an extra-musical motivation, often of a religious nature. Strangely enough he provides no clue to the origin of the powerful impulses that seem to have inspired this movement. Once more the strings becalm, summoning a more thoughtful response. This time the impassioned outburst is cut short as the string serenity and pianistic impatience become reduced to the following dialogue:

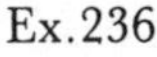

The piano now turns its comment into an expressive melody, the strings supplying an Alberti accompaniment. The mood darkens; the dialogue is repeated with modal inflections, its rising and falling second worked up to a passage of reconciliation in which the once serene opening is made to tremble like an orchestra of balalaikas.

Ex.237

For maximum sonority the pianist should vibrate in contrary motion. There is a short, valedictory coda in which the rising and falling second retreats once more into the calm from which it emerged.

The finale, in sonata form, is enacted against a fierce accumulation of semiquavers. The pianist's non-stop torrent is successively punctuated by the following string motif:

Ex.238

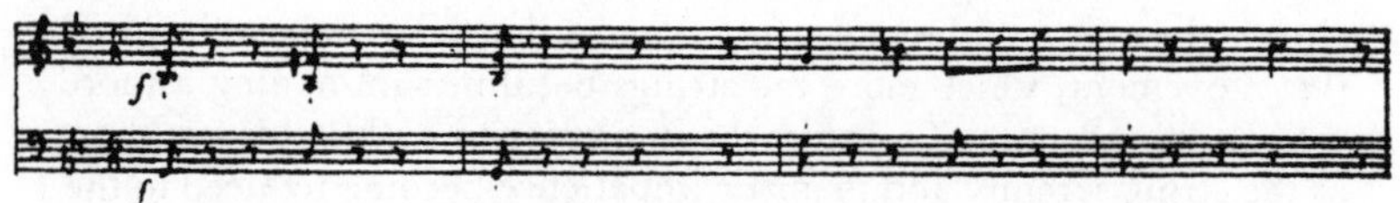

– a more flowing second subject,

Ex.239

– a foreshortening of Ex.238,

Ex.240

and an extension of figure (a),

Ex.241

to form the following brand-new melody, adding a darker dimension to the recapitulation as well as breadth to the design.

Ex.242

The surprise, however, comes in the coda as the pianist's continuing stream of semiquavers wavers, falters and stops, only to be taken up with renewed energy by his colleagues. The pianist now raps out the original string motif (Ex.238). The roles are reversed and the momentum increased in a jubilant marriage of tonic and dominant harmony which brings the work to its rousing conclusion.

Altogether the Trio is one of Alkan's most classical compositions. Although its gossamer scherzo and powerful slow movement make an immediate impact, the originality of the outer movements only reveals itself on closer acquaintance. Repeated hearings unlock unsuspected depths and subtleties that lurk beneath the terse severity of the opening movement and which nourish the brusque vitality of the finale.

Sonate de concert op.47 in E major for Cello and Piano

Some seventeen years separate Alkan's Trio and this last and most expansive chamber work, the Cello Sonata. It followed immediately in the wake of that tremendous spate of creative energy that culminated, in 1857, with the publication of the minor-key Studies op.39, the first two sets of *Chants* and a host of smaller compositions. Despite Alkan's plea of poor health he gave the first public performance with his friend Auguste Franchomme in Erard's concert rooms on April 27th that year. Nine years earlier Franchomme had introduced the last three movements from Chopin's Cello Sonata in the rival Pleyel rooms and it is widely accepted that, as its dedicatee, he had helped to fashion its cello part. Speculation that Franchomme might also have had a hand in the sonorous and effective writing in Alkan's sonata is silenced by the discovery, in the library of the Paris Conservatoire, of the cellist's personal copy dated March 23, 1857, with a humorous inscription thanking him for the addition of a pedal-point. The work is in fact dedicated to James Odier and it also exists in a version by Casimir Ney for viola and piano. Cast in four broadly conceived movements it is possibly the most brilliant and certainly one of the most original and rewarding works for the medium to come out of the nineteenth century. Its neglect, even by so eclectic an artist as Casals, indicates the total eclipse into which Alkan's music must have passed by the earlier part of the twentieth century. Even so it still seems extraordinary that no cellist of the older school should have stumbled across the work or, if he did, should have failed to recognise it for the masterpiece it undoubtedly is. Its republication in a scholarly edition by Hugh Macdonald should restore the work to its rightful position as the most important missing link between the cello sonatas of Beethoven and Brahms. Despite its romantic fervour the work is severely rooted in the classics and while it offers every opportunity for display it also exacts an uncommon degree of technical and musical discipline, especially from the pianist who, despite the forceful brilliance of his part, must not overwhelm his partner. From the outset tempo is crucial. At a tepid *allegro commodo* the opening subject will sound like a watery 'Song without words'. Alkan's ♩ = 160 *allegro molto* on the other hand sets the movement soaring on its urgent trajectory.

Ex.243

A note of anxiety in the following exchanges is confidently cast aside as a fierce major ninth launches a proliferation of motifs to form the second subject in B major.

Ex.244

The continuation seems so spontaneous that one is hardly aware of the tight logic that controls its course.

Ex.245

Note how, later, the piano's dotted rhythms are gathered into the following contractions:

Ex.246

Thoughout its progress this second group ranges freely and boldly within the gravitational field of B, its tonal identity clinched by a further lyrical exchange.

Ex. 247

This complex yet concise exposition ends belligerently with an insistent triplet motif distilled from Ex. 247, a contrary-motion flourish and an emphatic octave leap.

Ex. 248

A three-bar transition brings about the essential repeat as it spells out an unsuspected relationship between Ex.247 and the three-note anacrusis that opened the movement (Ex.243).

So far Alkan's fugitive anxiety and fiery optimism have been held in check. They are now let loose in an elaborate development as the stark octave leap plunges downwards in a series of chromatic steps. Its course is twice arrested by a rattling diminution of the opening anacrusis as it summons forth a brand new theme in C minor. Arising from the depths of the cello it is immediately answered in D minor by the piano whose last two minims become transformed into a cello ostinato beneath stalking developments of the triplet figure in Ex.248.

Ex.249

Tension mounts as a bold sequence fusing the triplet motif with the contrary motion scale leads off in A minor followed by questioning exchanges of the anacrusis. The whole episode, repeated with added urgency in F minor, heralds a return of the second subject (Ex.244) its fierce optimism tempered by disquiet as it lurches violently from the unsettled key of C sharp minor to the polarised one of G minor. It continues on its speculative path until the cello, sensing an apparent affinity between the falling thirds of Ex.245 and the opening, seizes the initiative. As the ear is prepared for an important pronouncement in G sharp major the cello slyly slides up a semitone to announce the main subject in A major. Is this the recapitulation?

Some returns start in the subdominant. The piano decides otherwise and inflects its harmonies, causing the cello to falter. After two such hesitations both instruments hurl themselves furiously into further trenchant exchanges until, for the last time, the bold sequence takes hold of the argument, guiding it adroitly to the threshold of the home dominant. Here the mood softens for the most magical of returns in which a web of counterpoint yields the following exquisite resolution.

Ex.250

Despite a development of almost bewildering resourcefulness Alkan has yet to spring his greatest surprise. Hardly has he established a normal recapitulation than that immigrant theme Ex.249 that appeared at the outset of the development rises once more, and in its correct key of C minor. It now slots so naturally into its host surroundings that one hardly appreciates the audacity of Alkan's innovation, yet it adds incalculably to the overall design. Its continuation is so contrived that the sudden fierce ninth of the second subject arrives from a tritonic modulation giving it the maximum potency possible. From here on it is plain sailing, but with one exception. Alkan's bold tonal plan tempts the cello, that most impulsive of instruments, to introduce the lyrical subject (Ex.247) a minor third too high. Tactfully but firmly its partner sets it right and the movement ends in high spirits with a double octave leap.

The second movement, in Siciliano style, is one of Alkan's most whimsical offspring. Amiable yet sly, it woos and teases the listener with its lilting rhythms and wry counterpoint. Alkan's ♩. = 80 may seem too impatient for the wealth of harmonic detail in store but at too slow a tempo this movement can easily stagnate and may come dangerously close to the ♩. = 66 of the following Adagio. Its key of A flat is constantly enhanced by quaint inflections. Flattened ninths abound. Note how charmingly the cello steals in taking its cue from the piano outline.

Ex.251

The leisurely continuation through C minor with a radiant glimpse of G major is paved with harmonic piquancies. As it settles in the dominant, E flat, the interweaving of parts becomes animated by a gentle 'spinning song' accompaniment which also enlivens the bittersweet harmony.

Ex.252

The section is rounded off by the following scherzando phrase, the piano's continuation conveying its relationship with Ex.252.

Ex.253

A few side-slips of harmonic mystification invite the cello to graft a complementary tune on to the opening phrase (Ex.251) in F minor.

Ex.254

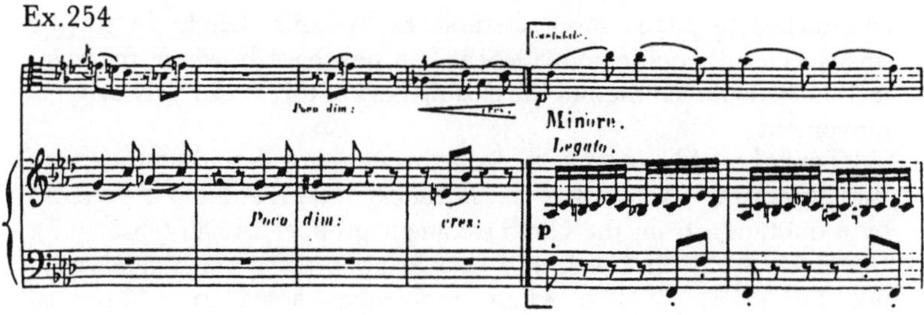

The piano continues to weave its spell of chromatic intrigue but just as its texture becomes denser and its counterpoint more anxious the cello side-steps adroitly to lead off a regular recapitulation in the home key. The narrative is now tightened and harmonic shadows lengthen as cello and piano reverse their roles. Once more we reach the point of recapitulation in this extended binary movement. Had Alkan laid down his pen at this moment no-one could have anticipated the surprise in store. Psychologically the listener is both stimulated and bewildered as the following strange sequence creates the impression of crumbling tonality.

Ex.255

The 'spinning song' is now reduced to a subterranean rumble as the opening subject from the first movement, in a newly cut 6/8 coat, holds court in this alien environment. The result, surrealistic but convincing, is made more credible by Alkan's delight in tracing unsuspected thematic coincidences – a penchant nowhere more infectiously deployed than in the closing bars of this stunningly original movement.

'If only I could have my whole life over again I should set the entire Bible to music' wrote Alkan in the 1860s, and his Adagio is prefaced by a quotation from the Old Testament prophet Micah (ch.5. v.7): 'As a dew from the Lord, as a shower upon the grass, that tarrieth not for man...' The whole movement floats in a mystical atmosphere familiar to those who have already charted its distilled after-glow in the late works for pedal-piano or organ. The form is rhapsodic and alternates two contrasted ideas. The first, a soaring melody for the cello in the neutral key of C major, is fashioned from moonlit fragments heard at the outset.

Ex.256

The second idea is one of Alkan's most atmospheric inventions in which the piano's mysterious supplication shimmers high above a plucked accompaniment. Hypnotic in its rhythmic ambiguity this cello pizzicato is later transferred to the piano and it invests the entire movement with an air of timelessness.

Ex.257

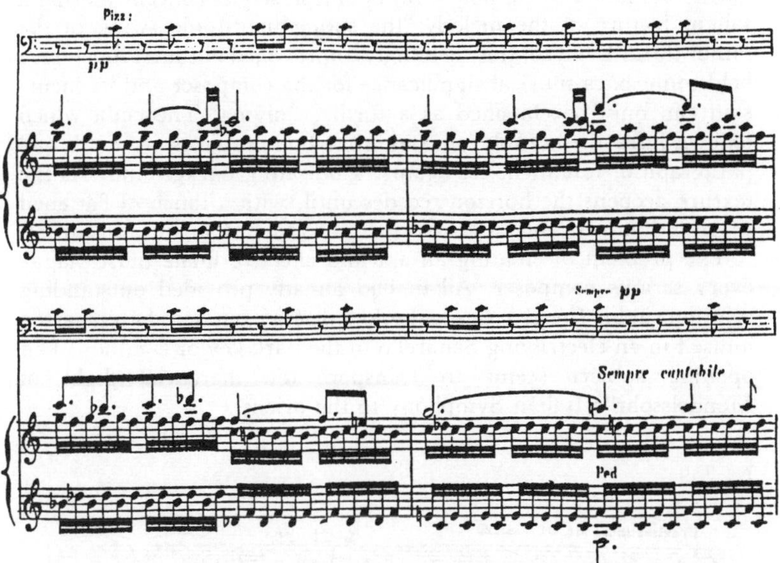

These tentative phrases are later gathered into an eloquent statement by the cello. Its continued pursuit in a dialogue with the piano produces a calm intensity of expression that shares a marked spiritual affinity with the famous cello episode in Franck's Symphonic Variations. Precise moments of identification may be fugitive but a cumulative impression of contained ecstasy, shared by both composers, reminds us that Franck might easily have been present at this work's première. On its third and last appearance the opening cello melody emerges from an alien tonality only to be cut short by a dramatic discord.

Ex.258

Interval fanciers will note how its unison sequel concentrates on a salient feature of the melody: the submediant-tonic swing of the minor third. Even so, this seemingly unprovoked outburst must have held some extra-musical significance for the composer and its incursion can only be classified as a further enigma! The coda which follows fuses memorable phrases from both subjects into a broad paragraph of fulfilment set against a pulsating background. As the texture deepens the horizon recedes until, with a touch of flattened seventh, it hovers and fades with the reluctance of an autumn sunset.

The problem of creating an apt and effective finale must plague every serious composer. Alkan had already provided outstanding solutions in his *Grande sonate* and solo *Symphonie* but here he surpassed himself in an electrifying Saltarello in the dark key of E minor. The opening subject seems to transport the mercurial flight of Mendelssohn's Italian Symphony to the orient.

Ex.259

Note the powerful imitations in line 3.

On each of its six returns this rondo theme is enhanced by ingenious transformations like these venomous acciaccaturas that barb its fifth appearance:

Ex.260

. . . or the following bizarre combination consumed by its own augmentation.

Ex. 261

Vigorous exchanges between the instruments (Ex. 262) beget a fine flow of cello melody adding breadth to the sonata-rondo design.

Ex. 262

Here, as throughout the movement, the ceaseless gathering up of triplets never allows the obsessional vitality to flag, except perhaps in a strange passage near the end marked 'stanco' (exhausted).

Ex. 263

Elsewhere some darkly conspiring sequences suggest an extension of moods engendered by Chopin's solo Tarantella, though such passages as the following unaligned counterpoint could hardly have come from *that* pen.

Ex.264

The last few pages are pursued with a pitiless fury that devours every obstacle in a final devastating avalanche. In the excitement Ex.253 becomes detached from its sequel, yet despite such far-flung freedom of form, every aspect of the design is accounted for and integrated with classical authority.

Alkan included the sonata in the programme of his *Petit concert* on April 30, 1875, surprisingly enough not with the sixty-six-year-old Franchomme but with his younger contemporary Léon Jacquard (1826-1886). The writer in the *Revue et gazette musicale* (May 2, 1875) commented on the pianist's prodigious memory, his absolutely personal approach to the keyboard and a loftiness of style which was equally matched by its poetry. 'The cello sonata' he continues, 'with its wealth of melody and most taxing *Finale alla saltarello* was superbly executed. It received an ovation'.[1] The technical difficulty of this final movement renders its performance an 'event'. Alkan may have realised this when he made a brilliant arrangement for four hands. In this form it can be strongly recommended to piano duettists as an applause-winning wind-up to their programmes; yet it must remain only a partial substitute for the breathtaking *tour de force* that crowns Alkan's finest chamber work.

[1] It is interesting to note that at this same concert the sixty-one-year-old composer was also joined by Saint-Saëns for a performance of Mozart's F major Sonata for four hands. Certain passages in the younger composer's own Cello Sonata in C minor op.32 strongly suggest that Saint-Saëns was not hearing Alkan's Cello Sonata for the first time.

13 Orchestral and Vocal Music

It has been traditionally claimed that Alkan was a frustrated symphonic composer turned away from large-scale orchestral projects by lack of opportunity. If this is true, pianists have profited from posterity's misfortune. Unlike Chopin who strayed cautiously outside his piano kingdom, or Liszt who only later found his orchestral feet, Alkan wrote with a natural ease for orchestra, voice and various chamber combinations; his Conservatoire training would have seen to that. His self-confessed misanthropy however must have militated against the organisation of concerted performances outside his immediate circle. Joseph d'Ortigue, a close neighbour of Alkan in the early 1840s, described the thirty-year-old composer as 'craggy and timid; on the one hand shy, on the other too proud to further his public career.' The youthful success of his first *Concerto da camera* was never repeated. The only subsequent performances of Alkan's compositions during his creative career were largely those he was able to promote himself within his limited means. Consequently, he restricted himself to writing music that could readily be published and brought to the notice of a small elite. Had either of his attempts in 1832 and 1834 to secure the *Prix de Rome* proved successful, he might have pursued a different course. The competitors are required to produce a cantata on a given text. Despite the strict conditions imposed on candidates Alkan must have found the medium congenial for his will included a generous bequest for the foundation of a yearly prize for the composition of a cantata.

Alkan's two *Prix de Rome* manuscripts may be examined in the Bibliothèque Nationale in Paris. In 1832 he was a runner-up to the future composer of *Mignon*, his friend Ambroise Thomas, two years his senior. Alkan's setting of the libretto by Pastoret *Hermann et Ketty* is scored for soprano, tenor and a modest orchestra of double woodwind, two horns and strings. Tuneful and fluent, it is well worth examining with a view to a possible performance. His second and last attempt was unsuccessful. Ironically enough the winner in 1834 was Antoine Elwart whose *Histoire de la Société des Concerts du Conservatoire* we consulted for the precise details of Alkan's concerto début. If Elwart is still remembered it is solely as a music historian. In the light of such unsuccessful candidates as Saint-Saëns and Ravel, or the several abortive attempts by Berlioz, Alkan's failure should not deter us from exploring the score of his second cantata on a libretto by Gail. *L'entrée en loge* for tenor and full orchestra is signed May 19, 1834. Its lightly scored opening sounds inviting.

Ex.265

With one exception the rest of Alkan's vocal music is of slender importance. A *Romance du phare d'Eddystone* which he performed in 1845 in Erard's salons with an English singer, Elizabeth Masson, must be presumed lost. A review described it as 'a pretty and modest flower of melody.' Two settings of Hebrew texts date from 1847 and 1857. *Etz chazzim hi* for unaccompanied mixed voices, notable for the purity of its four-part writing, is in a style similar to the devotional pieces among his *Vingt-cinq préludes* op.31 published that same year. The later piece is a vehement *Halelouyoh* for SATB with piano or organ accompaniment. *Stances de Millevoye* (1859) for female voices (SSA) and piano also shares its plaintive character with some of the preludes – no.16 in C minor in particular. The melancholy refrain alternates with a sad little piano interlude, its broken cadences contrasting with the chaste vocal lines, often in parallel thirds and sixths.

A sparkling *Pas-redoublé* (quick march) for wind band belongs to another world. The manuscript is dated Oct.1, 1840 and the piece, which plays for a little over two minutes, is well worth publishing. Brilliantly scored for military band it simply requires the replacement of a few obsolete instruments like the ophicleide by their modern equivalent. How best to describe it? Bracing, invigorating and unmistakably French; its dactylic gaiety matched by a sense of continuous growth from its opening call to attention to a final flourish from triple-tongued trumpets. Offenbach would have loved it. But what could have prompted the twenty-six-year-old composer to have written such a piece? Perhaps his flute-playing brother Ernest was attached to a concert band or military academy and commissioned it. One can but speculate.

Of all Alkan's enigmas the fate of the missing B minor symphony, Alkan's only purely orchestral work, announced in 1844, remains the most tantalising. We learn from *La France musicale* (Nov.7) that he hoped to mount a performance that season, yet the work was never tried out. Twenty years later Alkan declined an invitation to submit an orchestral work for Pasdeloup's *Concerts populaires*. Possibly a large-scale symphony might have proved unsuitable but Alkan may also have felt disinclined to allow his name to be associated with this newly-formed rival to the *Société des Concerts du Conservatoire*.[1] Certainly there seems no evidence from Alkan's meticulous life-style or his attitude to earlier compositions to suggest that he might have destroyed so important a work as his only orchestral symphony. We learn from his will that all his manuscripts passed to his brother Napoléon. 'These manuscripts' he explains 'many of which have been published by the firm Richault, are contained in four bound volumes, and I intend to gather into one or two boxes the remainder of this group of manuscripts finished and unfinished. Otherwise they will be found here and there, some at my address, others in my office at Erards.' Napoléon's great-grandson, Cyril Ray, believes that important family documents were deposited by his grandmother with family lawyers and so the trail is not completely cold. Meanwhile we must rest content with the following tantalising account of the work

[1] Alkan had also just refused a solo engagement from George Hainl, the newly appointed conductor of the Conservatoire concerts. Hainl later married the pianist Marie Poitevin. It was she who gave what was probably the first performance of Alkan's *Ouverture* (in 1876) and the first complete performance of his solo *Symphonie* (in 1877) as well as introducing such smaller works as *La voix de l'instrument* (1875) and *Super Flumina Babylonis* (1876). A former pupil of Delaborde, she became the dedicatee of Franck's *Prelude, Chorale and Fugue.*

by Léon Kreutzer, son of a celebrated violinist, as it appeared in the *Revue et gazette musicale* in 1846:

'The unpublished symphony which Mr. Alkan was willing to show me borrows nothing from the capricious forms which the modern symphony has adopted. It is divided, like the symphonies of Haydn, Mozart and Beethoven, into four movements. The first allegro in B minor is in four time and of moderate speed. The opening motif, perhaps slightly too calm, lends itself perfectly to the developments which the composer's art knows how to draw from a subject. This motif, which appears in all the parts and which the voices of the orchestra give and take from each other, is often interesting and never ceases: here it appears in its entirety, there broken up into fragments, like the ever-changing river which sometimes flows peacefully along, and sometimes, crashing against the rocks, foams and gushes in the sunlight, a luminous spray. In the second movement we noticed in particular a passage where the flutes, clarinets and bassoons remain on a held note while various strings play the theme, interrupting each other. It is a very simple effect, but a striking one. The scherzo, composed in the style beloved of Mozart, is highly spirited. The clarinet phrase which forms the trio is accompanied by strings (alternately viola and cello) and is very charming. However, we regret that Mr. Alkan had not used more of those bold, fantastic orchestral effects which Beethoven employed so happily, and which seems inherent in this compact, joyful triple rhythm.

'As we have never studied philology, and even if we know a little French – perhaps, alas, our readers think the opposite – the Coptic, the Syriac, the Sanscrit and the hieroglyphic languages of the Orient are sealed books to us. The composer ought to give us more explanation of certain Hebrew characters in red ink which decorate the first page of the Adagio, and which looked to us as complicated as a game of 'spillikins', thrown on the table at random. It is the verse from Genesis, no less: 'God said: "Let there be light" and there was light'. 'Will there ever be a better theme to inspire a composer! In his celebrated oratorio Haydn painted a marvellous picture of the world before the sovereign finger of the Creator raised it from the void. Those obscure harmonies, muffled and funereal, admirably express the silent horror of fathomless chaos: but despite our profound veneration for Haydn's genius we ought to acknowledge that the most unfortunate of all the chords and the most paltry of conclusions announce the explosion of light. Alas! great master, it is not the advent of the splendid sun which you convey, but rather that of a fairy-light. Without a doubt Mr. Alkan remained at some distance from Haydn in the first part of the piece, but the crescendo is superlatively achieved, and the wind unisons mingled with the rapid scales and the broad string chords ought to produce the most grandiose effect. It seemed to us as we consulted these pages that a brighter sun was about to burst through the clouds which surrounded us and let us distinguish more clearly the characters we were seeking to discern. The finale of the symphony is not of the same stature as the first three movements. Its melody is not sufficiently distinguished; however, in its development the most skilful treatment can be seen.'

It seems quite possible that should Alkan's volume containing the symphony ever be discovered it might equally well include such compositions as the missing 'quintets and sextets for strings' mentioned by Joseph d'Ortigue in the *Revue et gazette musicale* (March 3, 1844). As we have seen, Alkan also spoke of unpublished chamber works in a letter to Fétis on July 25, 1847; works he was holding for publication at a later date. From our examination of the cantatas and the recently discovered orchestral parts of the first *Concerto da camera* it is clear that Alkan was already a skilled orchestrator in his teens. His two chamber works, written before the age of twenty-eight, confirm a disciplined and individual handling of large, classical forms. The B minor symphony was the thirty-year-old composer's most ambitious work to date. Its rediscovery would not only provide evidence of the direction his genius might have taken him in a less personally hostile environment; it could well enrich our perspective of French symphonic developments in the nineteenth century by forging a missing link between the seditious masterpieces of Berlioz and the more traditional examples by such classically trained contemporaries as Saint-Saëns and Franck.

We can only be grateful that the fugitive symphony was not also joined by a minor masterpiece that Alkan had the foresight to publish in 1859, probably at his own expense. That rare compound of freakish imagination and classical discipline that hallmarks so much of the composer's work is arrayed to unique advantage in his *Marcia funebre sulla morte d'un pappagallo* (Funeral march for a dead parrot). This celebrated study in mock pathos remains to this day *sui generis*, an inimitable monument to Jaco, Alkan's operatically-trained parrot who seems to have taken a posthumous hand (or claw) in its creation and perhaps, even in anticipating its libretto; who knows?

> 'As-tu déjeuné, Jaco?
> Et de quoi?
> Ah!'

The march is scored for mixed voices (SSTB) and woodwind; and what an acute and imaginative ear for instrumental timbre Alkan displays by allocating the accompaniment to three oboes and bassoon. One can think of no other combination that could evince such piquant parrot cries as this bizarre quartet. A bare, instrumental prologue betokens the stiff upper lip until its C minor pathos spills over into such delectable sequences as the following chromatic landslide, its progress unpredictable yet inevitable.

Ex. 266

A half-close provides the cue for a tenor and bass recitative before the wind prologue returns, providing the harmonic framework for this bold vocal refrain.

Ex. 267

Alkan adds the following footnote: 'This reminiscence is solely due to an ornithological accident. I pray you, connoisseurs of *La gazza ladra* (the thieving magpie), do not attribute the slightest impertinence to the deceased parrot's song.' The section is repeated above a chromatic wail, rising to a stern unison descant, an impassioned resolution and double bar. The mood now lightens in the relative major E flat for Alkan's setting of 'Et de quoi?' accompanied by grotesquely contrasted twiddles from oboe and bassoon. Its continuation provides an ideal foil to the *portamento* style of the second episode. Here only the most detached delivery compatible with the constant bandying of the syllables 'de quoi' will do justice to this feast of onomatopoeic allusion as oboes and bassoon cluck their approval. The second episode demonstrates Alkan's classical vigilance at a moment when emotion threatens sobriety. The controlling factor here is a strictly organised fugue in four voices (Ex.268) with two counter-subjects, stretti and pedal; to the pedant a paradigm of contrapuntal skills, for the harmonist a minefield of unclassified asperities whereas the innocent ear hears simply what it is meant to hear: the sustained simulation of funereal wailing.

Ex.268

p
Ah! Ah!
p
Ah! Ah! Ah! Ah!

p
Ah! Ah! Ah! Ah!
Ah! Ah! Ah! Ah! Ah!
Ah! Ah! Ah!
p
Ah! Ah!

Ex.269

S
S
T
B
Chorus
Oboes
1
2
3
Ah! Ah! Ah!
Ah! Ah! Ah! Ah!
Ah! Ah! Ah! Ah! Ah! Ah!
Ah! Ah! Ah!

One should add that both the chromatic subject (Ex.268) and the lugubrious octave leap (in Ex.269) have been biding their time within the earlier textures. Note also how this anguished climax overlaps the final impassioned return.

Ex.270

After a brief reprise the sopranos bestow a valediction, the bassoon adds its blessing and all join in a sumptuous crescendo and diminuendo in the final liberating glow of C major.

Alkan's Erard pedal-piano (in Paris Conservatoire Museum)

14 Organ or Pedal-piano?

This chapter is directed at a future generation. It concerns the mainstream of Alkan's final creative period, a period that produced some of his greatest compositions including works that may one day prove indispensable to the organ repertory. Until all this music receives a full and independent study, preferably by an organist who is also a concert-pianist, its significance can hardly be realised. I believe that it contains some of the profoundest and most varied works for its medium since Bach. If such a claim strikes the reader as wildly improbable, wilfully irresponsible – even as fanatical – I can but urge my organ colleagues 'Search and ye shall find. How is it possible that an essential part of the organ repertory, considered vital by such a master as César Franck, could remain so obscure that Alkan's name is only known in organ circles as the dedicatee of Franck's own *Grande pièce symphonique?* The answer is twofold. To start with, the music has long remained out of print, an omission that must and will be remedied.[1] Meanwhile photocopies should be obtained from international libraries. Secondly, and perhaps more seriously, it has been claimed that Alkan wrote nothing specifically for the organ. This is not quite true but it brings us face to face with the whole convoluted problem of organ versus pedal-piano.

Like Schumann, in his Canons and Sketches op.56 and op.58, Alkan was already writing for the pedal-piano in the mid-1840s. His obsession with the instrument, however, dates from the early 1850s when Erard's placed a pedal-piano at his disposal, enabling him to immerse himself in the great organ works of Bach. Alkan wrote enthusiastically to Fétis who was eager to hear this instrument, describing it as 'the new *piano à clavier de pédales'* – (presumably an improved design), adding that he considered it both 'ancient and modern'. In 1855 he was displaying Erard's latest models at the Paris International Exhibition and a surviving sketch by Alkan emphasising the importance of the instrument may have been

[1] Since writing these words Billaudot have issued opp.54 & 72, together with Franck's selection of Alkan's *Prières* and *Grands préludes.* Opp.64, 66 & 69, the *Douze études* for pedals alone and *Bombardo-Carillon* (among others) remain unavailable.

intended as the basis for an introduction to this event. It can be summarised as follows:

1. French organists pay little heed to the clarity demanded by Bach's writing. The pedal-piano can reproduce this and could popularise these works.
2. It should restore a healthier style to both piano composition and performance by substituting true part-writing for the current vogue of endless arpeggios nourished by the vulgar abuse of the sustaining pedal.
3. It opens up a host of new colours unobtainable on either the piano or the organ.

Alkan's attitude to the organ, after obtaining his *premier prix* for the instrument at the Paris Conservatoire in 1834, must remain a mystery. In a centenary article by Theodor Bolte we are told 'since it was denied Alkan to work as an organist in a church or synagogue he practised his brilliant organ technique on one of Erard's pedal-pianos'.[1] In view of Alkan's close friendship with such organists as Franck and Lefébure-Wély, both of whom held key organ posts in Paris, it seems inconceivable that he would not have enjoyed at least an intermittent access to some of the city's finest organs to try out his compositions; yet of all the music under discussion only one publication is ascribed to organ alone. On the other hand several works assigned specifically to the pedal-piano would seem equally effective, if not more so, on the organ, whereas certain pieces entrusted either to organ or pedal-piano must prove ineffective if not impossible on the organ. Fortunately, like the keyboard works of Bach, much of this music transcends its medium, making an equally valid though different impression on either instrument.

Apart from the *Vingt-cinq préludes* op.31, all Alkan's works for organ or pedal-piano were published between 1859 and the early 1870s. Their chronology is approximately as follows: *Benedictus* op.54 (pedal-piano) 1859, *Petits préludes sur les huit gammes du plain-chant* (organ) 1859, *Treize prières* op.64 (organ or pedal-piano) 1866, *Onze grands préludes* op.66 (pedal-piano) *c*1866. *Onze pièces dans le style religieux* op.72 (organ, harmonium or piano) 1867, *Impromptu sur le choral de Luther* op.69 (pedal-piano) 1866. That op.66 and op.72 are each comprised of eleven original pieces with the addition of a transcription from Handel's Messiah indicates their complementary conception. There is also that four-foot-freak, the *Bombardo-Carillon* for pedal-board duo of 1872, presumably written as a joke to play at a *petit concert* with Delaborde; and there is a set of *Douze études* also for

[1] In the *Neue Zeitschrift für Musik*, Nov 27, 1913.

the pedals alone (for organ or pedal-piano) of diabolical difficulty published together with the *Impromptu* op.69 in the 1860s. (A set of twelve fugues for pedal-piano listed in Pazdirek's catalogue probably refers to these studies).

Clearly, most of this music requires varying degrees of adaptation when played on the organ; but, as Franck demonstrated in his three-volume edition selected in 1889 from Alkan's *Prières* and *Grands préludes* together with one of the *Pièces religieux*, the problem is in no way insuperable. Works that resist the medium, like the great *Impromptu* op.69, may be played on one piano with a third hand supplying the pedal part; a compromise sanctioned by Alkan himself. It must be admitted, however, that such a work could only make its full and unique impact on the instrument for which it was designed. Another piece that seems to me to demand the clanking resonance and attack of the pedal-piano is *Deus Sebaoth* no.8 from the *Prières* op.64, also known as 'Dieu des armées'. Played on the organ, its Hebraic fervour and minatory energy become too easily debased into fairground jollity. On a normal piano a third hand can complete the notes precisely as Alkan requires but with a loss of the bold dynamic freedom conveyed by a single player. Vianna da Motta's arrangement for two hands offers a valiant solution, yet despite the jettisoning of essential notes the texture becomes unwieldy and the pedal must be abused in a manner abhorrent to Alkan. Above all, one loses that extra physical dimension engendered by the constant entry of the pedal part and the powerful effect this has on the rhythmic tension. The very opening, with its bold threefold imitation, makes this clear.

Deus Sebaoth is only one of several unique works whose ultimate secret must remain locked within their enigmatic pages until a suitable instrument can be located, resurrected or reconstructed and a performer with the necessary will, temperament and perseverance persuaded to master it. Meanwhile a sizeable proportion of this music, with some minor adjustments of register, will go perfectly well on the organ.

The little plainchant preludes of 1859, for organ, manuals alone, should be known to all organists. These tiny pieces pass progressively, in as many minutes, through the eight Gregorian modes. The discipline imposed by a stylistic problem invariably puts Alkan on his creative mettle. Ranging from the Hypophrygian ferocity of the fourth prelude to the wistful artlessness of the sixth (Exs.272 and 273) they seem to stand outside the barriers of time and place. The set as a whole is indivisible and homogeneous and it reveals, perhaps more than any other work of his, Alkan's essential spiritual modesty.

Despite their spare, two-stave presentations the *Onze pièces dans le style religieux* op.72 are important, medium-sized pieces of strongly

Ex.271a Alkan: *Deus Sebaoth*

marked character. They are all possible and, with few exceptions, effective on the organ – most players making judicious use of the pedals. In many of these pieces, the fourth for instance, Alkan seems to rediscover the rich vein of his earlier *Vingt-cinq préludes* op.31 but with the wisdom of age and the breadth of experience. The opening piece has a dignified, processional character. The third, incorporated in Franck's edition, is a strangely haunting fugue while the seventh

Ex. 271b *Deos Sebaoth* as arranged by Vianna da Motta

is one of Alkan's most beguiling short pieces. Once discovered, its lilting refrain might easily become the familiar mainstay of every other organist's repertoire. Harmonic surprises, however, abound and a wonderful series of modulations just before the return should

Ex.272 Prelude no.4

prevent it from ever becoming hackneyed. The penultimate piece is a lumbering carillon in the Dorian mode while the set ends, apart from the closing transcription, with an absolute oddity. Its ingredients include a frail little song, a more reassuring sequel and a strangely groping chorale in five time. Progress is constantly challenged by the incursion of a stern, bare octave which threatens

Ex.273 Prelude no.6

the key centre. Neither the ingenious combination of the song with its sequel nor a majestic return of the chorale can exorcise this sinister visitation. The piece ends bleakly, inevitably, its song reduced to a single strand as beckoned by two final warning signals from the bare octave it seems to wilt and vanish into an alien environment.

Although op.72 was originally ascribed to ‘organ, harmonium or piano' the title page of the Costallat reprint simply advises piano or harmonium. If Alkan intended these pieces for harmonium, as their thin, bare textures so often suggest, one should not forget that this often maligned instrument is capable of an expressive power quite beyond its domestic image as a makeshift organ.

The two mighty sets of *Treize prières* op.64 and *Onze grands préludes* op.66 contain some of Alkan's most impressive music. From the thirteen *Prières* Franck selected nos. 1, 2, 5, 6, 8, 9 and 11 as suitable for the organ, adding nos. 3 and 7 from the *Grands préludes*, of which he was the dedicatee, to his series. Vianna da Motta also transcribed eight of the *Prières* for solo piano. The twelth has an infectious, polka-like swing about it quite unsuited to the organ, but in Motta's arrangement it makes a captivating, if hardly 'prayerful' piano solo, especially towards the end where a three-note carillon chimes in 'Ivesian' contradiction to the prevailing rhythm. The only other *Prières* that prove non-viable on the organ are the third and seventh, both wonderful pieces; but neither, despite Vianna da Motta's brave attempt, may be encompassed by two hands alone. No.3 is a daunting study in tremolando confined to the nether regions, the feet projecting a sombre melody between the hands. Motta shows how it is possible for two hands to smuggle these notes into the texture but the result remains an artistic absurdity. The seventh is one of the grandest of all these pieces with a spread of texture only possible on the pedal-piano. The very wide spacing of its second subject marked 'deux pédales' is the *locus classicus* of untranslatable writing for the instrument, sounding both muddy and muddled in its solo adaptation.

The ten remaining pieces go well on the organ and although some of the writing in the fourth may not feel particularly organistic under the hand it can be made to sound most effective. The opening *Prière* generates its own quiet mysticism by hypnotic repetition, rhythmic ambiguity and a probing tonal ambivalence delicately poised between C minor and G major. The second piece is an amiable three-part invention while the fourth contrasts pastoral episodes, well-suited to the organ, with some bold footwork beneath a persistent trill which may prove troublesome. The fifth, a monothematic adagio with pedal solos, seems equally adaptable to either instrument, whereas the sixth contains a piece of central mystification that cries out for organ timbre as a sustained major second favouring E flat minor resolves disarmingly into D major. Although Franck did not include the tenth and thirteenth *Prières* in his collection they seem to me among the most effective on the organ. No.10 in B flat major, a processional above a staccato bass, is full of Alkan's unpredictable twists and turns, not least in its minor-key ending. An outburst boosted by crunched chromaticisms contrasts strangely with a chorale-like episode juxtaposing unrelated diatonic harmonies. The eleventh *Prière* lays the ghosts of some of Alkan's earlier compositions, notably *Ouverture* and the Cello Sonata. I know of nothing in music more affirmative than the opening of the concluding *Prière*; but Alkan hastily abandons it for a swaggering march. Any initial shock of wilful incongruity is soon dispelled, however, as both ideas are brought into ever closer relationship until they become almost indistinguishable in a final resounding paean.

Unlike the *Prières*, Alkan's *Onze grands préludes* were written specifically for the pedal-piano. As one might expect their style is more consistently pianistic and, according to Bolte, Vianna da Motta arranged some of them for piano duet. Even here however several of these pieces, as well as the two included in Franck's rather cautious selection, may be effectively adapted for the organ. Only the sixth, one of Alkan's most bizarre inventions, and the formidable tenth resist the medium. The latter, above its bouncing ostinato, is marked scherzando, but at Alkan's ♩ = 92 it takes on the ferocity of a wild Cossack dance. Arranged for two pianos it would make an electrifying showpiece. The remaining nine preludes will all yield to varying degrees of modification although one or two may, on first acquaintance, appear perversely incongruous. The intense passion locked within the jaunty rhythms of no.4, for instance, seems mocked by its frivolous facade; yet it is this very contradiction that releases tensions absolutely unique to this composer. Like no.6, a piece of irresistible perversity, it extends moods already encountered in the *Trois petites fantaisies* op.41.

The whole series, including the final transcription from Handel's Messiah, proceeds in a sequence of related major and minor keys descending in thirds: F major, D minor, B flat, G minor etc. It opens with a foot-tingling homage to Bach's F major Toccata and continues with yet another return to Alkan's 'happy and glorious' rhythm ♩♩♩| ♩.♪♩ beneath a chirping upper mordent pedal-point. An exciting and disruptive piece, it cocks a snook at propriety and calls for some breathtaking virtuosity. The third prelude is compounded of three distinct elements: a severe recitative for pedals alone, a doleful refrain in the tenor register, and a celestial answering motif in the treble. After their separate introduction all three are interwoven into a passionate crescendo, the piece ending with an imposing restatement of the opening recitative six octaves deep. While the fifth prelude is a richly textured adagio, the seventh 'alla giudesca' is a congregational piece in Jewish devotional style. Arresting in manner but impersonal in substance it seems to me the least interesting of the set. The stormy passion that erupts so vividly in the final coda of Alkan's *Sonatine* op.61 is harnessed more rigorously in the eighth prelude. As rhythmic incisiveness is its life-blood, especially in a vigorous pedal motif, it will sit less happily on the organ; yet it is such a darkly cogent piece that it is well worth transcribing.

The last three preludes consummate three contrasted aspects of Alkan's genius: his inner calm, his wild abandon and his mysticism. The D flat prelude no.9 shares with some of Bruckner's great adagios a spacious inevitability that links both composers to Beethoven's final period. Its timeless pulsation requires delicate handling by pianists and careful registration from organists lest it chatters rather than purrs. In the absence of the instrument for which it was devised its richly-stranded texture may only be achieved by two players at one or more pianos, yet its long-breathed paragraphs demand the unity of a single mind. For this reason alone the organ seems to offer the better solution. Although, as we have seen, it is unsuited to the penultimate piece the organ serves the final *Grand prélude* magnificently. Here we enter the world of mysticism. An enigmatic recitative with questioning responses gropes its way from darkness towards light. After several abortive attempts at resolution it is gathered up into a passage of sumptuous sonority as unstable tonalities descend precariously above a huge dominant pedal enhanced by pungent acciaccaturas. The prelude ends with a mighty unison affirmation of its opening recitative.

If comparison with the work of his French contemporaries shows that Alkan's pedal requirement in these works is far in advance of its time, the *Douze études d'orgue ou de piano à pédales pour les pieds seulement* (Twelve studies for the pedal-board alone) are of such spine-chilling difficulty that one wonders if their dedication to his friend Lefébure-Wély 'the Auber of the organ' was meant as a joke – and a rather savage one at that in view of Wély's own cautious writing for the pedals. Could he, or any other of Alkan's contemporaries, have coped with the following example?

Ex.274 Pedal Study no.9

When one reflects that these studies were published in the 1860s at a time when pedal technique in France had only just emerged from the Dark Ages, Alkan's achievement appears well-nigh inexplicable; an isolated freak. To understand how it may have come about we must turn to an investigation of the Paris organ world of the mid-nineteenth century by David Gammie[1] and François Sabatier[2].

Alkan and Franck both graduated from François Benoist's organ class at the Paris Conservatoire at a period when Bach's organ works were still considered unplayable in France. Few organs had adequate pedal-boards and fewer organists availed themselves of a pedal-piano on which to work up the necessary technique. Franck himself was

[1] Incorporated in a lecture to the Alkan Society in London, March 1984.
[2] See Sabatier's excellent 'L'oeuvre d'orgue et de piano-pédalier'. This includes mention of Cavaillé-Coll's letter to Lemmens dated 22/9/1853, praising Alkan's 'marvellous' performance of Bach's F major Toccata BWV540.

only shocked into acquiring an upright model on his appointment to St. Clotilde, Paris in 1858 and, despite his later championship of Bach, his own writing for the pedals remained comparatively undemanding. Only the little-known enthusiast Alexandre Boëly (1785-1858) had been pursuing Bach within his own small circle, having acquired a pedal-piano as early as 1842. His compositions, surely among the first for this instrument, might be well worth exploring. Saint-Saëns held him in high esteem. But Boëly only operated on the fringe of his profession and his activities remained stillborn. The first event to shake the French organ world out of its apathy was a visit by the Breslau organist Adolf Hesse to inaugurate a new organ at St. Eustache, Paris in 1844. His pedal technique in such works as Bach's F major Toccata, later to be one of Alkan's specialities, astounded the Parisians. And when, eight years later, Hesse's brilliant pupil Nicholas Lemmens came to demonstrate the new instrument at St. Vincent-de-Paul in January 1852 the organ loft was packed with such famous musicians as Zimmerman, Gounod, Thomas, Stamaty, Boëly, Wély, Franck and, of course, Alkan. Writing in the *Journal des débats* Joseph d'Ortigue tells us that Lemmens's feet executed such incredible gymnastics that more than one organist might have considered himself fortunate if he could have done as much with his hands. In 1854 Lemmens returned to Paris to cause a further sensation by applying such feats to Erard's latest concert-grand pedal-piano completed in February 1853.

This event, perhaps, more than any other must surely have awakened Alkan to the undreamt-of possibilities of pedal technique. At the same time the pedal demands of Franck, Lefébure-Wély and other organists of the French school remained basic and simple. It was not until Widor took over the organ class at the Conservatoire in 1890 that a far more disciplined approach to organ playing, and the pedals in particular, replaced the semi-improvisational, inspirational teaching of Franck. To this end, Alkan's pedal-piano was brought back into service when Vierne acted as Widor's repetiteur. Widor's successor Marcel Dupré, doyen of twentieth-century organ virtuosi, considered Alkan's pedal studies, used in conjunction with scales, the complete and indispensable foundation of pedal technique. These strange and unique études emphasise once more Alkan's prophetic vision, his artistic isolation and his increasing relevance to a later generation.

Despite Dupré's advocacy, their dedication to an organist and the alternative suggestion of organ or pedal-piano on their title pages, the register (AA—e^1) and style of Alkan's twelve pedal-board studies confirms their pedal-piano origin. Nicholas King, who has made a special study of all Alkan's music for organ or pedal-piano, describes their technical challenge as 'fearsome' and at times 'contortionist' especially on the straight pedal-board of the period.[1] Nevertheless, all these studies are far more than exercises in fleet-footed dexterity. They are equally exacting musically, reminding us of Delaborde's refined performance on the pedal-piano, which included works by Alkan in the Hanover Square Rooms, London in 1871. 'To the practised foot' wrote *The World of Music* 'any gradation of intensity is as accessible to Broadwood's pedal-board as to the practised hand'. The first and simplest study is in the tradition of Bach's solo cello suites; the third an expressive fugue in three voices; the seventh a furious chromatic study, while the ninth is a scherzo. The last two studies contrast a deep and sombre adagio with a closely-knit set of variations on a stark ground bass. Although the idea of a public performance would be too monstrous to contemplate, the whole series might well be studied to advantage by enterprising organists and especially in conjunction with Alkan's two most important single works for the pedal-piano: *Benedictus* op.54 and *Impromptu sur le chorale de Luther 'Un fort rempart est notre Dieu'* op.69. Although both compositions contain passages that might sound magnificent on the organ their more pianistic textures would require drastic revision. Presumably Alkan was able to play them both on his pedal-piano even with its straight pedal-board; yet the textural complexities of the Impromptu in particular make inhuman demands on a single player. For this reason alone Roger Smalley has transcribed both works for two pianos, redistributing the parts in the most masterly manner. Whereas the Benedictus is a strangely haunting work with a gripping climax, the effect of the Impromptu, in this arrangement, is overwhelming. Roger Smalley's claim[2] that it emerges as one of the three greatest works for the medium from the Romantic era is no exaggeration. 'Only the Brahms St. Antony and Reger-Beethoven Variations', he writes 'can measure up to it'. Dr. Smalley has kindly contributed the following commentaries:

Benedictus op.54 moves from the lowest reaches of the keyboard to the highest, from lento to alla breve, from a gloomy D minor to an effulgent D major, from darkness to light. This interpretation connects with both the words of the Benedictus ('Blessed is he who goes in the name of the Lord') and Alkan's lifelong preoccupation with the struggle for spiritual redemption (see especially the second movement of the *Grande sonate* op.33).

[1] In a letter to the author.

[2] In a letter to the author. The distinguished organist Gillian Weir, who is also acquainted with Alkan's pedal studies, questions however the advantage of a curved pedal-board.

Ex.275 Benedictus op.54: main themes

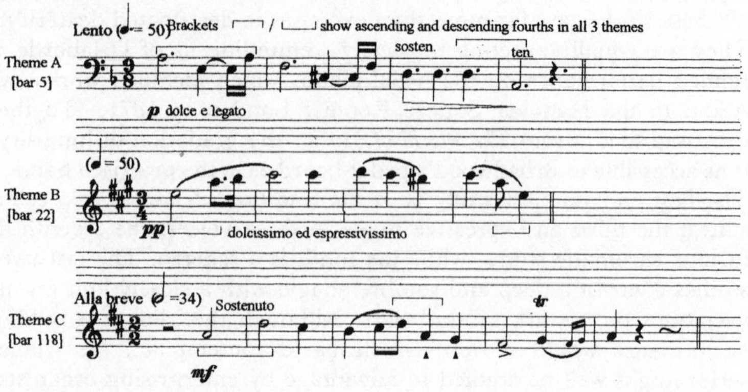

Over a drum-like ostinato a sombre theme in the tenor register (theme A) strives painfully upwards. This is immediately contrasted with an ethereal melody in A major (theme B – Alkan's marking is *dolcissimo ed espressivissimo*) floating high above its luxuriantly rippling accompaniment. Note that the descending fourth which opens theme A is inverted to form the beginning of theme B. Just as this second theme seems to be taking wing it collapses into the initial ostinato and theme A, this time treated canonically in F minor. Once again theme B interrupts, now in C major and more extensively developed. The pace quickens ('un poco più mosso') and, via an ecstatically rising series of sequences, the music mounts to a powerful climax in F major. This subsides on to the dominant of D major and the alla breve sets off in this key with a march theme (theme C) once again featuring rising and falling fourths. D major may have been reached but the struggle is not yet over. A central development section, built over a series of ingeniously decorated pedal points, ranges widely in tonality before leading back to theme C presented in canon over a thunderous pedal part in quavers. At the very moment of resolution theme A suddenly returns in a triumphant D major to provide an abrupt (only 5 bars) but satisfying conclusion to this powerful, if somewhat enigmatic work.

The *Impromptu sur le chorale de Luther 'Un fort rempart est notre Dieu'* op.69 is curiously titled – nothing could be less impromptu than this elaborately wrought single movement of 421 bars, lasting about 15 minutes.

Alkan's use of Luther's famous chorale melody (known in English as 'A mighty fortress is our God') is highly inventive, functioning at different times as a passacaglia bass, theme for variations, and fugue subject. Although played without interruption the work is divided by measured pauses into four distinct parts, which suggest a four-movement sonata structure – first movement, scherzo, slow movement and finale.

One very interesting feature is that although the same pulse (mm. = 63) is maintained throughout the entire work the illusion of several different speeds is created by applying different units to this unchanging pulse Thus the first part is in ¢ (𝅗𝅥 = 63), the second in 6/8 and 12/8 (𝅗𝅥. = 63), the third in 3/4 (𝅗𝅥. = 63), whilst the fourth returns to ¢ (𝅗𝅥 = 63).

After an initial unison presentation of the first two phrases of the chorale melody (8 bars – tonality E flat major) the first part is subdivided, by Alkan's characteristically meticulous use of double bar lines, into twelve variations, of steadily increasing momentum, brilliantly contrived on several levels – registral, textural and rhythmic. For the first eight variations the theme remains in the bass, in nine and ten it moves to the tenor, in eleven to the alto and in twelve to the soprano (these designations are used somewhat loosely, since the writing is not consistently in four parts).

In each of the first four variations a different figuration is superimposed on the theme. The next six variations, however, are grouped into three pairs, with the same figuration persisting through two repetitions. So far all the variations have been eight bars long. In variation 11 Alkan uses the entire chorale melody for the first time, adding another fourteen bars to the original eight. Variation 12 repeats these fourteen new bars, whilst omitting the first eight bars. Rhythmically there is a gradual increase in the numbers of subdivisions, progressing from the minims and crotchets of the initial theme, through crotchet triplets, quavers, quaver triplets and semiquavers to the twelve semiquavers in the time of a minim of the twelfth variation. This final subdivision means that the figurations are now equal in speed to the 6/8 semiquavers of the following scherzo which is in two halves. In the first the entire theme – still in E flat – is played in a vigorous dotted rhythm, the phrases being separated by cascades of arpeggios curiously reminiscent of the decorations of the central chorale in Chopin's C sharp minor Scherzo. For the second half the tonality changes to C major, the first eight bars of the theme being presented in augmentation, joined later by its own diminution in G major and followed by two diminutions in canon suggesting C minor and G minor. A skeleton of this section will give some idea of the complexity of Alkan's musical thought (Ex.276).

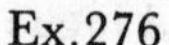
Ex.276

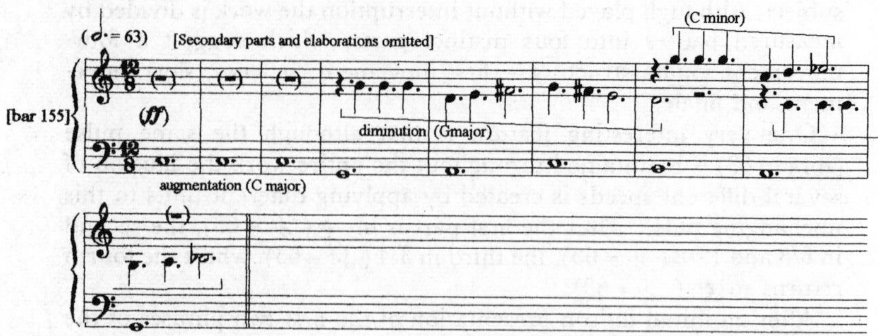

The slow movement which follows is in C minor. After a richly chromatic four-part harmonisation of the first eight bars each half of the chorale is developed in a series of elaborate canons, both direct and inverted. Then in a central section Alkan combines both halves of the theme – the second half played sostenuto, the first staccato and decorated with an increasing number of highly impolite grace notes.

Ex.277

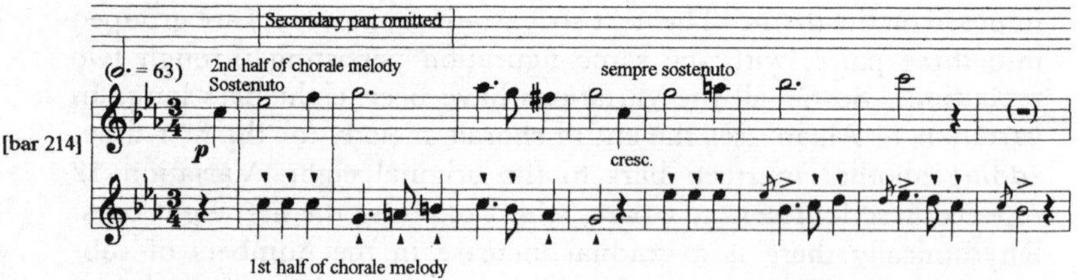

This third part evaporates in a wonderfully laid-out coda, in which a bizarre harmonisation of the chorale is enclosed by chromatic slitherings in the pedal part below and a continuous patter of staccato quavers above.

The hypnotic mood thus created is abruptly broken by the stridently dramatic four-bar introduction to the final fugue, whose subject consists of a speeded up version of the first two phrases of the chorale:

Ex.278

For its episodes this magnificently developed four-part fugue (which runs to 106 bars of mainly semiquaver movement in ¢) draws extensively on motives *a*, *b*, and *c* from Ex.278 – the last two being run in canonic chains at a distance of only one quaver. At its climax, after 17 bars of a modulating four-part stretto over a decorated dominant pedal point, the fugue breaks off and the complete chorale is announced in massive block chords accompanied by a tumultuous pedal part in broken octaves. How typical of Alkan that he did not finish at this point but ends with an almost self-effacing, reticent statement of the concluding four bars of the chorale marked *piano*.

While this chapter for the first edition of my book was in proof stage, the Cambridge organist, Dr John Wells, confounded my strictures about the third *Prière* and the tenth *Grand prélude* by performing both pieces at a public recital. Since then John Wells has recorded these and some of the other *Prières* and *Préludes.* We now have recordings (mostly by Kevin Bowyer) of all thirteen *Prières* op.64, the *Impromptu sur le choral de Luther* op.69 and the *Petits Préludes sur les 8 gammes du plain-chant.* There still remains the challenge of recording the *11 Grands préludes et un transcription du Messie de Haendel* op.66 and the *11 Pièces dans le style religieux, et un transcription du Messie de Haendel* op.72 in their entirety (see Discography).

An additional piece of the Alkan jigsaw puzzle has come to light. We now know for certain that the *Impromptu sur le choral de Luther* op.69 appeared in print in 1866, for that year Alkan sent a signed copy to his old colleague, Franz Liszt. The copy is now in the Liszt Museum, Budapest.

15 Alkan's Creative Personality

It seems impossible to study Alkan's generous output without becoming bemused by the sheer variety of its style and scope. Only a Beethoven, the sceptic may claim, could sustain his identity within such limits and although this broad spectrum of creative activity may yet prove Alkan's trump card it also has its dangers. Many different Alkans may seem to emerge on as many different occasions blunting his image and thwarting his assessment. Futhermore, this very profusion must prompt the intelligent musician to ask if such diversity is compatible with originality. In short, does Alkan's creative personality remain intact whether he adopts an earlier manner or anticipates a later one; whether he expresses himself in a twelve-bar vignette or an epic concerto?

It would be difficult to think of any universally established composer whose flavour and style are not immediately recognisable to those familiar with his music. Alkan's younger contemporary Saint-Saëns is something of a test case. His detractors dub him the chameleon among composers, a skilled eclectic whose underlying anonymity is cloaked in a multitude of styles. Does not his Second Piano Concerto start like Bach and end like Offenbach? Yet this engaging piece could hardly be mistaken for the work of any other composer. If Saint-Saëns' music affords glimpses of Beethoven, Mendelssohn, Schumann, Chopin and Liszt, with even a hint of Wagner, its overall impression remains essentially French in its clarity of form and texture, its glittering brilliance and its cool lyricism; all qualities, incidentally, he shares with Alkan. Should we agree with Tovey's gibe that Saint-Saëns was the most talented composer who was not a genius, then we must see this limitation not so much in a want of individuality but rather in Saint-Saëns' lack of emotional involvement and spiritual depth.

Alkan's stylistic versatility is of a different order. Where Saint-Saëns slips nonchalantly in and out of his various styles Alkan is more selective and often uses a particular example as a spring-board to release a special aspect of his many-sided imagination. For instance, an angular two-part invention in the baroque manner provides the ideal framework for a prophetic display of gritty Stravinskian counterpoint in his Gigue op.24. No matter what style Alkan adopts it is always sharply etched so that his voice remains unique and unmistakable. Although it may not be difficult to pin-point various musical elements that find their place in a composer's unique voice the way in which they are assimilated and unified is one of the profounder mysteries of the creative mind.

No investigation of Alkan's creative personality would be complete without some consideration of the part played in its formation by his Jewish background. Such titles as *Prières*, *Psaume*, *Super flumina Babylonis* remind us of his biblical studies and suggest an involvement in traditional Hebrew sources. Alkan's *Ancienne mélodie de la synagogue* displays unmistakable parallels with a Hassidic dance: *Rikud.*[1] Both the Alkan and this traditional source use a cantorial mode called *Ahava Rabba*:[2]

and each settles for G as its final note.

Ex.279a *Rikud*

Ex.279b Alkan: *Ancienne mélodie de la synagogue* (*Vingt-cinq préludes* op.31 no.6)

Alkan is also frequently drawn to the Dorian mode and the following example, also from his *Vingt-cinq préludes* sounds overtly Hassidic

[1] S. Naumbourg: *Recueil de chants religieux et populaires des Israelites* (Paris, 1874).

[2] I am indebted to Alexander Knapp for this and other details concerning Hebrew sources. See also Gérard Ganvert's study 'Alkan, musicien français de religion juive' in François-Sappey's *Alkan.*

Ex.280 *Vingt-cinq préludes* op.31 no.20

Only a handful of Alkan's compositions, however, disclose such a palpably Hebrew ambience and his most characteristic melodies seem more often to evolve from various elements, Hebrew among them. Raymond Lewenthal hedges his bets by describing the famous theme from *Le festin d'Esope* as Hasidic in character if not in origin. The following comparison would seem to support this view.

Ex.281a *Utso Etso* (traditional Hasidic melody)[1]

Ex.281b Alkan: *Le festin d'Esope*

I believe that Alkan's theme may have sprung to life as a synthesis of this traditional source and the Minuet from Mozart's G minor Symphony which he had already arranged for piano in the 1840s.

Ex.282 Mozart: Minuet from the G minor Symphony K550, transposed for comparison.

Whether or not this unlikely union was the result of conscious effort is immaterial; the strength and originality of Alkan's invention lies in its arresting simplicity.

[1] Velvel Pasternak: *Songs of the Chassidim* (New York, 1971)

Among the collections of Hebrew melodies by Naumbourg, Pasternak and others the overwhelming majority of Alkan-like turns of phrase that crop up from time to time are simply features absorbed into Jewish music from a western non-Jewish environment. Alkan's eclecticism made full use of any stimulus to hand and his ethnic background should not be exaggerated. His roots take their nourishment from many sources; from the French harpsichordists to late Beethoven; from Domenico Scarlatti to his friends and contemporaries, Mendelssohn and Chopin, but always transmuting it into something new and vital. Such cross-pollination may be true of all creative artists – no man is an island – but it is more demonstrably so in the case of Alkan who seems often at pains to disclose a source where others might seek to hide it.

It might be thought that Alkan's alleged anticipation of Mahler could throw some further light on a common racial heritage. Both were Jews. Both were eclectics and both were great performers; Alkan as a pianist, Mahler as a conductor. But it is in their music, in their obsessive rhythms, their acid harmony and counterpoint that the resemblance becomes most marked. Again one must be careful not to read too much into superficial similarities between these two composers of a different generation. There is nothing overtly Hebrew about their shared penchant for marches. Schubert also had it. Nor is their obsession with drum beats a peculiarly Jewish phenomenon. Although Alkan's premonition of the pungent bitterness of Mahler's harmonic language in such works as *Le tambour bat aux champs* or his Funeral March for a Dead Parrot has been frequently emphasised, the actual feeling invoked by the two composers is quite different. Where Mahler's emotional centre tends to be narcissistic Alkan's remains objective. He stands aloof, detached, presenting his most harrowing ideas in a cooler climate and larger perspective. The ostinati, the stark Neapolitan inflections common to both composers are, surely, only the symbols of their creativity; finger-prints perhaps but not their creative personalities. The *Esquisse* below displays none of these features, nor is it particularly Jewish in flavour yet to anyone familiar with Alkan's music – with the *Vingt-cinq prélüdes* op.31 or the *Petits préludes* for organ – its authorship is unmistakable.

Ex.283 *Esquisses* op.63 no.26

The elusive charm of this modal fragment stems from its chaste economy, its cool stepwise movement and Phrygian colouring. Although modality plays a more important part in Alkan's music than it does with his contemporaries it is no more an essential ingredient than his ethnic background or his fascination with five-beat rhythms. Alkan's harmonic originality must be sought in his radical, at times almost perverse treatment of a language that remains simple, diatonic and familiar. The hypnotic atmosphere of *La chanson de la folle au bord de la mer* is induced by the bizarre spacing of the most basic counters of harmonic small-talk. Often it is the strange 'orchestration' of a simple chord or an unaccustomed inversion that will wring new meaning from a well-worn progression, as in the following gruff resolution in the solo *Symphonie*.

Ex. 284

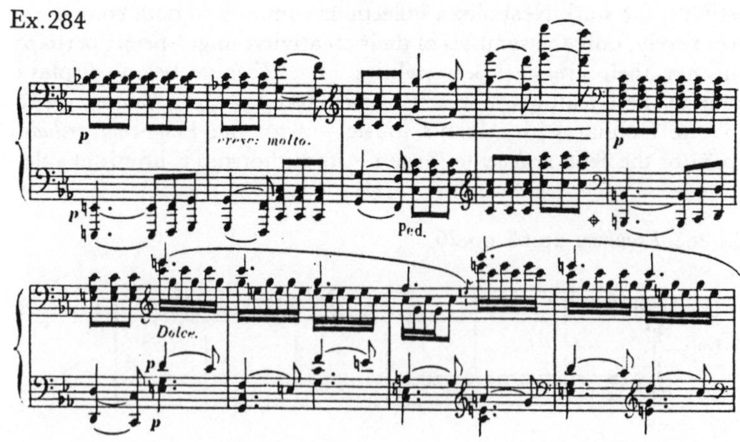

The characteristic Neapolitan colouring of so many of Alkan's cadences is often enhanced by a harmonic overlap or unusual juxtaposition. Note how the incipient Neapolitan pull in the following example crystallises into a stark confrontation of triads in root position and in opposed registers.

Ex.285 *Réconciliation* op.42

Alkan's attitude to other harmonic features such as false relations and appoggiaturas is similarly uncompromising. *Réconciliation* yields a host of such specialities, often held captive to his frequent pedal points.

Ex.286 *Réconciliation* op.42

Many of Alkan's most elaborate harmonic situations are brought about by the delayed resolutions of clustered appoggiaturas. The last two pages of his cadenza to Beethoven's Third Piano Concerto almost defies analysis as its tortured dissonances grind against a double pedal-point provided by its central trill. Although this whole extraordinary passage, (see pages 246 and 247), may be explained away by the long-delayed overlap of its resolutions, one has the uneasy impression that the familiar world of tonality has been placed under siege.

Alongside his frequent use of pedal points and ostinati, the most immediately striking aspect of Alkan's harmonic style is the surrealistic modulation. The fugitive clouding of harmonic identification that precedes the return in *Promenade sur l'eau* (from *Les mois*) may seem as ephemeral as a whiff of perfume yet it can give the unsuspecting listener a nasty turn. However bland Alkan's harmonic scheme its consequence can never be anticipated. There is nothing, for instance, in the classic elegance of the trio in the third movement of Alkan's *Sonatine* op.61 to prepare us for the booby-trap which plunges us into an alien underworld, yet its structural logic makes it totally convincing. Similarly the abrupt return from B minor to G minor in the Barcarolle op.65 is as unpredictable as it is inevitable.

We have noted the original and arresting appearance of Alkan's music on the printed page. This is partly due to its meticulous layout and boldly engraved dynamics; the composer was fastidious about the way his music was set out. Yet the symmetry and order of his marching regiments of notes are even more symbols of the crucial role played by rhythmic persistence in his music, a device he uses more exhaustively than any other composer before the twentieth century with the sole exception of Beethoven. In Alkan's case this rhythmic preoccupation is only part of a wider tendency illustrated by the way he will pin our attention on a specific facet of his invention; a rhythmic or melodic cell, a curiosity of texture or spacing – even an isolated note – pursuing its possibilities with ruthless singlemindedness. It is this *obsessional* aspect of Alkan's style that gives it its unique power and which provides the vital clue to the impulse that underlies all his widespread creative activity.

In his revealing study of creative motivation, *The Dynamics of Creation*, Anthony Storr describes traits of the obsessional personality citing three famous musical examples: Beethoven, Rossini and Stravinsky. Dr. Storr stresses the need of the obsessional to control both self and environment. Rossini and Stravinsky, he tells us, exhibit the meticulousness and extreme tidiness so characteristic of their kind. With Alkan these characteristics, exacerbated no doubt by his isolation, are carried to the edge of fanaticism. Thus his lifestyle becomes a ritual in which the rigidity of a domestic routine that leaves nothing to chance is only matched by the meticulous timing of each item, even each movement, in the programmes of recitals advertised to start 'à neuf heures très précis'. In Beethoven's case, as his sketch books indicate, it is in the actual act of creation, in the order he imposes on his material, that he most clearly discloses his obsessional character. At the heart of Alkan's creativity there is also this fierce obsessional control. It provides the driving force in his major works inducing an inexorable momentum even in so slow a movement as the finale of his *Grande sonate*. It powers and controls the relentless trajectories of the finales in the solo *Symphonie*, *Concerto* and *Sonatine* while his obsession with a specific idea can border on the pathological: witness the 414 repetitions of a single note in *Fa* and the way he will occasionally ram a point home with the insistence of a steam-hammer.

The originality of Alkan's piano writing is also rooted in the obsessional and the systematic. His preoccupation with the technical possibilities of his instrument forces him to squeeze every conceivable permutation out of his keyboard and pedal-board invention. It also accounts for such deliberate juxtapositions as the second and third *Esquisses* entitled *Le staccatissimo* and *Le legatissimo*; the one an extension of Scarlatti's brilliant keyboard technique, the other akin to Couperin's more lyrical writing. Although a comprehensive review of all Alkan's pianistic innovations is beyond the scope of this book many have been noted in their context. It is the obsessional aspect of his writing, however, that makes his demands quite different in degree from those of his contemporaries Schumann, Chopin, and Liszt. It calls for the cultivation of a rigorous rhythmic discipline offset by kaleidoscopic tonal refinements. It requires the courage to burn one's boats at the outset of each pianistic adventure; an apparent paradox only explained by the obsessional's need to rebel against the stultifying restriction of total control. Above all it demands a physical, mental and moral staying power beyond that required for any other music of the period. It is perhaps significant that no major pianist, apart from the composer himself, responded to the challenge during his life-time. The unfulfilled attempts by Busoni and Petri to promote Alkan's piano music in the earlier part of the twentieth century have already been discussed in Volume 1. I have long been convinced that the one great pianist of a succeeding generation who might have clinched their pioneering work is Rudolf Serkin. To my surprise I only learnt while working on this final chapter, and from Mr. Serkin himself, that he was introduced to Alkan's compositions at the outset of his career by no less an artist than Fritz Busch. How perceptive of Busch to recognise in the young Serkin that unusual combination of insight, courage and classical perspective so vital to Alkan's purpose. Serkin was impressed by the music, but after serious thought decided that the study of such taxing

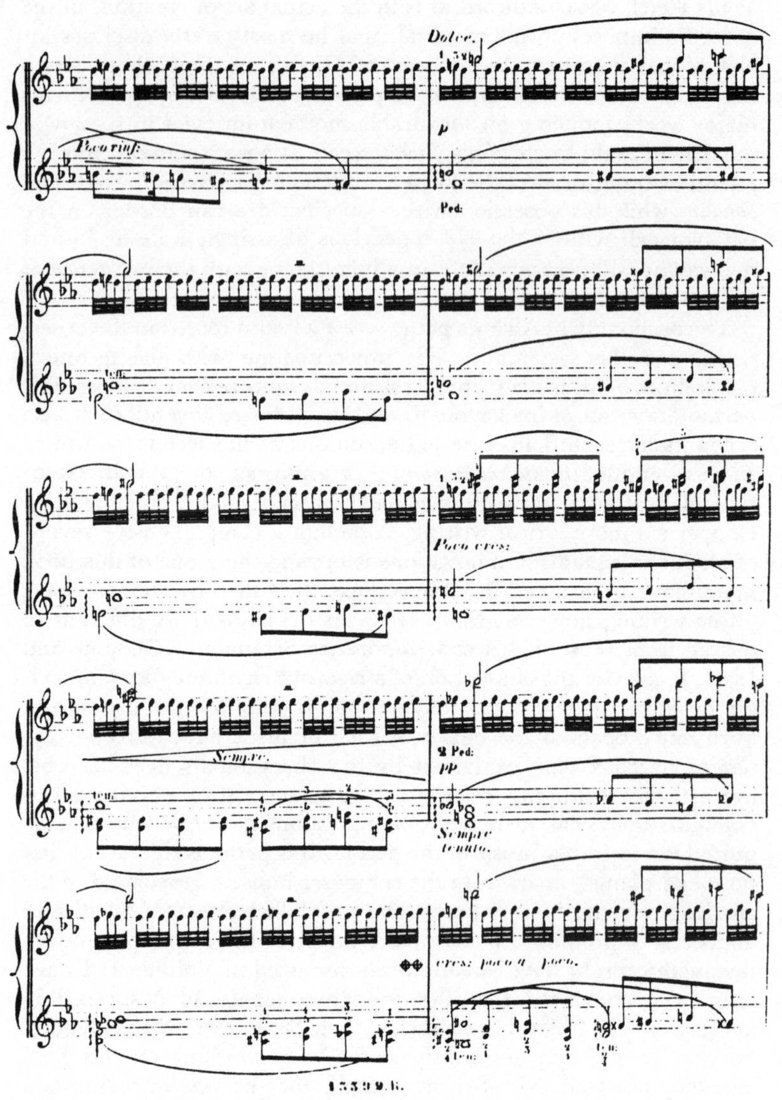

Alkan: from Cadenza to Beethoven's C minor Concerto

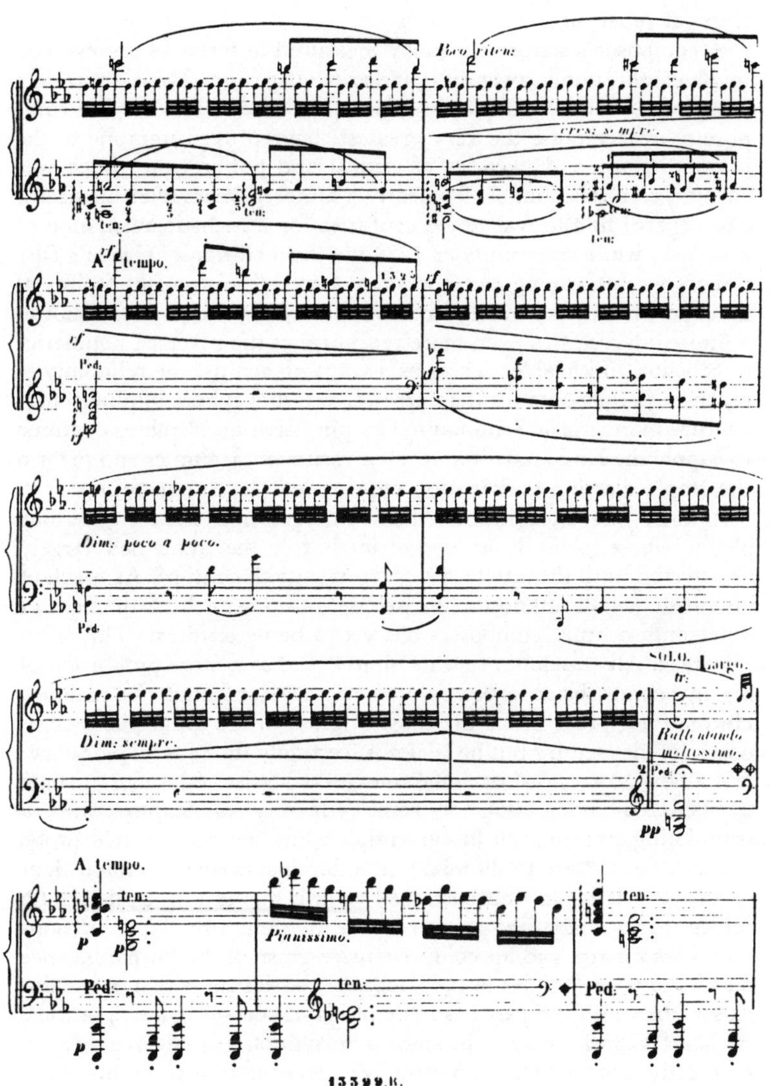
Poco riten:
cres: sempre.
ten:
A tempo.
Ped:
Dim: poco a poco.
Ped:
SOLO. Largo.
tr:
Dim: sempre.
Rallentando moltissimo.
Ped:
pp
A tempo.
ten:
Pianissimo.
Ped:
13399.R.

scores was incompatible with the demands of his ever-widening classical repertoire.

A composer's stature is usually measured in terms of professional involvement, public awareness and critical acclaim. These are widely accepted as reliable indicators of creative excellence. Yet few composers, even among the very greatest, have proved immune to the manipulations and vagaries of critical and public taste. Bach was considered unfashionable for nearly a hundred years after his death; Monteverdi had to wait three centuries for a realistic evaluation of his work, while as recently as 1928 the third edition of Grove's Dictionary was informing its readers that 'Vivaldi mistook the facility of an expert performer for the creative faculty that he possessed but to a limited degree'! In even more recent times the reversed popularity of Sibelius and Mahler serves as a warning against the reliability of received judgements. In the narrower yet vital sphere of nineteenth-century piano music Schumann, Chopin, Liszt and Brahms continue to supply the Romantic literature for recital programmes and to form the staple diet for examination requirements in our institutions.

Against this background Alkan emerges like some mysterious planet whose orbit is so eccentric that it has remained largely undetected until the latter part of the twentieth century. As much of his music is still unknown, his precise location in the firmament of nineteenth-century composers has yet to be determined. This is no easy task. Alkan seldom repeats himself and so a large proportion of his music must be absorbed before a true assessment can be realised. He may not prove to be the most original of the great piano composers of his century but he is almost certainly the most exploratory. His ability to surprise by some unexpected twist of harmony, some unsuspected modulation or some curiosity of texture adds a stimulating freshness to his invention while the way he will probe beneath the surface to illuminate the familiar in an unfamiliar light or to place it in an unaccustomed setting makes him a disturbing rather than a reassuring composer. At the same time his excursions into *le genre ancien* and his comprehensive grasp of the formal balance and forgotten subtleties of the Viennese classics show that he retains closer links with the past than any of his important contemporaries. At heart a traditionalist, in spirit a revolutionary, Alkan might be succinctly described as a subversive conservationist. In his finest work this apparent paradox combines with his obsessional character to produce music of challenging power, sustained intensity and classical pedigree; music that is different in kind and degree from that of any other composer.

Appendix 1

Origin of the Five-beat Bar in Alkan's Music

In 1852 the *Revue et gazette musicale* published a series of articles by Fétis concerning the future development of music. His investigation of quintuple rhythms (Oct.24) drew an immediate response from Alkan dated that same Sunday evening. He tells Fétis how one of his friends, a musically cultivated Spaniard who had lived in Paris, discussed five-beat rhythms with him. Alkan's friend cited the *Zorcico*, a national Basque dance, as an example of the naturalness to man of the five-beat bar. Alkan himself also claimed that, unlike certain people, he felt no aversion to five time. The Spaniard played with one hand a special flute with only three holes but a range of three octaves, while the other hand beat out the quintuple rhythm on a tambourine. 'The tunes that had five beats' he explained 'acquired an added or prolonged beat to become 6/8 in the more civilised centres of Spain.' Alkan adds that in the past Chopin had played him Polish folk tunes whose rhythm changed even from one side of a river to the other.

In a second article, on Oct.31, Fétis reproduced a *Zorcico* that Alkan had remembered and quoted from his friend's repertoire; but it is really in 3/4 plus 2/4 time with a strong accent on the 3/4 bar.

Alkan admits that, little by little, the sense of accentuation which his Spanish friend had given him tended to wear off. 'Nevertheless several years ago I published chez Brandus, under the title *Deuxième recueil d'impromptus*, three airs in five-time and one in seven. No longer remembering which was the strong beat, in the examples given below I placed the accents differently in each of the three airs in five-time. As for the one in seven-time, returning to it later on I realised that it was simply a theme in 6/8 with an elongated last beat. Alkan concludes by quoting the motifs of the first three *airs à 5* (Exs.287a, b and c).

Ex.287b

Ex.287c

On playing the first air (Ex.287a) from time to time, Alkan, like his friend Hiller, discovered people who seemed to like it while others found it most disagreeable.

Appendix 2 Documents

FRANCE

Chantilly

Bibliothèque Spoelberch de Lovenjoul

E 863, fol. 92–3
Alkan to Georges Sand; [Nov. 23, 1849].
Thanking the authoress for the invitation to attend the first performance of her play *François-le-Champi*.

Paris

Archives Nationales

AJ^{13} 117
Vicomte de la Rochefoucaude to the Théâtre Royal Italien, Feb.24, 1828.
Letter (draft) concerning Alkan père's request for singers.

AJ^{13} 120 (bundle I, no. 146).
Zimmermann, presumably, to M. Lubert, Directeur de l'Académie Royale de Musique, February 1828.
Requesting that Alkan should perform at one of the *concerts spirituels*.

AJ^{37} 71
Auber enthusiastically recommending Marmontel for the *Légion d'honneur*; Nov.30, 1858.

F^{21} 1291
Alkan recommended for the post of 'professeur de solfège' at the Conservatoire, October 1836.

Two letters, one from Zimmermann.

Eight letters concerning Alkan's application for the post of 'professeur de piano' at the Conservatoire; Aug.28–Sept.3, 1848.

O^3 1606 (212)
Official record of Alkan's request to use certain singers for his concerts; May 15, June 16 and Aug.20, 1827.

O^3 1671
Alkan père asks for his son's free pass to the Opéra and Théâtre Italien.

O^3 1825
Requests made by Alkan and his father for the use of singers, halls, etc. at various times; letters dated Jan.10 and Feb.19, 1826, May ? and May 15, June 16 and Oct.20, 1827.
Vicomte de la Rochefoucaude to Alkan, March 22, 1826. Letter and testimonial, subscribing the sum of 100f towards the boy's concert.

Archives de la Seine

Birth, marriage and death certificates of Alkan, his sister Céleste and most of his brothers. Some of these were destroyed in 1871 and only partially reconstructed shortly afterwards. The birth and marriage certificates of Alkan Morhange (i.e. Alkan's father) and Julie Abraham (Alkan's mother) have not been found here. Either the documents were destroyed in 1871 or the two were not born or married in Paris.
Déclarations des mutation par décès (Declaration of the transference of property through death): Charles Valentin MORHANGE dit Alkan.
1525 Morhange fol.6–52; Dec.10, 1888
1596 Complément fol.6–52; Dec.24, 1888
2756 fol.6–52; Dec.3. 1890
For a full list and further accounts of these documents, see Brigitte François-Sappey's 'Dossier de pièces d'archives'.
Bibliothèque Historique de la Ville de Paris.
Fonds Sand: G3288–98.
Eleven letters from Alkan to Georges Sand, from the late 1840s to the late 1850s. Two letters relate to the post of 'professeur de piano' at the Conservatoire in 1848: G 3288 and G 3297.

Bibliothèque Nationale, Département de musique
Lettres: 'Ch. V. Alkan'

Eight letters from Alkan.

1 To Madame de Lauzanne; no date.
2 Addressee unknown; April 17, 1873.
3 Addressee uncertain; Sept.9, 1836.
Concerning the post of 'professeur de solfège' at the Conservatoire.

4 Addressee unknown; no date.
Alkan sends complimentary tickets to 'Madame'.

5 To Professeur Lassigne; no date [1850s].
Inviting a musician to play 'chez le Prince Troubetzkoi'.

6 To 'mon cher Thomas' [probably Ambroise Thomas]; no date.
Declining an invitation.

7 Addressee unknown; [1855?].
Containing an article, to be published, entitled 'Piano à Clavier de Pédales'. Probably written for the Paris Exposition of 1855 at which he demonstrated the Erard pianos and pedal-pianos.

8 To [Jules] Armingaud; no date [1870s?].
'I should be grateful if you would give me my cupful of mallow or camomile in return for the small tot of rum which I should be delighted to offer you.'

GERMANY

Cologne

Historiches Archiv
73 letters from Alkan to Ferdinand Hiller, mostly from the 1860s and 1870s.

GREAT BRITAIN

London

Private Collection
Photocopy of a short, incomplete list of Alkan's works written up to 1844, in his own handwriting; [mid-1840s?].

SWEDEN

Stockholm

Musikmuseet: Daniel Fryklund collection
Twelve letters by Alkan, all but one written to Fétis, mostly in the 1850s.
Some were acquired from the collection of Wilhelm Heyer, Cologne. See Fryklund's article 'Contribution à la connaissance de la correspondance de Fétis' in *Svensk Tidskrift för Musikforskning*, 1930, p.115.

Appendix 3
The Alkan Society of Great Britain

The Alkan Society was founded in 1977 by John White and others. John was a retired teacher of chemistry who was also a church organist and a keen amateur pianist. The inaugural meeting was held in the Waterloo Room at the Royal Festival Hall in London and the attendance was encouraging enough to go ahead with the formation of the Society. Ronald Smith was invited to be the President and John White was the Secretary for many years. Charles Hailstone was the first discographer and produced several editions of his Discography.

Although the membership was widely scattered, the meetings in London usually attracted a satisfactory attendance. They were held in a variety of venues, including the historic Coram Foundation in Brunswick Square, which has connections with Handel, the Guildhall School of Music, the Royal College of Music, Kensington Town Hall, the City of London Boys' School, and various churches. Most meetings included live performances, and artists taking part included Hamish Milne, Stephanie McCallum, Jack Gibbons, Nicholas King, Roger Smalley, and Ronald Smith himself. Speakers included the composers Harold Truscott, Chris Dench and Erica Fox, and the musicologists Ruth Jordan and Hugh Macdonald. Professor Macdonald is the author of the Alkan article in the current edition of the 'New Grove' and in one talk he described his research in compiling the catalogue of works for the article, Alkan having been upgraded by the editors to require a complete list. In recent years we have held single all-day meetings with several sessions, rather than short evening meetings, and the attendance has been very encouraging, many members making long journeys to be present.

The Vice-Presidents include several distinguished musicians, such as Professor Wilfred Mellers, formerly of York University, and Professor Hugh Macdonald, now at St. Louis, the composer Roger Smalley, who has produced some splendid performing editions for two pianos of works by Alkan for the pedal-piano, and the pianist Richard Shaw.

The Society has a collection of music scores, recordings, books and articles, many donated by members, which is held in the library of the Guildhall School of Music and Drama. The collection of music is not yet complete, but, with the help of members with access to libraries and other sources abroad and our French counterpart, we keep extending it.

When the Society was formed, the number of available recordings was extremely small, and very few scores were in print. Now Richard Shaw's extended Discography runs to well over forty CDs, quite apart from the older recordings on LP, and the majority of the works have been reprinted. They are mostly published by Billaudot (distributed in the UK by United Music Publishers). Thanks to our French colleagues, with whom we exchange information, the publication of other out-of-print works continues steadily.

Since Alkan's music has the reputation of being technically demanding, the Society decided to produce an edition of some of the shorter pieces which would be within the compass of younger or amateur players. The pieces were chosen by John White and Ronald Smith, who also wrote introductory comments. 'Alkan in Miniature' was published by Billaudot.

One of our meetings was held in the Musical Museum in Brentford, and with their help a cassette was made by Symposium Records of all the available piano-roll recordings of Alkan's music (see the Discography). Symposium also produced cassettes of piano music played by Robert Rivard, and an organ recital by Nicholas King.

1988 saw the centenary of Alkan's death. On the anniversary itself, there was a recital in the Wigmore Hall of the three chamber works, played by James Clark (violin), Moray Welsh (cello) and Ronald Smith (piano). The recital was received with enthusiasm, and the players subsequently went into the studio at Nimbus and recorded all three works. For various reasons, some technical, some not, the recordings remained unedited, and the projected CDs were long delayed. Appian are now releasing these CDs to coincide with the publication of this book.

Later in 1988 an Alkan Festival (largely the brain-child of member Eliot Levin) was held in London, with several recitals on the South Bank as well as an organ recital in St Giles, Cripplegate. We also held a piano competition in which Alkan's music was a compulsory component; this was won by John Lenehan, who gave a Purcell Room recital during the Festival as part of his prize. After the Festival, Symposium Records produced an all-Alkan CD which included several first recordings, some involving artists associated with the Festival. The CD included Ronald Smith's performance of *Les Regrets de la Nonnette*, using the newly discovered manuscript.

John White was succeeded as Secretary by Brian Doyle, who worked very hard for several years to continue John's fine efforts. The membership continues to expand and while many members live in the UK, we also have support in the USA, Australia, Japan, Germany, Holland, Sweden, Norway, Belgium and France.

In 1989 the Bulletin contained news of a festival in Husum, Germany devoted to 'Rarities of Piano Music'. A small amount of Alkan had been played there in its first two years (1987 & 1988) by Rainer Klaas, but the third festival featured Alkan as its main composer, with a recital by Ronald Smith and a performance of the Concerto for Solo Piano by Marc-André Hamelin. I attended and wrote about the Festival in our Bulletin. The article led to an invitation to succeed Brian Doyle as Secretary, and I have continued in the post ever since.

Recent years have seen a series of new performers playing Alkan in concert and in recordings. Many members have attended key performances, such as those of the complete Op.39 *Etudes* in giant three-part recitals by Jack Gibbons in London and Oxford. He later recorded the set, together with a dozen shorter pieces, for ASV. Ronald Smith has continued to play much of the music, including a return to the Husum Festival in 1995. Marc-André Hamelin has played the Concerto for Solo Piano in London, Birmingham and Guildford; his live recording of the Op.76 *Etudes* at one of his Wigmore Hall recitals has been highly praised; and he recently gave a rare performance of the *Grande Sonate*, again at the Wigmore. Leslie Howard, best known for his recordings of Liszt's complete piano works, has also performed the *Symphonie* in London. The availability of recorded performances has gone well beyond what we could imagine in 1977, and with so many young pianists of outstanding ability eager to play Alkan's music, we can remain optimistic for the coming Millennium.

Peter Grove, Secretary, Alkan Society
Salisbury, July 1999

Details of the Alkan Society can be obtained from the Secretary, Peter Grove, 21 Heronswood, Salisbury, Wiltshire SP2 8DH, England. Tel/Fax: +44-1722-325771.

Appendix 4
A short history of the Société Alkan

At the completion of my studies, having the opportunity to spend a year on something else of my choosing, I decided to devote myself to a project on French music. A short time previously, the chance hearing of some works of Charles-Valentin Alkan on the radio had aroused my enthusiasm. In order to consider the subject more deeply, I made contact in the summer of 1984 with Jean-Yves Bras, whose work on behalf of this French composer was well known, and almost straight away the decision was made to found a French association, along the lines of the British Alkan Society. Several contacts enabled us to form a group which met on December 4th, 1984 and comprised of Jean-Yves Bras, Gérard Billaudot, François Derveaux, Constance Himmelfarb, Laurent Martin and myself. We officially founded an association having 'the aim to promote the music of Charles-Valentin Morhange, known as Alkan, French composer, born 1813 and died 1888', and we elected Jean-Yves Bras as the first President. This modest event was followed on June 18th, 1985 by an inaugural concert at the headquarters of Editions Billaudot which was announced in the press and on the radio. Georges Guillard and Laurent performed several pieces by Alkan before some fifty invited guests, and Martin gave what was probably the first French performance of the Trois Grandes Etudes op.76. Five months later the first edition of our Bulletin appeared; this set out the main directions of our activity. At this stage we numbered some thirty members.

The organisation of concerts was one of our first priorities. Thus on November 29th, 1985 Stephanie McCallum came to give a performance of the *Trois Grandes Etudes* op.76 together with the *Nocturne* op.22 and *Le Tambour bat aux champs* op.50 bis, which was recorded for distribution on cassette. A serious problem, however, was apparent: the concert hall was half empty...

Our principal plans of action were rapidly drawn up and defined at the first General Meeting, on December 4th, 1985. We resolved to restore the composer's tombstone, which was at risk of being obliterated, and to place a memorial plaque on one of Alkan's residences; to commemorate the centenary of his death in 1988, in particular by organising a festival, a competition and a conference, by the publication of a book, and the performance of transcriptions by Mark Starr on Radio France, and by a special edition of a postage stamp, and the striking of a medal, etc. We also resolved to promote wider knowledge of Alkan by encouraging recordings, by making pianists aware, by publishing, and by organising concerts; and we resolved to set up a documentary source.

Gradually the essential means were put together to ensure the longevity of an association whose members were so widely dispersed. We soon published the first edition of our Alkan discography, which has been regularly updated ever since.

From the end of 1987, in spite of the weak results obtained, we tried to organise ourselves by forming different working groups. In vain: the centenary of the composer's death was disappointing. Of the numerous projects proposed, not one succeeded. A few concerts, however, did see the light of day, including the one we organised in collaboration with the Jewish community. The year closed with a splendid all-Alkan concert by Ronald Smith at the Bösendorfer Centre on December 13th.

At the General Meeting in December 1988 some important changes were made, including the appointment of Jacques-Phillipe Saint-Gérard to the organising committee, and the election of Laurent Martin to the position of President. Since then, the composition of our committee has remained unchanged. As Laurent Martin remembers with pleasure, one might think that Alkan's spirit began to favour us from the day that restoration of his tomb was proposed. At the beginning of 1988, when he was rightly elected 'Man of the Year' for the Auvergne, our new President launched a subscription for the restoration of the memorial, giving two benefit concerts in March. The participation of the British Alkan Society and of SACEM (the Society of Authors, Composers and Music Publishers) enabled us to have the work done during the summer of 1990.

A new dynamic fell into place. The association established a sales service to members of all available Alkan recordings and books. On May 22nd and 23rd, 1989 Laurent Martin performed the complete *Préludes* op.25 in preparation for his subsequent recording. The following year was launched the drawing up of a collective publication on Alkan, the first in French, for which Brigitte François-Sappey, the editor of the project, succeeded in attracting the interest of the prestigious publisher Fayard. On May 22nd and 30th and June 6th, Laurent Martin organised a series of three concerts entitled 'Romantic Spring', to which he invited Alan Weiss and Margit Haider.

The year 1991 marked an important stage both for our association and for the success of Alkan in France. In the autumn of that year Fayard published the symposium edited by Brigitte François-Sappey, and it was received very favourably. At the same time, we discovered in a private collection the first known example of the score of *Variations sur un thème de Steibelt* op.1, which was rapidly republished by Edition Billaudot. Since then, the momentum has continued, and the relative regularity of the release of new recordings is a good indicator.

The quarterly bulletin of the association is established as a vital weapon, testifying in no small way to the remarkable faithfulness of its members. It is simultaneously an information letter, giving maximum distribution to news which is soon out-of-date, and a bulletin for a learned society, where one can read both historic texts which are difficult to find and recent in-depth studies. We have published several documents which have never been published before, like the notes taken by Marie Auroc during her lessons with Alkan (February 1996), or the facsimile of a music manuscript discovered in the Netherlands by Frank Leoni (March 1997).

At the present time, several important projects are in progress, and should be completed in the next two years: the establishment of a complete catalogue of Alkan's works and the publication of his correspondence. Both projects are based on the most exhaustive use possible of the sources of information available throughout the world.

By this tenacious action, the Société Alkan is building a solid reputation and shows itself to be an important partner for both performers and musicologists, enabling a synergy for which isolated individuals could not hope. It is up to us to succeed brilliantly with the bicentenary of the composer's birth in the year 2013!

François Luguenot,
Secretary, Société Alkan,
Paris, January, 1999

List of works

The problem of dating the composition and publication of Alkan's music is formidable. Few autographs of his published works have come to light; and where there are no *dépôt légal* dates and library entries cannot be dated, publishers' addresses, plate numbers, contemporary advertisements, the occasional première or dedication, even a restricted keyboard compass often supply our only evidence. A rough catalogue dating from the mid-1840s in Alkan's hand only demonstrates that a memory that could recall a complete concerto after thirty years was incapable of dating compositions accurately less than a decade after their publication. Probably Alkan was impatiently disinterested in such matters.

Dates in brackets indicate dates of publication, those without refer to dates of composition. Unless stated otherwise MSS are in the Bibliothèque Nationale, Paris.

Items marked with an asterisk are currently missing. The author would greatly welcome any further information about the whereabouts of these missing items, any MSS not mentioned below, and any dates of composition/publication which need revision.

COLLECTED WORKS

Ch. V. Alkan: oeuvres choisies, edited E. Delaborde and I. Philipp, published Costallat & Cie (Paris, *c*1900), reissued by Costallat's successor, Billaudot. These use the plates of Richault and others.

The Piano Music of Alkan, edited R. Lewenthal (Schirmer, New York, 1964). Adapted from the original plates.

Ch. V. Alkan: oeuvres choisies pour piano, edited G. Beck, *Le pupitre* xvi (Paris, 1969)

KEYBOARD

Works are for piano, unless stated otherwise.
op. no.

1 Variations on a theme from Steibelt's *Orage* Concerto (*c*1827)
2 Les omnibus, variations (1829)
3 Il était un p'tit homme, rondoletto (*c*1830)
4 Rondo brillant, piano with string quartet *ad lib* (*c*1833)
5 Rondo on Rossini's *Largo al factotum* from *Il barbiere di Siviglia** (*c*1833)
[8] See op.16
12 Rondeau chromatique (1833)
12 3 Improvisations (dans le style brillant) (1837)
13 3 Andantes romantiques (1837)
15 Souvenirs: 3 morceaux dans le genre pathétique (1837)
16 3 Scherzi (1837)
These last four sets of pieces were published as a series, numbered Books 1 to 4 respectively; also known collectively as 12 *Caprices*.
16/4 Variations on Donizetti's *Ah segnata è la mia morte* [*sorte*] from *Anna Bolena* (1834)
16/5 Variations on Bellini's *La tremenda ultrice spada* from *I Capuleti e i Montecchi* (1834)
16/6 Variations quasi fantaisie sur une barcarolle napolitaine (1834)
16 6 Morceaux caractéristiques (*c*1838); later published as op.8 and also as numbers 1, 4, 5, 7, 8 and 12 of Les mois [op.74], *qv* below.
17 Le preux, étude de concert (1844)
[17] See Finale, below
[18] A misprint in Marmontel's *Les pianistes célèbres* for op.13, perpetuated in Grove V.
22 Nocturne (1844)
23 Saltarelle (1844)
24 Gigue et air de ballet dans le style ancien (1844)
[24] See op.27
25 Alleluia (1844)
26 Marche funèbre, 1844 (1846)
[26] See Fantaisie à 4 mains sur *Don Juan*, below
26b/c See op.32/1 iii and i
27 Marche triomphale, 1844 (1846); called 'Marche héroique' before publication. The early edition published by Schlesinger of Berlin has op.27 on the title page, but op.24 on the first page of music.

27 Le chemin de fer, étude (1844)
29 Bourrée d'Auvergne, étude (1846)
31 25 Préludes, piano/organ (1847)
32/1 4 Impromptus (1849)
i Vaghezza (published separately in 1847, and sometime appeared as op.26c); ii L'amitié (1845); iii Fantasietta alla moresca (1847, and sometime as op.26b).
32/2 Deuxième recueil d'impromptus, 3 airs à 5 temps et 1 à 7 temps (1849)
33 Grande sonate (1847)
[34] Scherzo focoso (1847); first published by Brandus without an opus number
35 12 Etudes, in all the major keys (1847)
37 3 Marches quasi cavalleria (1857)
38 Deuxième recueil de chants (1857)
39 12 Etudes, in all the minor keys (1857)
i Comme le vent
ii En rythme molossique
iii Scherzo diabolico
iv–vii Symphonie:
iv Allegro moderato
v Marche funèbre
vi Menuet
vii Finale
viii–x Concerto:
viii Allegro assai
ix Adagio
x Allegretto alla barbaresca
xi Ouverture
xii Le festin d'Esope (variations)
40 3 Marches, piano duet (1857)
41 3 Petites fantaisies (1857)
42 Réconciliation, petit caprice (1857)
45 Salut, cendre du pauvre! (1856)
46 Minuetto alla tedesca (1857)
47 Finale (Saltarelle) from the Cello Sonata, arranged for piano duet (*c*1869?)
50 Capriccio alla soldatesca (1859)
50bis Le tambour bat aux champs, esquisse (1859)
51 3 Menuets (1859)
52 Super flumina Babylonis, paraphase of Psalm 137 (1859)
53 Quasi-caccia, caprice (1859)
54 Benedictus, pedal-piano/piano 3 hands (1859)
55 Une fusée, introduction et impromptu (1859)

57 Deuxième nocturne (1859)
57 Troisième nocturne (1859)
60 Ma chère liberté et ma chère servitude: deux petites pièces (1859)
60bis Le grillon: quatrième nocturne (1859)
61 Sonatine (1861)
63 48 Motifs, esquisses (1861)
64 13 prières, organ/pedal-piano/piano 3 hands (1866)
65 Troisième recueil de chants (*c*1866)
66 11 Grands préludes, and a transcription from Handel's *Messiah,* pedal-piano/piano 3 hands (*c*1866)
67 Quatrième recueil de chants (*c*1866)
69 Impromptu sur le choral de Luther 'Un fort rempart est notre Dieu', pedal-piano/piano 3 hands (1866)
70 Cinquième recueil de chants (*c*1872)
72 11 pièces dans le style religieux, and a transcription from Handel's *Messiah,* organ/harmonium/piano (1867)
[74] Les mois (late 1830s?)
Op. no. and title later given to the 12 morceaux caractéristiques, *qv* below.
75 Toccatina (*c*1872)
[76] 3 Grandes études (*c*1838–40)
i Fantaisie, right hand alone
ii Introduction, variations et finale, left hand alone
iii Etude à mouvement semblable et perpetuel, both hands
Originally published without an opus number.

KEYBOARD WORKS WITHOUT OPUS NUMBERS

Album-leaf ('Pour Monsieur Gurkhaus') dated Nov. 5,1863
24-bar recurring canon without conclusion, in G major.
MS sold Sotheby, London, May 28, 1986, lot 331.

Album-leaf, 'Apassionato' in D major (incomplete), dated Oct. 9, 1847.
MS 2943. Later published (varied) as 'Délire' in the *Esquisses* op.63.

Album-leaf, 'Etude' in D major (incomplete), pedal-piano, dated Dec. 17, 1872. MS 2945.

Album-leaf, 'Praeludium' in C minor, organ, dated Feb. 16, 1850. W24.42, p.70.

Alla-barbaro; see Etude, 'Alla-barbaro'

L'amitié (1845); see op.32/1 ii

Bombardo-carillon, pedal-piano 4 feet/piano duet (1872)

Caprice ou étude (1843); title given to the later publication of op. 13/2 by A. Diabelli & Co, Vienna.

Chapeau bas! Deuxième fantasticheria (*c*1872)

Désir (1844)

12 Etudes, pedals only, organ/pedal-piano (*c*1869?)

Etude in a minor (1840) published in *Encyclopédie du Pianiste Compositeur* edited by Pierre-Joseph Zimmermann

Etude, 'Alla-barbaro'

Fantasie à 4 mains sur *Don Juan* (1844); later called op.26.

Fantasticheria (*c*1867)

Finale, piano duet (*c*1838–40); later called op. 17.

3 Grandes études; see [op.76] above

Impromptu, F# major (1844)

Jean qui pleure et Jean qui rit, due fughe da camera (*c*1838–40)

12 Morceaux caractéristiques (late 1830s); later called Les mois and op. 74 *qv* above.

'Palpitamento' in A major, dated April 22nd, 1855. MS, unpublished.

Petit conte (1859)

Petits préludes sur les 8 gammes du plain-chant, organ (1859)

Pro organo, C minor, album-leaf, organ, 1850;
MS in W24.42 p.70, dated Feb. 16, 1850.

'Les Regrets de la Nonnette; petite mélodie pour piano', dated July 7th, 1854. MS, unpublished.

Souvenirs de musique de chambre;
see Transcriptions below.

Souvenirs des concerts du Conservatoire;
see Transcriptions below.

Variations à la vielle, supposedly on a theme from Donizetti's
L 'elisir d'amore actually from *Ugo conte di Parigi* (*c*1838–40)

Variations on a theme from Donizetti's *Ugo conte di Parigi** (1842); published by Mechetti, Vienna. Very likely a later edition of the Variations à la vielle *qv* above.

Zorcico, danse ibérienne (1969);
photograph of MS in Bibliothèque Nationale, Paris. First page is reproduced in *Ch. V. Alkan: Oeuvres choisies,* ed. G. Beck (see Collected Works above).

TRANSCRIPTIONS

The three main collections are:

Souvenirs des concerts du Conservatoire: partitions pour piano seul (1847)

Marcello, Psalm 18 'I cieli immensi narrano'
ii Gluck, *Armide* 'Jamais dans ces beaux lieux'
iii Gluck, *Iphigenie en Tauride* 'Choeur des scythes'
iv Haydn, Symphony No.36 [actually No.94 'Surprise'] Andante
v Gretry, *Les deux avares* 'La garde passe, ii est minuit
vi Mozart Symphony No.40 in G minor (K550) Menuet; performed by Alkan in April 1844.

Souvenirs des concerts du Conservatoire, deuxième série (1861)

i Handel, *Samson* 'Choeur des prêtres de Dagon'
ii Gluck, *Orphée:* Gavotte
iii Haydn, String Quartet in D, op.64/5: Finale
iv Mozart, Motet *Ne pulvis et cinis [Thamos, König in Ägyptenl* 'Ihr Kinder des Staubes' K345/336a.
v Beethoven, *Bundeslied* op. 122
vi Weber, *Oberon* 'Choeur des filles de la mer'

Souvenirs de musique de chambre (*c*1869?)

i Rigaudons des petits violons de Louis XIV
ii Bach, Flute Sonata in Eb, BWV 1031: Siciliano
iii Haydn, String Quartet in D minor, op.76/2: Menuet
iv Mozart, String Quartet in A, K464: Andante
v Beethoven, String Quartet in Bb, op. 130: Cavatina
vi Weber, Piano Trio: Scherzo

Beethoven, 3rd Piano Concerto, op.37: 1st movement (1859); with extended cadenza by Alkan.

Beethoven, Choeur des derviches des *Ruines d'Athenes** (?)

Beethoven, Symphony No. 7 op. 72, transcribed for 8 hands, by 1837*

Meyerbeer, *Le prophète:* Ouverture (*c*1849)

Mozart, Piano Concerto in D minor, K466, 1860 (1861);
with cadenzas by Alkan for the outer movements.

Mozart, Symphony in G minor [K450], Menuet (1842).

CHAMBER MUSIC

4 Rondo brillant, piano with string quartet *ad lib* (*c*1833)

21 Grand duo concertant, piano and violin (*c*1840)

30 Trio, piano, violin and cello (1841)

47 Sonate de concert, piano and cello (1857); also with cello part revised for viola by Casimir Ney*. Alkan arranged the Finale for piano duet (see Keyboard Music above).

Album-leaf, 'Allegro agitato' (incomplete) in F minor, string quartet, dated June 6, 1846. MS in British Library: Hirsch IV 1455, p.20. Dedicated 'à son confrère P. Cavallo'.

Other chamber works, now missing, include 'quintets and sextets for strings' composed by 1844 and perhaps others composed by 1847 (see p.214). These may well have been among the MSS mentioned in Alkan's will (see p.212)*.

ORCHESTRAL WORKS

10 Concerto da camera, A minor, piano and full orchestra (1832).

Deuxième concerto da camera, C # minor, piano and strings (1834); MS string parts in Alkan's hand are in the Bibliothèque Nationale, Paris. The full score and parts are now available from Billaudot, Paris.

Pas redoublé, wind band, 1840;
MS2944, score dated Oct.1, 1840.
The original parts are missing*; unpublished.

Symphony in B minor*, 1844 or earlier; see pp.212–214.

VOCAL MUSIC

Trois anciennes mélodies juives arrangés pour Mademoiselle Zina de Mansouroff, for voice and piano (nos.1 & 2) and voice and organ/ harpsichord (no.3). MS dated 11/10/1855.

Hermann et Kitty (words by de Pastoret), Prix de Rome cantata 1832; MS 2749. Unpublished.

L'entrée en loge (words by Gail), Prix de Rome cantata, 1834; MS 2750. Unpublished.

Romance du phare d'Eddystone*, voice and piano, 1845

Etz chajjim hi, SSTB voices (1847)

Halelouyoh, SATB voices and piano/organ (1857)

Marcia funebre sulla morte d'un papagallo, SSTB voices, 3 oboes and bassoon 1858 (1859)

Stances de Millevoye, SSA voices and piano (1859)

2er [sic] verset du 4le Psaume ... for voice and piano. MS incomplete, dated 19/5/1855.

Bibliography

Beck, Georges, 'Ch. V. Alkan: oeuvres choisies pour piano' (*Le Pupitre*, 16, Paris, 1969)

Bellamann, Henry, 'The Piano Works of C. V. Alkan' (in *Musical Quarterly*, 10, 1924)

Berlioz, Hector, *Grand traité d'instrumentation* (Paris, 1843)

Berlioz, Hector, tr. D. Cairns, *Memoirs* (London, 1969)

Bertha, Alexander de, 'Ch. Valentin Alkan ainé: étude psycho-musicale' (in *Bulletin français de la société Internationale de Musique*, 5, 1909)

Blanchard, Henri, 'Auditions musicales. C. Valentin Alkan' (in *Revue et Gazette Musicale*, 16, May 13, 1849)

Bloch, Joseph, *Charles-Valentin Alkan.* Dissertation, Harvard University, (Indianapolis, privately printed, 1941)

Bolte, Theodore, 'Charles Valentin Morhange Alkan zur 100. Wiederkehr seines Geburtstages' (in *Neue Zeitschrift für Musik,* 80, 1913)

Dannreuther, Edward, 'Alkan' (in *Grove's Dictionary*, ed. H. C. Colles, 1927)

Davis, Lawrence, *César Franck and his Circle* (1970)

Dean, Winton, *Bizet: His Life and Work* (1965)

Delacroix, Eugène, ed. A. Joubin, *Journal* (1932)

Dieren, Bernard van, *Down among the dead men* (1935)

d'Indy, Vincent, 'Impressions musicales d'enfance et de jeunesse: III. adolescence' (in *Les Annales Politiques et Littéraires*, 95, 1930)

Elwart, Antoine., *Histoire de la Société des Concerts du Conservatoire...* (Paris, 1860)

Fétis, François-Joseph, *Biographie Universelle des Musiciens* (Ist edition, 1837-44, and 2nd edition, 1860-5)

Fétis, Francois-Joseph, 'Revue Critique. C.-V. Alkan' (in *Revue et Gazette Musicale* 14 (1847) pp244-6

François-Sappey, Brigitte, ed., *Charles Valentin Alkan* (Paris, 1991)

François-Sappey, Brigitte, 'Dossier de pièces d'archives' (in François-Sappey's *Charles Valentin Alkan,* 1991)

Fryklund, Daniel, 'Contribution à la connaissance de la correspondence de Fétis' (in *Svensk Tidskrift för Musikforskning,* 12, 1930)

Ganvert, Gérard, 'Alkan, musicien français de religion juive' (in François-Sappey's *Charles Valentin Alkan,* 1991)

Gorer, Richard, 'A nineteenth-century French romantic' (in *The Listener,* 36, 1946)

Hallé, Charles, ed. Michael Kennedy, *Autobiography* (1972)

Harding, James, *Gounod* (1973)

Harding, James, *Saint-Säens* (1965)

Himmelfarb, Constance, 'L'interprète à travers la presse musicale' (in François-Sappey's *Charles Valentin Alkan,* 1991)

Lewenthal, Raymond, *The Piano Music of Alkan* (New York, 1964)

Liszt, Franz, 'Revue critique. Trois morceaux dans le genre pathétique, par C.-V. Alkan...' (in *Revue et Gazette Musicale,* 4 (1837)

Luguenot, François, 'Catalogue de l'oeuvre d'Alkan' (in François-Sappey's *Charles Valentin Alkan,* 1991)

Macdonald, Hugh, 'Alkan [Morhange], (Charles-) Valentin' (in *The New Grove Dictionary of Music and Musicians,* ed. Stanley Sadie, 1980)

Macdonald, Hugh, 'The Death of Alkan' (in *Musical Times,* 114, 1988)

Marmontel, Antoine, 'Ch.-Valentin Alkan' (in *Les pianistes célèbres,* Paris, 1878)

Murdoch, William, *Chopin: His Life* (1934)

Naumbourg, Samuel, *Recueil de chants religieux et populaires des Israelites* (Paris, 1874)

Niecks, Frederick, 'More glimpses of Parisian pianists of another day. Personal recollections. Ch. V. Alkan' (in *Monthly Musical Record,* 48, 1918)

Pasternak, Velvel, *Songs of the Chassidim* (New York, 1971)

Piggott, Patrick, *The Life and Music of John Field* (1973)

Sabatier, François, 'L'oeuvre d'orgue et de piano-pédalier' (in François-Sappey's *Charles Valentin Alkan,* 1991)

Schonberg, Harold, *The Great Pianists* (1964)

Schumann, Robert, *Music and Musicians: Essays and Criticisms* (tr., ed. and annotated by F. R. Ritter; 2nd series,1880)

Searle, Humphrey, 'A plea for Alkan' (in *Music & Letters,* 18, 1937)

Shaw, Richard, *Alkan's Life and early Works.* Dissertation, Edinburgh University (1974)

Sitsky, Larry, 'Summary Notes for a Study on Alkan' (in *Studies in Music,* 8, University of Western Australia, 1974)

Smalley, Roger, 'A case of neglect: two virtuosos' cadenzas for Beethoven' (in *Music & Musicians* 20/9, 1972)

Sorabji, Kaikhosru, 'Charles Henri Victorin Morhange (Alkan)' in *Around Music* (1932)

Starr, Mark, [Orchestrations of Op.39, nos.4-7, 11 & 12] (Carl Fischer, New York, 1986)

Starr, Mark, Alkan: Concerto for piano and orchestra [orchestration of Op.39, nos.8-10] (photocopy, 1987)

Storr, Anthony, *The Dynamics of Creation* (1972)

Vapereau, Gustave, *Dictionnaire universal des contemporains* (Paris, 1858)

Discography

Recordings are CDs unless specified otherwise. The layout of each entry is as follows: Performer, date of recording, recording company, number, date of registration. To assist identification the nationality of some companies is given in brackets. For further information on the early piano roll recordings, see below. Where a company has issued a recording in a number of different formats, each item is separated by a comma, with the date of release (where known) indicated at the end of that company's issues. Reissues are separated by a semi-colon. Issues by a separate company follow a full stop.

SOLO PIANO

Op 1 **Variations on a theme from Steibelt's *Orage* Concerto**
Laurent Martin rec 1992 Marco Polo, 8.223657 (1994)

Op 12 **Rondeau chromatique**
Osamu Nakamura rec 1989 Epic/Sony, ESCK 8001 (1988)
Laurent Martin rec 1992 Marco Polo, 8.223657 (1994)

Op 12 **Improvisations dans le style brillant**
Robert Rivard rec 1988 Symposium (UK), 1057 [cass] (1988)
Laurent Martin rec 1990 Marco Polo, 8.223500 (1993)

Op 15 **Trois morceaux dans le genre pathétique**
no.2 **Le Vent**
L. Johnson. HMV, MBLP 6006 [LP mono]
Harold Bauer [piano roll] Keyboard Immortal Series KBI 4A 102 [LP]; Symposium 1002 [cass] (1983)

Op 16 **Tre Scherzi**
Ronald Smith rec 1987 EMI, EG 7 69630 1 [digital LP], CDM 7 69630 2 [CD], EG7 69630 4 [cass] (1988);
EMI Angel, TOCE 6240 [CD]. Arabesque (USA), Z6604

Op 17 **Le Preux, étude de concert**
Osamu Nakamura rec 1989 Epic/Sony, ESCK 8001 (1989)
Laurent Martin rec 1990 Marco Polo, 8.223500 (1993)

Op 22 **Nocturne**
Ronald Smith rec 1984 EMI, EG 27 0187 1 [LP], MC 27 0187 4 [cass] (1985); Arabesque (USA), 6523 [LP], Z6523 [CD], 7523 [cass] (1985)
Stephanie McCallum rec 1985 Société Alkan (France) [cass] (1986)
Alan Weiss rec 1989 Fidelio (Netherlands), 8839 (1990)
Jack Gibbons rec 1995 ASV, CD DCS 227 [2 CDs] (1995)

Op 23 **Saltarelle**
Bernard Ringeissen rec 1971
Harmonia Mundi, HM 927 [LPL 2863] [LP] (1977); MHS 1344 [LP]; HM B40.927 [cass]; HMA 190 927 [CD], HMA 43 927 [cass] (1988)

Op 24 **Gigue et Air de ballet dans le style ancien**
Osamu Nakamura rec 1989 Epic/Sony, ESCK 8001 (1989)

no 1 **Gigue**
Bernard Ringeissen rec 1971 Harmonia Mundi, HM 927 [LPL 2863] [LP] (1977); MHS 1344 [LP]; HM B40.927 [cass]; HMA 190927 [CD] , HMA 43 927 [cass] (1988)
Ronald Smith rec 1984 EMI, EG 27 0187 1 [LP], MC 27 0187 4 [cass] (1985); Arabesque (USA) 6523 [LP] Z6523 [CD], 7523 [cass] (1985)

Op 25 **Alleluia**
Osamu Nakamura rec 1989 Epic/Sony, ESCK 8001 (1989)
Laurent Martin rec 1992 Marco Polo, 8.223657 (1994)

Op 26 **Marche funèbre**
Ronald Smith rec 1970 EMI, HQS 1247 [LP] (1971). Arabesque (USA), 6516 [digital LP] (1984)
Ronald Smith rec 1994 Appian, APR 7032 [2 CDs] (1999)

Op 27 **Marche triomphale**
Ronald Smith rec 1970 EMI, HQS 1247 [LP] (1971). Arabesque (USA), 6516 [LP] (1984)

Op 27 **Le Chemin de fer, étude**
Osamu Nakamura rec 1989 Epic/Sony, ESCK 8001 (1989)
Laurent Martin rec 1990 Marco Polo, 8.223500 (1993); Naxos, 8.553434 (1995)

Op 29 **Bourrée d'Auvergne, étude**
Osamu Nakamura rec 1989 Epic/Sony, ESCK 8003 (1989)

Op 31 **25 Préludes dans tous les tons majeurs et mineurs**
Laurent Martin rec 1989 Marco Polo, 8.223284 (1990); partially [nos. 1, 13, 17 & 25] reissued in: Naxos, 8.553434 (1995)
Olli Mustonen rec 1990 Decca, 433 055-2 (1991); London (USA), 433055

no 1 **Lentement**
Laurent Martin rec 1989 Naxos, 8.553434 (1995)
Huseyin Sermet rec 1991 Valois (France), V 4659 (1992)

nos 2 **Assez lentement, 3 Dans le genre ancien, 4 Prière du soir, 5 Psaume 150me**
Huseyin Sermet rec 1991 Valois (France), V 4659 (1992)

no 6 **Librement mais sans secousses**
Huseyin Sermet rec 1991 Valois (France), V 4659 (1992)

no 8 **La Chanson de la folle au bord de la mer**
Ronald Smith rec 1968 [on Viennese piano of 1851] Oryx "Collectors' Series" 1803 [LP] (1969)
Ronald Smith rec 1977 EMI, SLS 5100 [3 LPs] (1978). Arabesque (USA), 8127 [3 LPs]. EMI (France), CDM 7 64280 (1992). Appian, APR7031[2 CDs] (1996)
Huseyin Sermet rec 1991 Valois (France), V 4659 (1992)
Jack Gibbons rec 1995 ASV, CD DCS 227 [2 CDs] (1995)

no 9 **Placiditas**
Huseyin Sermet rec 1991 Valois (France), V 4659 (1992)

no 11 **Un petit rien**
Ronald Smith rec 1968 [on Viennese piano of 1851] Oryx (UK) "Collectors' Series" 1803 [LP] (1969)
Ronald Smith rec 1977 EMI, EG 27 0187 1 [LP], MC 27 0187 4 [cass] (1985). Arabesque (USA), 6523 [LP], Z6523 [CD], 7523 [cass] (1985)

no 12 **Le Temps qui n'est plus**
Ronald Smith rec 1968 [on Viennese piano of 1851] Oryx "Collectors' Series" 1803 [LP] (1969)
Ronald Smith rec 1977 EMI, EG 27 0187 1 [LP], MC 27 0187 4 [cass] (1985). Arabesque (USA), 6523 [LP], Z6523 [CD], 7523 [cass] (1985)
Alan Weiss rec 1989 Fidelio (Netherlands), 8839 (1990)
Huseyin Sermet rec 1991 Valois (France), V 4659 (1992)
Jack Gibbons rec 1995 ASV, CD DCS 227 [2 CDs] (1995)

no 13 **J'étais endormie mais mon coeur veillait...**
Ronald Smith rec 1968 [on Viennese piano of 1851] Oryx (UK) "Collectors' Series" 1803 [LP] (1969)
Ronald Smith rec 1977 EMI, EG 27 0187 1 [LP], MC 27 0187 4 [cass] (1985). Arabesque (USA), 6523 [LP], Z6523 [CD], 7523 [cass] (1985)
Laurent Martin rec 1989 Naxos, 8.553434 (1995)
Ronald Smith rec 1989 Danacord (Denmark), DACOCD 349 (1990)
Huseyin Sermet rec 1991 Valois (France), V 4659 (1992)
Anthony Goldstone rec 1993 Amphion (UK), PHICD123, PHI 123 [cass] (1993)
Jack Gibbons rec 1995 ASV, CD DCS 227 [2 CDs] (1995)

no 14 **Rapidement**
Huseyin Sermet rec 1997 Valois (France), V 4808 (1998)

no 15 **Dans le genre gothique**
Ronald Smith rec 1968 [on Viennese piano of 1851] Oryx (UK) "Collectors' Series" 1803 [LP] (1969)
Ronald Smith rec 1977 EMI, EG 27 0187 1 [LP], MC 27 0187 4 [cass] (1985). Arabesque (USA), 6523 [LP], Z6523 [CD], 7523 [cass] (1985)
Huseyin Sermet rec 1997 Valois (France), V 4808 (1998)

no 16 **Assez lentement**
Ronald Smith rec 1968 [on Viennese piano of 1851] Oryx (UK) "Collectors' Series" 1803 [LP] (1969)
Ronald Smith rec 1977 EMI, EG 27 0187 1 [LP], MC 27 0187 4 [cass] (1985). Arabesque (USA), 6523 [LP], Z6523 [CD], 7523 [cass] (1985)

no 17 **Rêve d'amour**
Huseyin Sermet rec 1997 Valois (France), V 4808 (1998)

no 25 **Prière**
Laurent Martin rec 1989 Naxos, 8.553434 (1995)

Op 32 no 1 **1er Recueil d'Impromptus**
Laurent Martin rec 1992 Marco Polo, 8.223657 (1994)

Op 32 no 2 **2e Recueil d'Impromptus: 3 Airs à 5 temps et un air à 7 temps**
Laurent Martin rec 1992 Marco Polo, 8.223657 (1994); partial reissue (nos 1 & 3) in: Naxos, 8.553434 (1995)

Op 33 **Grande Sonate**
Ronald Smith rec 1973 EMI, HQS 1326 (1974) [LP]; CDM 7 69421 2; EG 7 69421 4 [cass]; EMI Angel, TOCE 6239.

Arabesque (USA), 8140 [LP]. EMI (France), CDM 7 64280 2 (1992)
Pierre Réach rec 1979 RCA (France), RL 37243 [LP] (1979). Musical Heritage Society (USA), MHS 4875 [LP] (1983)
Osamu Nakamura rec 1990 Epic/Sony, ESCK 8004 (1990)
Alan Weiss rec 1989 Fidelio (Netherlands), 8839 (1990)
Pierre Réach rec 1991 Vogue (France), 645 006 (1991); Koch Discover, DICD 920362 (1997)
Marc-André Hamelin rec 1994 Hyperion, CDA66794 (1995)

2nd Movement "Quasi-Faust"
Raymond Lewenthal rec 1965 RCA, LM 2815 [LP mono], LSC-2815 [LP stereo]; RB 6660 [LP mono], SB 6660 [LP Stereo] (1966); GL 42689 [LP stereo], GK 42689 [cass] (1979); Elan, CD 82276, remastered: BMG High Performance Series 633310 (1999)

Op 35 **Douze Études dans tous les tons majeurs**
Bernard Ringeissen rec 1990 Marco Polo, 8.223351 (1993); partial reissue (nos 6, 8 & 10) in: Naxos, 8.553434 (1995)
Stephanie McCallum rec 1992 Tall Poppies Records (Australia), TP 055 (1994)

no 5 **Allegro barbaro**
Ronald Smith rec 1968 [on Érard piano of 1855] Oryx (UK) "Collectors' Series" 1803 [LP] (1969)
Ronald Smith rec 1977 EMI, SLS 5100 [3 LPs] (1978). Arabesque (USA), 8127 [3 LPs]. EMI (France), CDM 7 64280 2 (1992). Appian, APR7031[2 CDs] (1996)
Jack Gibbons rec 1995 ASV, CD DCS 227 [2 CDs] (1995)
William Fong rec 1995 Olympia (UK), OCD020 (1995)

no 6 **Allegramente**
Bernard Ringeissen rec 1990 Naxos, 8.553434 (1995)

no 7 **Lento-appassionato**
Raymond Lewenthal Columbia, M 30234 [LP] (1971); CBS 61117 [LP] (1981)
Bernard Ringeissen rec 1990 Naxos, 8.553434 (1995)

no 10 **Chant d'amour - Chant de mort**
Ronald Smith rec 1994 Appian, APR 7032 [2 CDs] (1999)

no 11 **Posément**
Ronald Smith rec 1994 Appian, APR 7032 [2 CDs] (1999)

no 12 **Andando**
Bernard Ringeissen rec 1990 Naxos, 8.553434 (1995)
Ronald Smith rec 1994 Appian, APR 7032 [2 CDs] (1999)

Op 37 **Trois Marches quasi da cavalleria**
no 1 **Molto allegro**
Bernard Ringeissen rec 1971 Harmonia Mundi, HM 927 [LPL 2863] [LP] (1977); MHS 1344 [LP]; HM B40.927 [cass]; HMA 190927 [CD] (1988). Also Heugel's promotional *Carnet de Notes 34* [LP] (1971)
Ronald Smith rec 1984 EMI, EG 27 0187 1 [LP], MC 27 0187 4 [cass] (1985); Arabesque (USA) 6523 [LP] Z6523 [CD], 7523 [cass] (1985)

Op 38 **1er Recueil de Chants**
Osamu Nakamura rec 1989 Epic/Sony, ESCK 8004 (1990)
Jacqueline Méfano rec 1995 2e2m collection, 2e2m 1005 (1996)
no 1 **Assez vivement**
Ronald Smith rec 1994 Appian, APR 7032 [2 CDs] (1999)
Jack Gibbons rec 1995 ASV, CD DCS 227 [2 CDs] (1995)
no 6 **Barcarolle**
Robert Rivard rec 1988 Symposium (UK), 1057 [cass] (1988)

Op 38 **2e Recueil de Chants**
Jacqueline Méfano rec 1995 2e2m collection (France), 2e2m 1005 (1996)
no 2 **Fa**
Ronald Smith rec 1968 [on Viennese piano of 1851] Oryx "Collectors' Series" 1803 [LP] (1969)
Ronald Smith rec 1984 EMI, EG 27 0187 1 [LP], MC 27 0187 4 [cass] (1985); Arabesque (USA) 6523 [digital LP] Z6523 [CD], 7523 [cass] (1985)
Alan Weiss rec 1989 Fidelio (Netherlands) 8839 (1990)

Op 39 **12 Études dans tous les tons mineurs**
Ronald Smith rec 1977 EMI, SLS 5100 [3 LPs] (1978), partly reissued in EMI (France), CDM 7 64280 2 [CD] 1992 (see Études nos 1, 2, 3, & 12). Arabesque (USA), 8127 [3 LPs]. Appian, APR7031 [2 CDs] (1996)
Jack Gibbons rec 1995 ASV, CD DCS 227 [2 CDs] (1995)
no 1 **Comme le vent**
Michael Ponti rec 1970 Vox Candide, STGBY 653 [LP]

(1972); CE 31045 [LP], Vox CDX 5151, FSM 31 045, Vox Box 5151 (1996)
Ronald Smith rec 1977 EMI (France), CDM 7 64280 2 (1992)
Bernard Ringeissen rec 1989 Marco Polo, 8.223285 (1990)

no 2 **En rythme molossique**
Michael Ponti rec 1970 Vox Candide, STGBY 653 [LP] (1972); CE 31045 [LP], Vox Box 5151 (1996)
Ronald Smith rec 1977 EMI (France), CDM 7 64280 2 (1992)
Bernard Ringeissen rec 1989 Marco Polo, 8.223285 (1990)

no 3 **Scherzo diabolico**
Michael Ponti rec 1970 Vox Candide, STGBY 653 [LP] (1972); CE 31045 [LP], Vox Box 5151 (1996)
Bernard Ringeissen rec 1971 Harmonia Mundi, HM927 [LPL 2863] [LP] (1977); MHS 1344 [LP]; HM B40.927 [cass]; HMA 190927 (1988)
Ronald Smith rec 1977 EMI (France), CDM 7 64280 2 (1992)
Bernard Ringeissen rec 1990 Marco Polo, 8.223351 (1993); Naxos, 8.553434 (1995)

nos 4-7 **Egon Petri rec c1952-3 Pearl, GEMM CD 9966 (1992). Symphonie**
Symposium, 1145 (1993).
John Paul Bracey VLR LP 1512 [LP mono] (before 1964)
Raymond Lewenthal RCA, LM 2815 [LP mono], LSC-2815 [LP stereo]; RB 6660 [LP mono], SB 6660 [LP stereo] (1966); GL 42689 [LP stereo], GK 42689 [cass] (1979); Elan CD 82276, remastered: BMG High Performance Series 633310 (1999)
Ronald Smith rec 1969 Unicorn, UNS 206 [LP] (1970)
Michael Ponti rec 1970 Vox Candide, STGBY 653 [LP] (1972); CE 31045 [LP], Vox Box 5151 (1996)
Bernard Ringeissen rec 1989 Marco Polo, 8.223285 (1990); partly reissued (no 5) in: Naxos, 8.553434 (1995)
Mark Salman rec 1993 Titanic (USA), Ti-220 (1994)
Stephanie McCallum rec 1995 Tall Poppies (Australia), TP081 (1996)

no 5 **Marche funèbre**
Bernard Ringeissen rec 1989 Naxos, 8.553434 (1995)

nos 8-10 **Concerto**

John Paul Bracey VLR LP 1512 [LP mono] (before 1964)

John Ogdon rec 1969 RCA, LSC-3192 [LP] (1972); LSB-4078 [LP] (1973)

Ronald Smith rec 1968 EMI, HQS 1204 [LP] (1970). The first movement is performed with cuts devised by Ronald Smith.

Stephanie McCallum rec 1990 MBS, MBS 24 CD (1991)

Osamu Nakamura rec 1990 Epic/Sony, ESCK 8005 (1990)

Marc-André Hamelin rec 1991 Music & Arts, CD-724 (1992)

no 8 [orchestrated Klindworth]

Dmitri Feofanov (pf), Razumovsky Symphony Orchestra, cond Robert Stankovsky rec 1995 Naxos, 8 553702 (1998)

no 10 **Allegretto alla-barbaresca**

Malcolm Binns Concert Artist/Fidelio Records (UK), STLPX 8017 [LP]; FED-TC-1017 [cass] (1967)

no 11 **Ouverture**

Bernard Ringeissen rec 1989 Marco Polo, 8.223285 (1990)

no 12 **Le Festin d'Esope**

Raymond Lewenthal RCA, LM 2815 [LP mono], LSC-2815 [LP stereo]; RB 6660 [LP mono], SB 6660 [LP stereo] (1966); GL 42689 [LP stereo], GK 42689 [cass] (1979), Elan CD 82276, remastered: BMG High Performance Series 633310 (1999)

Ronald Smith rec 1968 [on Érard piano of 1851] Oryx (UK) "Collectors' Series" 1803 [LP] (1969)

Michael Ponti rec 1970 Vox Candide, STGBY 653 [LP] (1972); CE 31045 [LP], Vox Box 5151 (1996)

Ronald Smith rec 1977 EMI (France), CDM 7 64280 2 (1992)

Carl Axel Dominique Dag Visa (Sweden), DAG 02-1002 [LP] (1986)

Geir Henning Braaten rec 1989 Victoria (Norway), VCD 19002 (1990)

Alain Weiss rec 1989 Fidelio (Netherlands), 8839 (1990)

Bernard Ringeissen rec 1990 Marco Polo, 8.223351 (1993)

Marc-André Hamelin rec 1994 Hyperion, CDA66794 (1995)

Op 41 **Trois Petites Fantaisies**

Ronald Smith rec 1977 EMI, SLS 5100 [3 LPs] (1978); Arabesque (USA), 8127 [3 LPs]. Appian, APR7031 [2 CDs] (1996)

Daniel Capelletti René Gailly (Belgium), CD87 007 (1988)

Huseyin Sermet rec 1997 Valois (France), V 4808 (1998)

no 2 **Andantino**

Pierre Réach rec 1979 RCA (France), RL 37243 [LP] (1979)

Op 45 **Salut, cendre du pauvre!**

Osamu Nakamura rec 1990 Epic/Sony, ESCK 8005 (1990)

François Bou rec 1990 Adda (France), 581 285 (1991)

Laurent Martin rec 1992 Marco Polo, 8.223657 (1994)

Op 46 **Minuetto alla tedesca**

Ronald Smith rec 1970 EMI, HQS 1247 [LP] (1971); Arabesque (USA), 6516 [LP] (1984)

Op 50 **Deux Caprices**

Malcolm Binns Concert Artist/Fidelio Records (UK), STLPX 8017 [LP]; FED-TC-1017 [cass] (1967)

Ronald Smith rec 1968 [on Viennese piano of 1851] Oryx "Collectors' Series" 1803 [LP] (1969)

Osamu Nakamura rec 1992 Epic/Sony, ESCK 8016 (1992)

Ronald Smith rec 1994 Appian, APR 7032 [2 CDs] (1999)

no 2 **Le Tambour bat aux champs**

Raymond Lewenthal Columbia, M 30234 [LP] (1971); CBS 61117 [LP] (1981)

Stephanie McCallum rec 1985 [live] Société Alkan [cass] (1986)

Ronald Smith rec 1984 EMI, EG 27 0187 1 [LP], MC 27 0187 4 [cass] (1985); Arabesque (USA) 6523 [LP] Z6523 [CD], 7523 [cass] (1985)

Osamu Nakamura rec 1992 Epic/Sony, ESCK 8016 (1992)

Op 51 **Trois Menuets**

Osamu Nakamura rec 1992 Epic/Sony, ESCK 8016 (1992)

no 3 **Tempo nobile**
Pierre Réach rec 1979 RCA (France), RL 37243 [LP] (1979)

Op 52 **Super flumina Babylonis, paraphrase**
Laurent Martin rec 1992 Marco Polo, 8.223657 (1994)

Op 53 **Quasi Caccia**
Osamu Nakamura rec 1992 Epic/Sony, ESCK 8016 (1992)

Op 57 **2e et 3e Nocturnes**
2e Nocturne: Andantino
Bernard Ringeissen rec 1971 Harmonia Mundi, HM927 [LPL 2863] [LP] (1977), MHS 1344 [LP], HM B40.927 [cass]; HMA190 927, HMA43 927 [cass] (1988)

Op 60 **Ma chère liberté, et Ma chère servitude**
Jacqueline Méfano rec 1996 2e2m collection, 2e2m 1005 (1996)
Osamu Nakamura rec 1992 Epic/Sony, ESCK 8016 (1992)

Op 60 bis **Le Grillon, nocturne**
Osamu Nakamura
rec 1992 Epic/Sony, ESCK 8016 (1992)

Op 61 **Sonatine**
Raymond Lewenthal Columbia, M 30234 [LP] (1971); CBS 61117 [LP] (1981), Elan (USA), Elan 82284
Ronald Smith rec 1970 EMI, HQS 1247 [LP] (1971); CDM 7 69421 2, EG 7 69421 4 [cass]; EMI Angel (Japan), TOCE 6239. Arabesque (USA), 6516 [LP] (1984)
Bernard Ringeissen rec 1971 Harmonia Mundi, HM927 [LPL 2863] [LP] (1977); MHS 1344 [LP]; HM B40.927 [cass]; HMA 190927 (1988), HMA43 927 [cass]
Daniel Capelletti René Gailly (Belgium), CD87 007 (1988)
Pierre Réach rec 1991 Vogue (France), 645 006 (1991). Koch Discover, DICD920362 (1997)
Marc-André Hamelin rec 1994 Hyperion, CDA66794 (1995)

Op 63 **48 Motifs (Esquisses)**
Laurent Martin rec 1990 Marco Polo, 8.223352 (1992); partial reissue (nos 1-5, 8, 10, 13, 16, 18, 21, 32, 43 & 48) in: Naxos, 8.553434 (1995)

Osamu Nakamura rec 1992 Epic/Sony, ESCK 8016 (1992)

no 1 **La Vision**

Raymond Lewenthal Columbia, M 30234 [LP] (1971); CBS 61117 [LP] (1981)

Ronald Smith rec 1970 EMI, HQS 1247 [LP] (1971); Arabesque (USA), 6516 [LP] (1984)

Laurent Martin rec 1990 Naxos, 8.553434 (1995)

no 2 **Le Staccatissimo**

Alan Weiss rec 1989 Fidelio (Netherlands), 8839 (1990)

Laurent Martin rec 1990 Naxos, 8.553434 (1995)

Huseyin Sermet rec 1991 Valois (France), V 4659 (1992)

Jack Gibbons rec 1995 ASV, CD DCS 227 [2 CDs] (1995)

no 3 **Le Legatissimo**

Alan Weiss rec 1989 Fidelio (Netherlands), 8839 (1990)

Laurent Martin rec 1990 Naxos, 8.553434 (1995)

no 4 **Les Cloches**

Ronald Smith rec 1968 [on Viennese piano of 1851] Oryx (UK) "Collectors' Series" 1803 [LP] (1969)

Ronald Smith rec 1984 EMI, EG 27 0187 1 [LP], MC 27 0187 4 [cass] (1985); Arabesque (USA) 6523 [LP], Z6523 [CD], 7523 [cass] (1985)

Laurent Martin rec 1990 Naxos, 8.553434 (1995)

Jack Gibbons rec 1995 ASV, CD DCS 227 [2 CDs] (1995)

no 5 **Les Initiés**

Laurent Martin rec 1990 Naxos, 8.553434 (1995)

no 7 **Le Frisson**

Raymond Lewenthal Columbia, M 30234 [LP] (1971); CBS 61117 [LP] (1981)

no 8 **Pseudo-Naïveté**

Laurent Martin rec 1990 Naxos, 8.553434 (1995)

no 10 **Increpatio**

Ronald Smith rec 1968 [on Viennese piano of 1851] Oryx (UK) "Collectors' Series" 1803 [LP] (1969)

Ronald Smith rec 1984 EMI, EG 27 0187 1 [LP], MC 27 0187 4 [cass] (1985); Arabesque (USA) 6523 [LP], Z6523 [CD] 7523 [cass] (1985)

Alan Weiss rec 1989 Fidelio (Netherlands), 8839 (1990)

Laurent Martin rec 1990 Naxos, 8.553434 (1995)

Huseyin Sermet rec 1991 Valois (France), V 4659 (1992)

no 11 **Les Soupirs**

Raymond Lewenthal Columbia, M 30234 [LP] (1971); CBS 61117 [LP] (1981)

Ronald Smith rec 1984 EMI, EG 27 0187 1 [LP], MC 27 0187 4 [cass] (1985); Arabesque (USA) 6523 [LP], Z6523 [CD], 7523 [cass] (1985)
Alan Weiss rec 1989 Fidelio (Netherlands), 8839 (1990)
Laurent Martin rec 1990 Naxos, 8.553434 (1995)
Huseyin Sermet rec 1991 Valois (France), V 4659 (1992)
Jack Gibbons rec 1995 ASV, CD DCS 227 [2 CDs] (1995)

no 12 **Barcarollette**
Raymond Lewenthal Columbia, M 30234 [LP] (1971); CBS 61117 [LP] (1981)

no 18 **Liedchen**
Laurent Martin rec 1990 Naxos, 8.553434 (1995)

no 21 **Morituri te salutant**
Ronald Smith rec 1968 [on Viennese piano of 1851] Oryx (UK), "Collectors' Series" 1803 [LP] (1969)
Ronald Smith rec 1984 EMI, EG 27 0187 1 [LP], MC 27 0187 4 [cass] (1985); Arabesque (USA) 6523 [LP], Z6523 [CD], 7523 [cass] (1985)
Alan Weiss rec 1989 Fidelio (Netherlands), 8839 (1990)
Laurent Martin rec 1990 Naxos, 8.553434 (1995)
Huseyin Sermet rec 1991 Valois (France), V 4659 (1992)

no 29 **Délire**
Ronald Smith rec 1968 [on Viennese piano of 1851] Oryx (UK),"Collectors' Series" 1803 [LP] (1969)
Ronald Smith rec 1984 EMI, EG 27 0187 1 [LP], MC 27 0187 4 [cass] (1985); Arabesque (USA) 6523 [LP], Z6523 [CD], 7523 [cass] (1985)

no 32 **Minuetto**
Laurent Martin rec 1990 Naxos, 8.553434 (1995)

no 34 **Odi profanum vulgus et arceo: favete linguis**
Joachim Draheim FSM Audite, 53 179 [LP] (1978)

no 39 **Héraclite et Démocrite**
Raymond Lewenthal Columbia, M 30234 [LP] (1971); CBS 61117 [LP] (1981)

no 41 **Les Enharmoniques**
Ronald Smith rec 1968 [on Viennese piano of 1851] Oryx (UK), "Collectors' Series" 1803 [LP] (1969)
Ronald Smith rec 1984 EMI, EG 27 0187 1 [LP], MC 27 0187 4 [cass] (1985); Arabesque (USA) 6523 [LP], Z6523 [CD], 7523 [cass] (1985)

no 43 **Notturno-innamorato**
Laurent Martin rec 1990 Naxos, 8.553434 (1995)

no 45 **Les Diablotins**
Raymond Lewenthal Columbia, M 30234 [LP] (1971); CBS 61117 [LP] (1981)
Ronald Smith rec 1970 EMI, HQS 1247 [LP] (1971); Arabesque (USA), 6516 [LP] (1984)
John Bingham Deutsche Harmonia Mundi/EMI Electrola (RFA), HM 065-099 843 & EMI 1C 065-99 843 [LP] (1979)

no 46 **Le premier billet doux**
Ronald Smith rec 1968 [on Viennese piano of 1851] Oryx (UK), "Collectors' Series" 1803 [LP] (1969)
Ronald Smith rec 1984 EMI, EG 27 0187 1 [LP], MC 27 0187 4 [cass] (1985); Arabesque (USA) 6523 [LP] Z6523
Alan Weiss rec 1989 Fidelio (Netherlands), 8839 (1990)
Huseyin Sermet rec 1991 Valois (France), V 4659 (1992)

no 47 **Scherzetto**
Raymond Lewenthal Columbia, M 30234 [LP] (1971); CBS 61117 [LP] (1981)
Alan Weiss rec 1989 Fidelio (Netherlands), 8839 (1990)
Huseyin Sermet rec 1991 Valois (France), V 4659 (1992)

no 48 **En songe**
Ronald Smith rec 1968 [on Viennese piano of 1851] Oryx "Collectors' Series" 1803 [LP] (1969)
Ronald Smith rec 1984 EMI, EG 27 0187 1 [LP], MC 27 0187 4 [cass] (1985); Arabesque (USA) 6523 [LP] Z6523
Laurent Martin rec 1990 Naxos, 8.553434 (1995)
Jack Gibbons rec 1995 ASV, CD DCS 227 [2 CDs] (1995)

Op 64 **13 Prières pour orgue,** transcribed for piano by José Vianna da Motta

no 12 **Allegretto [da Motta's collection: No 8]**
Ronald Smith rec 1970 EMI, HQS 1247 [LP] (1971); Arabesque (USA), 6516 [LP] (1984)

Op 65 **3e Recueil de Chants**
Jacqueline Méfano rec 1992 2e2m collection (France), 2e2m 1002 (1995)

no 6 **Barcarolle**
Raymond Lewenthal rec 1965 RCA, LM 2815 [LP mono], LSC 2815 [LP stereo]; RB 6660 [LP mono], SB 6660 [LP stereo] (1966); GL 42689 [LP stereo], GK 42689 [cass] (1979), Elan CD 82276, remastered: BMG High Performance Series 633310 (1999)
Ronald Smith rec 1968 [on Viennese piano of 1851] Oryx "Collectors' Series" 1803 [LP] (1969)

Pierre Réach rec 1979 RCA (France), RL 37243 [LP] (1979)
Ronald Smith rec 1984 EMI, EG 27 0187 1 [LP], MC 27 0187 4 [cass] (1985); Arabesque (USA) 6523 [LP], Z6523 [CD], 7523 [cass] (1985)
Huseyin Sermet rec 1991 Valois (France), V 4659 (1992)
Marc-André Hamelin rec 1994 [live] Danacord, DAOCD 429 (1995)
Marc-André Hamelin rec 1994 Hyperion, CDA66794 (1995)
Jack Gibbons rec 1995 ASV, CD DCS 227 [2 CDs] (1995)

Op 67 **4e Recueil de Chants**
Jacqueline Méfano rec 1992 2e2m collection (France), 2e2m 1002 (1995)
Osamu Nakamura rec 1992 Epic/Sony, ESCK 8021 (1992)

no 6 **Barcarolle**
Bernard Ringeissen rec 1971 Harmonia Mundi, HM927 [LPL 2863] [LP] (1977); MHS 1344 [LP]; HM B40.927 [cass]; HMA 190927 (1988)

Op 70 **5e Recueil de Chants**
Stephanie McCallum rec1990 MBS (Australia), MBS 24 CD (1991)
Jacqueline Méfano rec 1992 2e2m collection (France), 2e2m 1002 (1995)
Osamu Nakamura rec 1992 Epic/Sony, ESCK 8021 (1992)

no 6 **Barcarolle**
Ronald Smith rec 1984 EMI, EG 27 0187 1 [LP], MC 27 0187 4 [cass] (1985); Arabesque (USA) 6523 [LP], Z6523 [CD], 7523 [cass] (1985)

Op 74 **Les Mois**
Daniel Capelletti René Gailly (Belgium), CD87 007 (1988)
Osamu Nakamura rec 1989 Epic/Sony, ESCK 8003 (1989)
François Bou rec 1990 Adda (France), 581 285 (1991)

no 2 **Carnaval**
Ronald Smith rec 1984 EMI, EG 27 0187 1 [LP], MC 27 0187 4 [cass] (1985). Arabesque (USA) 6523 [LP], Z6523 [CD], 7523 [cass] (1985)

no 6 **Promenade sur l'eau**
Ronald Smith rec 1984 EMI, EG 27 0187 1 [LP], MC 27 0187 4 [cass] (1985). Arabesque (USA) 6523 [LP], Z6523 [CD], 7523 [cass] (1985)

no 10 **Gros temps**
Raymond Lewenthal Columbia, M 30234 [LP] (1971); CBS 61117 [LP] (1981)
Ronald Smith rec 1984 EMI, EG 27 0187 1 [LP], MC 27 0187 4 [cass] (1985). Arabesque (USA) 6523 [LP], Z6523 [CD], 7523 [cass] (1985)
Jack Gibbons rec 1995 ASV, CD DCS 227 [2 CDs] 1995)

Op 75 **Toccatina**
Raymond Lewenthal Westminster, XWN 18362 [LP mono] (1956)
Werner Hass Philips, 6504.077 & 837 916 AY [LP] (1968), 4FM 10001 (LP)
Ronald Smith rec 1984 EMI, EG 27 0187 1 [LP], MC 27 0187 4 [cass] (1985). Arabesque (USA) 6523 [LP], Z6523 [CD], 7523 [cass] (1985)
Alan Weiss rec 1989 Fidelio (Netherlands), 8839 (1990)
Huseyin Sermet rec 1991 Valois (France), V 4659 (1992)

Op 76 **Trois Grandes Études pour les deux mains separées et réunies**
Stephanie McCallum rec 1985 [live] Société Alkan (France), [cass] (1986)
Ronald Smith rec 1987 EMI, EG 7 69630 1 [LP], CDM 7 69630 2 [CD], EG7 69630 4 [cass], (1988); EMI Angel, TOCE 6240 [CD], Arabesque (USA), Z6604
Laurent Martin rec 1990 Marco Polo, 8.223500 (1993)
Marc-André Hamelin rec 1994 [live] Hyperion, CDA66765 (1994)

no 3 **Étude à mouvement semblable et perpétuel pour les deux mains**
Bogdan Czapiewski Gdynia Wifon (Poland), ST LP 054 [LP] (1983)

no 3 **Étude à mouvement semblable et perpétuel pour les deux mains,** arr McDowell
Austin Conradi [piano roll transfer, c1923] Symposium (UK), 1002 [cass] (1983)
Ernest Hutcheson [piano roll transfer, 1923] Symposium (UK), 1002 [cass] (1983)

12 Études pour les pieds seulement
Osamu Nakamura rec 1992 Epic/Sony, ESCK 8020 (1992)
Impromptu
Osamu Nakamura rec 1989 Epic/Sony, ESCK 8003 (1989)
Petit conte
Raymond Lewenthal Columbia, M 30234 [LP] (1971); CBS 61117 [LP] (1981)
Ronald Smith rec 1984 EMI, EG 27 0187 1 [LP], MC 27 0187 4 [cass] (1985). Arabesque (USA) 6523 [LP] Z6523 [CD], 7523 [cass] (1985)
Osamu Nakamura rec 1992 Epic/Sony, ESCK 8016 (1992)
Les Regrets de la nonnette
Ronald Smith rec 1991 Symposium (UK), 1062 (1992)
Ronald Smith rec 1995 [live] Danacord (Denmark), DACOCD449 (1996)
Zorcico, danse ibérienne
Bernard Ringeissen rec 1971 Harmonia Mundi, HM927 [LPL 2863] [LP] (1977); MHS 1344 [LP]; HM B40.927 [cass]; HMA 190927 (1988), HMA43 927 [cass]

TRANSCRIPTIONS FOR PIANO

Souvenirs des Concerts du Conservatoire
no 6 **Menuet de la Symphonie en mi bémol no 39 de Mozart**
Osamu Nakamura rec 1989 Epic/Sony, ESCK 8003 (1989)
Souvenirs de Musique de chambre
no 2 **Sicilienne de la 2e Sonate pour clavecin et flûte de J. S. Bach**
Penny Loosemore Symposium (UK), 1062 (1992)
no.3 **Menuet du Quatuor op76/2 de Haydn, no.4 Andante du Quatuor en la majeur K464 de Mozart, and no 5 Cavatine du 13e Quatuor en si bemol majeur op.130 de Beethoven**
Osamu Nakamura rec 1992 Epic/Sony, ESCK 8020 (1992)
1er Mouvement du 3e Concerto pour piano de Beethoven, arrangé pour piano seul avec cadence
Thomas Wakefield Symposium (UK), 1062 (1992)
Marc-André Hamelin rec 1994 [live] Hyperion, CDA66765 (1994)

PIANO, FOUR HANDS

Op 25 **Fantaisie à 4 mains, sur Don Juan**
Anthony Goldstone & Caroline Clemmow rec 1988 Symposium (UK), 1037 [CD & Cass] (1988)
Duo Alkan: Alberto Baldrighi & Anne Colette Ricciardi rec 1997 Agora (Italy), Agora 105 (1997)

Op 40 **Trois Marches**
Isobel Beyer & Harvey Dagul FHM (UK), FHMD 9110, FHMC 9110 [cass] (1991)
Huseyin Sermet & Jean-Claude Pennetier rec 1997 Valois (France), V 4808 (1998)
Bombardo-carillon, pour quatre pieds seulement, played four hands
Caroline Clemmow & Anthony Goldstone rec 1991 Symposium (UK), 1062 (1992)

ORGAN/PIANO À PÉDALIER

Op 64 **13 Prières**
Kevin Bowyer rec 1988 Nimbus, NI 5089 (1988)

no 1 **Andantino**
John Wells rec 1988 Ribbonwood (New Zealand), RCD 1001 (1989)

no 2 **Moderato**
[arr Franck] Ton van Eck Polygram, 6814 769 [LP] (1982)
John Wells rec 1988 Ribbonwood (New Zealand), RCD 1001 (1989)
[arr Franck] Pierre Pincemaille rec 1994 Solstice (France), SOCD 116 (1994)

nos 3 **Poco adagio, 4 Moderatamente, 5 Adagio, 9 Doucement, 10 Assez lentement**
John Wells rec 1988 Ribbonwood (New Zealand), RCD 1001 (1989)

no 11 **Andantino**
John Wells rec 1988 Ribbonwood (New Zealand), RCD 1001 (1989)
Christopher Herrick rec 1998 Hyperion, CDA67060

nos 12 **Allegretto, 13 Largement et majesteusement**
John Wells rec 1988 Ribbonwood (New Zealand), RCD 1001 (1989)

Op 66 **11 Grands Préludes et un transcription du Messie de Hændel**

no 1 **Allegro**

Nicholas King Symposium, 1059 [cass] (1988), 1059 (2000); 1062 (1992)

John Wells rec 1988 Ribbonwood (New Zealand), RCD 1001 (1989)

no 3 **Andantino**

[arr Franck]

Polygram, 6814 769 [LP] (1982)

Ton van Eck

no 9 **Langsam**

Nicholas King Symposium (UK), 1059 [cass] (1988), 1059 (2000); 1062 (1992)

John Wells rec 1988 Ribbonwood (New Zealand), RCD 1001 (1989)

no 10 **Scherzando**

John Wells rec 1988 Ribbonwood (New Zealand), RCD 1001 (1989)

no 11 **Lento**

Nicholas King Symposium (UK), 1059 [cass] (1988), 1059 (2000); 1062 (1992)

Op 69 **Impromptu sur le Choral de Luther: "Un fort rempart est notre Dieu"**

Kevin Bowyer rec 1988 Nimbus, NI 5089 (1988)

Op 72 **11 Pièces dans le style religieux, et un transcription du Messie de Hændel**

nos 1-5, 7, 9-11

Nicholas King Symposium (UK), 1059 [cass] (1988), 1059 (2000); 1062 (1992)

Bombardo-carillon, pour quatre pieds seulement,

[see Piano, four hands above]

Petits Préludes sur les 8 gammes du plain-chant

Georges Lartigau Motette (Germany), M 10 760 [LP] (1984)

Kevin Bowyer rec 1988 Nimbus, NI 5089 (1988)

Nicholas King Symposium (UK), 1059 [cass] (1988), 1059 (2000); 1062 (1992)

Pro Organo

Pierre Pincemaille rec 1994 Solstice, SOCD 116 (1994)

CHAMBER MUSIC

Op 4 **Rondo brillant pour piano et cordes**
Christine Stevenson (pf) & the Morhange Ensemble rec 1991 Symposium (UK), 1062 (1992)

Op 21 **Duo concertant, for piano and violin**
Danièle Renault-Fasquelle (pf) and Pierre Hommage (vln) rec 1988 Adda, 581209 (1992)
Trio Alkan: Rainer Klaas (pf) and Kolja Lessing (vln) rec 1991 Marco Polo, 8.223383 (1992)
Ronald Smith (pf) and James Clark (vln) rec 1992 Appian, APR 7032 [2 CDs] (1999)
Oliver Gardon (pf) and Dong-Suk Kang (vln) rec 1992 Timpani, 1C1013 (1992)
Huseyin Sermet (pf) and Tedi Papavrami (vln) rec 1992 Valois (France), V 4680 (1993)

Op 30 **Trio for piano, violin and cello**
The Mirecourt Trio: John Jensen (pf), Kenneth Goldsmith (vln) and Terry King (vc) Genesis, GS 1058/9 [2 LPs] (1975)
Ronald Smith (pf), James Clark (vln) and Moray Welsh (vc) rec 1992 Appian, APR 7032 [2 CDs] (1999)
Trio Alkan: Rainer Klaas (pf), Kolja Lessing (vln) and Bernhard Schwarz (vc) rec 1991 Marco Polo, 8.223383 (1992)
Oliver Gardon (pf), Dong-Suk Kang (vln) and Yvan Chiffoleau (vc) rec 1992 Timpani, 1C1013 (1992)

Op 47 **Sonate de concert, for piano and cello**
Edward Auer (pf) and Yehudi Hanani (vc) Finnadar, SR 9030 [LP] (1981)
Trio Alkan: Rainer Klaas (pf) and Bernhard Schwarz (vc) rec 1991 Marco Polo, 8.223383 (1992)
Huseyin Sermet (pf) and Christoph Henkel (vc) rec 1991 Valois (France), V 4680 (1993)
Ronald Smith (pf) and Moray Welsh (vc) rec 1992 Appian, APR 7032 [2 CDs] (1999)
Oliver Gardon (pf) and Yvan Chiffoleau (vc) rec 1992 Timpani, 1C1013 (1992)
Carl-Axel Dominique (pf) and John Ehde (vc) rec 1997 Caprice, CAP 21563 (1997)

String Quartet fragment
Members of the Morhange Ensemble rec 1991 Symposium (UK), 1062 (1992)

ORCHESTRAL MUSIC

Op 10 **1er Concerto da camera**
Marc-André Hamelin (pf), BBC Scottish Symphony Orchestra, cond Martyn Brabbins rec 1993 Hyperion, CDA66717 (1994)
Dmitri Feofanov (pf), Razumovsky Symphony Orchestra, cond Robert Stankovsky rec 1995 Naxos, 8 553702 (1998)

Op 10 **2e Concerto da camera**
Michael Ponti (pf), Südwestfunk Kammerorchester, cond Paul Angerer rec 1973 Vox Turnabout, TV 43740 [LP] (1979); FSM 53033 [LP]; CDX 5098 [2 CDs] (1993)
François Bou (pf), Ensemble 2e2m, cond Paul Méfano rec 1990 Adda, 581 285 (1991)
Anthony Goldstone (pf), Morhange Ensemble rec 1991 Symposium (UK), 1062 (1992)
Marc-André Hamelin (pf), BBC Scottish Symphony Orchestra, cond Martyn Brabbins rec 1993 Hyperion, CDA66717 (1994)
Dmitri Feofanov (pf), Razumovsky Symphony Orchestra, cond Robert Stankovsky rec 1995 Naxos, 8 553702 (1998)

Concerto da camera no 3 [reconstructed Hugh Macdonald]
Dmitri Feofanov (pf), Razumovsky Symphony Orchestra, cond Robert Stankovsky rec 1995 Naxos, 8 553702 (1998)

Pas redoublé, for Wind Band
Leicestershire Schools Band, cond Mark Fitz-Gerald Symposium (UK), 1062 (1992)

VOCAL MUSIC

Psalm 41, verse 2
Rachel Yakar (sop) and Jacqueline Mefano (pf) rec 1991 2e2m collection (France), 2e2m 1005 (1996)

Etz Chajjim Hi
Les Jeunes Solistes, cond Rachid Safir rec 1991 2e2m collection (France), 2e2m 1005 (1996)
The Kentish Opera Singers, cond Mark Fitz-Gerald Symposium (UK), 1062 (1992)

Halelouyoh
Les Jeunes Solistes, cond Rachid Safir rec 1991 2e2m collection (France), 2e2m 1005 (1996)

The Kentish Opera Singers, cond Mark Fitz-Gerald Symposium (UK), 1062 (1992)

Marcia funebre sulla morte d'un pappagallo

Alfred Genovese, Leonard Arner, Henry Schuman (oboe), Loren Glickman (bsn), singers from the Metropolitan Opera Studio, cond Raymond Lewenthal Columbia, M 30234 [LP] (1971); CBS 61117 [LP] (1981)

Nell Froger (sop), Anne Bartelloni (ms), Bruno Boterf (ten), Francois Fauche (bass), Ensemble 2e2m, cond Paul Méfano rec 1990 Adda, 581 285 (1991)

The Kentish Opera Singers, Rachel Porter, Hazel Todd, Alison Turnbull (oboe), William Waterhouse (bsn), cond Mark Fitz-Gerald Symposium (UK), 1062 (1992)

3 Anciennes mélodies juives

Rachel Yakar (sop) and Jacqueline Méfano (pf) rec 1991 2e2m collection (France), 2e2m 1005 (1996)

MISCELLANEOUS

Grotesqueries of Alkan. Raymond Lewenthal talks about Alkan, and demonstrates at the piano

Raymond Lewenthal Columbia, BTS 24 [small bonus record accompanying Columbia M 30234 [LP] (1971)] [LP] (1971); CBS 61117 [LP] (1981)

Barcarolle op. 65/6, arranged Jascha Heifetz

Forgotten Gems from the Heifetz Legacy, Encore Duo: Sherry Kloss (violin) and Mark Westcott (piano) Kloss Classics (USA), KC 1816 (1999)

PIANO ROLLS

Op 15 **Souvenirs. Trois Morceaux dans le genre pathétique**
no 2 **Le Vent**
Harold Bauer Duo Art 6446; Aeolian A921

Op 27 **Le Chemin de fer, étude**
Rudolph Ganz Hupfeld 14744/51330

Op 31 **25 Préludes dans tous les tons majeurs et mineurs**
no 6 **Ancienne mélodie de la synagogue**
Egon Petri Welte-Mignon B520
no 13 **J'étais endormie mais mon coeur veillait...**
Charlton Keith Hupfeld 14624/51623

Op 35 **12 Études dans tous les tons majeurs**
no 1 **Allegretto**
Louis Closson Hupfeld 14176/53220

no 2 **Allegro**
Louis Closson Hupfeld 14177/53691
no 3 **Andantino**
Michael von Zadora Hupfeld 13078/51935
no 5 **Allegro barbaro**
Michael von Zadora Hupfeld 13079/55692
Louis Closson Hupfeld 14178/55086

Op 46 **Minuetto alla tedesca**
Unknown pianist Aeolian 1143

Op 50 **Deux Caprices**
no 1 **Capriccio alla soldatesca**
Louis Closson Hupfeld 14179/53219
Egon Petri Welte-Mignon B519
R Singer Virtuola 4420
no 2 **Le Tambour bat aux champs**
Louis Closson Hupfeld 14180/53221
R Singer Virtuola 4420
Michael von Zadora Welte 3648

Op 63 **48 Motifs (Esquisses)**
no 1 **La vision, no 2 Le Staccatissimo, no 10 Increpatio**
Michael von Zadora Hupfeld 13076/51934
no 18 **Liedchen, no 24 Contredanse, no 42 Petit air**
Michael von Zadora Hupfeld 13077/55690

Op 76 **Trois Grandes Études pour les deux mains separées et réunies**
no 3 **Étude à mouvement semblable et perpétuel pour les deux mains,** arranged McDowell
Austin Conradi c1923 Welte-Mignon C7010
Ernest Hutcheson 1923 Duo Art 6144

Index to Alkan: The Music